The Glastonbury Zodiac

This book
is dedicated to
my Patron Saint
St. Keyne

[My thanks are due to the Royal Society of Arts for their kind permission to reproduce Mrs. Maltwood's map and air-photos. I would also like to thank my sister Judith Lucas for her unstinting help with the index and proof-reading.]

Mary Caine (1978)

Cover shows Arthur of Avalon on front and Gemini on the back.

Facing painting by Osmund Caine.

ISBN 0 9506834 2 6

© MARY CAINE 1978

25 KINGSTON HILL KINGSTON SURREY

All rights reserved. No part of this publication may be reproduced, stored in a retrieval system, or transmitted, in any form or by any means, electronic, mechanical, photocopying, recording or otherwise, without the prior permission of **Mary Caine**.

Contents

CHAPTER 1. THE ZODIAC: A General Survey   19

Glastonbury's notables, legendary and historic. The Secret of the Lord. Earthworks. The 12 Hides. The stars fit their effigies. The Cauldron, proto-Grail. This Zodiac the key to Celtic poems and folk-lore, Arthur's Round Table and Grail-Quest, our national saints and emblems. Description of Zodiac. The Girt Dog. Three changes, Aquarius, Cancer, Libra. The First Zodiac? A compendium of all knowledge. Some famous men who favoured astrology.

CHAPTER 2. KATHERINE MALTWOOD   31

Birth, youth and marriage. A prophetic sculptress. Perlesvaus, or the "High History". Arthur's knights as the seasons; allegory of the soul's life-path, based on Avalon's landscape-figures. Her books. The Maltwood Museum, Vancouver.

CHAPTER 3. WHO MADE IT? WHEN? AND WHY?   35

Who made it? When? Why? The Zodiac is natural, aided by man. A Space-Time Pattern, embodying evolution's aim—recognised by early settlers. "Prepared by God for the salvation of Mankind". Antiquities of different periods. The Trinity. Zodiac the fount of all myth and religions.

CHAPTER 4. ARIES   43

A Paschal lamb. Templars' sign. Jason's Golden fleece. Aries=Spring=Gawain, who revives dying sun as mumming plays' doctor. Gawain fails at Grail-Castle. The Waste Land. Gawain and the Green Knight, a sun-myth.

CHAPTER 5. TAURUS   49

Bull of Dawn. Taliesin's "Buarth Beirdd". The ox and the Avanc. Aldebaran, the Bull's-eye. A line to Antares in Scorpio. Zodiac geometry. Bulls of Connaught and Ulster. Bull-sacrifice. Bel and Beltane. Taurus-Joseph.

CHAPTER 6. GEMINI 57

Blake's "Jerusalem". Did he know the Christ-head in Gemini? Head a British camp; beacon-tumulus his pineal gland. Lynchets on Lollover his ribs. The Cromm Cruach, Bowed One of the Mound. St. Patrick. Prometheus. Castor and Pollux. Orion. Horus. Atlas. Geometry of Ship's masts. King Fisherman. Gemini's Christian symbolism. Christ in Britain? Jesus-Yesse. Lyonesse. Second Twin. The Griffon. Perceval, Galahad.

CHAPTER 7. CANCER. A SHIP 64

Ship expresses Cancer better than a crab. Maternal sign. Did Sumerians cut it? Sargon I. in Britain. Phoenicians. Mummers' horse-boats. Taliesin. Solomon's Ship. Hiram of Tyre. Gilgamesh. Noah-Menes-Minos-Menu, the Measurer. Sumerians-Cimmerians-Cymry? Arthur's glass ship Prydwen.

CHAPTER 8. LEO 73

Taliesin's Leo. Somerton, Sumer-town. The Cath Palug. Lleu-Lancelot. The Four Grail Hallows. Lion and Unicorn. A Jewish Leo-legend. Romans on Leo. William of Malmesbury's Leo prophecy. Miracles and coincidences. The Pilgrim's Path. Stoke-sub-Hamden's fire-signs. Somerton's inn-names. "This other Eden". Ecliptic path on Leo's tongue. Sanctuary knockers. Tristram and the little dog. Hercules' Nemean Lion. The Cary river.

CHAPTER 9. VIRGO 80

The Triple Goddess. Mother Carey and Davey Jones. Christianity's starry origins. Babcary and Virgin-Birth. The Fosse Way notch. Virgo's wheatsheaf. St. Bride. Ceridwen. Black Annis. Wimble Toot. Ceres-Carey-Ceridwen-Kerin-Keyne. Her Well. Keinton Mandeville. Keynsham. Ceres-Persephone. Guinevere. Camelot-Camillus. Eve of Yeovil.

CHAPTER 10. LIBRA. A DOVE 91

Dove at Barton-St-David brings light, inspiration. Three Bars of Light. Dove a better sign than scales for Libra. Why displaced? The Awen. The Logos or Word. Plough-stars fall on the Dove. Minos. Taliesin again. The Brood Hen. Arianrhod's Turning Castle. Doves and divas. Draco, Park Wood Butleigh. Hydra. Ten signs or twelve? Iona, David John. Davey Jones. Columba. Columbus and America. Some Dove river-names.

CHAPTER 11. SCORPIO   98
Elusive sign. My alternative figure. Mistletoe. Lucifer-Mordred. Stone on the equinoctial line. Arthur's death-gate into Avalon. His incest. Battle of Camlann. Scorpio's character. Ditcheat—St. Christopher as Scorpio. Hornblotton's caduceus and the pineal. Alford's Scorpion. Callixtus. Lydford's empty graves. Arthur and Brutus. The Fall of Man and Troy.

CHAPTER 12. SAGITTARIUS-ARTHUR   111
Ahura, Osiris, Hu. Bel of Baltonsborough. Hercules-Melkarth. The sun-king. An old Breton Legend. Arthur Harrows Hell. Not a centaur, a mounted warrior-king. Chiron. "The king must Die". Crucified on the Tree of Life. Patron saints. Arthur's dream—The Zodiac Wheel of Fortune. Somerset's first Somersault.

CHAPTER 13. CAPRICORN   118
Ponter's Ball, unicorn-horn. Lion and Unicorn. Templars, Guardians of the Grail. Glastonbury, "Roma Secunda". The Gilded Goat. Virgin and Unicorn. The White Hart. Merton College's Zodiac. The Tor's "Cave of the Rising". Gog and Magog. The Cornucopia. Sagittarius, dying, revives Capricorn. "Puntes Bal". Capricorn = Man throughout Time. Pan and Bran. The singing, severed head. Skull in the well. Cauldron of inspiration. Capricorn = Merlin. Oannes-Jonah. Esau-Enkidu. Chronos, Old Father Time. Plutarch's visitors to Britain.

CHAPTER 14. AQUARIUS   129
Eagle and Waterpot. Chalice Well, Glastonbury Tor. Water-carrier bears the Water of Life. Joseph of Arimathea, the Grail and Blood Spring. The Phoenix, resurrection-sign. Actis fields and Heliopolis. Ganymede and Mount Ida. Chaldean Zu, Indian Garuda. Lleu and Gronw. Attar the Eagle. Perceval reborn. The Burning Castle. Phoenix and evolving universe. "Five changes of the Grail". Joseph's silver cruets. The Wells clock. The Tor's earthquake. Perceval, "perceive-all", "Pierce-the-Vale". Man Know Thyself. Christ at Heliopolis. Golden cup and fountain. Glastonbury's tree, lopped and bare.

CHAPTER 15. PISCES   139
Two Fish and a Whale. The Abbey's whale-jaws. A fish swallows the sun. The Salmon of Wisdom. The Mabon imprisoned. Nodens. The Maimed Fisher-King. Pomparles Bridge and Excalibur. Arthur's ecliptic grave. Joseph of Arimathea on Wearyall Hill. The Twelve Hides. Joseph's accurate timing. His Thorn a calendar-peg. Joseph II. Wallyer's Bridge. Perceval and the Castle of the Whale. Draco's stars. Pisces sums up the Zodiac.

CHAPTER 16. THE GIRT DOG OF LANGPORT — 147

The Somerset Wassail Song. The Guardian of the Mysteries, drawn by river Parrett. Hercules and Cerberus. Many place-names. Dormarth, "Death's Door". A planned triangle of forts? The Great Dragon Line. Cabal, Arthur's dog. Arthur, Gwythyr and Gwyn. The Tor's maze. The Questing Beast. Alfred at Athelney. A "sop to Cerberus". Alfred's British descent—the royal Secret. Asser. Alfred's renaissance. Swithin, Christian Druid. Guthrun baptised at Aller. Drayton's Polyolbion.

CHAPTER 17. THE ZODIAC IN SOME SUMERIAN MYTHS — 153

Epics of Creation and Gilgamesh. Khassisadra-Cassiterides, Britain's tin-islands. Chaldean Culdees. Ceridwen's, Medea's Cauldron. Gilgamesh's Zodiacal adventures. Parrett-Euphrates. Avalon-Arallu. Sumeria's Summerland.

CHAPTER 18. WAS BRITAIN PART OF ATLANTIS? — 156

Sunken lands of Ys and Lyonesse. Plato's date for Atlantis' sinking. The Santorin heresy. The Ice Age melts. Hesiod's western Titans in the Hesperides. The Book of Enoch. Proto-Phoenicians. The Cabiri. Io and Europè—rapes and abductions. Atlantean Bull-cult. Atlas and Gadir. Albion and Erin, Titans. Plato's Atlantean maze. Ariadne's maze. Druid tree-alphabet the earliest letters. Atlas, Enoch, Idris, Noah. Noah's Sapphire Book. Bath's sulphur springs. Genesis' "Sons of God". Hermes Trismegistus and magi. 9000-year-old cities. Men into apes? Evolution not automatic.

CHAPTER 19. THE SOMERSET ZODIAC IN GREEK MYTH — 167

Hercules in Britain? His Twelve Zodiacal Labours. Ulysses too goes west. And Perseus. Medusa-Ceridwen-Virgo. Atalanta's Atlantic apples. Melanion-Meleagant and the moon-boar. Carpo and Camillus at Camelot. Jason of Gemini and the Arian Golden Fleece. Theseus and the Minotaur in the maze. Daedalus, Icarus, Minos. Hecateus on Hyperborean Britain. Latona and Apollo, British-born. Abaris and Pythagoras.

CHAPTER 20. BRUTUS OF TROY AND GOGMAGOG — 178

Britains old straight tracks. Watkins' leys. Norman Lockyer's star-alignments. Three Zodiac ley-patterns. Gog and Magog. Brutus at Totnes. Geoffrey of Monmouth's account. London, New Troy, Troytown mazes. Oxford's Magi. Tam-Isis. Holy Ileum. Trojan Law, Troy-weight. Whit-mounds and Toots. Seven stars, seven steps to perfection. The Awenyddion.

CHAPTER 21. THE ZODIAC IN CELTIC POETRY 185

Kept secret. Taliesin's tale—an initiation-myth, repeated in Chaldea. "The Hanes Taliesin" interpreted. His three births. "Preiddu Annwn" —Arthur harrows Hell. The Battle of the Trees. A druid riddle. "Song of the World". The Ox-pen of the Bards. Zodiac a royal secret. Math the mathematician. Merddin's "Avallenace". Caradoc-Cerdic. Taliesin on Leo.

CHAPTER 22. THE ZODIAC IN THE MABINOGION 202

Arthur's antiquity. First Branch—Pwyll Prince of Dyfed, and Rhiannon, moon-goddess. Hafgan and Pwyll, summer and winter kings. The Beheading Stroke. Pryderi, born in a stable. Rhiannon's penance. Third Branch—Manawydan, son of Llyr. The Waste Land. The wise shoemaker. The vanishing castle, fountain and golden bowl. Manawydan catches a mouse. Fourth Branch—Math and the Moon-maiden. Gwydion's trickery. Pryderi's pigs. Arianrhod's virginity-test. Lleu's instant birth. More tricks from Gwydion. Lleu's false wife; his death and revival. His vengeance. The Second Branch—Bran and Branwen. The cauldron revives dying soldiers in battle. The Giants' Iron-House. Bran's severed head replaces the burst cauldron. Buried in Tower Hill. Four Independent Native Tales. 1. Prince Macsen, emperor of Rome in Wales. 2. Llud and Llefelys—gadflies and swine. 3. Culhwch and Olwen—Giant Ysbadadden sets Culhwch impossible tasks to win his daughter. 4. The Dream of Rhonabwy—Arthur's giant knights. A group of later Romances. 1. The Lady of the Fountain. 2. Peredur son of Efrawg; the Welsh Perceval. 3. Gereint son of Erbin—Faithful Enid, jealous Gereint, the dwarf king and the Hedge of Mist.

CHAPTER 23. JOSEPH OF ARIMATHEA 228

The tin-trader in Britain? A symbol of Gnostic, Johannine Christianity, Mary the Vessel. John and Peter. Apocryphal Books; 1. The Acts of Pilate. 2. Questions of Bartholomew. 3. The Story of Joseph of Arimathea. 4. Obed. 5. The Healing of Tiberius. The Golden Legend. 6. The Acts of Magdalen. The Coming of the Saints. Fecamp's legend. First century missionaries in Europe. Early writers' confirmation. Robert de Borron's "Joseph". Henry II and Eleanor. What *was* the Grail? An Ark? Evelake or Avallach, and Nasciens in Sarras. Melkin's prophecy. Gildas and Nennius. William of Malmesbury. The Twelve Hides again. Joseph in British folklore. St. Anna of Cornwall and Brittany. The Priddy Legend. Wookey Hole. Morien Morgan on the Babe in the Boat, a Druid rite. William Blake. The legend of Crewkerne. Joseph and ley-lines. King Harold, the flint cross and Waltham Abbey. Animals set to find leys. The Zodiac and the Precessional Ages.

CHAPTER 24. ENGLISH HISTORY FITS THE ZODIAC. 255

Examples from 770 AD to the present.

List of Illustrations

	Page
"Arthur of Avalon" by Osmund Caine	5
Glastonbury Tor	19
"Great Dragon Line"	21
Mrs Maltwood's Zodiac Temple of the Stars in Avalon	24
Girt Dog of Langport	24
Mary Caine's suggested alterations of Scorpio, Libra and additions of a second twin and Draco	24
Katherine Maltwood's Portrait	29
Maltwood Museum	31
Aries	42
Aries (Map)	43
Taurus	48
Taurus (Map)	49
Mrs Maltwood's Gemini	54
Gemini	56
Gemini (Map)	57
The Three Bars of Light	60
Cancer (Map)	64
Cancer	65
Leo (Map)	71
Leo	72
Tympanum, Stoke-Sub-Hamden Church	77
Virgo (Map)	80

	Page
Wimble Toot	85
Virgo's Head and Wheatsheaf	87
Libra – Dove	90
Libra (Map)	91
The Maltwood Scorpio	98
Scorpio	99
West Lydford	107
Sagittarius (Map)	108
Sagittarius	109
Capricorn (Map)	118
Capricorn	119
Cadbury Castle "Camelot"	126
Aquarius	128
Aquarius (Map)	129
Chalice Well	134
Pisces (Map)	136
Glastonbury Abbey	142
Great Dog	146
Girt Dog of Langport (Map)	147
"Owl Faces" and Chalk-Cut Figures	184
Troy Town Maze	184
"Fall of Satanas"	232
Jerusalem	287
Joseph of Arimathea	286

Foreword
By Geoffrey Ashe

Nostradamus, in the sixth book of his famous and cryptic Prophecies, has a couple of lines which have so far baffled his commentators.

> Dedans la terre du grand temple celique
> Nepveu a Londres par paix faincte meutri.

> In the land of the great heavenly temple
> A nephew at London is murdered through a false peace.

Whatever the second line may mean (and I shall be offering a suggestion in a moment), the reference to London proves that 'the land of the great heavenly temple' is England. What could Nostradamus, a French astrologer in the sixteenth century, have meant by this temple? Hardly a church. All Christian countries had churches, and there was nothing so obviously distinctive about any English one. Stonehenge? It was little known, and those who did know it were unaware of its nature. What then?

Since I first noticed Nostradamus's phrase, I have often wondered why no one seems to have applied it to the Glastonbury Zodiac. Coming from an astrologer it would fit very well. The Zodiac is the theme of Mary Caine's book, and when she mentions Nostradamus, as she does near the end, I suspect that she is right to draw attention to him.

What is the Glastonbury Zodiac? Over the past few decades, it has become a part of the mythology of that spellbinding and sacred place. In the eyes of some, it is the key to it all—to the legends of Joseph of Arimathea, of the Holy Grail, of King Arthur and the rest. In the eyes of others it is a fantasy, an apocryphal extra. According to those who favour it, Glastonbury is part of a huge and ancient circle of figures which are outlined in the landscape by hills, water-courses, woods, trackways. These, when taken together, are seen to compose a diagram of the zodiacal signs. Their significance is confirmed by apt place-names and local lore, showing that tradition preserved memories of them even when their original character was forgotten.

Katharine Maltwood, who announced her discovery of the Zodiac in 1935, called it the Temple of the Stars. When something is alleged to have been made thousands of years ago, and to have been known among bards and myth-makers through most of its existence, it is natural to object that no one can be proved to have mentioned it in writing before 1935. But I think Nostradamus's *grand temple celique*, which is very like 'temple of the stars', must be admitted to call that criticism in question.

Is the Zodiac literally there or not? Mary Caine knows far more about it than I do, and her readers must decide for themselves. My own feeling is that it is not there as, say, the Egyptian pyramids are, but that this is not the whole story. To take the negative first, it does seem to me that Zodiac enthusiasts have claimed too much. Mrs. Maltwood, for instance, was led to it by what she decided were allusions in a mediaeval romance, *The High History of the Holy Grail*. The author of that strange book certainly knew Glastonbury, and he has a few passages which you can read as referring to Zodiac figures if you wish, but there is no necessity to do so. They make sense without. Again, it is often asserted that the figures are plainly seen from the air, and in aerial photographs. That may be true for people who are looking for them. If the same aerial photographs were shown to a group who had not been told what to look for, I doubt very much if they would pick out the figures.

As I said, however, this is not the whole story. I am reminded of the Rorschach ink-blot test, or of seeing pictures in the fire. People see what they are attuned to see. Those who are attuned do see the figures in the Glastonbury landscape, and no amount of prompting or wishful thinking could make them do it if the landscape did not supply the materials of the vision—hills, water-courses and so forth, suitably placed. You could not see a Zodiac (so far as I know) by looking at the Isle of Wight, because the materials are not there. You would not find what you needed to make the pictures.

Why the landscape round Glastonbury should have this character, and whether it is due to chance or to human work or to subtler agencies hinted at by Mary Caine, I have no idea. I would say, though, that if you discuss the figures in a purely objective way, as if they could be proved and accounted for like a prehistoric burial or a Roman villa, you are discussing them wrongly. Those who do not see them do not see them, and should not be argued with, or treated as obstinate or wilfully blind. What matters is the experience of those who do see them—the wide-ranging meditations which they can set in motion, the complex imagery which they can conjure up. It may be urged, and it often is, that none of this could have happened to anybody before aircraft were invented, because it was then impossible to get high enough above Glastonbury to make the figures out. That may be a strong argument against their being crudely and literally 'there', to be taken in at a glance. It is not so strong against the notion of the landscape's inhabitants building up the figures in their imagination as they explored its features, and retaining them and passing them on to others. After all, good maps were being made long before flying.

The great merit of Mary Caine's treatment is that it leans away from the archaeological (I am tempted to call it the pseudo-archaeological) and towards the psychological and spiritual. It is about the experience of a Zodiac-finder, of someone who does see, who responds in this way to this unique piece of England, and who lets the vision work. Her vision is not everybody's, but it can be shared—exhilaratingly shared—and she may be right in supposing that it has occurred among poets and magicians for many centuries.

Lastly, let us return to Nostradamus. If we accept that prophesying can happen at all, there is a way of construing his second line which shows how the event he foresaw could have evoked the 'temple' for him. 'A nephew at London is murdered through a false peace'. It would be odd to describe the victim as a nephew unless it was an uncle who killed him. In 1685 the Duke of Monmouth, whom many believed to be the rightful king, led a rebellion which collapsed. He was brought to London and put to death by his uncle, James II. The 'peace' or pacification was false, because the cruelty of James's repression left a bitterness that helped to dethrone him only three years later. And the thought of this executed nephew might well have brought a Somerset 'temple' into Nostradamus's mind, because the heart of the rebellion, was precisely, Somerset. Monmouth's army camped twice in Glastonbury Abbey, and fought its single disastrous battle at Sedgemoor, less than ten miles away.

Geoffrey Ashe

The Glastonbury Zodiac

The Vale of Avalon hovers half in this world, half out of it. Dominated by the astonishing pyramid of Glastonbury Tor, it has magnetised to itself more than its fair share of mystery and legend, saints, demons, giants and national heroes.

In prehistoric times the Tor was long the seat of Gwyn ap Nudd, lord of the Celtic Annwn or Hades. Shrouded in swirling mist he hunted the souls of the dead with his hell-hound pack, their baying mingling with the storm-winds until Celtic St. Collen banished him with holy water. Or did he? Baying hounds may still be heard today, though the local kennels will allay our fears.

Here came Joseph of Arimathea, the wealthy Phoenician tin-trader (or so they say) bringing his nephew Jesus as a boy. It is this legend that prompted William Blake to write,

> *"And did those Feet in ancient time*
> *Walk upon England's mountains green?"*

It was to Avalon, they will tell you, that Joseph returned, fleeing from Jewish persecution after the Crucifixion; coming with twelve followers and bearing that precious Cup of the Last Supper, the Holy Grail. Glastonbury indeed is chief among the famed hiding-places of that elusive Vessel.

It was part of the Silurian kingdom of western Britain, whose famous sons Caradoc and Arviragus defended the land with such heroism against the Roman invasion. (The blood of their royal house flowed equally freely in Rome's amphitheatres; no less than five martyrs did this family, exiled in Rome, provide to cement the foundations of Christianity.)

Arthur and Caradoc, they say, are buried in the Abbey; Arviragus and his successors are said to have given Joseph and his followers the "Twelve Hides of Glastonbury" to maintain them and their church in perpetuity

Here Arthur kept his court and Round Table; here his knights set out on their quest of the Grail, already by that time long withdrawn from the unworthy eyes of men. It was a family affair, this Quest, for Arthur and his chief knights were said to have descended from Joseph himself.

Here centuries later Alfred hid from the Danes, burnt his cakes and emerged to defeat his enemies inspired by a vision of the Virgin at the Abbey. Here he baptised Guthrun the Dane, and (apparently imitating Arviragus' gift to Joseph,) *"gave him many fine houses."*

If St. Collen banished demons from Glastonbury, so did St. Beon, who has a church there as St. Benignus. St. Bride has another, her stay being remembered also by a well; her bell until recently was kept at Chalice Well. St. Patrick of Ireland and St. David of Wales were both reputedly abbots of the Abbey, and St. Dunstan undoubtedly was.

Such an impressive roll-call of kings, saints and heroes may perhaps be sufficiently accounted for by the age and magnificence of the Abbey, the cradle of Christianity in Britain—and by the numinous nature of its foundation-legend. But even here magic and mystery prevails. The abbey, says William of Malmesbury, was known in Norman times as the *"Secret of the Lord"*, and called *"a heavenly sanctuary on earth."* Though some said that Joseph had built the first wattle church, it was also rumoured that *"it was not built by human hands, but by the Lord Himself for the salvation of men."* This rumour reached the ears of St. Augustine, who scratched his head and passed the conundrum to Pope Gregory for solution at top level. The Saxon biographer of St. Dunstan also records it in the year 1000.

But before the Christian beginnings, what could have attracted Joseph to Avalon in the first place? And Jesus? What was this otherworld of Gwyn ap Nudd, where Caradoc was buried, that struck awe into Celtic hearts long before Joseph hallowed it with his little wattle church?

It looks as if there was something of importance here, something which breathed out myth and legend long before the first Christians settled in these marshes. Something, perhaps, which magnetised them there. But what?

Copious evidence of prehistoric interference with the landscape can be seen on every side; there were obviously early and important settlements here. There is hardly a hill that has not been terraced or fortified; tumuli and other earthworks abound. The Tor, already impressive enough, has been laboriously terraced into something reminiscent of a Chaldean Ziggurat, or a step-pyramid. Its influence on the whole area is hypnotic; it is a constant reminder of eternity—a gnarled prophetic finger pointing to another and disturbing dimension. Impossible to resist its imperial bidding for long; it impels us to ascend and contemplate wider horizons.

It seems to be the apex of an enormous symmetrical triangle of terraced forts—evidence of neolithic town and country planning on the grand scale? Twelve miles to the south-west is Alfred's Burrow, Athelney, thought by some to be artificial, and terraced like the Tor. Like the Tor it is crowned with a ruined church. Twelve miles south-east of the Tor is the ramparted hill of Cadbury Castle, the traditional Camelot. This too was once crowned by a church of Celtic or early Saxon date, as recent excavations have revealed. (Cadbury Castle's spring used to be called Arthur's Well; it is said that his knights can still be seen on moonlight nights, lances glittering between wall and ditch.)

What is contained within this suspiciously geomantic pattern? On what secret do these hills look down?

The answer to this question is the answer to all the previous questions. It is the Secret of the Lord, to which title Glastonbury Abbey only later succeeded—the Original *"Twelve Hides"* of the *Glastonbury Giants or Zodiac*.

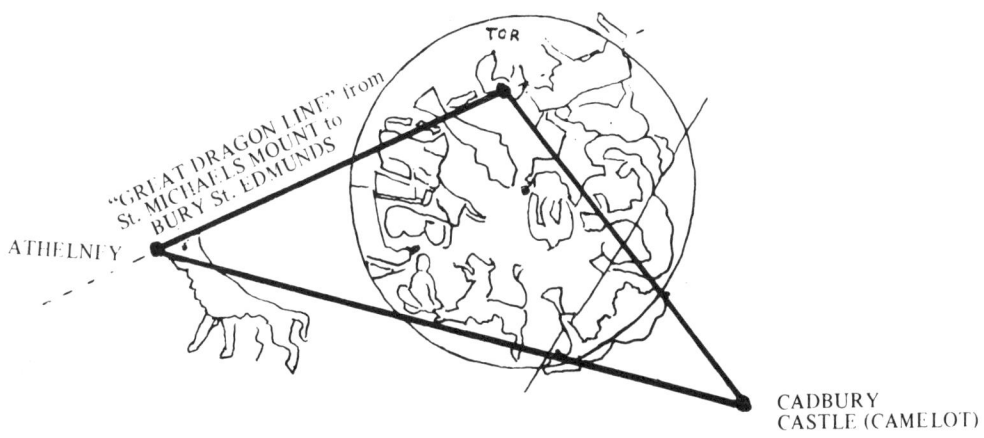

Here is the missing link that will be found to bind together into one coherent whole all the multifarious legends of Avalon; the great magnet that attracted all its pagan gods and demons, and the later concourse of saints and heroes. Here is the vast and original enigma, key to all Avalon's mysteries; the fount and source of that continuous spring of romantic inspiration and heroic endeavour that was once called the *"Matter of Britain."*

Here is the earthly counterpart of the Caer Sidi of the Celts, a great Star-Temple, reflecting in its natural contours and streams the Zodiac in the heavens. *So accurately indeed does it mirror the heavenly pattern that the stars of the Zodiac fit over its earthly effigies when the planisphere is scaled to the map of Avalon.*

It is of this Zodiac that Taliesin the British bard sang in his mysterious poem *"The Spoils of Annwn"*, telling how Arthur descended into its Underworld to rescue Gweir (Man) and carry off the inspirational and rejuvenating Cauldron of the Goddess Ceridwen. (Bran or Bryan in Irish myth also harrowed hell in a glass diving-helmet. Arthur's vessel was a Glass Ship. Both versions must record Mystery teachings from Druidic times.) Long before Joseph ever came, something very like the Grail was already being sought by a prehistoric Arthur in Avalon's Annwn.

This Zodiac recurs throughout the stories of the Welsh Mabinogion and all Arthurian myth—as will be demonstrated in a later chapter. With its key many obscurities in Celtic literature may be deciphered, many a closed door in the dark labyrinth of our archives unlocked, revealing treasures lost to us for centuries. Here indeed are the *"Thirteen Treasures of Britain"* hidden so well by Merlin that their very nature has been forgotten, and since embroidered out of all recognition.

Here too are the *"Chief Master-Works of the Island of Britain,"* remembered in the old Welsh Triads. And here is the ancient wonder that gave Britain its first name, *"Clas Merddin"*—the school of Merlin, the mage, who embodied the Druidic teachings for which Hyperborean Britain was so famed in Greece.

Here is the first Round Table; of which the Norman *"Queste del San Graal"* says, *"The Round Table was constructed, not without great significance, upon the advice of Merlin. By its name it is meant to signify the round world and round canopy of the planets and the elements in the firmament, where are to be seen the stars and many other things".*

No wonder William of Malmesbury called Glastonbury a Heavenly Sanctuary on Earth!

This Star-Temple explains the mystery of Arthur's long-awaited return. *"A mystery to the world, the grave of Arthur"*, as the old Welsh Song of the Graves puts it. The first Arthur, we now see, was the sun-god whose path is through the Zodiac, dying and resurrecting each year, each day.

Here we shall also find the strands which knit together many half-forgotten scraps of folk-lore; Mother Cary and Davy Jones, Gog and Magog, the Lion and Unicorn, St. George and the Dragon, Britannia and her wheel, the Celtic Salmon of Wisdom, and many another.

Here are the first Jacks of Giant and Beanstalk fame, pitting themselves against the first Giants of folklore; here the first Sleeping Beauty, her somnolent court enmeshed in the thorn-hedge of the Enchantment of Logres; Glastonbury Tor by its name and fame is the first Glass Mountain of European fairy-tale. The first wise Cobbler, the first Cunning little Tailor, are to be found not far from the Tor; here lies the first enchanted circle of Arthurian knights, sleeping around their golden treasure-trove.

The identity of this Zodiac with the Cauldron of Ceridwen, and therefore with the Grail has already been indicated; but the implications of this may not immediately become clear. That is, that if we embark on a study of this ancient system of knowledge we are following in the footsteps of the Knights of the Round Table; undertaking in fact, whether we realise it or not, nothing less than the Quest of the Holy Grail.

In the foregoing paragraphs some very big claims have been made for the Glastonbury Zodiac—claims which cannot be substantiated in a few sentences. To justify them will be the task of the ensuing chapters of this book. But the biggest claim of all is made by the Grail itself.

For this is not just an archaeological antiquity, of interest only to scholars. Both Cauldron and Christian Grail were said to possess three essential properties; both were inexhaustible, satisfying the hunger and thirst of those privileged to find them; both inspired the scholar and the poet; and both bestowed the gift of eternal youth, rejuvenating the diseased, the aged and the weary.

Whether such a claim belongs only to the realm of Faery, or whether it has any validity in actual, literal fact, can only be judged ultimately by each for himself at the crucial bar of personal experience.

Description of the Zodiac

That this antiquity has lain so long forgotten is due, paradoxically, to its immense size. It is literally too big to be seen.

These giant figures—one of them is five miles across—lie stretched over the Vale of Avalon in a great circle ten miles in diameter. Glastonbury Tor is its northern sighting point; Somerton and Lyte's Cary bound it on the south. The effigies are formed and outlined by hills, contours, earthworks, roads, paths, ancient field boundaries, and by natural and artificial waterways. They consist of the twelve signs of the Zodiac in their correct order, with a thirteenth figure, the largest of all, lying outside the circle to the southwest. This is the great dog of Langport, who guards the sacred abode of Annwn, just as Cerberus guarded the gates of Hades.

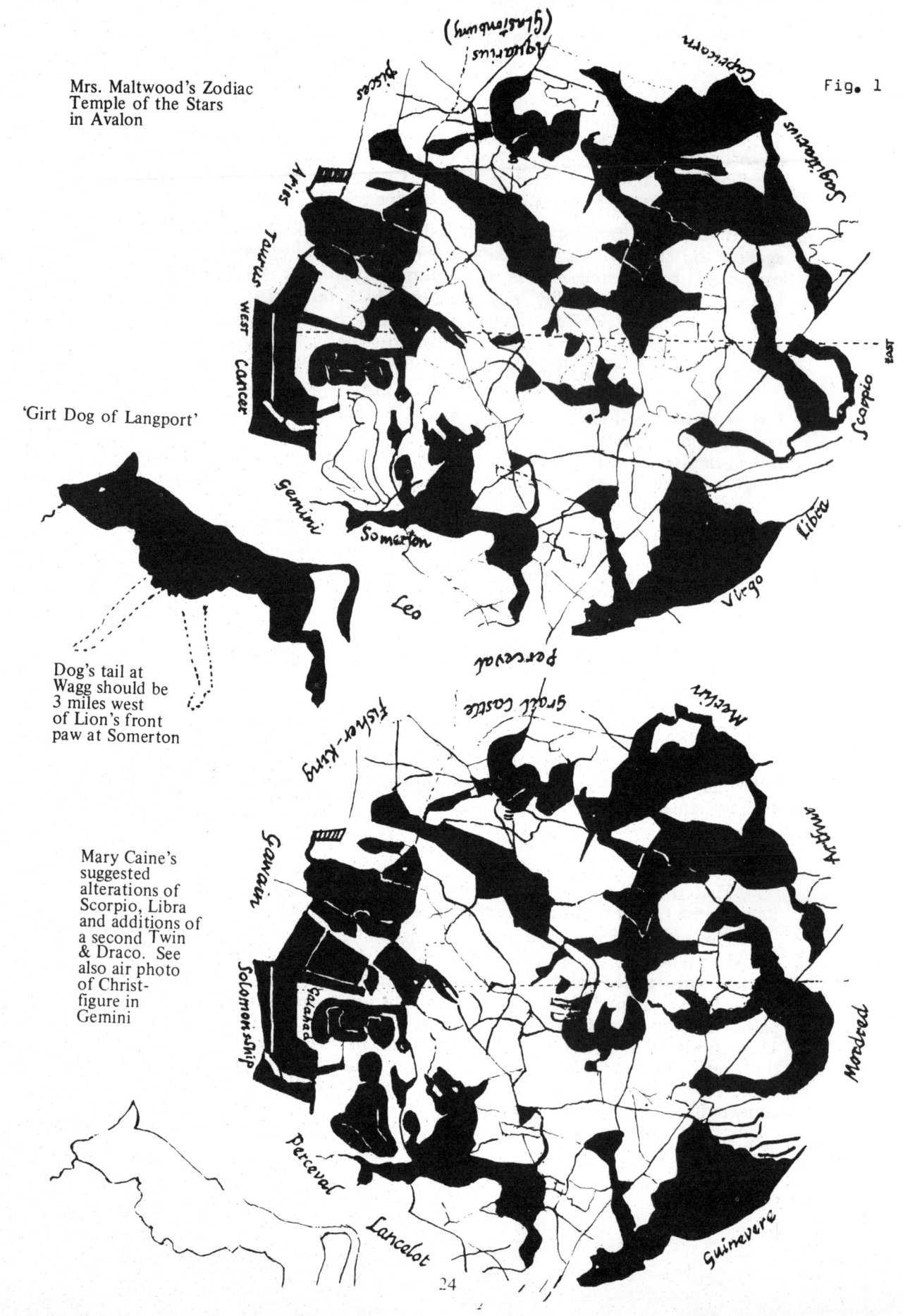

Fig. 1

Mrs. Maltwood's Zodiac Temple of the Stars in Avalon

'Girt Dog of Langport'

Dog's tail at Wagg should be 3 miles west of Lion's front paw at Somerton

Mary Caine's suggested alterations of Scorpio, Libra and additions of a second Twin & Draco. See also air photo of Christ-figure in Gemini

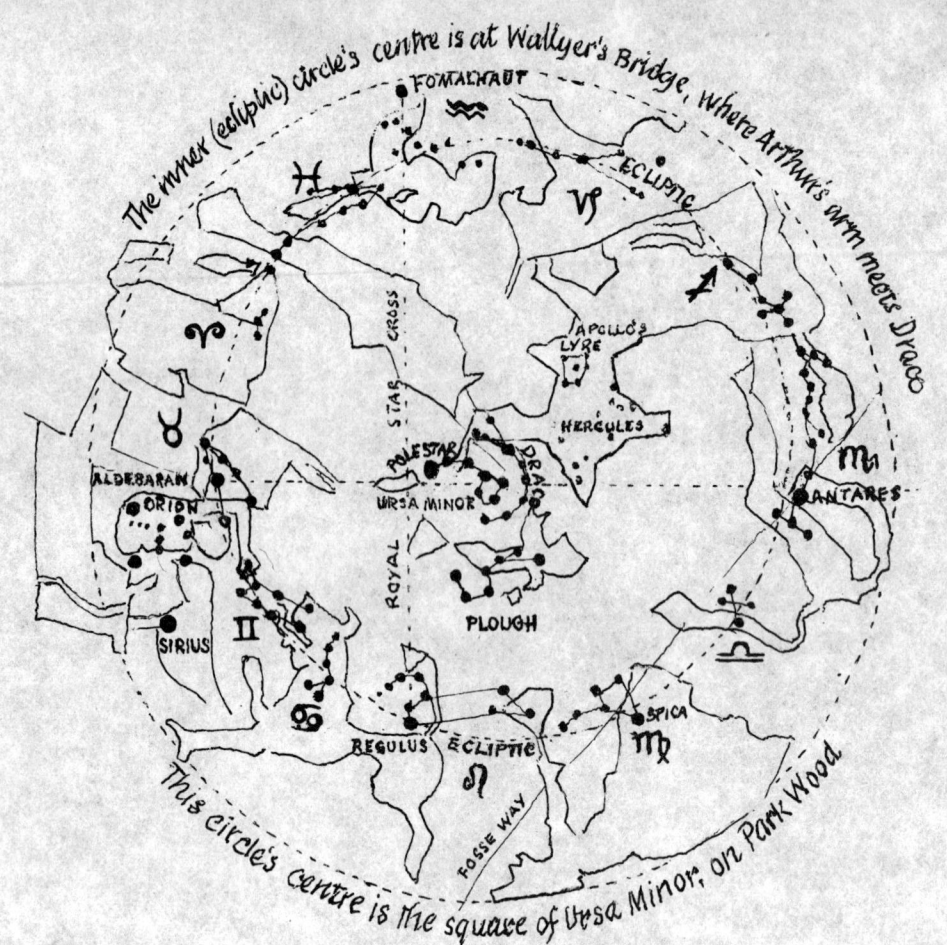

Three signs differ from the Zodiac with which we are familiar; instead of the usual man with a water-pot at Aquarius, we find a phoenix. Libra and Cancer appear at first sight to be missing, and only reveal themselves later, Libra as a dove, Cancer as a boat; both signs being moved slightly to the west of their normal positions. There are three fish in Pisces, not two; Cetus the whale making a monstrous addition to this sign. In the chart of the heavens Cetus, though a near neighbour of the fishes, lies just outside the path of the ecliptic. It would be wrong however to regard him as a gate-crasher in the charmed circle, for the part he has to play in the drama about to be unfolded is crucial. Indeed, in every case where our British Zodiac differs from the familiar pattern the effect is to restore significance to the whole design, to irradiate it anew with its original meaning, long since overlaid and forgotten. Study of its component parts leads inevitably to the conviction that here, in the Somerset version, we are seeing one of the earliest Zodiacs of all; one whose design is nearer to the intentions of the first designers than those with which we have hitherto been familiar. Such a conviction is strengthened by comparing the elements of the Avalon circle with Chaldean, Greek and Celtic mythology, and leads to the startling conclusion that most, if not all these apparently unrelated myths stemmed originally from the Zodiac. This great pyrotechnic work had it, seems, the power to throw off saga and legend with the prodigality of a Catherine Wheel throwing out centrifugal sparks. By its light the minor alterations of the versions that have been handed down to us will be seen as bad copies, the result of generations of misinterpretation and imperfect transmission of its original myths. That even these bad copies still retain sufficient magnetism to make the astrological column the most avidly devoured section of our daily press is a tribute to its original power.

The Somerset Zodiac, however, will be found to restore to this battered and derided symbol of symbols its original order and consequence, its self-proving logic, its lost philosophy. For the secret it enshrined was the teaching of the ancient mysteries; a vast and harmonious compendium of every kind of knowledge embracing science, mathematics, astronomy, agriculture, medicine, history, psychology, philosophy, poetry, clairvoyance and mysticism; into whose school Pythagoras, that founder of Greek thought, was proud to be initiated.

The Zodiac key will unlock the doors which divide the religions of the world from each other, for it provides a common basis for them all, an open-plan mansion in which all may intercommunicate and recognise their common inspiration. It will also unlock the doors of specialist study in all the arts and sciences, revealing unsuspected correspondences between them of structure, relationship and proportion, thus providing a common language for all. Many of the greatest minds throughout human history have recognised this.

Isaac Newton silenced the astronomer Halley's derision of astrology with the famous remark, *"I have studied the subject, sir—you have not!"*

The discoveries of Tycho Brahe and Kepler owed much to it. Kepler finding a correspondence between the notes of the musical scale and the distances of the planets from one another. Jung's psychology was enriched by studying astrology; he has said that before long every university would have its chair of astrology. Einstein too expressed respect for the subject. Recent studies of the proportions of mediaeval cathedrals have revealed deliberate correspondences to the mathematical proportions of the musical scale, and thus to the Zodiac whose pattern adorned their doorways. Mozart, Hindemith and Holszt, among others, have expressed this pattern in music; Shakespeare, Goethe, Chaucer, have seen it at work, and illuminated their poetry with its system; T.S. Eliot is no mean successor in this tradition. In Philosophy Kant and Leibnitz are but two in a line of succession which stretches back through Plato and Pythagoras into prehistory. This is no list of second-raters, dabblers or pedants; it is indeed only a small selection from the ranks of genius who have been illumined by the ancient science.

There are signs that some scientists today are awakening to this rich heritage, so long neglected. Max Muller remarked that many of the greatest men of his own day study astrology, but most keep their opinions to themselves, for fear of the derision of lesser minds.

Genius is distinguished from normal competence or scholarship by its ability to draw upon the unconscious. The Zodiac pattern seems to be imprinted on the unconscious mind no less than upon the earth and the stars—how else can we account for its persistence through the ages and throughout the globe?

KATHERINE MALTWOOD AT WORK

KATHERINE MALTWOOD

THE MALTWOOD MUSEUM OF HISTORIC ART AT ROYAL OAK, VICTORIA, B.C. AN OUTSTANDING EXAMPLE OF GOTHIC REVIVAL ARCHITECTURE. IT WAS THE MALTWOODS' HOME FROM 1939

2: Katharine Maltwood

Sole credit for discovering the Glastonbury Giants belongs to this remarkable woman. Born Katharine Sapsworth at Woodford Green, Essex, on the 17th April, 1878, her father was a man of substance who seems (from a photograph) to have been mayor of the town. They lived at Higham Lodge, a large Italianate house. She studied sculpture at the Slade under Sir George Frampton, and was soon exhibiting at the Royal Academy. Her work, always monumental in feeling, shows her preoccupation with mystical themes; but perhaps the most extraordinary thing about it is how often her subjects foreshadow her Zodiac, as yet undiscovered. Such titles as *"Wounded Centaur", "Magna Mater", "Plucking Feathers from the Eagle's Tail"* are strangely prophetic. This last is Z-shaped, a somewhat strained design. Was she intuitively spelling Z for Zodiac? Her lofty studio in a mews off Kensington High Street inspired reporters with awe, being divided into shrines by gold lamé curtains hung from ceiling to floor. These housed sculptures like *"The head of a Buddhist priest"*; the whole effect induced hushed reverence, as letters from her visitors testify. Reading them, one feels that here was a purposeful incarnation, solemnly conscious of her mission. Her photographs show her as stately, handsome, commanding—even in old age.

She married John Maltwood, as tall and handsome as herself; a childhood sweetheart. One is glad to hear that he was poor (her father called him *"the pauper"*). But he grew wealthier than her father; she never lacked for this world's goods, though from her marriage it seems she never sought them. They were undoubtedly necessary for the task she had to perform, and one has the impression that they moved under Fate to fulfil it. He lived to the great age of 100. *"She was"* he wrote to me, *"a goddess."*

By 1911 they were living at Tadworth, where she sculpted the font of the Church of the Good Shepherd. No less prophetically, she used the theme of the Trinity, depicting it with a creative hand, a paschal lamb, a dove.

In 1914 she exhibited another prophetic piece; *"Canada awakening to her Destiny"*. How could she know then, before World War I, that they would emigrate to Canada at the onset of World War 2?

We can learn more of her character and outlook from a novel, *"The House of Fulfilment"*, whose heroine was closely modelled on Katharine Maltwood. It was written by a friend, a Mrs. Barrington of New York, using the pen-name of Adams Beck, and published by Fisher Unwin in 1927. The story is set in India, its characters questing for enlightenment through the wisdom preserved in its monasteries.

But for Katharine Maltwood India was not the end of the trail; she was destined to rediscover the ancient mystical heritage of her own country. The book, interesting as it must be to Zodiac researchers, was written too soon.

For about that time she became aware of Arthurian legend, and was asked to draw an itinerary of the Grail-Quest in Avalon for *"The High History of the Holy Grail"*, a Norman-French manuscript newly translated into English by Sebastian Evans, for Dent's *"Everyman"* edition.

It is easy to see the impact this highly mystical—and mysterious—manuscript must have had upon her. She had, unknowing, long been preparing herself for it. It is an early "Pilgrim's Progress" with calendrical overtones; its chief knights typify the four seasons—Gawain, Spring; Lancelot, Summer; Arthur, Autumn; Perceval, Winter; it is essentially an allegory of the soul in its quest for self-fulfilment through the seasons of human life.

Studying its text, which purports to have been written at Glastonbury Abbey, she found that the castles and adventures of the knights accurately corresponded to places in the Vale of Avalon. Following their encounters with dragons, giants, lions and other alarming fauna on the map, she was amazed to find that she too was confronted by a huge lion, its underside accurately drawn by the river Cary from Somerton to Lyte's Cary; its back traced by an ancient road, Somerton Lane.

A geographical giant revealed itself next, contoured by Dundon and Lollover Hills. An astrologer friend with whom she discussed these strange finds suggested from their relative positions that they might be Leo and Gemini of the Zodiac—and it was not long before the whole consort of Glastonbury Giants was restored, after centuries of oblivion.

Perhaps only a sculptor could find such earth-sculptures? Certainly the artist's habit of visualising must have helped her to see what is plainly there though no-one before her had noticed it. But it must have been her mystical training that earned her the right, the affinity, to rediscover the Mysteries of Britain, still vibrating faintly on a wave-length no-one else could hear.

The High History of the Holy Grail, she began to realise, set out the secret location of these long-lost Zodiac effigies in the Avalon landscape. It was the search for these that was the Quest of the Grail—at once an outward and an inward quest, for Arthur's knights were searching both for their own signs and the Geminian image of the Perfected Man.

She too gave herself over to the search, abandoning sculpture. They went to live for 25 years on the Polden Hills in a Victorian fairy castle, from which she could overlook the landscape of her quest. She wrote her book, *"Glastonbury's Temple of the Stars"* (published in 1935 by John Watkins, London) in its tower. (Looking south-east to the bold contour of High Ham, between her Dog and Gemini Babe, did she reflect on the odd coincidence that her birthplace was named Higham Lodge?)

She also produced an *"Aerial Supplement"* with the help of Huntings Aerofilms, a series of aerial photos of the effigies; but this is alas out of print. *The "Temple of the Stars"* her second book *"The Enchantments of Britain"* are now published by James Clarke. This last was the result of many years' study of comparative mythologies, gathered during her frequent travels all over the globe, during which she and her husband amassed a large collection of art treasures. After her death in 1961 their home *"Thatched Lodge"* in Victoria, British Columbia, was bequeathed to Victoria University as the Maltwood Memorial Museum. Here their treasures are exhibited and her voluminous notes stored. It also houses much of her sculpture.

She also bequeathed her fortune to the Royal Society of Arts in the hope that it might be used for further research into her Zodiac. But the nature of her discovery has been an embarrassment to that august body, and the interest has so far been diverted to less controversial archaeological projects, despite requests from those devoted to furthering her work.

How ironic that a large Zodiac, carved on the building opposite, faces the Royal Society of Arts in John Adam Street. Is this mysterious coincidence a further embarrassment to its officers?

Though the icy materialism of her day is now beginning to crack, the thaw has hardly as yet reached *"establishment"* circles. Katharine Maltwood, that lone pioneer, born under Aries, suffered the fate of most of her kind, dying without reaping the reward of recognition for her splendid labours.

This book, such as it is, is a tribute not only to her discovery, but to herself. She spoke of her work as unfinished, and invited further research; I therefore hope that the few additions and amendments I have made meet with her posthumous approval. Time itself will correct any errors. Chief of these additions is the Messianic figure I found within her Gemini effigy; I am sure she must approve of Him.

Her books might be described as *"slim volumes"*—but their size is deceptive. To open them is like opening a small but bulging suitcase whose contents tumble all over the floor; try to repack them and one needs several large trunks to contain them. Each item is a collector's piece, each paragraph needs a whole chapter of proof with attendant reference. And though her books are liberally sprinkled with such assurances, many of her statements are so startling, so contrary to accepted beliefs that the reader is impelled to verify them where he can. But many years of such testing has left me with a real respect both for her erudition and integrity; an opinion entirely endorsed by those I have met who knew Katharine Maltwood. Many references can be run to earth by reading the bibliography at the end of her *"Temple of the Stars"*; a fascinating exercise for those who are waking to the lure of the British Mysteries.

But despite the painstaking evidence she has given, her find has been dismissed in academic circles as too *"inherently improbable"* to warrant serious investigation. (Most modern discoveries in science would have been dismissed in the same terms, a century ago.) So Mrs. Maltwood's critics have not risked looking into her Pandora's box before rejecting it. There is a certain worldly wisdom in such a course, though it hardly confers the right to an informed opinion on her work. For those who actually lift the lid of her box will never be able to close it again. Its contents will tease, nag, and pursue them, distract them from their course, upset their calculations, preconceptions and values, expose them to ridicule and hostility, and give them a new and disturbing view of themselves and the universe.

There are certain subjects which, if we wish to preserve the even and relatively meaningless tenor of life, are best left alone. The Glastonbury Zodiac is one of them.

3: Who Made It? When? And Why?

For those intrepid enquirers whose curiosity outruns their discretion, these must be the first questions.

There can be no doubt that this Zodiac, in essence, is *natural*. Its huge figures, moulded by hills and lesser contours, part-outlined by rivers and streams whose course is determined by them—the whole complex measuring some ten or twelve miles across, thirty miles round, can hardly be the unaided work of man.

No, it was modelled by a vaster hand; whether we like to call it Nature, Cosmic Forces, or simply God.

Mrs. Maltwood herself conceded this, though her thesis that it was developed by metal-seeking Sumerians in Britain has obscured the fact. It is however an important fact, and ignoring it has led some enthusiasts into strange byways. Supermen, Atlanteans or flying-saucer-men, capable of superhuman feats like moving mountains have been put forward as the Zodiac's creators. Glastonbury Tor alone must have been quite a handful. Alas for such theories! It has been found by archaeologists to have been a natural formation, even at its preposterous summit.

But such notions at least recognise the superhuman nature of such a project; one far too great to have been carried out by puny creatures like ourselves. The trouble is that they miss the whole point—which is *to recognise that Nature works to a pattern*.

The first civilised men undoubtedly recognised this. They realised that this pattern operated not only on matter but on Time; that it was in fact a *Space-Time pattern*. The traditional Zodiacs of Egypt and Chaldea, Greece and Rome, not to mention those of ancient South America and China, are the diagrams they made to demonstrate their knowledge. They are not simply a picture of the stars of the ecliptic belt (though they are that too) but a pattern from which a vast and complex philosophy was derived, a cosmology which involved not only the shapes taken by the constellations as seen from earth, but the shape and character of all earthly formations, including the human race. Being a Time-pattern as well as one that governed form in space, it was a pattern that implied orderly progress toward an aim. This aim could only be the aim of Evolution itself. This, no less, they found expressed within the pattern.

It is too early to examine this Aim in detail, for this must depend upon a study of the effigies, their character and relationships; enough for now to suggest that its fulfilment was not seen as automatic, but on the contrary dependent on the exercise of free-will; and that it aimed at *ever-increasing consciousness or awareness*. This is not a new suggestion. It is as old as the ancient system of Astrology—and has been put forward anew in our own time by such thinkers as Julian Huxley and Teilhard de Chardin, men of otherwise widely divergent views—and without benefit of astrology.

The natural origin of this Star-Temple seems to be endorsed by a strange passage written by St. Dunstan's biographer in 1000 AD. *"There is"*, he says, *"on the confines of western Britain a certain royal island called in the ancient speech Glastonia... dedicated to the most sacred of deities. In it the earliest neophites of the Catholic rule, God guiding them, found a church not built by art of man, they say, but prepared by God Himself for the salvation of mankind.."*

This is usually taken to refer to the little wattle church, long vanished, around which the magnificent abbey was erected, stage by stage, in successive ages. Some said this little church was built by Joseph of Arimathea, but some, remembering the legend that it was not built by merely human hands, suggested that Jesus Himself was the builder. He was after all, a carpenter, and Cornish tradition insists that he visited Britain with his tin-trading Phoenician uncle Joseph.

I would suggest however that Dunstan's biographer was *referring to the Glastonbury Zodiac*, which still breathed out an aura of mystery and sanctity inherited from Druidic ages, an aura inherited by the abbey in Christian times.

Yet human hands—and feet—have certainly played a part in the development of this astonishing design, for the roads and paths which delineate much of the effigies, the aptly-placed lynchets, the canals which define the Ship and the Whale, are undeniably man-made. The question most difficult to answer is how much of it is deliberately developing the design, and how much is the inevitable result of natural siting; extensions permitted or encouraged by the terrain. The paths and roads that help to outline these figures all lead purposefully towards farms, villages, towns; and settlements must grow up around a water-source. It looks as if most if not all such roads and habitations are simply developments of natural resources.

WHO?

So the question *"Who made the Zodiac?"* must it seems have a dual answer; it was made by Nature in the first place, and continued by man—

because, as Kipling would say, *"He Had To"*. He is still at it, quite unconsciously, for the Zodiac can be seen on 20th century maps perhaps more clearly than in the past; the paths are widening into motor roads, and some roads are becoming dual carriage-ways.

Yet this is not to say that the design was unknown, unrecognised. There is indeed much evidence in early writings to show that it *was* known—as we shall see. And though this knowledge was kept secret, it was all the more highly valued for that; and it is unimaginable that those in the know should not have helped the design along when opportunity offered. The man-made rhines or canals for instance that entirely draw the Ship, or the tumulus that models the nipple on Virgo's breast, or the lynchets defining Taurus' horns on Hatch Hill, or the rampart of Capricorn's long straight horn, seem deliberate.

WHEN?

The second question *"When was it made?"* must then take us back to the geological ages when the hills were first formed and the streams first began to flow. But this was only the beginning; its continuous development embraces all the ages of man down to the present day; and if this is so there is no reason to suppose that its evolution should not continue into the future. On the contrary, now the Zodiac is more openly known, this defining process is likely to accelerate. The Dove Centre recently founded on Libra's Dove is only one example. Such developments are also indicative of the way awareness increases the speed of evolution.

WHY?

The third question, *"Why was it made?"* has already been answered by Dunstan's biographer with commendable succinctness. It was prepared, he tells us, for the salvation of mankind.

What a flavour of infinity there is about all these answers! We come to it in our usual state of partial consciousness, expecting a clear yes or no, and get both yes *and* no at once; this in itself is a hint (to those of mystical bent) that we are in touch with infinity. The word *"mystic"* has a religious flavour, but this inherent contrariness is not confined to probing saints; it is encountered by the artist in the disciplines of perspective, (where, as for the mathematician, parallel lines meet in infinity) and by the physicist, for whom the search for the ultimate particle of matter ends in limitless energy, and whose neutrinos have the alarming capacity to be in two or more places at once.

Such discoveries in physics, spread by television, paperbacks and communication media generally more widely and immediately than ever before, are doing much to change the climate of thought from the materialism of Mrs. Maltwood's day. Our children can consider the claims of this Zodiac more seriously than our fathers. Like the Red Queen in Alice, they are practising *"believing in at least six impossible things before breakfast"*. In such a climate the assertion that the Zodiac of Glastonbury was *"prepared by God Himself for the salvation of man"* is not so easily dismissed as monkish credulity or mediaeval superstition; it reads as a statement that simply needs translating into 20th century terms.

How then can a pattern of twelve shapes in a circle do so much for the human race? A formidable task for any designer!

The Trinity, demonstrated by this Zodiac, is for instance a recognition of the basic forces behind all creation, observable in light, colour, electricity and the structure of the atom. Only three signs are human. These three signs, Sagittarius, Virgo and Gemini, are placed in an equilateral triangle across the circle. Here, surely, is the Trinity of all ancient religions—Father-God, Mother-Goddess, and their semi-divine son(s). The second Twin I found does not really make a fourth human figure, for Gemini, who is Man on earth, is divided against himself, half-animal from his Mother Earth, half-divine from his sun-god Father. All old religions explained man's dual nature by Twin-myths; they survive unchanged in modern Zodiacs. But their meaning has been lost. The Somerset Zodiac restores it by showing them as part of the ancient *"family"* Trinity. This Trinity was itself lost to Zodiacs when the Greeks added another human figure, the Watercarrier at Aquarius. Our Zodiac restores it, for here Aquarius is an eagle or phoenix.

In what later Zodiac may we plainly read the Fatherhood of God, the Brotherhood of Man? Or see the process of Creation depicted? Here in Avalon Sagittarius is unmistakeably kingly, something a centaur can never be; he is indeed a dying god, dragged like the dying sun from his sky-mount by the Sea-Leviathon in Pisces. It is the battle between light and darkness, Creation and Chaos. As he sinks he sends a last shaft of light, of energy, in the form of the Dove to quicken Virgo—virgin-soil—with life. (There would be no life on earth without the sun.) Their Geminian sons, unlike the animals that surround them, have free-will to sink back to the animal state or rise to the Godhead that engendered them.

In what other Zodiac may we see these possibilities in Gemini's Twins? Yet here on Dundon Hill the foetal form of the northern Twin contains the Perfected Man. The Babe, man as he is; the Christ, man as he is destined to become. To emphasise the point, Aquarius, a resurrecting Phoenix, rises on strong wings from Glastonbury Tor's hill of resurrection, illumination, self-fulfilment. (He is a Watercarrier too—Chalice Well is in his beak.)

Here then at Glastonbury is the star-lore of all the ages; the source of all religious teachings. The Trinity is common to all. The Christian Trinity is there too with its Holy Spirit or Dove, though the Word or Logos came from earlier teachings still. Here is the first Annunciation, Virgin-Birth, Passion, Crucifixion, Resurrection of the son of God and Man, call him Bel, Krishna, Christ, Dionysus, or what you will—for the same myths belong to them all.

Here the Babe lies in the manger, watched by ox and ass; for he lies in Cancer's cradle, whose constellation contains the Manger stars and those of Asella, the Asses. Taurus the ox nuzzles his arm. (Man is born helpless, say the stars, utterly dependent on parental care; a debt he must repay. Yet his potential is such that domestic animals adore him, working to increase his wealth and strength—another debt he must repay.

The story of the Messiah is continued when we see that the same vignette of the Messianic figure in the boat gives us the Baptism in Jordan at Bethabara (also called Bethany, *"place of a boat"*). John the Baptist is perhaps the second or mortal Twin here, seeing Jesus as one *"whose shoe I am unworthy to unlatch"*. The Logos-Dove flutters overhead. In Star-lore this is the dawning of self-awareness, idealistic youth awakening to his mission.

The same picture gives us the entry into Jerusalem on the Asella stars, the ass and her foal, the Passion, kneeling with bowed head in Gethsemane; flagellation—(both hands of the Geminian Messiah are tied above his head)—and the crucifixion between two thieves. (Gemini is ruled by Mercury, god of thieves.) Such is the young sun-hero's path, faithfully imitating his father the old sun-god, who dies continually to give life and hope to his creation.

Here too is the original Fisher of men, the first Good Shepherd—for Orion had these titles before Christ, and the stars of Orion fall upon our Gemini's effigy.

The resurrection is portrayed by Aquarius' Phoenix, rising from its own ashes. For death, say the stars, is not the end; it is only the end of a day, a cycle, the beginning of a new life better or worse according to our efforts. Aquarius too is the Man with the Waterpot who led the disciples to the Upper Room in Luke's gospel. It is the place of Pentecost, where new vision and understanding enlightened the mourners, flooding them with courage so that many begin to tread the path that only one could tread before.

It is the story of Evolution and its purpose that this Zodiac tells, no less; and this story has been preserved in the Mysteries of all cultures.

It seems right to describe the true path of Evolution for Man first; but the Zodiac also abounds with warnings of the consequence of failing to follow it. The first Garden of Eden is here, with Sagittarius as Adam, Eve as Virgo, Cain and Abel as the Gemini twins. The serpent Draco twines about the pole-star Tree of Life, tempting Eve with Avalonian apples. Wisdom born of experience, trial and error?

The Ark of the Flood is there too, with its Noah surrounded by his Zodiac animals; a story that appears in myth the world over, and has always been taken as a dire warning to mankind not to press Evolution's patience too far.

This economical compendium is the source of myths the world over, as I hope to shew in later chapters with some examples from ancient Egypt,

Chaldea, Greece and Britain. By such parables were the initiates in the Mysteries instructed. Well might our Zodiac have been prepared by God himself for the salvation of men.

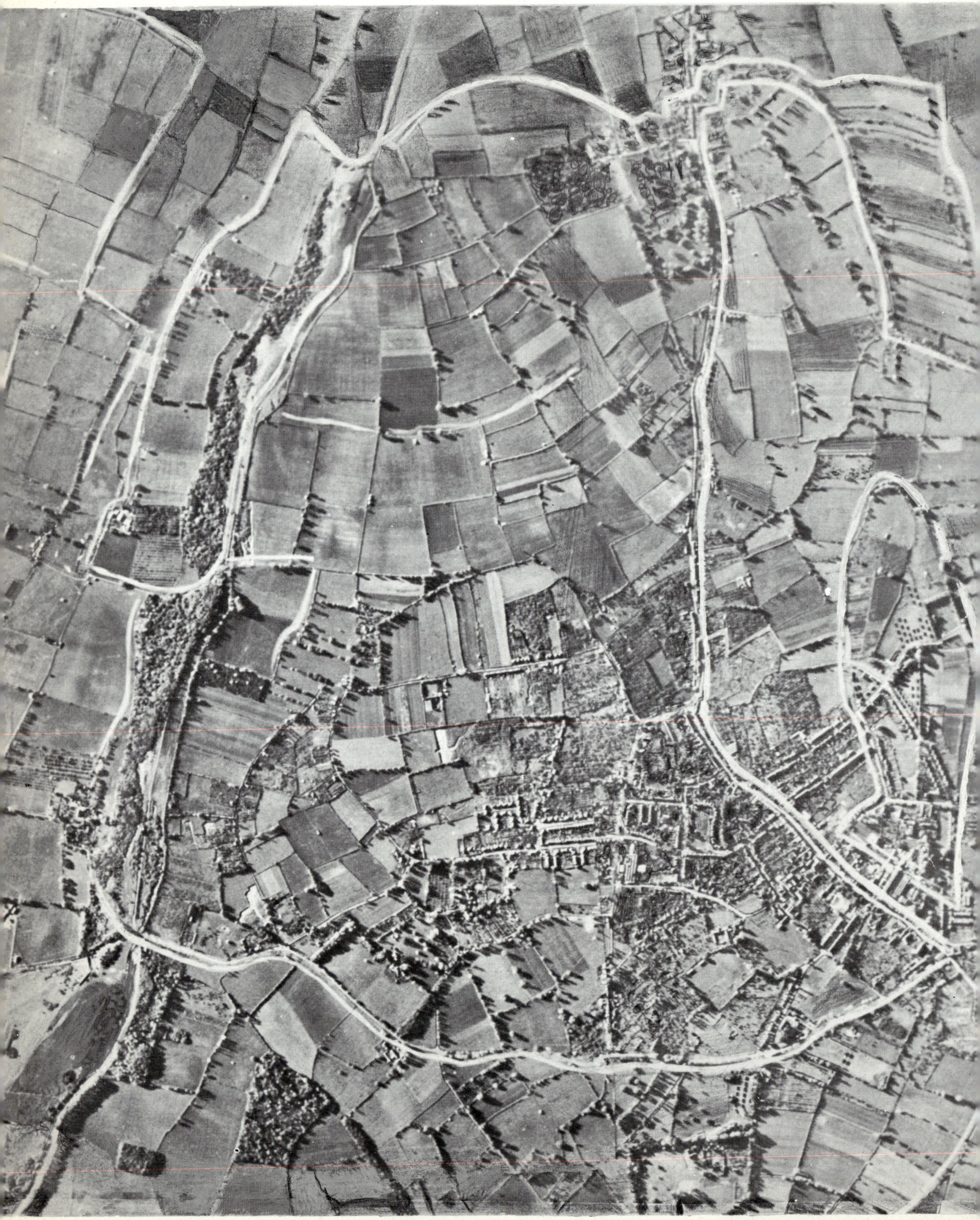

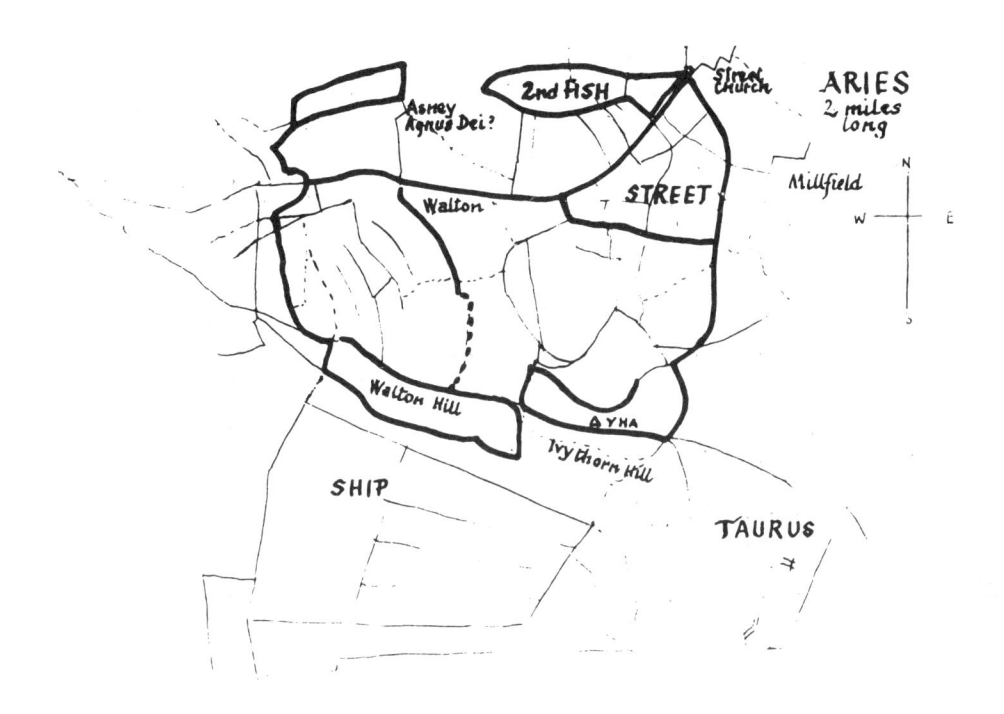

4: Aries

This figure, the Zodiac's first sign since ancient Egyptian times, is a Paschal Lamb, not a Ram, its head reverted at Street, its feet tucked underneath. A favourite insignia of the Templars, it is carved on a mediaeval farm together with an eagle at Lower Wick, on the Glastonbury Eagle's eastern wing. Templars, their astrological Mysteries expressed by the Zodiac, owned much land in Somerset; this may have been one of their farms. An ivory Lamb and Flag was found at a Templar farm at Chedzoy, near Bridgwater. Templars, known as Guardians of the Grail, must often have trodden the ancient road from Bridgwater to Street that draws the Lamb's back atop the Polden Hills. From here they could map the Zodiac landscape below with discerning eye; southward lay Gemini's effigy, whose great head on Dundon Hill may well be the *"head"* they were accused of worshipping. And worshipful it is, as we shall see.

Mrs. Maltwood discovered the Zodiac while living at Chilton Priory, a Victorian castle on this old road. The name *"Portway"* where this track draws Aries' underjaw, proclaims that it went past Bridgwater to the ancient British port of Dunball on the mouth of the Parrett. At Walton on his haunch, it branches south-east to draw his legs and Taurus' neck. This is Ivythorne Lane, equally ancient, for it yielded a flint scraper. At Ivythorne Farm some standing stones mark the beginning of a footpath that draws the bent-back forefoot.

Mrs. Maltwood surmised that a Templar who knew this landscape well must have written the *"High History"*, so accurately does it describe these effigies. Of this area it says: *"The king of Wales was lord of this land"*. Walton Hill—*Welsh* or Waellas' town—contours Aries' body, its fieldshapes accurately drawing his haunches. The young Aries has seen battle, for earthworks here have left scars. This is not surprising, for the wedge-shaped hill forms a natural defence westward. This wedge governs Aries' triangular shape; not only his head is three-cornered. The third road completing his triangle is the old tin-track from Cornwall to the Mendips through Somerton and Glastonbury, drawing his breast and the back of his head. Did Joseph of Arimathea, the *"tin-man"* travel this road to the Mendip mines?

Sheep grazing on Walton Hill have made Street aptly famous for sheepskin rugs. And how right that the town should also be famed for its shoes; one of the Piscean Fish springs from Aries' head, and in astrology Pisces rules the feet!

The Greeks identified Aries with the Golden Fleece which was hung in the Temple of Ares (Mars) in Colchis, guarded by the dragon or whale Cetus until Jason captured it. In our Zodiac, Aries is still guarded by the Whale Cetus, while Geminian Jason waits his chance in his ship Argo, just beneath. (Jason's connection with the Zodiac is further examined in the chapter on Greek myth.) The Golden Fleece appears on Aries' back in summer as rippling fields of corn.

But let us return to our own traditions. In Britain this Zodiac is the origin of the Round Table, round which Arthur and his chief knights sit as the Houses, months and seasons. Some Celtic scholars had already suspected that Arthurian legend was sun-myth, before Katharine Maltwood discovered the Glastonbury Zodiac; her find offers confirmation of their theories.

The High History, her main Arthurian text-book, treats of four knights who she suggests represent the four seasons or quarters of the year. Perceval stands for winter, at the eagle of Aquarius, Gawain for Aries and spring, Lancelot for Leo's summer quarter, and Arthur himself is the dying sun of autumn, signed by **Sagittarius**. The High History states that Arthur once had 366 knights—the number of days in the sidereal year—but that due to his fading vigour he only had 25 left.

Aries is the first sign of the Zodiac; Gawain is the first of Arthur's knights. Arthur says of him *"Thou art the first to move this Quest"*. His brash impulsive youth also identified him with Aries. In the old mumming plays, seasonal in content, Gawain is cast as the doctor who revives the old sun.

> *"Of wounds and healing lore had Sir Gawain learnt more*
> *Than any man alive to make the sick knight thrive..."*

says Chretien de Troyes

Only the young spring sun can revive the dying year.

An early Grail Romance tells us that when Gawain was presented with the mysterious spectacle of the Grail procession with its lance dripping blood into the cup, *"so soon as Sir Gawain asked about the lance the waters flowed again through their channels, and all the woods were turned to verdure"*. Surely this is Aries, the first *"April Rainer"* who can turn the Waste Land of winter into spring. But he did not manage it at his first visit to Grail Castle, which was an ignominious failure. He first goes there quite unprepared, in all the assurance and ignorance of youth, and is dumbfounded by the mystic parade. Only if he can ask the meaning of it can the mysterious Fisher-king be cured. But he cannot, so the king grows worse and a blight falls upon the whole land. It becomes the Waste Land, and Gawain is ignominiously kicked out to bloody his thoughtless head against brick walls until his own sufferings and those he inflicts on others bring him to a sadder, wiser frame of mind: one where he is ready and eager to ask the fundamental questions about life. These are the Grail Questions. Interestingly, he is not required to answer them; to ask them is enough to bring the streams gushing forth, to grow hair on the bald-headed women, to enable sheep to lamb and sterile cows to calve, and the dying king to recover and rejoice. What a parable for today! There's more to it than simply seasonal myth.

Celtic myth records a fascinating trait of Gawain's: his strength waxed till midday, but waned rapidly after that. The day of the young spring sun is short. Gawain must have had to fight his battles before lunch. He is impetuous, like March winds, repentant like April showers; but he has little staying power. Though he is the first to start the Grail Quest, he gives up impatiently before achieving it. (Aries the pioneer likes starting things but never stops to finish them.) By contrast Leo, Lancelot, the high sun of summer, blazes with steady ardour—his love for Guinevere, his only passion, ceases only with death.

As both Gawain and Lancelot are fire-signs, it is hardly surprising that Gawain's people in the High History mistake Lancelot for their lord. Both knights, being sun-gods, undergo the same Beheading Test—an odd return-match characteristic of solar heroes.

The Tale of Gawain and the Green Knight is the best-known version of this. A monstrous figure, green from his hair to his toenails, rides into

Arthur's hall, challenging anyone to cut off his head on condition that a year later the beheader shall himself be beheaded. All are abashed, save Gawain - who is quite incapable of seeing a year ahead. Characteristically bold and thoughtless, he obliges the Green Knight with a sweeping blow; only one blow is allowed in this game. But the Green Knight picks up his head from the floor, dusts it carefully and replaces it, and reminding Gawain of his bargain, rides away none the worse. Gawain, having acted in haste, repents at leisure. But honour demands the fulfilment of his pledge, and one year later he seeks the Green Knight's castle. Here he is warmly entertained — too warmly - for his host's wife nearly seduces him. Extricating himself politely from what was surely an initiate's test of chastity, he puts his head on the block at the appointed time, only accepting a safety-belt from his seducer, guaranteed to preserve him from harm. A wise precaution, one might think - but no. The Green Knight's axe falls, but just grazes his neck. The graze was for accepting the belt made of the lady's hair; had he really stuck his neck out, explains his executioner, he would have got off scot free. We are undoubtedly among the Mysteries of Britain - not only seasonal myth but a morality play. Virtue defeats winter, death and hell, and wins summer or paradise.

The Green Knight's odd colour makes him a Green Man or Nature Giant. It may also be due to the ambiguous Celtic word Glas, which can mean green, grey, or transparent. In some versions of the story the challenger is a Grey Huntsman - like Gwyn ap Nudd, wild hunter of Glastonbury Tor. In the first pages of the Mabinogion this huntsman is Arawn, king of the Celtic Underworld of Annwn, who must exchange an annual death-blow with Hafgan, all clad in white as the Summer king. In south Wales until the 19th century this ritual battle was enacted between the white Summer King and the winter King, clad in furs and armed with a blackthorn club. Summer always won, for this was a May-Day rite.

Gawain's Welsh name, Gwalchmai, means Hawk of May. He is also Gwalchaved, Hawk of Summer. But it is his Spanish variant, Gavrilan, which firmly connects him with Aries in April. His name is in fact found under various guises all over Europe, and his Grail Castle on the Tor is no less universal as the Glass Mountain. Against its misty, grey-green, transparent backcloth much of European folklore is enacted. For all folktales are but the Mysteries, told and retold to the young in heart.

Youthful Aries has a Youth Hostel. Surely no accident! Superbly placed for views on Ivythorne Hill's prehistoric hill-top track, it looks north to Wearyall and the towering Tor, west to the Ship's flat sea-moors stretching out to Severn sea, south to Gemini, sculptured by Dundon and Lollover. Eastward the track beckons uphill to Taurus' muscular neck, his head crowned by the Hood Monument. Where better for the young adventurer to begin the Quest of the Grail?

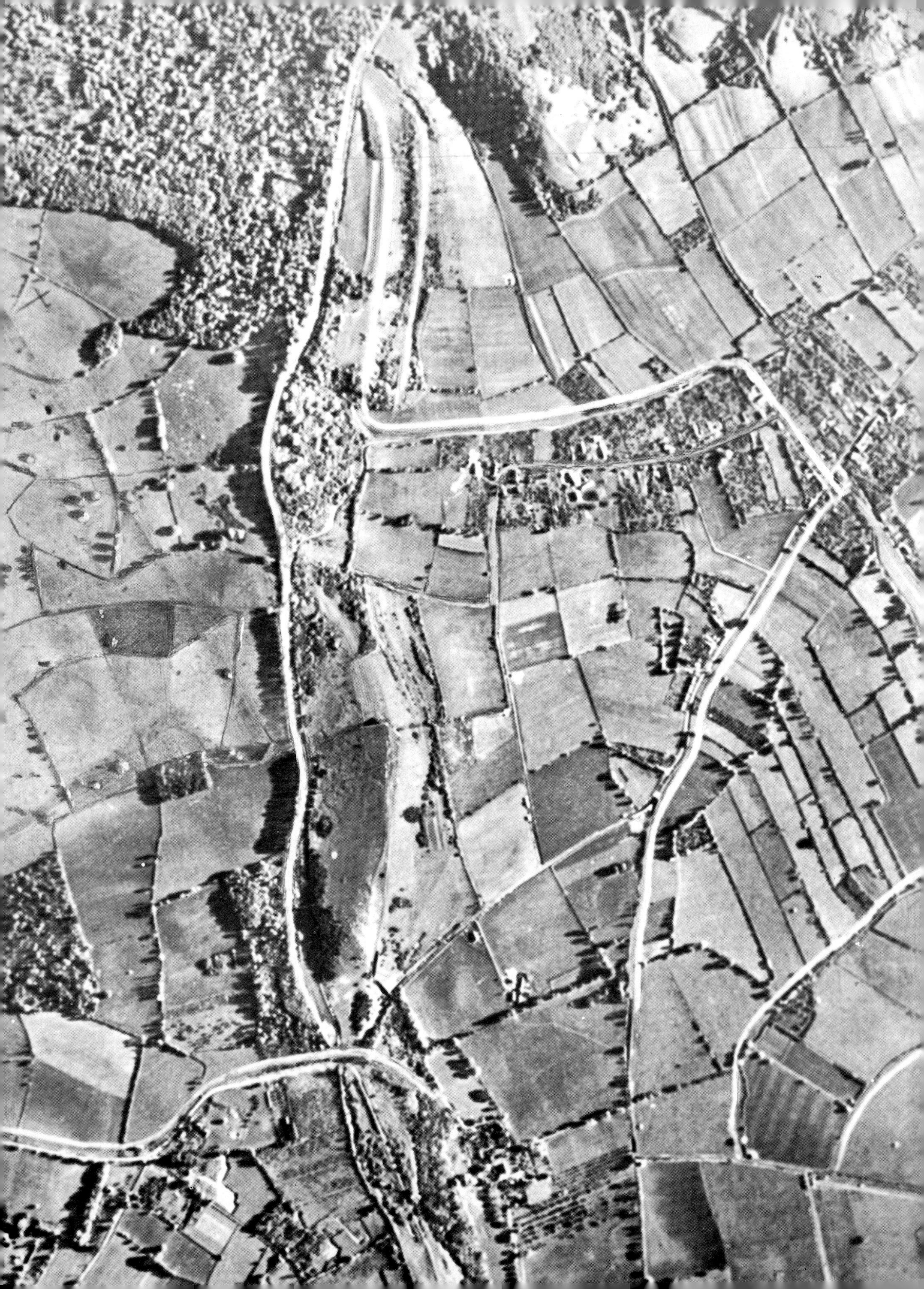

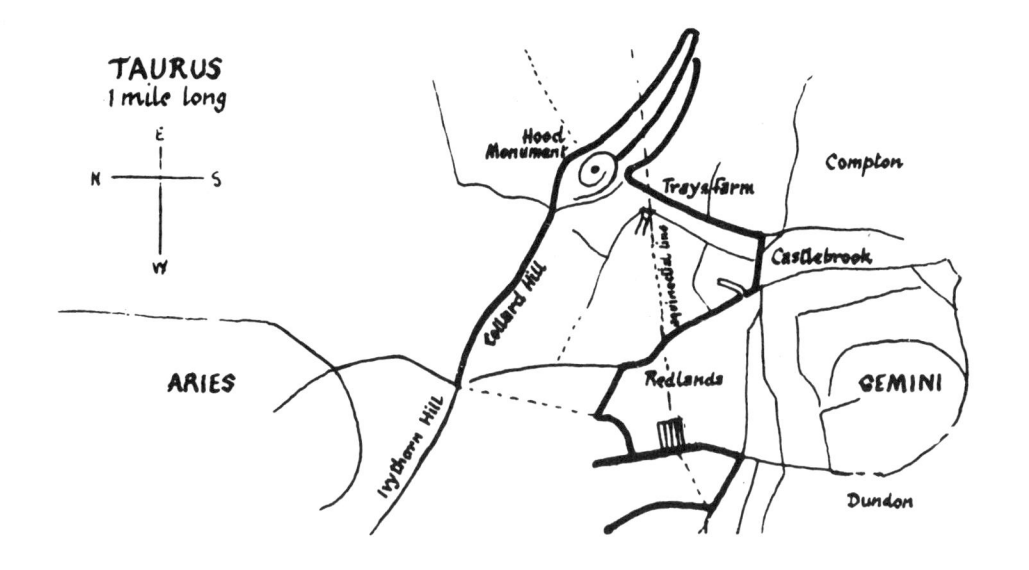

5: Taurus

*"Then let the giver of the mead-feast cause to be proclaimed—
I am the cell; I am the opening chasm; I am the Bull Becr Lled.
I am the repository of the Mystery; I am the place of re-animation...
As for him who knows not the ox-pen of the Bards
May fifteen thousand overpower and afflict him at once."*

Taliesin's Buarth Beirdd

Luckily Mrs. Maltwood has saved us from this dreadful fate by finding the ox-pen of the Bards, and indeed the Bull Becr Lled (bull of dawn) at Compton. The ox-pen can only be the Zodiac itself. Davies (who translates this poem from the Welsh in his *"Mythology and Rites of the British Druids"*, 1809) says that the Bull of Dawn must be an idea dating from about 4500 BC, when for over 2000 years the Bull *"Opened the year with its horns"*. That is, the sun rose against the sign of Taurus at the spring equinox. And what else *can* it mean?

The bard Taliesin undoubtedly knew of the Zodiac, being heir to the astronomical (and astrological) Mysteries of Ancient Britain, and never ceased to taunt other bards with their ignorance.

He proclaims *"A holy sanctuary there is, on the wide lake; a city not protected with walls; the sea surrounds it. Demandest thou, O Britain, to what this can meetly be applied! Before the lake of the son of Erbin, let thy ox be stationed. The sacred ox of the patriarch is stationed before the lake"* (Taurus has his foot on the Ship's mast) *"ready to draw the Shrine"* (Argo, the Ark) *"to land out of the watery repository. It is the lake of the vessel of the lofty chiefs. The eagle or symbol of the sun, was placed aloft in the sky,"* (Aquarius, aloft on the Tor) *"that is, in the open aetherial temple, which is often so called. There was the representation of the path of Apollo—an image of the ecliptic, in which the pomp was conducted, preceded by a waving eagle. And this was done in the presence of the great sovereign, the sun himself."*

Can anyone doubt that Taliesin was describing the great ethereal Temple of the Stars? Its ecliptic path is marked on the head of Aries by an ancient sacred circle (now the round churchyard at Street, where there must have been a Celtic Cross, for it is marked *"Cross"* on the oldest O.S. Maps). The ecliptic line is also grasped between Gemini's upraised fingers and runs along Leo's tongue. Its full width is measured by Virgo's wheatsheaf and Aries' head. *"The patriarch"* must be Noah, who in Britain was called Menu, or Hu. Hu did quite a bit of irrigation with the help of his faithful ox, who burst his mighty heart drawing the Avanc out of the lake. In fact two effigies have been recovered from the periodic inroads of the Severn; the Avanc must be the huge Whale in nearby Pisces, also drawn by canals which keep the flooding river Brue within bounds.

Britain in fact had its own Flood legend, in which Hu or Menu (from which we derive our word minnow) was the only survivor—with his wife of course, who is described as the *"goddess of various seeds"*—Virgo. The animals he preserved are the creatures of the Zodiac. The flood was caused by Llyn Llion bursting its banks. Lyonesse! Nor was this a local affair—*"the whole world was overwhelmed"*.

Can this memory really go back to the Cancerian Age of the Ark, 6700 to 9000 BC? For at this period Britain and Europe lost much land to the west, Britain being finally cut off from the Continent.

Though Taurus is only represented by his head and foot in our Zodiac, he is clearly drawn, and by ancient roads. We must thank Venus who rules Taurus for the scenic beauty here; Glastonbury Tor can be seen through a screen of beeches on his collar—Collard Hill; southward lies Gemini asleep on Lollover and Dundon Hills. Between lies Redlands, remembered as the Red Launde of tournaments in the High History. Lynchets curving round Hatch Hill furrow his horns in true Taurean style, earthworks convolute his ear.

On the hillcrest, which crowns his head, he is further crowned by the Hood Monument, a tall 18th century obelisk. The impulse (however subconscious) to add a third horn seems to have been irresistible. Admiral Hood's apt name here makes one smile.

His eye at Tray's Farm was once a pond. Alas, this has recently been filled in. They built a cowshed on the hill immediately above it, and it began to smell intolerably of cows. How apt.

The farm's mediaeval remains shew that a monastery once hallowed this pre-Christian sacred place. The field near this Bull's-eye is marked on old O.S. Maps as a rifle range!

Taurus' eye-in-the-sky is the red star Aldebaran. Its earthfall on our map is not on his pond-eye, but on four little fields, differently orientated from their neighbours, on his foot. Here, if we draw a straight line through the pond-eye and through the Archer Sagittarius' eye to "Stone" in Scorpio, some of this Zodiac's marvellous geometry is revealed. *The Archer draws a bead on the Bull's-eye.* But further elucidation must await a later chapter.

Taurus recurs in Taliesin's poems. *"They know not the brindled ox with his thick headband, and the seven-score knobs on his collar"* he grumbles in *"The Spoils of Annwn"*. But we can recognise the Pleiades, nearer seven-score than seven, that fall on his collar, Collard Hill. In the Mysteries he signified strength, fertility. (Is the Hood Monument a phallic symbol?) But he is not easily subdued. Spanish bullfighting, Cretan bull-vaulting, Jason, Arthur or Hu ploughing Herculean furrows, are all allegories of will over wish, sinapse over sinew, brain over brawn. Natural vitality must be guided into constructive channels.

What happens when the Bull is master of the field? The Celts, an undisciplined lot, had reason to know. Reflect on their tragic saga of the Bulls of Connaught and Ulster. There, Queen Mab's envy of her husband's bull led to fratricidal strife and the death of many heroes; even the bulls in question finally ran amok and killed each other. Amid all this slaughter King Conchobar uttered the famous oath, which is found with variations from Ireland to eastern Europe, wherever the Celts have settled. *"The heavens are over us; the earth beneath, and unless the sky falls with all its stars about us—"*. Men swear by what they hold most sacred: surely this oath reflects the Somerset Zodiac, source and centre of the Celtic Mysteries, as its effigies reflect the stars?

Bulls bled profusely in the Taurean Age—though no more, one imagines, than in our own abbatoirs today—just more publicly. One hopes the horrors of the Taurobolium were not enacted in Britain. In this Roman rite the Mithraic initiate slit the tethered bull down its belly from a pit beneath, being thus bathed and *"purified"* in its blood. Romans loved this sort of thing, but Britons seem to have regarded bull-sacrifice as a regrettable necessity, just as we do today—if the bard Aneurin is anything to go by. *"But wounded art thou, severely wounded, thou delight of princesses, thou who lovedst the living herd. It was my earnest wish that thou mightest live, O thou of victorious energy. Alas! Thou Bull, wrongfully oppressed; thy death I deplore".* The R.S.P.C.A. couldn't put it better.

If Moses disapproved of Golden Calf-worship however, it was because it was by his time out-dated. His was the Arian Age, so with one eye on the precessing equinoxes he substituted the Paschal Lamb for the aging Bull. The Passover, some suggest, remembered the passing of the Taurean Age as well as the Red Sea. They derive its name from the Pesach, a hobbling cripple-dance imitating the lamed sun-king's gait, left over from Taurean times and danced at Easter. Tradition dies hard, as Moses found.

"Why do the women of Elis summon Dionysus to come among them with his bull-foot?" asks Plutarch. But of course he was the lamed sun-and-seed-god of spring fertility-rites, limping about with his heel in the air, only his toes on the ground, like a bull. We can now see why the all-important foot appears, even though there is no space in the design for more than the head. The bull with only the head and foot is normal in many old Zodiacs. In the Denderah Zodiac he lies down in the ship.

The Chaldean and Phoenician god Bel has given his name to the bull; *"bellan"* means to bellow. He is also present in the word Beltane, Taurus' May-Day feast; no doubt the reason for the great Tourney at the Red Launde near his foot.

The High History's Castle of the Trial is undoubtedly on this effigy. Here a bellowing copper bull was worshipped, guarded by two figures with flailing mallets. Perceval, a muscular Christian, incensed like Moses at this anachronistic adoration, drives forth the bemused worshippers, all but 13 being knocked flat by the flailing mallets. But the 13 survivors *"forsaking the Old Law for the New"* were baptised, and *"scattered themselves on every side among strange forests"*, making hermitages for themselves. The number is surely significant. Are they not the effigies of the Zodiac and the Guardian Dog? All groups of twelve, such as the twelve gods of Olympus, the twelve apostles, originate with the Houses of the Zodiac, which denote twelve distinctive human types. (Though the spectrum of human character is actually endless, for purposes of identification and study the divisions had to be made. The colour-spectrum is equally endless, but the same necessity has caused us to divide it arbitrarily into three main colours, then six, then into twelve.)

Esoteric Christians, trying to equate *"the Old Law"* with the New, allotted each apostle to a different Zodiac sign; St. Andrew was identified with Taurus, though why, is difficult to understand. At any rate, Dundon Church near Taurus is St. Andrew's. (The reason for this may be more interesting, however; Dundon Church is actually on Gemini, the Perfected Man, and *"Andrew"* means the androgyne or perfected Man of the Mysteries. This may well be a Templar dedication.)

The old Hebrews equated Taurus with Joseph, which makes good sense; for all three Biblical Josephs provide shelter for the young sun-god, like Taurus the Builder and Protector. Egyptian Joseph built granaries, and hints at the Grail in young Benjamin's sack of corn; Joseph, Jesus' foster-father the Carpenter protects him at Bethlehem like Taurus overshadowing Gemini, Joseph of Arimathea houses him in death in his tomb, and in myth at least bears him and the Grail westward, housing him in a ship.

Taurus in Arthurian legend must be Sir Ector, protector and foster-father of the young Arthur; (his name indeed is Hector, who protected Troy). And Ector's son sir Kay was the steward, who served dishes in Arthur's court. Bethlehem too means *"House of Food"*. Taurus the Provider, the Protector, appears in all myths.

Mary Caine's messianic figure contained within Mrs. Maltwood's Gemini child.

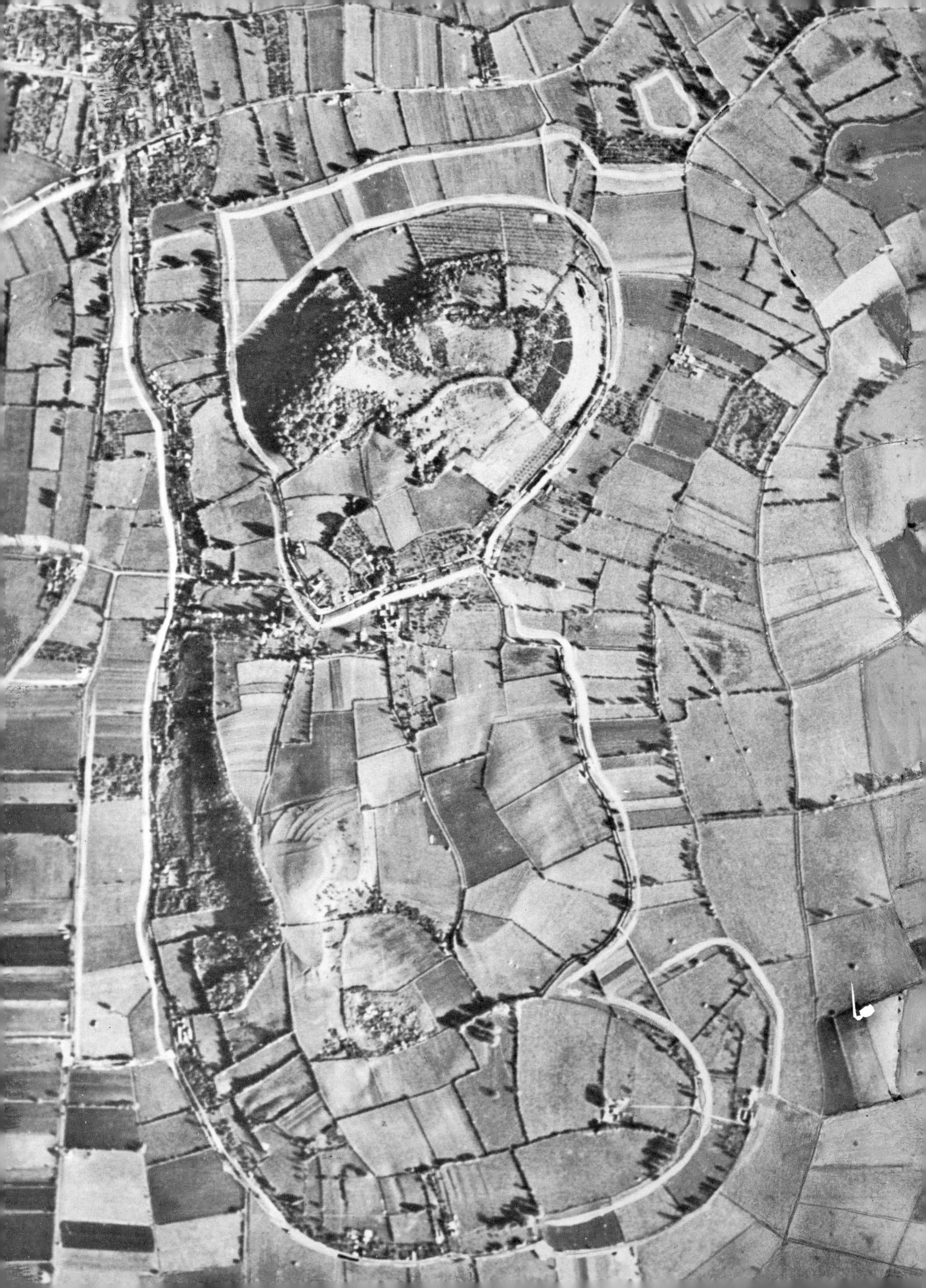

6: Gemini

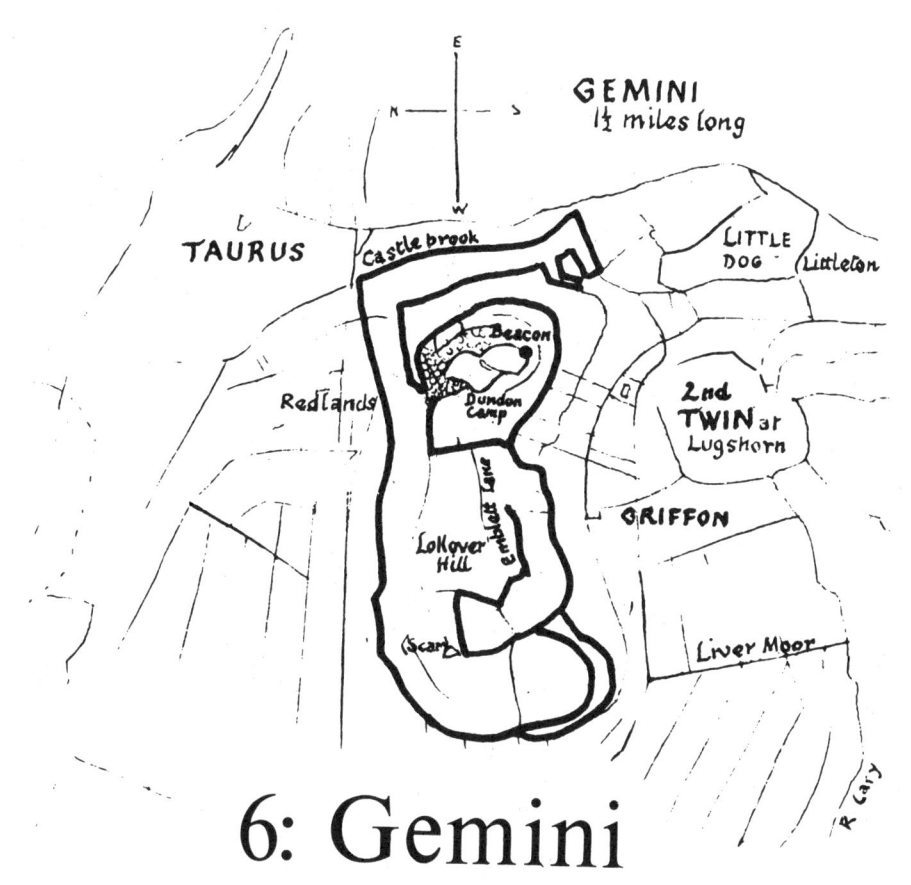

"And did those feet in ancient time
Walk upon England's mountains green?
And was the Holy Lamb of God
On England's pleasant pastures seen?
And did the Countenance Divine
Shine forth upon our clouded hills?"

Our Zodiac answers Blake's question with a resounding affirmative. Gaze at the Giant Babe, the Heavenly Twin of Dundon Hill and a second figure emerges from within, numinous as the Grail itself! Here is a twin-figure indeed; at once Child and Man, Bethlehem Babe and Suffering Saviour. Katharine Maltwood will I hope forgive this addition to her effigy; his beauty and grace only deepens the meaning of the Zodiac Trinity and indeed emphasises the message of the whole Zodiac. She was not one to reject such a cornerstone to her building.

This self-sacrificing figure mediates between all faiths, for Christ-like though he is, he was there before Christianity, typifying the self-giving of Bel, Tammuz, Adonis, Dionysus, Krishna and many another noble son of the sun.

Mysteriously unfolding from within the Babe, is he not every man's True Self, undeveloped, unrecognised, denied—and daily, hourly, self-betrayed? When the cock crows, the initiate feels this and weeps; for he has begun to see himself as merely the misshapen foetus of what he must become. Here, surely, is the goal of Evolution, towards whom all the other effigies turn in hope; the Genius lurking in the unconscious of us all. His head is the steep and rounded British Camp of Dundon Hill, the "fort of Don, or Wisdom". The Camp models the Baby's ear, and within this is a dip (perhaps once a dewpond) that makes the eye of the Christ or Krishna figure. A beacon-tumulus crowns the head at the place of the inspirational pineal gland; when lit in times past it could be seen right across the Severn in Wales. Truly here is the original Taliesin Radiant-Brow, inspired bard and Master of Celtic Mysteries! Tal-iesin means, literally, *"tall or raised-up Iesse—Jesus"*

His hair and beard grow just where they should, untended and unintended. It is Mother Nature who preserves her Son. She fed him with her wheatsheaf, which she, as Virgo, extends towards him—for an old tithe-barn, now ruined, once stuffed the Baby's mouth with corn. His eyebrow is still modelled near the entrance to an orchard by Dundon Smithy, though the eyeball is much obscured. A path from the church turns his jaw at right-angles to ascend to his ear on the Camp. Here many flints and bronze rings were found. (The church has a map of Gemini, drawn by a *young boy*—and two monuments by *twins* in the chancel. Coincidence?) Ancient lynchets terrace his ribcase on Lollover Hill, his body—though the odd name must surely remember the bowed head. For here is the Cromm Cruach, the Bowed One of the Mound—chief of thirteen *"gold and silver idols"* seen by St. Patrick on the shores of Britain. In the 7th century life of St. Patrick this idol *"bowed its head westwards, for its face was from the south"*—exactly describing Gemini—*"and twelve other images can be seen to this day, half-buried in the earth."* St. Patrick, said to have been an early abbot of Glastonbury, blessed this pagan idol with his staff or crozier, and a wound of red marl is there on his thigh to this day. It is an important mark, figuring in innumerable sun-god legends, not least in Christian, where it was caused by the lance of Longinus. The blood of the wounded God-man may account for the two Redlands, also Redlake, around his effigy. Liver Moor is also a blood-symbol, by his knee.

Ancients saw the liver as the seat of life, rather than the heart—hence no doubt its name—and prophesied by throwing them and watching the shapes they took. Several are in the British Museum, marked in cuneiform with divinatory meanings; one at Piacenza, used by Etruscans, *resembles our Gemini in shape.* (Etruscans, like Britons, claimed Trojan descent.) Our Gemini, *"the Liver"*, is still the giver of Life! Prometheus too gave life to men and was punished by Zeus who sent an eagle to peck his liver for ever. And in The Maltwood Zodiac an eagle-headed Griffon can be seen pecking at Gemini.

The stars of Gemini fall on our effigy's upraised arm; he is undoubtedly Pollux, immortal twin-brother of Castor the mortal Twin in Greek myth. Pollux, (whose name means Beautiful) begged Zeus to save Castor from death, so they were granted alternating immortality, each standing hostage in Hades for a period while the other enjoyed a holiday in Olympus. Pre-Christian brotherly love!

Cretan and Phoenician sailors prayed to the twins at sea, remembering how they saved Jason's Argo by quelling the storm-waves. Did not Jesus do the same?

Our Gemini is also Orion, for Orion's stars, most beautiful of constellations, fall upon his body. (The Giant Orion's head appears in some old Zodiacs between the Twins.) He too is solar myth, for an enemy put out his eye as he slept on the shore, and he had to sail over the western horizon to regain his sight. Some said he was killed while far out to sea by an arrow from Diana's bow. The sun cannot long survive the rising moon-bow. In Egyptian myth he is Horus, who while sitting with his father Osiris in the *"Boat of Millions of years"* was stung to death by Scorpio. Time stood still (Horus means Hour) until Thoth started things up again by uttering the Word; at this the life-fluid from Ra the sun entered Horus and revived him. This is not only a myth of the perpetual rebirth of nature after the ravages of autumn and winter, but a hint that the initiate, dying to his old self in the agony of Scorpio's self-analytical sting, will also be reborn.

Our Gemini it seems is also Atlas, King of Atlantis—for he bears the starry heavens on his upraised arm, pinching the line of the ecliptic between his fingers.

Atlas too lived on a mountain, in the Garden of the Hesperides, which as we shall see was identified by the Greeks with Britain *"in the far west, bordering the Ocean."* He held up the firmament on two great pillars; (Geminis astrological glyph, II) and these too are figured in this Zodiac's astonishing geometry.

Project the masts of Gemini's ship; they meet, in a triangular enclosure by Butleigh Cross in the circle's centre, bathing our Twin in a shaft of light like that which descended on the Dioscuri when they saved Jason's Argo. If they are extended west to cut the circle's circumference, this segment, Mrs. Maltwood found, corresponded to the thirteenth moon month (a secret of the Templars) being exactly a thirteenth of the circumference. Emblett Lane on Gemini's body may derive from the Greek Embolos, an insertion or intercalated time period to regulate the Calendar.

I used Eighteen foot Rhyne and the poopline marked Sale Piece to test her theory, and was astonished at the accuracy of the layout. These rhynes are man-made. Whoever made them must have orientated them on maps as accurate as our own.

Preposterous idea! The few attempts at cartography that survive from ancient or even mediaeval times are (from our superior standpoint) laughably vague and inaccurate. The whole theory is sheer coincidence. *But is it?*

The moon-month measurement occurs on the moon-boat, which in every myth is the young sun-god's vessel. Can this too be just coincidence? And if this ship is Cancer in disguise—well, Cancer too is ruled by the Moon.

But there is more to this Mystery than that.

It seems that Phoenician maps were better. Columbus knew the earth was round—indeed, pear shaped, a fact only rediscovered very recently. He had the now famous Pirie Reis map, dating it is said from 300 B.C. at least.

The Three Bars of Light

In Celtic myth the patriarch Hu (the British "Noah" in his Ark) was the Teacher of mankind. One of his symbols was the arrow-head, the wedge of cuneiform writing. The Giant Hu beheld three pillars of light, on which were inscribed all sciences and knowledge. Celtic records say *"When God pronounced his Name, with the word sprang light and life"*. Hu, *"Son of the Three Shouts"*, beheld the original language, which began with the Name of God. This Name, IA, when the I and A were put together, made the Broad arrow of the Druids, a sign of extreme antiquity still used on Government property today.

We can easily see, with Hu, how two of the pillars of light stream down the masts of his ship. But where is the third? It lies invisible, midway between the two, longitudinally. There is no line on the map to correspond, but we strike some significant places as we draw it. For it passes through Dundon's British camp, at once the Baby's ear and the Messianic eye, through the Baby's mouth, his heart, and strikes the open wound of red marl on his groin, where Orion's star Rigel falls. It is at once the Lance of Longinus and of the Grail-procession, and the sword of Orion. It is the shaft of self-seeing, piercing the initiate to the core, as he sits bent in introspection; the spear that lamed innumerable sun-gods, not least the Arthurian Fisher-King, as he plumbs his own depths in search of the Salmon of Wisdom. We have already noticed how well this tableau depicts the Bethlehem scene, the Baptism in Jordan at Bethabara or Bethania, the entry into Jerusalem on the ass and foal of Cancer's Asella stars, the Crucifixion scene, with the Christ between two Mercurial thieves. In the Mysteries womb and tomb are one; *"Beth"* in Hebrew reads Bedd in Welsh. It is both cradle and grave, where dying god and babe must bed together.

While the two arms of the god are bound above his head as if tied to a tree or flagellation-post, the Babe has only one arm raised. It is bent at the elbow, the right-angle reminiscent of a Mason's square, for he is the son of the Architect of the world, and a geometer in his own right. This aspect is expressed by Math son of Mathonwy in Celtic records (who taught the Greeks mathematics and gave the science his name). We have already seen something of what his measuring-rod could do, and will make his further acquaintance later.

As we begin to glimpse the nature of the Druids' teaching, it no longer seems so absurd to imagine that Jesus may have come to Britain. Cornish and Somerset legends have long asserted that He had the means, seeing tin-trading Joseph of Arimathea as his uncle. All that was lacking was the motive—and this the Glastonbury Zodiac amply supplies.

Shall we take Blake's question seriously for a moment?

Did He come, urged to it by the astrological Essenes of Qumran, who are thought to have taught his cousin John the Baptist, to study at this famous Druid Open University? Did he come to see himself in the Divine

Youth in the Boat? He inherited the title of *"True Shepherd"* from Orion; like the Fisher-king, He provided a mystical meal of fish on the sea-shore. He was careful to fulfil the prophecies which were foreshadowed in the Zodiac, as in the entry into Jerusalem on an ass, the choice of a Water-carrier as guide to the upper room, the re-instituting of the Last Supper, where the god-man was eaten from the days of Osiris onwards, and so on. And how strange that his very name should be here before him, waiting like Jason's Golden Fleece for him to put on!

For Jesus in Welsh is still Yesse, and this ancient form reveals the name's true meaning—the Essence of Man. And Esus or Hesus was the third person of the Druidic Trinity of Belinus the sun-god, Taranis the earth-mother and Esus their son, before Jesus walked the earth.

One is tempted to wonder whether the lost Arthurian land of Lyonesse was not in fact the land of *Leo the Lion and Esse the Giant,* celebrated in the Mysteries of Atlantis before the Flood changed Britain's face for ever.

Cornishmen supply a further motive for Jesus to come to Britain. They insist that Joseph married into the Silurian British Royal family of Caradoc and Arviragus. In mediaeval records he is sometimes called *"noble decurion"* —a Roman office not only military but also given to those in charge of mines. Both Cornish and Breton legends tell how he found the British princess Anna wandering on the cliffs, pregnant and turned out of doors. He rescued her, taking her by ship to Palestine, and married her to Joachim his brother, whereupon she gave birth to—the Virgin Mary! So Jesus to Cornishman and Breton was a red-haired Celt—at least on his mother's side. And that, come to think of it, is genetically the only side that counts. The main difference in the two accounts is that the Bretons thought of St. Anne as a Breton Duchesse, and said that she returned to her beloved Brittany to die. But as Cornishmen and Bretons are close cousins there is less contradiction here than might be thought. It also shews the age of the legend, which must date back to Celtic Christian times, when the royal families of Cornouaille and Cornwall were one.

This legend may explain the intriguing fact that Jesus in European art is usually depicted as auburn-haired. Artists have a nose for the Mysteries, and have become adept through the centuries in preserving by such innocuous means ideas which were too subversive for print. Another example is the frequent depiction of John the Baptist as the dark Twin, his cousin Jesus as the Fair. This idea that Jesus had a Twin belongs to the Mysteries, as our Zodiac demonstrates, and was discouraged by literal-minded Rome. Even now the writings of the Essenes' Dead Sea Scrolls are suppressed! Well might those ascetics have sent the Flower of *Jesse's* Rod to learn his part and see his Counterpart in Lyonesse, the Holy Land before the Holy Land.

THE SECOND TWIN

So far we have only considered the first Twin, and indeed Mrs. Maltwood did not discover the second, though she *did* see the effigy in which he lurks. This she said was a Griffon, a minor character in the High History.

But look within the Griffon as depicted in her *"Temple of the Stars"* and see the missing Twin, seated in yogic posture with his head at Lugshorn. He is the same size as his brother, and placed at right-angles to him; Bradley Hill models his body. His head, like the others, faces west; his head is near his brother's, as it should be, and is within the Griffon's.

The incident in the High History that shewed her this hawk-headed monster was an adventure of Lancelot's. He comes to the Castle of the Griffon, whose owner kept a menagerie of Griffons and a lion underground. Lancelot is able to escape by throwing a little dog to the monsters as a decoy. While they are diverted by it he slips past them, kills the lion and emerges in an orchard to be met by a charming damsel. This accurately describes the course of the river Cary, which draws Griffon, Lion and Virgin, passing Canis Minor's head (the little dog) at Littleton on the way. Is it another coincidence that the Griffon's eye is named *"Decoy Pond"*? It is another old pond that is now alas, being filled in.

Lancelot in killing the lion is overcoming his own love-nature, and accordingly repels the damsel's advances with ease.

Mrs. Maltwood identified her Griffon with the second Twin, and though she missed the boy within her monster, how right she was! The creature stood, she said, for the boy Perceval in Arthurian legend.

Perceval, the boy from the backwoods, worships Sir Galahad the perfected, Christ-like knight, as his ideal. And though at first his brash mistakes remind us of Gawain's trial-and-error career, he does at last achieve a chaste nobility equal to that of unworldly Galahad. Both sail away in Solomon's ship; both see the Grail, united in perfection; they are more identical than twins. Is Galahad not the immortal Twin of the Ship—Perceval his mortal half, struggling to realise his own true immortality? Is this not the Quest of the Grail? The brightest star of the heavens, Sirius, burns on Perceval's breast, lighting his way with hope; the earth poetically responds, marking the spot with welling springs in Grove Lane. An ancient track, aimed from Perceval's heart to Dundon Beacon, crosses the Cary river here at Grove Steyning Ford. Where better for a Druid Grove?

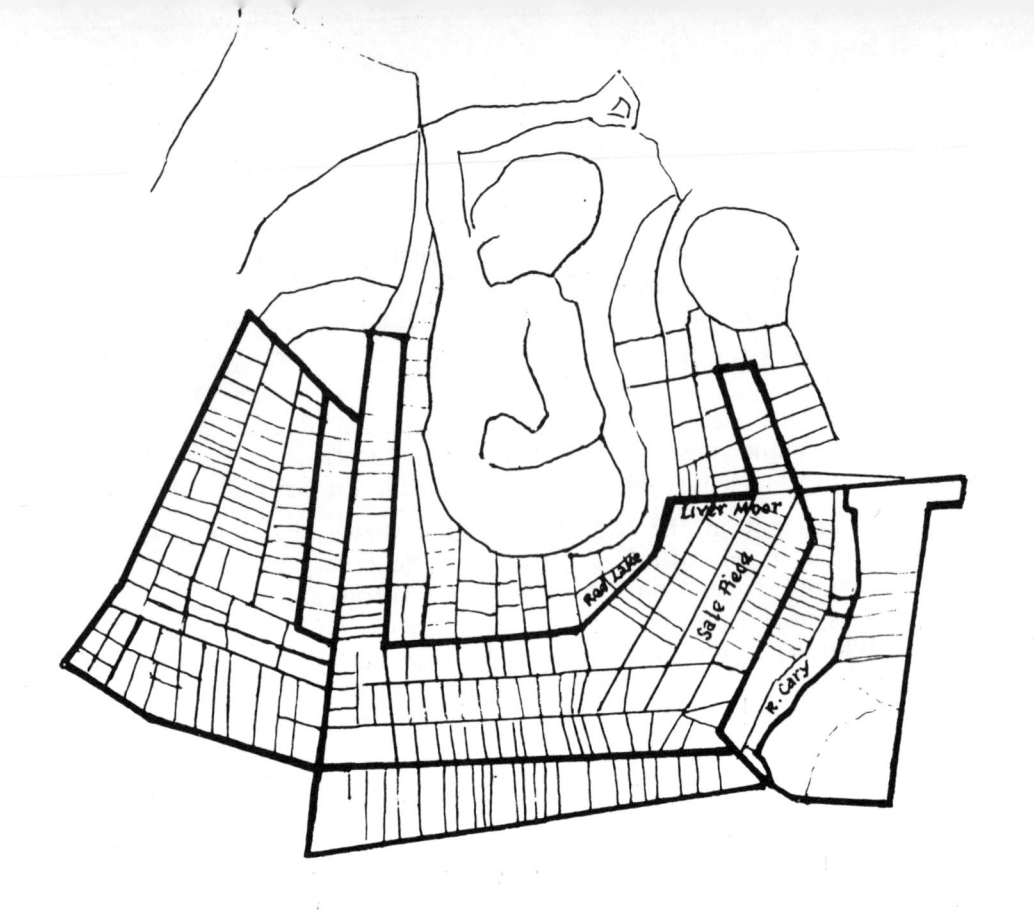

7: Cancer. A Ship

Zodiacs don't usually have ships! This undoubtedly man-made model has strayed in from Argo Navis, a constellation which belongs to this part of the sky. Does it do duty for Cancer's crab, which, like Libra, the Scales, is missing from the circle? Was it a sign to shew that the first recognisers and developers of the Zodiac came by ship? And if so were they from Sumeria, as Mrs. Maltwood concluded, or Atlanteans?

The answers to all these questions, though they must be speculative, need not, oddly enough, be contradictory.

This boat expresses the character of Cancer better than the Crab has ever done. It cradles a baby; Cancer is the Zodiac's maternal sign. It is crescent-shaped, like the Crab; Cancer is ruled by the Moon. Cancer is a water-sign; our vessel is so low-lying that despite the drainage-rhines that draw its planks it is still often flooded. Like the Whale in Pisces' water-sign, it is all drawn by canals. The stars of Lepus the hare fall upon it; the hare was sacred to the moon. To the Egyptians, Lepus was Osiris' boat, his funeral-barge, like Arthur's. How then can the Crab vie in symbolism with

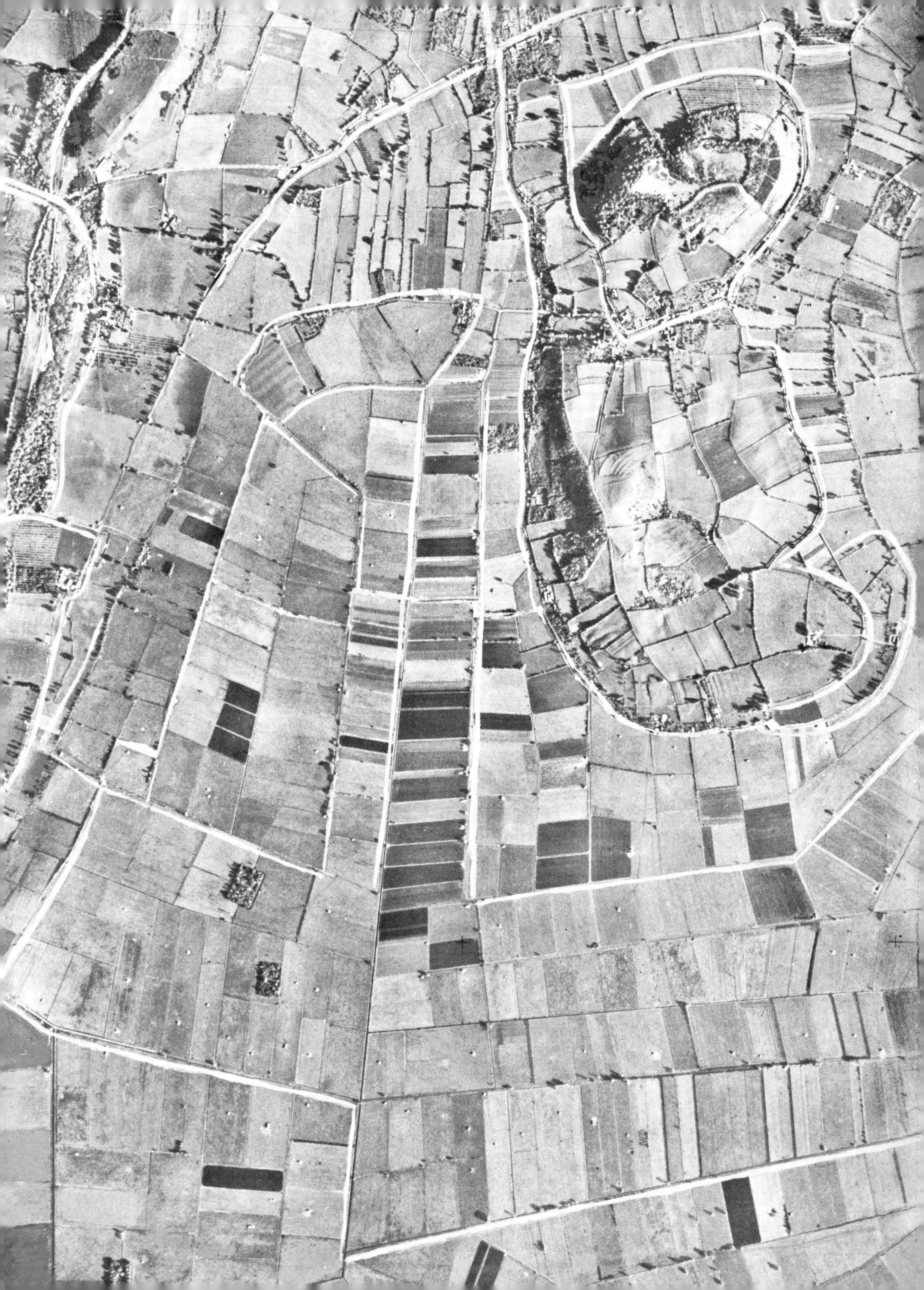

this poetic ship, at once Cauldron of Annwn, moon, womb and tomb? Let it scuttle away and bury its head in the sand for shame!

Cancer's period, from June 21 to July 20, is still in the solar calendar the time of gestation of new life, the time when the fertilised flowers of May-June begin to form the seeds of the future.

At this period the still-damp soil and waxing sun together produce maximum growth; our Ship's flat, green, improbable Looking-Glass country reflects Mother Nature's secrets with a bland half-smile.

This Ship hints at historical and prehistoric secrets too, involving Mrs. Maltwood's Sumerian traders and immigrants. Did Sumerians first carve this Ship by irrigation of the marsh round Gemini's hills, as her researches certainly suggest? Their expertise in irrigation, astronomy, their cuneiform letter-forms, their divination by livers, all point the same way. (Sargon of Akkad, 2600 BC, divined by this method.) This same Sargon, says Waddell's *"Phoenician Origin of the Britons"*, traded for metals in Britain. Certainly the Phoenician trade was ancient; their sailors had orders to sink their ships rather than allow pursuing Cretans to discover where they obtained their wealth . . .

Local legend remembers our Ship. They still say here that a ship once sailed up under the lee of Street and disappeared. And the great baulks of timber sometimes dredged up from this effigy almost fool you into belief. A magical Ship once berthed at Minehead too, without captain or crew; it is still commemorated there by parading a boat-like hobby-horse on May-Day, its quaint ox-tail recalling May's Taurus, his foot on the Somerset Ship's mast. This horse alternately leaps and crouches like a boat on the waves, to the refrain:

> *Awake St. George, our English knight-O,*
> *For summer is a-come, and winter is a-go!*

The Salisbury hobby-horse, now in the museum, was also paraded, but on St. John's Day, June 24th—the cusp of Gemini and Cancer. The Padstow hobby-horse still gladdens May-Day. All celebrate the young sun in his boat—or horse.

Taliesin throws light on this weird horse-boat, but before he can explain it we must know his story.

At first Taliesin was a nobody, little Gwion. Set to stir Ceridwen's cauldron, he accidentally swallowed three drops of its brew, intended for her son—and became inspired. He fled; vengefully she pursued. After much shape-shifting on both sides he hid in a wheat-grain, but she found and ate him; later she bore him, a helpless babe, and threw him into the sea in a coracle or bag. He was rescued, and evincing bardic genius, was renamed Taliesin. (A fuller account appears in the chapter on Celtic poetry.)

Describing his flight Taliesin says *"I fled in the form of a grain of wheat . . . She caught me in her fangs. In appearance she was as large as a proud mare . . . Then was she swelling out, like a ship upon the waters. Into the sea . . . she cast me; It was an auspicious moment for me when she happily suffocated me. God the Lord set me free".*

This night*mare* goddess, mother and midwife to Taliesin's three births, must be our Cancerian Ship. Taliesin himself is the Gemini Twins, at first mortal Gwion, at last an immortal bard. The quaint hobby-horse dances are vestiges not only of seasonal sun-myth but also the Druidic Mysteries of spiritual rebirth.

Taliesin's poems have been dated to the 6th century AD, but his material is of dateless antiquity. The bard himself is a shadowy figure; there seems to be more than one of him, occurring at different periods. Perhaps bards of special merit were honoured with the title. It is tempting to see the White Horse of Uffington and those weird horses on old British coins as representations of his mare-goddess Ceridwen. These belong to the Iron Age. She is at least as old as that, for her name is one with Ceres or Kore of the Mediterranean.

Which came first, Ceridwen or Ceres? Taliesin's descriptions fit our Zodiac, surely the oldest Zodiac in the world, so well that it seems the goddess's first home was here.

Here is another extract which betrays the bard's familiarity with its geography.

"May the heavenly god protect us from a general overflowing! The first surging billow has rolled beyond the sea-beach. A greater than he, Daronwy, there has not been, to afford us a sanctuary, round the proud celestial circle." Daronwy is Gemini, Don of Dun-Don. Ship and Whale were once again awash, the Zodiac's celestial circle menaced by Severn's waves. *"How woeful"* he laments, *"was the treatment of Kedwy and the Boat."* Ked is the Whale, also liable to floods—for elsewhere he speaks of *"Jonah in the belly of Ked."* The sea-mother in her ark, chest or kist-aspect is also called Kit and Cetti. (Cetus is the Whale.) Kit's Coty House dolmen in Kent remembers the same goddess Ceridwen, at once cradle and grave for man.

Our Boat appears in Arthurian legend too. Here it is known as Solomon's Ship, made by Sol the sun and his evil wife the moon, to last for all time till the perfect knight should come. In it hung three spindles, green, white and red, made from the Tree of Life, the Tree of Knowledge planted by Eve (presumably from an apple-pip) and the red tree under which Abel was slain. These we can recognise as the three bars of Light, waiting to inspire Geminian Galahad to fulfil the purpose of Time.

He, we are told, would be of Solomon's line—like Jesus.

Now Solomon's Temple was built to house the Ark of the Covenant; both Ark and Temple reflected cosmic and Caballistic measurements in their proportions, so Solomon's two Arks, the Hebrew and the British, have much in common.

But who helped Solomon build his Temple, giving him cedars of Lebanon and metal-workers? Hiram, Phoenician King of Tyre.

Did Solomon get his wisdom from the Celtic Salmon of Wisdom? Solomon and Salmon are in essence the same word.

Did Hiram pass on other ideas, gleaned from his contact with Britain?

The Masonic order looks back to Solomon as a Master Mason. But so is Somerset's Gemini in Solomon's Ship, his arm right-angled in a Mason's Square. The knowledge of cosmic proportions and star-alignments embedded in our Zodiac confirm his title; he represents the Architect of the Worlds. Such knowledge was used by all ancient temple-builders. Solomon's wisdom owed much to the Phoenicians of Tyre.

But long before Hiram's day, Sumerian Gilgamesh voyaged to the far west for wisdom. His epic pictures him as sleeping with bowed head in his boat. This Geminian image recurs in the death of Jason, crushed by the falling poop of his Argo while sleeping. Odysseus too was caught napping in his ship. Yet, Zodiacal as these myths undoubtedly are, where can we find such a figure in traditional Zodiacs? We are forced back to the Bowed One of the Mound of Dundon for their origin. Here the stars are faithfully reflected on earth as in a mirror, in shapes that truly give the heavenly message.

If Gilgamesh, travelling to Khassisadra (surely the Cassiterides or Tin Islands) in the far west, found these figures already there in 2500 BC or thereabouts, *how old are they?*

Did some Hyperborean Noah escape the floods of Atlantis in his Ark with its Zodiac animals and bring it to found the ancient civilizations of the east? Was Lyonesse sunk with Atlantis? The name of Jason's crew, the Minyans (sun-gods to a man), Egyptian Menes, Cretan Minos, Celtic Menu of the Menai Straits, are all derived from Menu the Measurer, and aliases for Noah. They are all culture-bringers from the sea. Conjure with the name Europa, Minos' mother, who was abducted screaming on the back of a swimming Bull to Crete, to see where she came from. Juggle with the name Atalanta, that chaste and much-chased Amazon who fell for those Hesperidean apples; with the Name of Atlas, king of Atlantis of that same western Hesperides garden, bearing the starry globe upon his shoulders.

Solomon's Ship, without moving from its Somerset haven, seems to have sailed round the world (like the moon it symbolises) planting seeds of civilization wherever it came to port!

Were those Sumerians, Cimmerians or Cymry not so much discovering new land to the far west, but *returning*, lemming-like, when time and tide allowed, to their long-lost Summerland home, fabled in their myth and history for its metals, its *"proud celestial circle"* of starry measurements?

Yet Atlantis, Lyonesse, are not merely sunken lands; they hold eternal magic as symbols of human consciousness, half-sunk and sundered since the Golden Age. When with Arthur they return, the Geminian breach will heal; the Covenant of the Ark, the Promise will be fulfilled.

King Arthur's Glass Ship *"Prydwen"* in which he plumbed the Underworld, to recover the lost Inspirational Cauldron and rescue Gweir (Man himself) is surely our Ship at **King's Sedge**moor. *"Prydwen"—"the beauty of Cosmic Order"*—fairly describes **the Z**odiac's ancient teaching. This Ship has much to teach about Man's lost self; the Quest of the Grail.

Take your stand on Lollover Hill, and let the glory of Lyonesse flood over you. (Gemini's pineal beacon on Dundon is now too overgrown, alas, and needs a brushwood fire to free it). Watch the Ship's sea-moors slip out to Severn Sea, earth fading into sky, Time into Eternity, dissolving both horizon and barriers of sense. See from the Dying Son the dying sun aflame, sinking once more into his mother's arms, clad in white samite, mystic, wonderful. Surely here if anywhere, we near the Vision of the Grail . . .

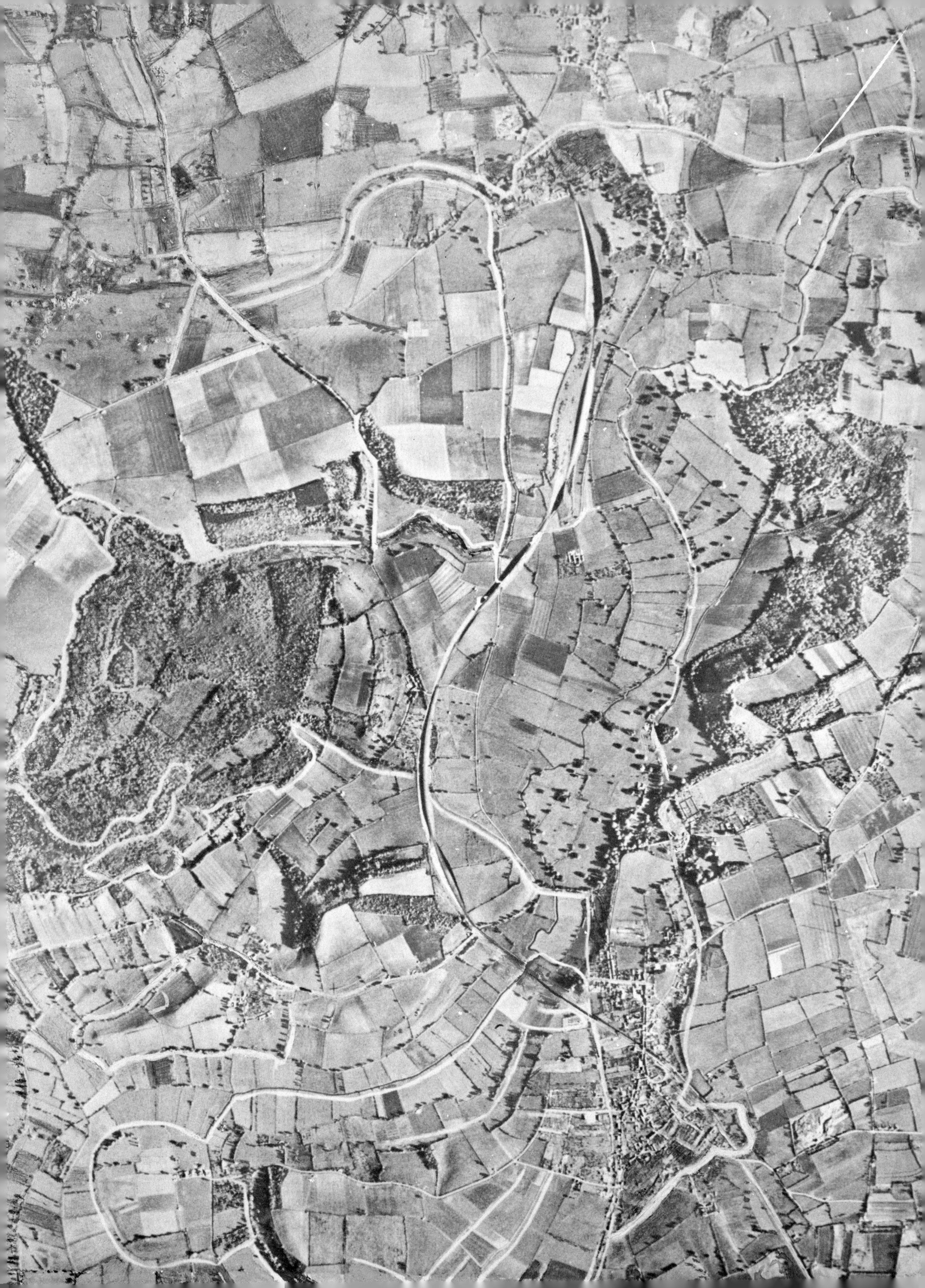

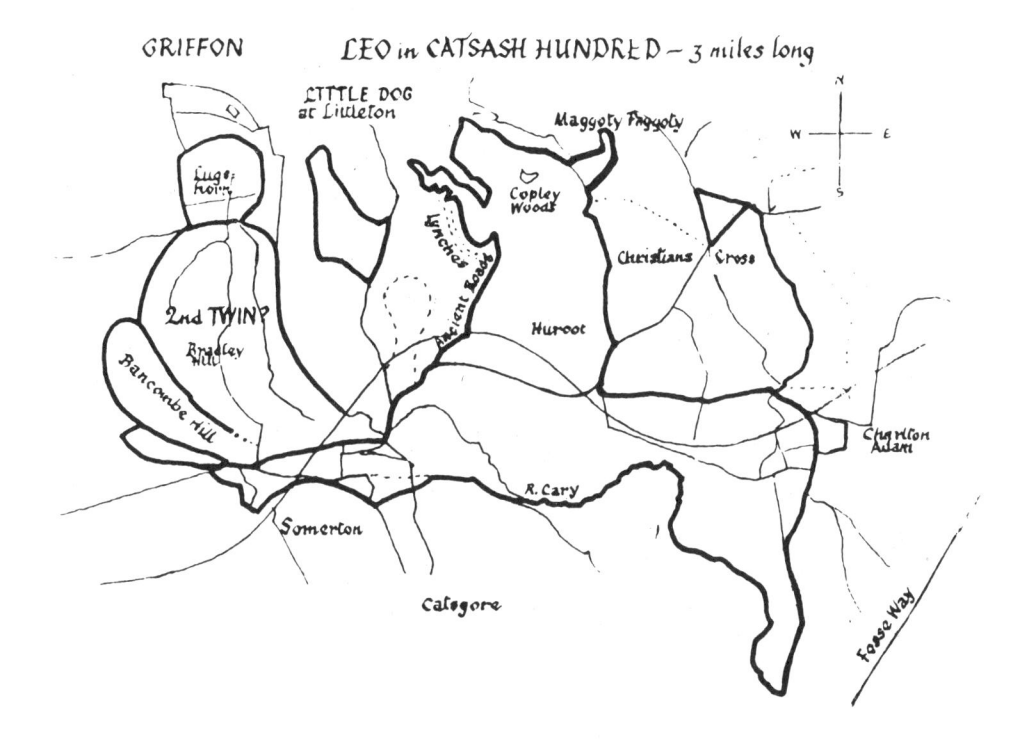

8: Leo

"*If ye are primitive bards, according to the discipline of qualified instructors, relate the great secrets of one world we inhabit*", Taliesin taunts his colleagues. "*There is a formidable animal from the city of Satanas, which has made an inroad between the deep and the shallows. His mouth is as wide as the mountains of Mynnau: neither death shall vanquish him, nor hand, nor sword. There is a load of nine hundred rocks between his two paws; there is but one eye in his head, vivid as the blue ice.*"

The rest of this poem is given in the chapter on Celtic poetry, but there is enough here to shew that Taliesin has one of our Zodiac nature-effigies in mind. And as the only one with paws is Leo, Mrs. Maltwood quotes it as referring to his effigy.

Leo, Britain's first heraldic lion, lies on the south of the Zodiac, with Somerton's *"load of nine hundred rocks"* on his front paw. Royal Leo protects the ancient royal Capital city of Wessex; the sun's own sign beams on the Summer County's seat of Saxon kings, once the county town.

Text-book history says that Richard I brought the heraldic lion to Britain from Asia Minor, but John of Glastonbury knew better, insisting that *Arthur's* arms were three red lions, inherited by British kings from Brutus, first king of Britain about 1100 BC. Brutus came from Troy, part of the ancient culture-complex of Babylon and Sumeria. But according to Waddell's *"Phoenician Origin of the Britons"*, Sumerians were trading with Britain and even migrating here long before Brutus' time. Somerset he claims was their capital, Somerset their seat. Among these migrants were the Cimmerians from the Black Sea and the Khassi, Catti or Cassi from the Caspian. Did these take their name from the heraldic lion-cat, and give it to the metals they were famed for working? Ireland and Britain were the Cassiterides—*"Tin Islands"*

Catt- and Cass- place-names besprinkle their kingdom on both sides of the Severn. Leo himself stands in Catsash Hundred; Arthur's helmet (Latin, cassis) is at Catsham. Silurian British kings inherited the ancient prefix in their name; Cassibelaunus throws in the asiatic god Bel for good measure. Somerton, *"city of Satanas"* belonged to these underground metal-miners. It was in the Underworld of the Titans, Satans or Giants of the far west, the clock of Satan or Saturn, Father Time.

Doubtless Plantagenet Richard, knowing the Zodiac secret of Britain, reinstated its ancient royal emblem and wore it on his *"Lion-heart"*. But long before this the Arthur of Celtic myth was hunting the Cath Palug, whose name means Lion of the month of Lug the sun-god. As they called the winter solstice Alban Arthan, Arthur sun of winter was hunting Leo sun of Summer. In Arthurian legend Arthur actually imprisons Lancelot, who symbolises Leo—but has to let him out again in due season. Leo's month, Lughnasad, is August. Celtic myth calls him Llew the long-handed—Leo, Welsh-style. His long hand was once the longest day, when the Royal Star Cross coincided with the compass-points, and Regulus, Leo's brightest star, was due south. Lancelot also means Lance of Light. The light-spear of Leo, Llew or Lugh, glints in Lancelot's name. His strength, courage, constant and too-loving heart proclaim Leo's astrological character. He lies too close by half to Virgo, while she, the seductive earth-mother, turns from etherial Arthur to Lancelot, preferring her sun-gods hot. It was Lancelot's earthbound heart that made him fail the Grail-Quest; by adultery with Guinevere he brought down the whole Round Table and the Fellowship he held dear.

> *"His honour rooted in dishonour stood*
> *And faith unfaithful made him falsely true"*.

He failed to hallow (or sublimate) the four Grail *"Hallows"*—These Hallows, Lance, Cup, Sword and Stone, recur throughout Arthurian legend. Lance and sword are male, cup and stone female. Lance into Cup, Sword into Stone.

These Hallows are clearly shewn in our Zodiac; the Three Bars of Light from Libra's Dove flood into the Ship, and the Water of Life from Aquarius pours into Leo's sign of the Cauldron. Both signs, or rather all four, symbolise the outpouring of Alpha the Word into Omega the Cauldron of Matter. Strange though it seems at first to find Leo, most masculine of Zodiac signs, playing this receptive or feminine part, it is endorsed by this Zodiac, for the stars of mother Cancer fall upon his neck, right in the path of the overflow from Aquarius, his opposite sign.

There is much to ponder on in this arrangement to illuminate the mystery of sex. Leo is masculinity personified. He is thus unable to receive the Aquarian illumination; his cauldron ♌ is upside-down! He cannot learn from weaker or more feminine sources, when domination or subjugation is his sole aim.

Dominant Leo's power is tempered by the Unicorn, as Capricorn, in this Zodiac. These two, Leo the Lion and Capricorn the Unicorn, summer and winter signs of the Zodiac, *still support our Royal Coat of Arms!* Grey Capricorn, ruled by Saturn, has often been the *"eminence gris"* who curbs and regulates the flamboyant king, reminding him that he too is only a subject of a higher power.

"The Lion and the Unicorn were fighting for the crown"

Leo signifies triumphant materialisation, the claims and clamour of the senses, of outer life. Mrs. Maltwood quotes a fascinating Jewish legend of the Middle Ages which illustrates this, and seems, from its imagery, to *stem from our Zodiac.* The Hidden Name, it tells, was secretly inscribed in the innermost recesses of the Temple, guarded by a sculptured lion. If, as was most unlikely, an intruder saw the Name, the lion would give such a supernatural roar that all memory of it would be driven from his mind. But Jesus knew this, evaded the lion, wrote the Name, cut his thigh open and hid it within the wound, closing it by magic. Once out of the Temple he re-opened the incision and took out the sacred letters. Gemini of the wounded thigh and the Three Bars of Light, the Name of God—guarded by Leo in the Temple of the Stars!

St. John seems also to have known this secret, for in Revelations 19. v 16, he wrote *"He hath on his thigh a name written, King of Kings, and Lord of Lords."* Christ is the secret king over Leo the king of men and beasts. Nor need we doubt that Gnostic St. John knew of Somerset's Temple with its apocalyptic teachings about Time and its purpose; the apocryphal gospels of the eastern early Church contain references to this Hades among the metal-mountains in the far west. But for these we must await the chapter on Joseph of Arimathea. Here perhaps is the greatest polarity of all—one whose tensions have been felt all through the Christian centuries, and which still wrack us today—the Lion of Rome versus the Unicorn of the secret Johannine church of the future. The once and future Church is indissolubly connected with Arthur, the once and future king.

But what does he mean, this lion that drives all memory of the Name from the minds of men? Is he not the roar of the outer world, that prevents us from receiving the voice of conscience, of self-analysis that would pierce our ear, our mouth, our heart, our loins—if our manes were not so thick; if our receptive cauldron were not so obdurately upside-down?

Leo's mane is thick, being tangled by Copley Woods; his head reared up on craggy Hurcot and Worley Hill. Does *"Maggotty Pagotty"* a ruined villa on his ear, echo prayers to the Mother and Father gods? The character of the country varies to an astonishing degree within the circle, and has an uncanny way of expressing the character of the Zodiac creatures. On the Lion's head it suddenly becomes rough and rugged, with deep chasms and steep quarries where Romans hewed marble to make the many villas whose remains have been found here. *"Ancient Roads"* leads to one of them from under his jaw. Romans belong on Leo. Do the names Hurcot and Huish remember Hu, Ahura? Somerton Lane's ancient track draws his back, and being—typically—too rough for cars offers peace and birdsong to the walker. Here one may follow nostalgically in Roman footsteps to Charlton Mackrell. Here there are more villas, old quarries and a Romano-British burial-ground, duly noted in the High History as the *"Graveyard Perilous"*. In these graves sun-discs were found (no doubt to remind the mourners of the resurrection-promise of the returning sun)—and, delightfully, *Lions' claws*, for no-one lays hold of life more ebulliently than Leo. To Zodiac pilgrims on this path it must seem fitting that there should be a burial-ground on his tail. His is a merry life of maximum involvement, but not a long one. He suffers too much from his heart, in every sense, for that.

The tuft of his tail, raised over his back, is at Christian's Cross, and is made by the crossing of ancient roads. A strange and hoary prophecy in William of Malmesbury's *"Antiquities of Glastonbury"* proclaims that *"Miracles should not cease until the great lion had come, having a tail fastened with great chains. Again, in what follows concerning the search for a cup which is here called the Holy Graal, the same is related, almost at the beginning."* Was it merely accident that Katharine Maltwood found this Lion first of all the effigies? When I found another Zodiac round Kingston, Surrey, Leo was the first to appear. But if Leo represents the outer world, is this not the only point from which the pilgrim can begin to penetrate the Mysteries?

As far as I can interpret the cryptic prophecy, it would seem to mean that miracles (which are only the working of laws we don't understand) will not cease until we begin to understand these laws. When we penetrate the Zodiac, this gives a key by which they can be understood.

These coincidences are themselves not the least of the *"miracles"* that attend the initiate's path. Indeed, as a mere beginner, I can only say that at first, far from ceasing, they seem to multiply. But Jung has been there before us and resolved our perplexity to some extent with his "law of synchronicity." No doubt this is only one of the numinous laws the pilgrim may come to understand on this astonishing path. Among occultists this phenomenon is known as *"outer life beginning to correspond with the inner."* Everybody has these coincidences, but not everybody pauses to reflect upon them, to try and interpret their meaning.

The miracles do not cease when the great lion appears, they increase—but cease to be regarded as miracles. They appear instead as part of a newly-perceived pattern. By practice we can learn to interpret these coincidences as guides to living; we find they come to warn or encourage us, often when they are most needed. A pilgrim's path exists quite literally in our Zodiac—for all inner facts have their outer counterpart—it touches every sign with the notable exception of Scorpio.

Tympanum,

Stoke-sub-hamden

Six miles south of Leo, at Stoke-sub-Hamden, a Norman tympanum over the church door secretly directs pilgrims to follow the ancient road from here to Somerton for the Zodiac, by depicting three fire-signs, Aries, Sagittarius and Leo, in delightful sculptured relief. Its three birds must also represent Libra, Aquarius and the Griffon. But only in this earth-Zodiac are these signed by birds! The tympanum's fire-signs are clearly Zodiacal, so it follows that the sculptor knew the Secret.

Somerton's leonine heart beats slowly now; its great days are past. But the pilgrim can be grateful that the tumult and shouting have been transferred to Yeovil, Somerset's new capital—for Somerton is left much as it was centuries ago. There is an Arthurian melancholy about its wide, quiet square; the sun slants long shadows from its mellow market-cross, aptly adorned with a lion's head. Of course there is a Red Lion inn, but the White Hart and the Unicorn are there too, fighting only to refresh Zodiac pilgrims with white bread and brown, washed down with good Somerset cider. The Globe too seems to remember the Zodiac, which *"signified the round world, the round canopy of stars, and many other things"*.

Here is the first Paradise-Garden (for the account of Eden has a Phoenician origin older by some centuries than the Genesis version) where Sagittarius-Adam is tempted by Virgoan Eve and fails the test. The serpent Draco's cider-apples are still potent! Does Charlton Adam, on Leo's tail, faintly remember the first failed initiate? An echo of this ancient secret reached Shakespeare's ear, inspiring him to say *"This other Eden, demi-Paradise"*. Shakespeare, one suspects, knew very well what he was saying, for he put these words into the mouth of John of Gaunt, a great student of the Mysteries, whose son became Earl of Somerset, his badge the Unicorn. The High History also calls Grail-Castle Eden.

Somerton's splendid church remembers it, for the legs of its Elizabethan Altar-table are carved to shew the Fall, the Expulsion, the Flood, and the quest for the Way Back via the Grail. The serpent tempts Adam and Eve, Adam works his passage with a hand-plough. Noah (or is it Esus the Woodcutter or Jesus the Carpenter?) builds the Ark and the Grail-cup surmounts a bible (or is it a cider-press? For there is veritas in vino too.) all surmounting an hour-glass. Angels and serpent-dragons sport on the roof; the Elizabethan pulpit proclaims *"Praise God for Ai"*—delicious punning on the broad-arrow Holy Name.

They had fun in church in bygone days. Balls found in the roof shew that sacred solar games were once played by parson and clerk with the congregation as fielders, though it looks as if the angels caught some of them too. But if religion was boisterous, secular life was religious, and a glass of Somerset's apple-wisdom was a sacred toast to Adam, George and Arthur, gardeners and ploughmen all.

Leo's tongue lolls out on Worley Hill, as if he were thirsty too, despite Chabrick Millstream that defines his muzzle and trickles down his neck to cool his summer heat. Blazing tar barrels were rolled downhill to celebrate the summer sun; Worley hill probably remembers these whorls of fire. What larks they had at Lughnasad. What gambolling on Somerton's Maypole Knap!

The midsummer ecliptic path of the sun rolls along Leo's tongue—surely no accident. This must have been a processional path. All brass lion-head knockers with a ring in their mouths must stem from Worley Hill's ecliptic path, as must the ancient custom of claiming sanctuary by laying hold of the knocker on some church and cathedral doors, as at Gloucester. Did it signify, Mrs. Maltwood wondered, the laying hold of the sun's path of righteousness? And is this what Gemini the Good Thief is doing, his fingers pinching the ecliptic? This merciful custom, designed to give criminals another chance, is thought to be pre-Christian.

Avalon has long been haunted by a Lion and a Giant, indeed the very name of Lyonesse may come from this association, as we have seen. In Arthurian legend the lion is fierce, but can be led by a fearless child. If Leo follows his nose he will find this child at Gemini.

Tristram, the *"sad one"* of Lyonesse must stem from the bowed Gemini figure. Tristram's identity was given away by a brachet or little dog, who recognised him and jumped up to lick his face. Here by Leo's upraised paw is Canis Minor at Littleton, jumping up to Gemini. But Gemini is Galahad too, and well might Leo-Lancelot love him, for he is his father. Galahad like Tristram is always associated with the ship, and in Arthurian legend Lancelot joins him for a six-month cruise. This must have been in origin a calendar-myth, symbolising the six summer months. They never meet again, the father who longs to see the Grail but cannot—the son who fulfils his father's highest ideals.

It was the River Cary, drawing Leo's underside so clearly, that revealed him to Mrs. Maltwood. (If the Lion came first in both our Zodiacs, is it not significant that Hercules' Twelve famous Labours also *began with the Nemean Lion*? For Hercules too was an initiate in the ancient Mysteries, and seems to have come to Britain, as we shall see.)

This little river never wastes a curve, and draws four of the Zodiac's southern effigies—a feat only matched by the equally astonishing river Brue, which draws four northern ones.

But it is time to follow the river eastwards to find Virgo, Lancelot's beloved queen.

VIRGO: 4 miles long

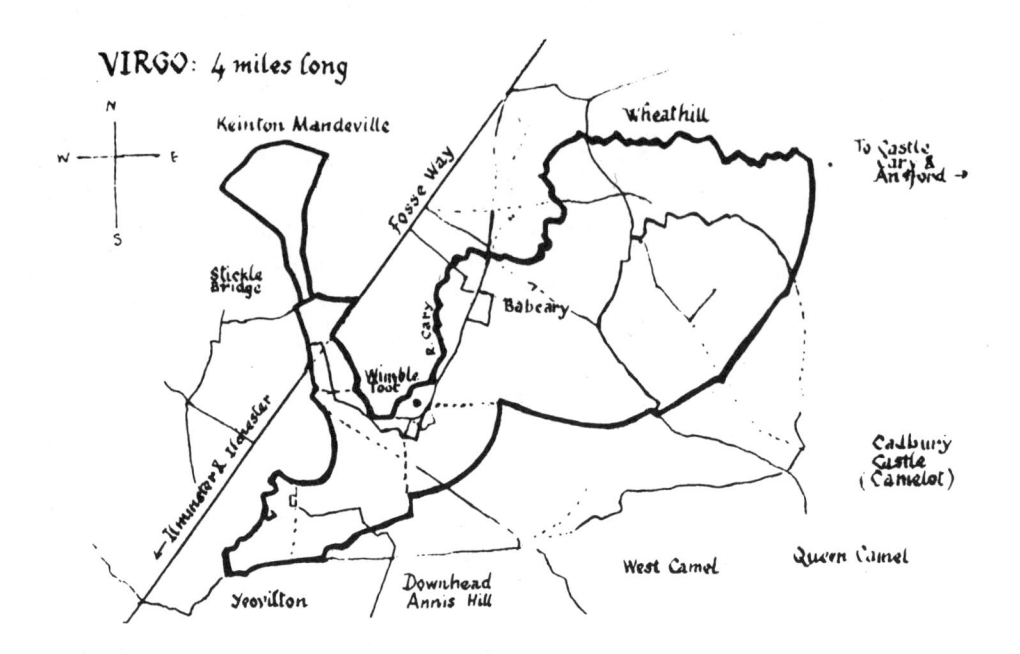

9: Virgo

Since the dawn of humanity, the goddess of Nature has been adored, feared and wooed in every tongue and clime; thus her names—like her moods—are legion. She is the Triple Goddess of earth, sea and moon (itself three-phased). Mother of all life, she devours her own children. She is both kind and cruel, smiling in spring and harvest, a screaming hag in winter. She is all women in one: seductive maid, fruitful mother, toothless crone; young, beautiful, capricious, faithful, patient and compassionate; old, hideous, and terrifyingly wise.

This is the guise in which she appears in our circle. Here must be Britain's first witch, complete with tall hat, broomstick and cauldron. The River Cary, rising from the Seven *Lady* Springs in Castle Cary, draws her front from top to toe. The Britannia Inn guards these springs, to help us recognise our tutelary goddess and draw fresh courage at her very source; Castle Cary's British Camp guards her too, reminding us that here is also Old Mother Cary, Britain's half-forgotten sea-witch. Her chickens still fly towards

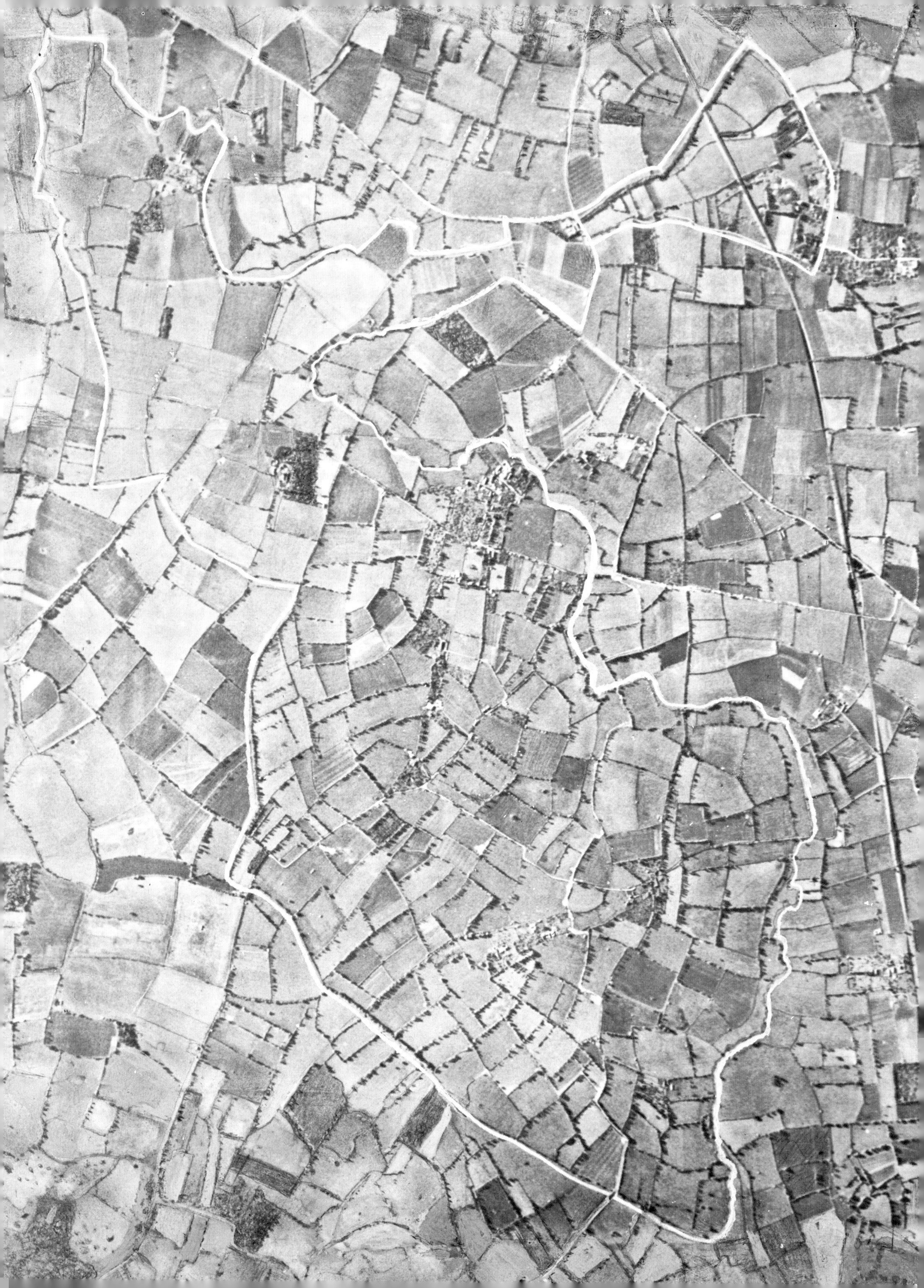

her from Aquarius and Libra, but her favourite is the Libran Dove of Barton St. David, for he is not only the Logos announcing her coming Virgin-birth, but also her rascally consort Davey Jones, with whom she sits at the bottom of the sea on his locker crunching dead sailors' bones. This at least is all we remember of her now, if we remember her at all. Charles Kingsley's Water Babies contains a portrait of her, and Stanford's Sea Songs carry a dire warning to young mariners *"If you want to make old bones, steer clear of old Mother Cary and that there Davey Jones!"*

Sad how the gods of the old faith become the devils of the new! Christians are reluctant to recognise Virgo as the Blessed Virgin. Yet Virgo's stars descend after harvest below the horizon, and the sun of the winter solstice rises from the same point—the Babe Sun in his mother's arms. It is Christ the *"True Sun's"* birthday too. Teucros of Babylon called this babe in his mother's arms Ysu. Her issue! The Abbé Chauve-Bertrand shews that the Church knows this better than she will publicly admit. His article entitled the *"Origins of Christmas"* makes it clear that the Annunciation was fixed by the spring equinox, Christ's birth then being at the winter solstice. In this the church merely followed the primordial custom of earlier Mysteries. *"We do not realise fully"* confesses the honest abbé, *"how much the liturgies owe to astronomy."* Yet the Virgin's birthday is celebrated in September, Virgo's month; surely the faithful must sometimes wonder, especially when they remember that the Wise Men read Christ's birth in the stars.

Templars however knew the secret, and our Lady appears in many a cathedral Zodiac of their time. Judging from architecture, the Church had its finest hour when it embraced astrology; its fortunes have not flourished since the Virgin disowned the Virago. Templar-inspired Parzifal understood this too. In Book IX the hermit tells the astonished hero,

"for the earth was Adam's mother, of the earth was Adam fed,
And I ween, tho' a man she bare here, yet still was the earth a maid . . .
Two men have been born of maidens, and God hath the likeness ta'en
Of the son of the first earth-maiden, since to help us He aye was fain."

Virgin-soil, ever reaped or raped, yet ever undefiled.

The name Babcary on Virgo's swelling womb clarifies the vexed question of the Virgin-Birth. Asking at the Post Office for any old legends which might preserve this memory, I was delighted beyond words to hear that *"a royal child was supposed to have been hidden here, long ago"*. I have since heard another version, that it was Henry II, hidden as a boy here in the wars of Stephen and Matilda. But all Plantagenet history is so imbued with sun-myth that this deterred me not a whit. It was under Henry and Eleanor that Arthur of Britain came once more into his own, and the Templars flourished and quested the Grail. And as Babcary is *"Babcari"* in the Domesday Book, Mother Cary was carrying her babe here before Norman times, let alone Plantagenet.

The helpful postmistress also told me that Cromwell's horses are said to be buried under Wimble Toot, the tumulus that marks Virgo's nipple. Shades of that Night-Mare Goddess once again! *"And they do say of Babcary, easy to get into, hard to get out of"* she added for good measure. Conception and birth! Surely a typical Templar joke?

It must be said that the stories were told before I volunteered the existence of Virgo to account for them. My informant had not until that moment heard of the Zodiac.

To Mrs. Maltwood (who seems to have missed these legends) the name Bab is Arabian for gate. Gates, she says play an important part in the Temple traditions, and nearby is the Fosse Way, whose straight path is broken to go respectfully round Virgo's hand. This notch exactly marks mid-September on the superimposed planisphere. But *"Gate"* or *"Baby"* at Babcary are not really at variance. Is not birth the gate to life?

The Fosse Way, that stern unbending old Roman, did not willingly make a bow to kiss her hand for the original track can still be seen crossing her wrist. Did scandalised Britons make the present diversion after their temporary Roman masters had gone? Or was it Mother Nature herself who made the new angle by seeing to it that the old track became too boggy to be practical? For so it is, as I am assured by a hard-riding Virgoan who knows all these local tracks.

At Stickle Bridge Virgo holds her broomstick, trident or wheatsheaf, a three-cornered object that does not inhibit fancy. It exactly marks the full path of the ecliptic, both in size and position (another feat of *"Chance"*!) Here stands Mary Magdalene's church, reminding us that the three Christian Marys were once the triple Goddess. Mary Magdalene was of course *"beyond the pale"* of respectable society, and Arthurian legend remembers the damsel beyond a paled bar. Is this Virgo, divided from the rest of the circle by the bar of the Fosse Way? Oddly enough, the name *"the Barton"* occurs here. Fifteen old stones edging a field suitably called *"Stones"* seem to mark something of long-forgotten importance here.

The wheatsheaf of course is essential to the harvest-goddess. She was placated at reaping by the harvesters who all bowed down before the last sheaf in the field (would we could see that ceremony now) and by the making of *"kern-babies"* or corn-dollies with the last ears of corn. These were also called Bride or Bridget babies by Goidelic Celts passing through here on their way to Ireland. There Bridget is also a triple goddess, or was, before she became a Christian saint. She is carved in stone on the Tor's tower, milking her cow, and Chalice Well possessed a cow-bell called Bride's Bell until it was taken, alas, some fifty years ago. The miracle-working saint is said to have visited Glastonbury when St. Patrick was abbot there, and still has her well at Beckery. Do these legends dimly recall our Virgo?

Virgo's landscape is suitably mild after Leo's rugged hills; undulating gently, it is full of cows and corn. What else should we expect? A priory at aptly-named Wheathill by her skirt once tried to Christianise her, but only caught her hem. Now it has gone, while she, all four miles of her, remains. She is big, too big for any creed's confines—yet graces every one.

The British Ceres, Ceridwen, she is still clothed in golden corn. As Black Annis the witch she shrieks in the wind on Annis Hill near her head, and lurks at Ansford, Castle Cary. But of course, she is not only the Virgin, but St. Anne her mother, the British princess. No wonder we have so many St. Anne's hills in Britain. Celts never made the mistake of taking the Gospel story too literally as mere history; they understood its inner meaning. Poets to a man, they saw the hills with their springs as so many breasts of the Nature Mother, every rivulet a stream of Liebfraumilch. Black Annis still persists in remote parts of our islands; Ireland has its mountainous Paps of Anu. She is, it seems, Danu of the Tuath de Danaan, Anu of Annwn, the Celtic Underworld!

Wimble Toot, Babcary

The Cary river lovingly rounds our Virgin's breast, its nipple-tumulus at Wimble Toot now happily preserved as an ancient monument. Wimble means an auger (a carpenter's bore) and this is interesting, for the goddess of the ancient Mysteries always had her *"pythoness"* or sybil, for divination or augury—a medium whose clairvoyance was stimulated by narcotic fumes from the cauldron on a tripod. She is often pictured in Greek art on this hot seat. Her mistress, the snake goddess, is shewn in the famous Cretan figurine. The word *"Toot"* is no less interesting. Translated from the old Welsh *"twt"* it is said to mean a look-out mound or hill—but Wimble Toot shews clearly that it once meant *teat*, as any tot will tell you, or any sailor over his bawdy tot of rum.

What junketings at harvest festivals must Wimble Toot have seen!

Ceres-Ceridwen of Somerset offers her wheatsheaf, all spangled with her stars, to her Son. This wheatsheaf, or Kern-baby, suggests the Goddess gave her name to Cornwall. (It is not and never has been good corn-growing country, with its Atlantic winds and rain.) Some say the Celtic tribe of Cornovii named it, but it may be the other way about; they took their name from the horn-shaped county. Latin Cornu means horn. Any horn? No, Britons always remembered their deities in their placenames and Cornwall, *"Kerniow"*, was Druidic; whose horn could it be if not the corn-horn or cornucopia of Ceres-Ceridwen, Cary of Kerin?

The ancient province of Kerin stretched from Cornwall to Somerset.

St. Keyne of Cornwall and Somerset has perhaps inherited the Goddess's character and name (though the r seems to have been elided). Remembered as a chaste Welsh princess of the 5th century AD, this daughter of King Brechan of Brecon was a determined virgin, fleeing across the Severn to Keynsham to escape her many suitors. Another chaste and much-chased Virgin! Here, being much bothered by deadly snakes in her woodland hermitage, she turned them all to stone—as we can still see from the many ammonites still found in Keynsham's limestone. This Celtic royal saint is also remembered at St. Keyne, near Liskeard, where she blessed the well for Women's Lib., ordaining that the first partner of any marriage at her church to reach her well and drink should *"wear the trousers"* ever after! A most unchristian whim, surely, and likely to cause much marital discord; but Celtic women were always more liberated than most, thinking nothing of going to war with or without their men, as Boadicea shews.

Snake-snaring matriarch, royal virgin—who is she but our goddess? It comes as no surprise then to find Keinton Mandeville on her wheatsheaf. Is it secretly *Main-de-ville, the town of Virgo's hand*? I ask because there is a mystery about this Norman name (no such town exists in Normandy from which the de Mandevilles could have come) and because Geoffrey de Mandeville was a Templar, though he disgraced the order. But unworthy as he was, he must have known the Secret. And because Sir John Mandeville two centuries later wrote up his fantastic travels which I suspect were an allegory of the Somerset pilgrimage, full of strange neverland animals. He was called a liar for his pains, but maybe we have taken him too literally. Sir John was an alchemist—nor was Mandeville his real name. Was it an alias to conceal and reveal at once the Star-Temple, its ecliptic measured by Virgo's wheatsheaf?

Alchemy, it is now recognised, was a cloak for Mysteries; the quest for the transmutation of base metals into gold was not just a literal one, though it was that too. Metaphysically it masked the quest for self-perfection—the fusion of the base qualities in man in the crucible of experience to produce the perfected Man.

By the snake-goddess hangs a true tale. Travelling through Virgo's effigy by car towards Keynsham we stopped to pick up a dead snake in the road. It isn't often one finds such a trophy; it was in perfect condition. I was already alerted to St. Keyne, as my mother's family come from that village in Cornwall, and we decided to explore the mystery further at Keynsham. But it was only when we arrived and were given a pamphlet on the saint that I read for the first time of her snake story.

Our informant did not believe she ever existed, because in Domesday Book the town is spelt *Cainesham*. My married name! With that snake in the boot of the car I could hardly agree that my saint did not exist. It seemed she was still very much alive. Nor is this the only hint she dropped us on our quest, for after a long session with the pilot of the plane that was to fly us over the effigies, spent explaining the significance of Virgo and her wheat-sheaf, we left Gatwick, our throats dry with exposition. The Queen's Head at Bolney on the London-Brighton run offered refreshment, and we were astounded to see the bar completely festooned with corn-dollies of every type of cereal! Each year adds another miniature sheaf to this collection, we were told. Horstead Keynes, Scaynes Hill and Keymer are all close by. The goddess is by no means confined to the Celtic west. We drank to her ubiquity, thankful for her encouragement. These are but two of the many astonishing coincidences that attend the quester's path: I could add many more.

But it is time to leave the Queen's Head in Sussex for the Queen's Head in Somerset. With her nutcracker jaws and wrinkled robe so cruelly drawn by the Cary river, Virgo is no fashion-plate, as Rag Lane on her throat seems to admit. A prosperous farm blots her face at Cary Fitzpaine, but the stars of Crater the Cup at her lips offer solace for this indignity. Old Cary-Ceridwen has had her day, but once she was young and beautiful; behind her sunken gums another face peeps out from the air-photograph, half-hidden behind farm buildings. A princess indeed! A deep ditch had apparently no other purpose than to carve her smiling mouth—now alas it is filled in and her mouth stuffed with potatoes. Her eyes are shallow depressions, clearly visible in the air-photo, which according to the farmer still fill with heavy rain. Were they once dewponds?

Distracted Ceres searched the world for Persephone—but she should look within *herself* to find her lost daughter, her true self, untouched by time or care. The map will not help her; only photography's X-ray eye can find this lovely creature.

Here of course must be Arthur's queen Guenevere, with the river Cam, Camel Hill, west Camel and even *Queen* Camel nearby, asserting her right to Camelot's crown. Queen Street runs south on to her wheatsheaf fromBarton St. David. The Round Table belonged to *Leodegrance* her father and king of Camelot; it was hers by matriarchal right, and only became Arthur's on her marriage. Leo, toward whom she leans in love, is both Leodegrance and Lancelot—whom she loved no doubt as a father-figure!

Camelot's ancient fort, now called Cadbury Castle, guards her from the east. Legend clings to it still, for it must have been chief of the camps of the kingdom of Logres, with its splendid ramparts cut into the solid rock. Those with second sight still see the lances of Arthur's knights, tipped with unearthly flame, as they pass on midsummer eve through the village along Halter Path Lane to Par Rock. This means *"fire rock", "Halter",* says Mrs. Maltwood, means *"altar".* Worshipped here was Camulos, the Goidels' sky god, identical with Etruscan Cadmillus and Baal. But Baal in the Bible was worshipped on Mount Carmel (where he was routed by Elijah's more potent fire)—and Camel Hill was therefore another mount Carmel. And indeed, amid this spectacular tumble of hills we feel ourselves in the Holy Land before the Holy Land. Is the Kingdom of Logres not the kingdom of the Logos, the Word?

It is only a small kingdom, but like Palestine, its importance bears little relation to its size; it is thought to have been bounded by the Axe, the Parrett and the Severn. But much can come from little, like the Pentecostal flames from the Upper Room, to light the whole world.

In which Holy Land, in which Eden, east or west, did Eve dwell? For Guinevere means White Eve and her name spreads far and wide, to Yeovilton and Yeovil, Ilchester and Ilminster, for all derive from Ivel or Gifl, Eve the Giver of all. If she is Evil, this is only because men can sometimes, all too weak, be destroyed by her charms. Such was the screaming Morrigan, or deceitful Morgan-le-faye, whom Arthur learnt to rue. But she is also Perceval's pure sister, who died that others might live. And whether they hate or love her, all yeomen are her husbandmen, for good or ill.

Once, approaching Ilchester, I expounded these name-derivations to two sceptics. In the splendid church an 18th century Bible, under glass, lay open at the story of Adam and Eve. Just another coincidence?

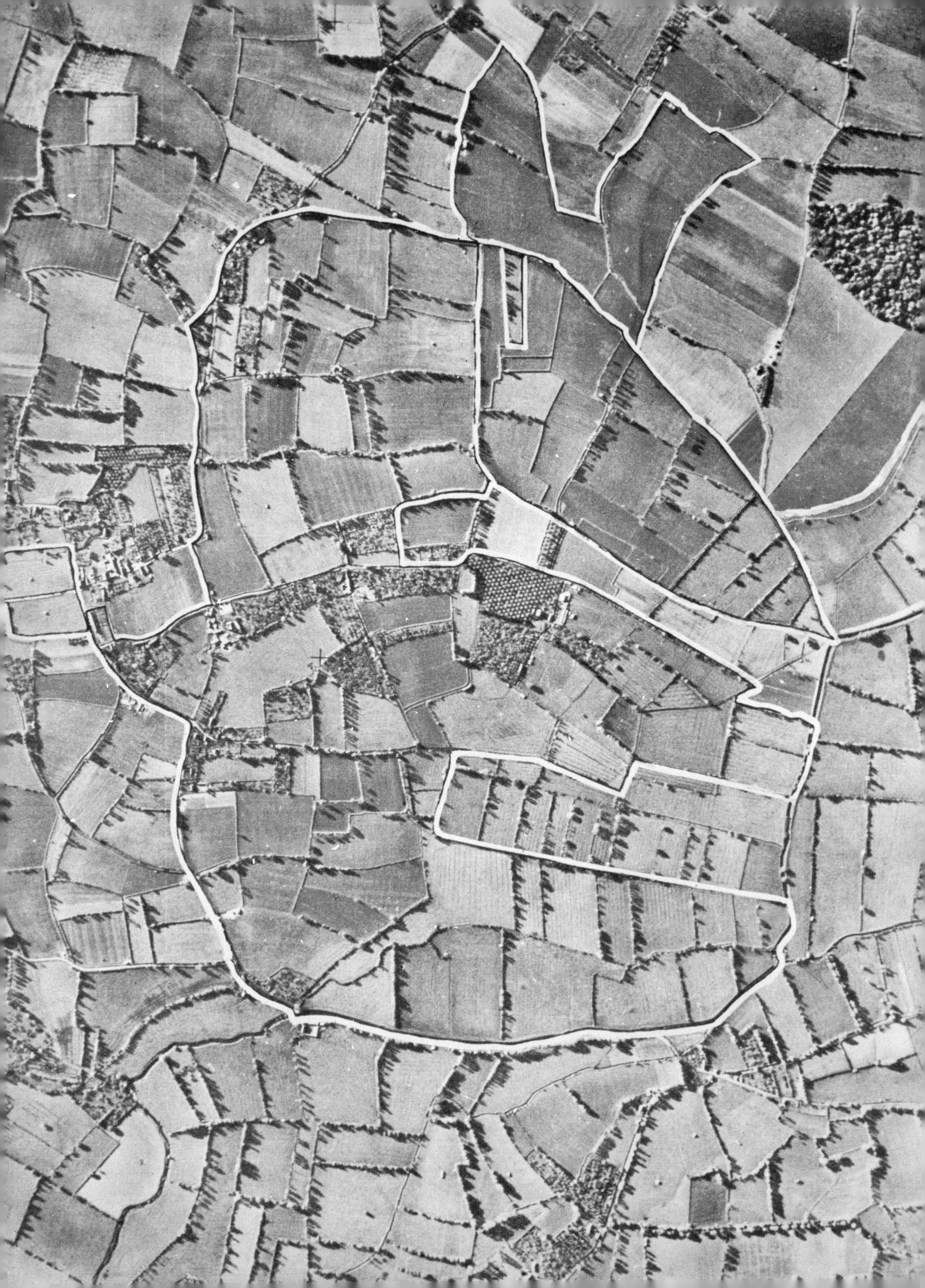

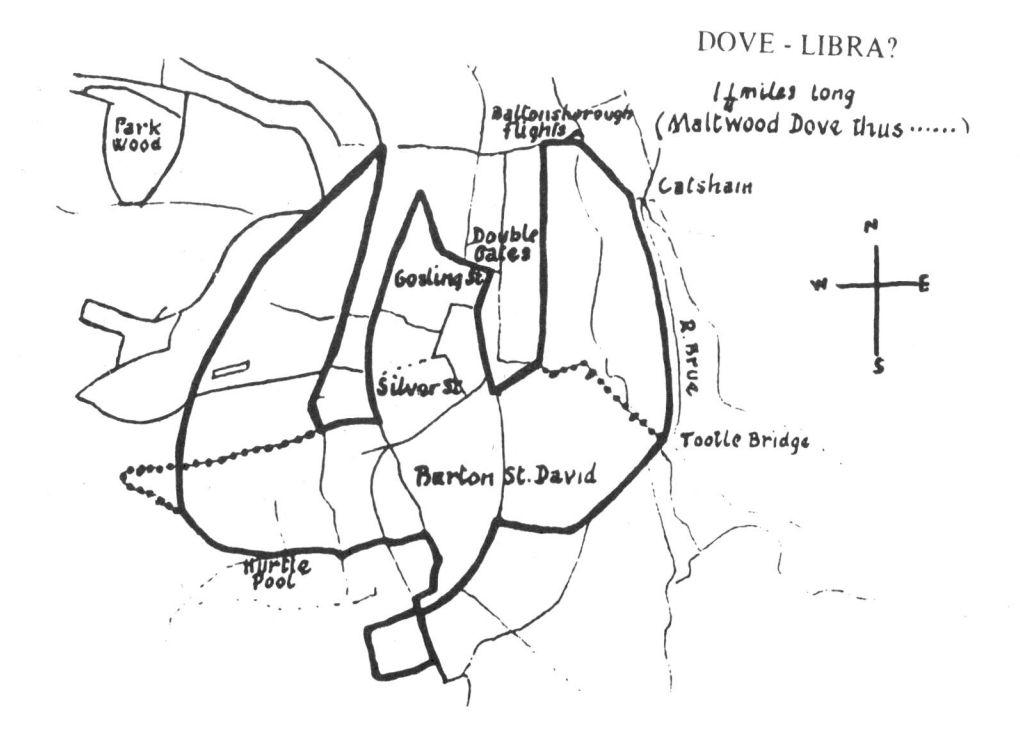

10: Libra. A Dove?

The gentle paths and streams of Barton St. David, near the circle's centre, preserve a bird, flying from the head of Arthur-Sagittarius—and, like the bird at Aquarius, about a mile across. Birds are soul-symbols the world over, and as both Druids and Egyptians saw the spirit as escaping at death in the form of a dove, to Mrs. Maltwood this bird flying from the dying god's head, must be a dove. Her effigy, with shorter wings than mine, imitates the twist of Arthur's body as if it had just wriggled free like a butterfly from its chrysalis. One wing, longer than the other (like Arthur's arms) touches a triangle at the circle's centre which she calls the Sacred enclosure, and exemplifies the Three Bars of Light, the three drops of blood from the Lance in the Grail Procession, and no doubt the three inspirational drops from Ceridwen's cauldron that inspired little Gwion too. From a spring in this enclosure the Three bars of light stream down the masts of the Ship, bathing Gemini in unearthly radiance, as in the Argo they illuminated the Twins, and as in the Baptism of Jordan, with the dove of the Holy Spirit hovering overhead. In our Zodiac also it is undoubtedly a light-bringer, a source of enlightenment and priests in the Mysteries, after bewailing the sun-god's death would shout *"Hail to the Dove, restorer of Light!"*

If Mrs. Maltwood's effigy indicates itself as the source of light, mine, with longer wings, brushes Arthur's head, so that the waters of the Brue that delineate it rush out here like life-blood down the little waterfall of Baltonsborough Flights into the wing of the dove. The name of these water-steps surely remembers the flight of the spirit of Bel. Musing on the Zodiac story at this peaceful and poetic spot, many things tumble fluidly into place. Both versions of the Dove are drawn on the map; together they make a kinetic picture of flight.

Here in fact *is* Libra (as Mrs. Maltwood herself supposed) and in a guise that eclipses the Scales in interpretive power. Its shape indeed echoes the Balance. What Libran would not prefer to be signed by a Dove? Libra is an air sign, its qualities peaceful, harmonising, communicative, graceful, inspirational. It lightens the Scales of Justice, for what is justice without mercy? The dove is the very symbol of divine mercy and no Libran would wish to exercise judgement without it. The Scales were only added to the Zodiac signs in stern Roman times, when justice was often merciless. They were formed from the death-Scorpion's claws, to weigh departing souls. Both Libra's and Scorpio's stars fall on the Scorpion, who points to Libra's Dove in no uncertain manner as if pointing, despite itself, to hope beyond its death-sting.

Why is Libra out of place, like Cancer? Why are they both disguised? To understand this we must examine further aspects of this communicative Dove.

For it has more than one message to convey; not only does it flood the young sun-god with recognition (*"This is My Beloved Son, in whom I am well pleased—"*) but it is flying from the old sun-god straight towards Virgo, who lies expectantly on her back awaiting it. The Dove of the Annunciation! It is also Noah's Dove, seeking a foothold of hope above the waters of Destruction—the Logos, descending Word, willing to begin all things anew, as at the Creation.

Its shape not only foreshadows the later Scales, but its body and wings form the arrowed Awen (which Druids pronounced A-hoowen), the three Bars of Light. Doves still coo A-hoowen; it means, literally, White-Wings.

But other birds have conveyed messages from the gods, and Barton St. David's Gosling Street and Silver Street remind us of the sacred swans of Leda and Lohengrin—even of old Mother Goose, whose rhyme hides the Secret beneath its nursery pinafore. For her goose laid golden eggs, or inspirational ideas, and her son Jack is Man himself; not very good, but not very bad. Doublegates on the Dove's tail seems to hint at Arthur's escaping doppelganger.

Though Libra's stars do not correspond with this effigy, the stars which *do* fall upon it are eloquent. For these are the Plough-stars, which the Chaldeans called Wul mo sarra—*"the Lord, Bel, Voice of the Universe"*. It is no accident that they fall upon the Logos-Dove. The full meaning of this star-fall does not immediately become clear. Only when one examines some of the titles of this, the largest constellation of all, does the aptness of this placement strike with full force. The Plough's seven great stars called forth Creation in seven days; they are also the Seven words from the Cross, *"Wul"* is a form of Bel, the self-sacrificing god, who though the Old Testament has given him a bad press, was nevertheless tried, found innocent, condemned and killed, restoring his people to hope again by returning from the grave, according to ancient Chaldean tablets.

Celts called the Plough or Great Bear stars David's Chariot, which helps to make sense of Barton St. David; also Arthur's Chariot, which explains why in Welsh, Arthur's name is said to mean both Ploughman and Bear. This chariot carried the sun-god's spirit during his nightly death, for like the sun it is an unfailing twenty-four hour clock. Other names for this greatest of all constellations are revealing—Thor's Wagon, Odin's Wagon, Car of Osiris, Wagon of our Saviour, the Brood Hen, and perhaps most intriguing of all— *"the Abode of the Seven Sages who entered the Ark with Minos".* Minos! In the Ark? It confirms our suspicions that Minos was in league with Menu the Measurer, and that the Ark of the Hebrews (and doubtless Noah's too) contained earth and star measurements, an ancient system of divine proportions underlying all created things. Menu, as all true Welshmen know, not only entered the ark, but *made* it in all its sublime proportions. But Minos, king of Crete, creator of the labyrinth? What has he to do with the ark? Only if he like Noah, was one of those patriarchs who fled sinking Atlantis to found new colonies in the Middle East, does this mysterious name for the Plough-stars make sense.

Europa, Minos' mother, hints that he sailed from Europe. (Rather mean of him, safely in his ark, to make his mother swim on that white bull to Crete.)

This starry chariot, ever turning round the Pole-star, explains Taliesin's mysterious boast—*"I have presided in a toilsome chair, over the circle of Sidin"* (the stars) *"while it is continually revolving between three elements; is it not a wonder to the world that men are not enlightened?"*

This was the last riddle in the long poem with which he confounded Maelgwyn's bards and freed Elphin from prison. It *is* surprising that they could not guess it, for Druids, like whirling dervishes, danced in circular patterns that imitated the movements of the stars. As Cynddelw the Bard put it, *"Rapidly moving in the course of the sky, in circles, in uneven numbers, Druids and Bards unite, in celebrating the leader."* No slow and stately measures here; they whirled at speed, heightening consciousness by imitating the intricate order and velocity of the heavenly bodies, which also whirl at colossal speed without collision.

Taliesin, presiding at the centre of this giddy scene, was within the *Brood Hen,* Ceridwen, who pecked him out of the heap of wheat in which he had so foolishly tried to hide, and swallowed him before his second birth.

Another Celtic name for Ceridwen was Arianrhod of the Turning Castle or Caer Sidi. Minos, it seems, brought a dim memory of her to Crete, calling his daughter Ariadne. And it was Ariadne who shewed Theseus, the initiate in the Mysteries, the way out of the labyrinth or *"turning castle"*. It was she in other words who was responsible for his rebirth. Greek and Celt tell the same story. But only in Welsh myth are the starry or Zodiacal origins of this *"Greek"* myth remembered; we shall examine it for further clues in a later chapter.

Our Dove, intermediary between these gods and men, betrays its function in its name; the very word dove is a past-participle of the verb *"to dive"*. It is in fact *"a diva"* or angel-messenger from heaven to earth. In our Zodiac it *"dives"* from the sun-god's head down to the earth-and-sea Mother, impregnating her with life. She, as Ked or Cetus the Whale, swallows him whole: for she is represented by three signs, Ship, Whale and Virgoan harvest-goddess—being the triple goddess of Earth, Sea and Moon.

See then how the Dove's wing is engulfed in the jaws of a serpent, whose neck drawn by the river Brue, extends from the nose of the Whale. Though this snake is not among Mrs. Maltwood's effigies (her snake's head being in nearby Park Wood), its credentials are excellent—*the stars of Draco curve along its neck when the planisphere is superimposed.*

Here must be St. George's, St. Michael's, dragon; the dark adversary who drags the sun-god down into the sea at sunset, and who is always defeated again at dawn. Draco's circumpolar constellation coils round the Eden Pole-Tree whose wisdom-apples are stars.

Park Wood, where Mrs. Maltwood's snake lurks, is shaped like the snake-embellished crown of Ancient Egypt—a strange coincidence.

Are there then *two* heads from the same neck? And if two, why not seven? For Draco had seven heads. Try the children's puzzle-game of finding the others on the map; they are all there, though for clarity only mine is illustrated here. Butleigh and Barton St. David are indeed alive with snakes—but we may safely tread, for St. Keyne has turned them all to stony paths. Her cell at Keinton Mandeville is but a mile away.

Hydra is another serpent implied in our Zodiac by the course of the river Cary. This river connects Libra and Cancer across the Zodiac, as the constellation of Hydra does across the sky. But its stars are so small and far apart it can hardly be said to be a constellation at all. Why then did the ancient astronomers bend over backwards to create Hydra out of such unpromising material? They must have wanted to connect Cancer and Libra for reasons of myth. But these two signs are both disguised and slightly displaced in our Zodiac—as if to give a clue to a Mystery.

Once, astrologers say, there were only ten Zodiacal signs—two being kept secret until the time was ripe to reveal them. Once there were only Ten Commandments, until Jesus revealed two more from the Book of Deuteronomy. Our two missing signs, like the two extra Commandments, have to do with love, human and Divine. Libra in our Zodiac plays the male part, penetrating the world, the sea of Cancer's maternal sign, to give it life and light.

The other serpent Draco tells the same story, connecting Libra and the Piscean Whale. Together they complete a cycle from air to sea and back again. Did the ancients know that all life began in sun-warmed water?

These signs sum up the message of the whole Zodiac, as Jesus' two commandments summed up the other ten. It is the story of Creation and its purpose. Life, it is surely saying, is seeded from above upon the earth, and not only seeded but fed and watered by continual nourishment from the same source—in order to return a harvest of sixty-fold, a hundred-fold, according to each creature's capacity, so that when the Reaper comes he can go home rejoicing, taking his sheaves with him. Christ's parables of the Sower and the Talents shew that He understood the Zodiac message.

Sunrays penetrate the *Ionised* layers of *"the boundless atmosphere"* plunging into the *Ionian* sea to inspire its great philosophy schools; St. Columba (the dove) plunged into the sea from Ireland to bring Christianity to *Iona*, an island of great Druidic sanctity already, long before he came. Hebrideans placated a sea-god called Shoni (Johnny!) who is likely to pre-date Christian St. John. It was however Johannine Christianity that Celts took to their hearts; his apocalyptic seership and cosmological outlook was so much their own that he has been supposed by some to be a Celt or Gaul from Galatia, a suspicion deepened by his traditionally slender, poetic, fair-haired representations in the catacombs and other early paintings.

If Celts loved inspirational John, they loved all Davids too, for dove and David have a common Welsh root in Duw Dovydd—*"God's messenger"*. Indeed, the commonest Welsh surnames commemorate this inspirational source. Jones, Davies, Evans, Owen (both forms of John) Howell or Hwyll, spirit . . . Under Gemini and thus ruled by Mercury, messenger of the gods, they rightly chose St. David with his pet dove for their patron saint. Legendarily an abbot of Glastonbury in the 6th century, he had a Virgin Birth. Very much so, for his mother was St. Nunn (remembered at Altarnun). But Nun in the Old Testament meant a fish—Joshua, son of Nun, was the son of a fish. David's father, King Seint, was obviously too seintly to have anything to do with his arrival on earth. In fact David was said to be born during a great storm at sea—the dove's descending splash!

Edouard Schure in his *"Pythagoras"* shews how the waterspout, a column of water from sea to sky, demonstrated to the ancients these moments of communication between heaven and earth. And this is doubtless what the birth-storm of David is intended to convey—for the word for dove in Celtic and Latin is Colomen, colombe, columba. In German it is taube (tube) and turtel (door or tower of telephonic communication). The first telephones were daffodil-shaped Daffydd's flower. David, with a D at either end, standing for Dol or door, signifies a tower, column or speaking-tube, open both ends to receive and relay messages from the Most High to earth. *Such a tower stands open on Glastonbury Tor.*

David, John . . . Is our Dove not Davey Jones, diving to join Mother Cary in his deep-sea Locker?

Druids taught eternal truths by analogies in natural phenomena. Taliesin saw a parallel in what is now known as the water-cycle, ever-circling *"between three elements"*, earth, sea and sky.

"Three fountains there are in his receptacles; one is the increase of salt water, when it mounts aloft over the fluctuating seas to replenish the streams. The second . . descends upon us when it rains through the boundless atmosphere. The third springs from mountain-veins; a banquet from the King of kings". Taliesin's own story and that of Jonah and the Whale and the boy on the dolphin, Perseus and the many heroes floating in their arks or chests on the sea . . . All these illustrate the *"water-cycle"* of man's descent into matter, his struggles to master it, his defeats and achievements, and his return, enriched by growing self-mastery and experience, to his spiritual home. I have found reason to call it the Iona Mystery, and am tempted to explain this in a Bardic jingle.

> *From the sun's bow*
> I, *Arrow-Word, speed down to*
> O, *the world—the brain; my light shaft bent at*
> N, *piercing dense element. I thread its maze, till raised again*
> to A — *my Alpha-source, enlightenment.*

That some such message is buried in the letters of the word Iona is clear. It is the same word as John, and the Johns of the New Testament are all manifestly heaven-sent messengers, as was the reluctant Jonah or Chaldean Oannes (Johannes) the prophet from the sea who instructed the Chaldeans.

> *"Johannes the Diviner was I called, and Merddin*
> *Now every king shall call me Taliesin—"*

sings the bard, who obviously understood all about it. Merddin or Merlin's name means *"from the sea"*. Arthur himself was said to be swallowed by a mighty fish being coughed up again after three days in its belly.

And how did the turtle get its name? Was it because it was seen as giving a protective shell for the turtle-dove, defenceless among the monsters of the deep?

Outside Barton St. David's church on this effigy stands a mediaeval statue, somewhat weathered, of the Welsh Patron Saint. But inside the church oddly enough is an old picture of quite another David, the Jewish king and bard, playing his harp. A case of mistaken identity? not a bit of it. The magic is in the name! All Davids are messengers from the most high, relaying the Seven Words of Creation in harmonious octaves.

In Arthurian legend the Dove flies like a sign from heaven across the hall of the Grail Castle, preceding the Grail Procession with its Hallows, flooding the scene with unearthly light, preparing the heart for revelations from another plane.

Columba the Dove conveys the Word from heaven to earth. Columba the Saint spread the Word from Ireland to Scotland. The *"colony"* is sustained by the *"column"* or connecting link from the parent culture overseas. Is it accident merely that *Columbus* connected America with Europe?

The little village of Barton St. David has a special link with the States; two of its presidents, the Adams, father and son, came from the old farmhouse near St. David's church, and their descendant Evangeline Adams (well-named) was well-known for her enlightening radio talks on astrology. The Dove of Barton St. David crossed the Atlantic to spread the Word.

Druids in Britain held the Dove of the Awen in reverence, and named many rivers after their inspirational source. The Spirit is clear like water, descending from the heights to fertilise and nourish the plains below. Such names as Avon, Dove, Dovey, Tavy, Columb, Culm and Colne are evidence of the cosmology expressed by our Zodiac and taught by the ancient philosophers and priests.

Scorpio – 1" to the mile
Suggested alternative

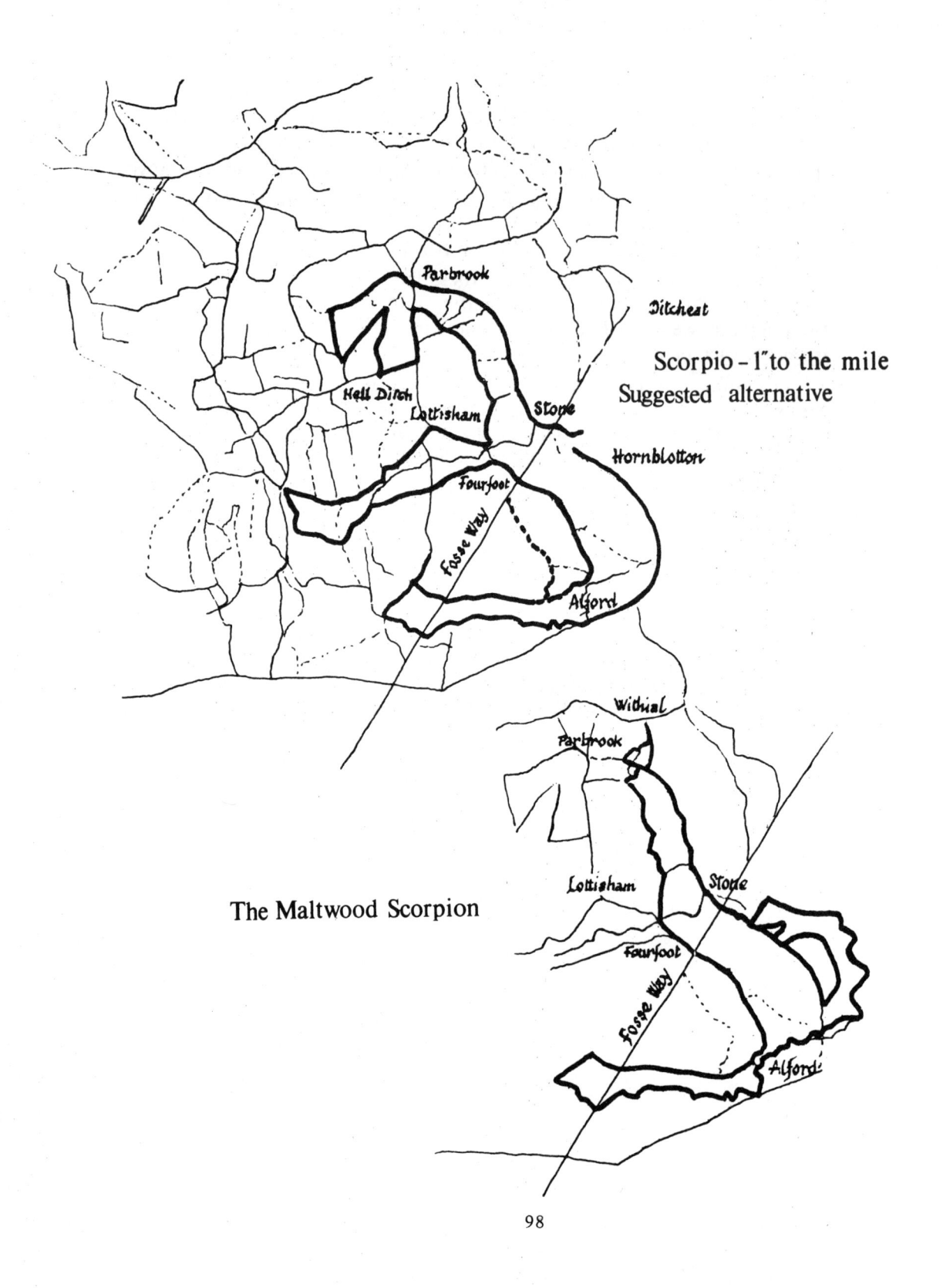

The Maltwood Scorpion

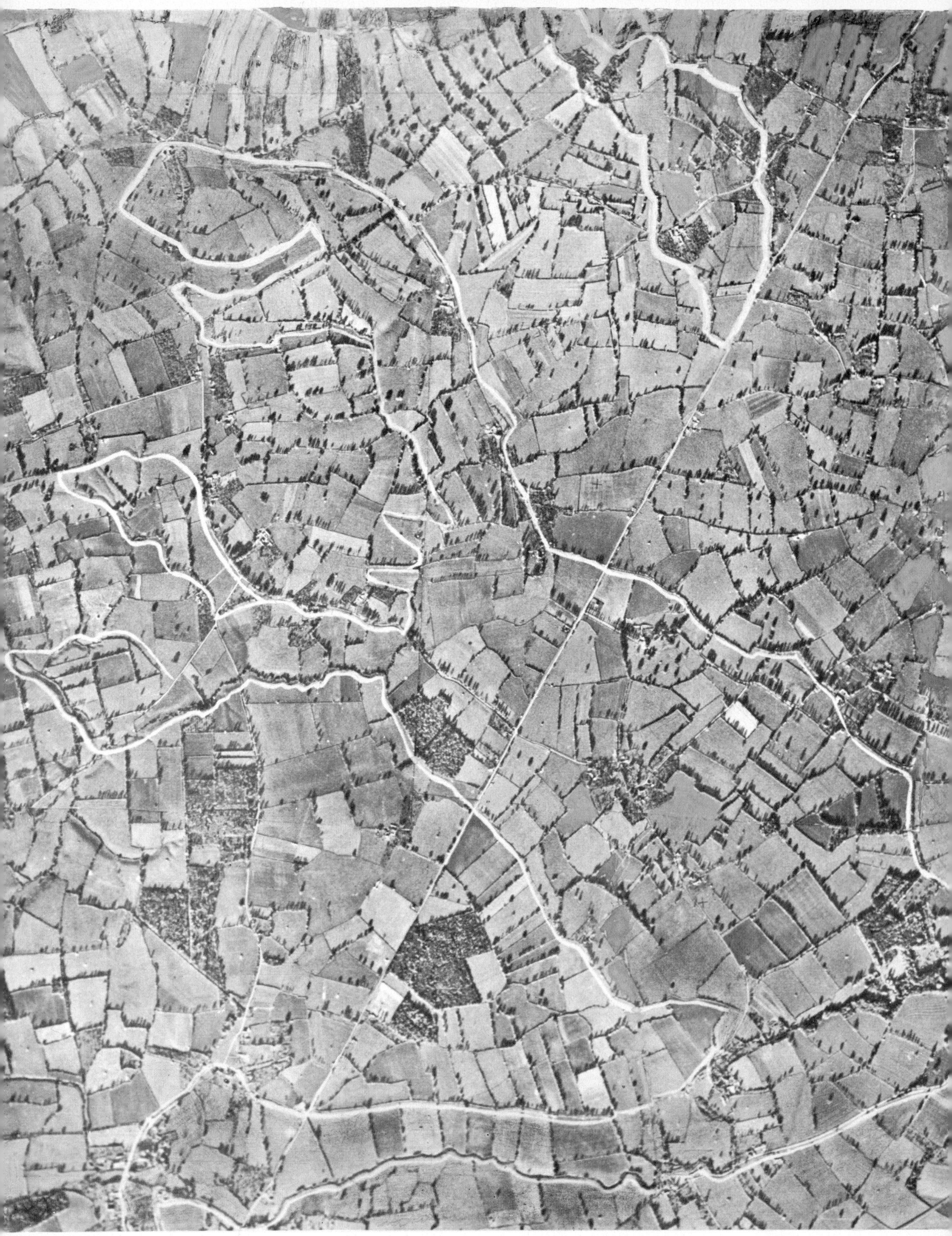

11: Scorpio

*I was buried near this dyke
That my friends may weep as much as they like.*

Epitaph by William Blake

Scorpio, which in astrology hides itself and works in secret, is this Zodiac's most elusive sign. Mrs. Maltwood's is the least convincing of her figures, and I have tried to find an alternative, using her effigy's outlines wherever possible.

Mrs. Maltwood's Scorpion has one outstanding feature, however; its tail stings Sagittarius' horse on the rump at Withial, a place in which gypsies gather mistletoe before sunrise on November 12th.

Mistletoe was the deadly dart that killed Baldur (or Bel) the Beautiful. This Norse myth is by no means the only one that has Celtic parallels (for both mythologies have their source in the Zodiac) and the parallel here is that Druids cut mistletoe from oaks with a golden sickle. Some have seen this as a ritual castration, from the shape of its berries and leaves, so both Norse myth and Celtic custom may symbolise the *"maiming"* of the sun in autumn and winter, its season of increasing impotence. The custom of kissing under the mistletoe at Christmas seems then to signify hope for the increasing power of the returning sun with its promise of fertility.

My Scorpion, the other way up, is at best tentative, and is offered more as an incentive to other researchers than as a definitive solution.

It curves its tail round Alford to its sting at West Lydford, nips Arthur's head at Catsham with one claw while the other, extending the tail of Mrs. Maltwood's, *"pinches his seat"* at Parbrook. *"Par"*, says Mrs. Maltwood, means *"fire"*, as in Par Rock, so Parbrook seems to mean *"fire-water"*—not a bad description of Scorpio's passionate water sign. To find the claws illustrated I used some of the many banked ditches which drain this flood-liable area. For all three water-signs in this extraordinary Zodiac are still flood-prone! Hornblotton's—(Horn-blow-town's) horn used to warn of the Brue's dangerously rising waters from the old church tower. The Brue seems at last to have been brought under better control, and many of these dykes are now dry and no longer marked on the map; one needs air-photographs to see their course.

Scorpio is the sign of *"fixed water"*—an apparent contradiction in terms; yet dykes *do* fix water. The elusive reptile might well be hiding in these drains.

A fury of banked ditches round Lottisham's Lower Farm revealed a possible head and mandibles, and focussed attention on a significant place-name. For Lot meant Light, as in Lancelot's Lance of Light; Llew, Lugh or Lud the British Light-god. But what has light to do with Scorpio's demon of darkness? Why, just this. Legend says that Lucifer's bright star once made Scorpio's constellation resplendent. After his fall this part of the sky became darkened, and the eagle which had hitherto signed this constellation was replaced by the malignant Scorpion. And Lucifer, though he be the very devil himself, is nonetheless the *light-bringer,* as his name implies. And who can Scorpio be in Arthurian legend but Mordred, son of Morgan-le-Faye whose husband was King Lot of the Orkneys—and no doubt of Lottisham too?

Provocative place-names abound; Hell Ditch runs south from Arthur's truncated arm as if to fend off this diabolical enemy; a Canute-like attempt to stem the tide of time, for November's sun is doomed. (Was Hell Ditch, like Blake's dyke, a wailing wall for mourners?) Scorpio has four legs on either side; look for them at Four Foot Farm and Bridgefoot Bridge. This emphasis on feet must irk the fallen Lucifer, now an earth-bound, creeping thing. The village of Stone, where Scorpio's star Antares falls, seems to echo the proud angel's fall with a dull thud. Alas, the stone that gave the place its name is now as elusive as everything else about this effigy; yet it must once have been an important marker, for this district is in White Stone Hundred. We have already seen that it must have marked the invisible equinoctial line that connects Sagittarius the Archer's eye with the Bull's-eye, right across the circle, from east to west. There is more to this orientation than meets the eye—to the Druids east was the world, west the otherworld. It is the direction all must take, Arthur was ferried down the Brue through Scorpio's gate of death into the haven-isle of Avilion. Entering through this eastern Zodiac portal, he *"died to the world".*

Two enemies assail the sun-god. The Whale from Pisces (apathetic matter, chaos) resists his struggle to mould it into conscious form, and by sheer dead weight drags him into the deep; Scorpio (envy, pride and passion) attacks him treacherously from behind, making from ungoverned emotion a flood that drowns his creation. Arthur not only has one foot in the grave; he is also between the devil and the deep. Arthur and Osiris have much in common; November was Osiris' death-month too. Plutarch tells us that the first to hear of Osiris' death were the Pans and Satyrs. Of course they were—Capricorn, ruled by Saturn and himself a goat, is Sagittarius' neighbour, sharing November with him. (Osiris was cut in pieces by his Scorpionic brother Set, and when Isis patiently found them all and joined them together again, only the genitals were missing. That mistletoe again!)

Judas was surely Jesus' Scorpio—his thirty pieces of silver November's thirty days. The sun-king is betrayed not by a stranger, but by a near relation or trusted follower—his nearest and dearest, both male and female. For Scorpio is the dark side, the dark twin, of the sun.

Persians called November Mordad, a death-name echoing Mordred, Arthur's nephew-son, who attempts to wrest from his father both wife and throne. He *should* have been Arthur's nephew, for he was the son of Arthur's sister Morgan-le-Faye, wife to king Lot—but he was, incestuously, his son.

For this lapse Arthur paid with his life. Forgive Arthur's incest—it is unavoidable in solar myth based on the Zodiac, where one female figure must do duty for daughter, sister, wife and mother; where fathers become sons or nephews, and twins are truly identical. We must not judge the gods until we understand the origin and meaning of their myths. Malory's Mordred is sheer sun-myth. Merlin predicted Arthur's death through a child born on May-Day, so Arthur massacred all the innocents with this unfortunate birthday by herding them into a ship and setting them adrift, crewless, out to sea. All drowned but Mordred, who clinging to a rock was saved, fostered secretly and eventually brought to Arthur's court with quite a sizeable chip on his shoulder. No wonder! It is a shock to find noble Arthur cast in Herod's role, but Zodiac students will recognise the old and young sun-kings at play. This incident gives us a new perspective on the Babe in the Boat, and Freudian insight on Mordred. (Oedipus, Paris, Moses, Jesus all survived Massacres of the Innocents.)

Arthur and Mordred fought their fatal battle of Camlann on a down beside Salisbury, not far, says Malory cryptically, from the sea. Stonehenge? Not most people's idea of a seaside resort, though it certainly records the sun-king's rise and fall. Was Malory hinting at the Zodiac, not far from the Severn estuary? Or was he simply recording that rival sun-kings fought their duels by water—a ford, a sea-shore?

Where *was* Camlann fought? On the Cam, near Camelot or Cadbury Castle, where Arthurian memory is still vivid? At Camelford, as Cornishmen claim?

Or is it wherever the sun goes down, turning water to flame? Camlann was known in the Triads as One of the Three Frivolous Battles of Britain, because it was accidentally caused. The tense armies ranged against each other held a parley at a spot midway between; both had orders to march at the first sign of a sword unsheathed. But an adder alarmed a nervous knight. He drew his sword to kill it—with inevitable results. The stars of the constellation Serpens fall upon Scorpio's effigy as well as his own. Mordred's adder!

Scorpio's character as shewn so far is hardly endearing, but his function in evolution is vital. He is the merciless critic, the tester, the analyst, without whose probing sting much corruption in society, the body, the psyche, would spread undetected. Unerringly Mordred picked on the Round Table's weakness, namely the clandestine affair between Lancelot and Guinevere. It was not so much Mordred that brought the Fellowship to ruin as its own internal strains; he was the magnet that polarised the opposition. (Scorpio is always magnetic.) His following included not only congenital malcontents, but many knights whose very loyalty to Arthur was scandalised by such goings-on in high places. Creation needs such testers, whatever their motives. Some have seen comets as exercising this function on a planetary scale. (Was the belt of asteroids another *"Round Table"* casualty?)

Scorpio in his higher aspects criticises himself as much as others: the legend that he stings himself to death with his own tail illustrates this—it is not apparently a fact of natural history. The Scorpionic House of Death is essentially the place of dying to the old self that the new may emerge. Lucifer-Scorpio, though black as coal, is only solar energy waiting to be raised from the libido's mine; its strong and secret passions must transcend earthly goals to find fulfilment. Nothing as it is is good enough for him, including himself.

Until he can reach this goal he is his own worst enemy, stinging himself with his own venom; but he was once signed by an eagle, and by *"dying to himself"* can rise again on strong pinions. The eighth House of Death, once the Stone of White Stone Hundred is rolled away, becomes the place of resurrection. So take heart, Scorpions—you too can become eagles!

It is the time for remembering with remorse. And there is much to remember, remember, in November; All Souls, All saints and their struggles, Armistice Day; Guy Fawkes night but re-enacts the ancient purge-fires of Samhain. Yet we avoid the thought of death, and the horrors of self-seeing—no wonder the Somerset Scorpion got forgotten. The Fosse Way doesn't want to know either, scuttling across his obliterated effigy straight as a die.

The river Brue traditionally has the honour of bearing Arthur's funeral barge westward into Avalon, from its rising on the western slopes of Salisbury plain. The river Alham, jealous of this honour, claims "Arthur's Bridge", near his horse's tail, at Ditcheat. Pronounced Ditch-at, it raises the question *"Ditch at what"*? At the Zodiac's eastern gate, of course. Arthur, passing westward from the world, enters the otherworld, borne on the rueful Brue through Scorpio's gate of Death.

Do not miss Ditcheat's magnificent church with its huge mediaeval mural. It is of St. Christopher, who also *"died to the world"*, passing through this river of self-humiliation. He is Scorpio at its best. Perhaps the artist realised this. Or was it intuition that placed this painting on this sign? Christopher, a soldier, like Martial Scorpio, would serve none but an invincible king. Passing from one defeated master to his conqueror, only to find that each in turn was conquered, he rejected the world and became a hermit, using his great strength to carry travellers across the river on his back. One stormy night he carried a child across the swirling water—but its weight increased until, staggering, he felt he was carrying the world itself on his shoulder. It was the Christ-Child—the Invincible King at last!

The whole story of Christopher echoes the complex message of the Zodiac. From Aries to Leo, the signs have been preoccupied with establishing the spirit in the flesh—coming to terms with the world. The body as an efficient machine must first be established, the sculpture roughed out, before the sculptor can afford to sit back and evaluate his creation. Virgo the critic is the first to see there is something lacking. Libra visualises new possibilities. Scorpio's penetrating tool corrects, destroys, remodels—for he alone has the demonic energy and ruthless standards necessary for such acts of destruction. (Anyone who has seen films of Picasso—a sun-Scorpion—at work, destroying his own marvellous creations as fast as he makes them in order to produce something nearer to his high vision, sees Scorpio at work. The fact that each picture destroyed would have fetched thousands on the market weighs with him not at all. His portraits of himself as Minotaur or monkey are equally typical of Scorpio's savage self-criticism.)

St. Christopher the swaggering soldier, testing one empire-building worldling after another, finds none good enough for him. Scorpio-like he swings from one extreme to another, to serve humble travellers in the most menial capacity, yet one that demands the utmost of his great strength. So, all unknowing, he waits upon the Lord, and when He comes He is even humbler than Christopher—a mere child. Thinking Him an easy burden Christopher finds himself in the position of Hercules, bearing Atlas' world-burden on his shoulders for a moment. But Atlas is our Gemini Babe and Christopher in ferrying him across the turbulent water, is his boat. There are overtones here of Charon, the ferryman who takes the dying across the Styx, river of death. Not by accident is this mural on Scorpio's death-sign! But Christopher is himself the dying man whom he carries across the river; the Christ-Child his new, true self, regenerated by higher values, new vision. The heavy burden of the sins of the world are his own past; it is this new sight of his old self which makes him stagger and nearly go under.

Christopher-Scorpio's staff sprouts at the top like Joseph of Arimathea's. (Joseph bore the Christ-Child to Britain across the water.) Ditcheat's old inn, *"The Green Tree"* surely remembers all this. The dead staff with sprouting top, like the snake-entwined Caduceus, is a symbol of energy redirected from its natural expression by conscious sublimation (not, repeat *not* by unconscious inhibition) to climb the spine and activate the pineal. Thus anger, lust, greed, envy etc., (all forms of energy destructive in their direct expression) can be by conscious alchemy transformed into understanding, compassion, generosity, admiration and emulation respectively— from which comes inspiration; not only the green leaves but the fruits of the spirit.

Hornblotton's church mural shews Moses holding up the snake-festooned Tau Cross in the wilderness; Alford church's pew-end repeats this Scorpionic theme with a dragon stinging its own head with its tail. Within this circle is a human head. *"See, human,"* it seems to say, *"Scorpions need not die by their own venom—they can fire themselves with their own energy on a higher level."* Other mediaeval pew-ends shew a Pelican in her piety. feeding her young with her own blood (does this self-maiming not say the same thing?), a Paschal Lamb, and a Green Man, chief among Nature-Giants. On a Victorian chancel screen the four Zodiac animals symbolise the evangelists. Heavens! Were these Victorians in the secret too?

The High History pictures Scorpio as a dead hermit, Callixtus, whose misspent life is being weighed against his last penitent years by squabbling demons and angels. Happily, the angels win by a whisker. The stars of the Scales fall in our Zodiac on Scorpio's claw (my Scorpion's tail) and Libra's judgements are always merciful. No doubt this is the message the author of the High History intended to convey; it certainly seems that he knew where to find Libra's judgement-scales. On Scorpio, the sign of touch and go—the sign of the Last Chance. No wonder there is more than a hint of desperation in the Scorpionic character. Will the dead staff bud again? Can the kundalini snakes be persuaded to climb the Caduceus Tree of Life?

The river Brue traces Scorpio's tail past Lovington's old mill to Lydford. *"Lyd"* is said to mean *"gate"*, but here it means more, being Lud or Lot the light-god's gate through death to the Otherworld—Lud's-ford. Rival sun-gods duelled at a ford, lake or sea-beach. Malory's Stonehenge-on-sea is poetry, not geography!

Lean over West Lydford Bridge and see the dying king emerge with weeping queens, to float past church and graveyard, river-lapped, where golden water-lilies reflect his setting sun. (The queens had to lean over too, to survive West Lydford's low bridge—but no matter.) On the opposite bank, East Lydford's church and churchyard are in ruins, and open lidded graves yawn wide, showing that Arthur is not there. For he, the sun, is risen. *"Unwise the thought, a grave for Arthur'* sang the bard. The Brue, river of rue, *encompasses his ruin by drawing both Scorpion and Whale;* its very name breathes ancient tragedy—the ruin of Bruin, Brian Boru the Bear.

Britain's early history was bardically known as the *"Brut"*—ostensibly from Brutus, its first-crowned king, from Troy. But Arthur ousts Brutus as the Brut's central theme, for in his Round Table and Grail-Quest he represents a culminating-point of Man's long struggle upwards from *"brutish"* beginnings. Was he not a champion against the Brute in Man?

Bards saw the Fall of Man, of Troy, of the Round Table, as a repeating pattern in history's tapestry; to them, Adam, Brutus, Jesus, Arthur, Galahad, were inextricably interwoven on its loom. (Was Ector, Arthur's foster-father, not Hector, Troy's last protector? And did Brutus not found London as Trinovant, New Troy?) It is the Tale of Man, no less; of the rise and fall of civilisations, over which bards and angels weep and hope. Banished *Brythons* wept as they *bruited* abroad their mournful lays in *Brittany*; *imbrued* in Saxon gore they homed once more to *Britain* in the Norman train. For there, they hoped and harped, Arthur would return; at his Round Table another Golden Age of Quest and Chivalry would dawn. And so, under Henry and Eleanor, the Plantagenets and Templars—for a brief moment, it did.

West Lydford

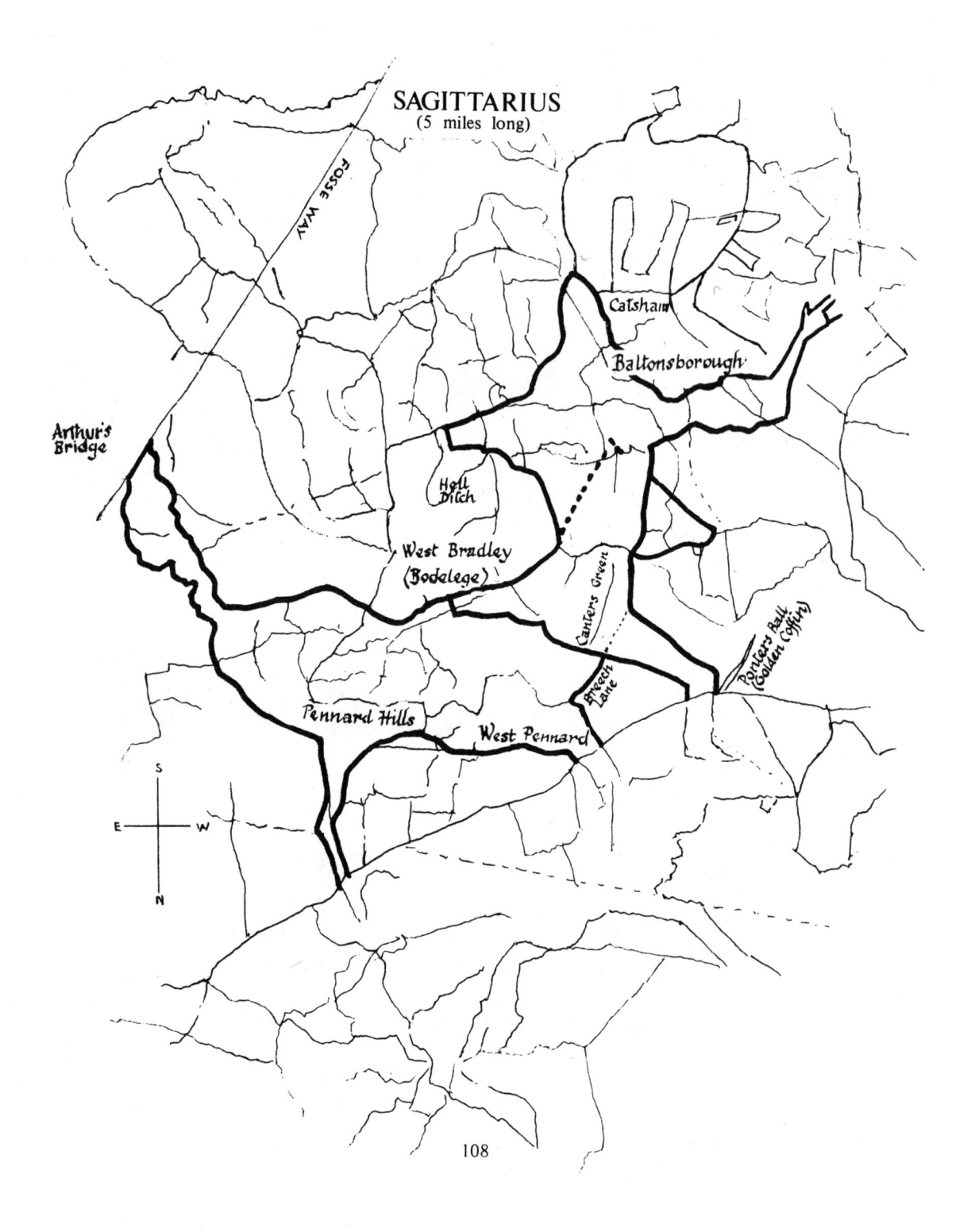

SAGITTARIUS
(5 miles long)

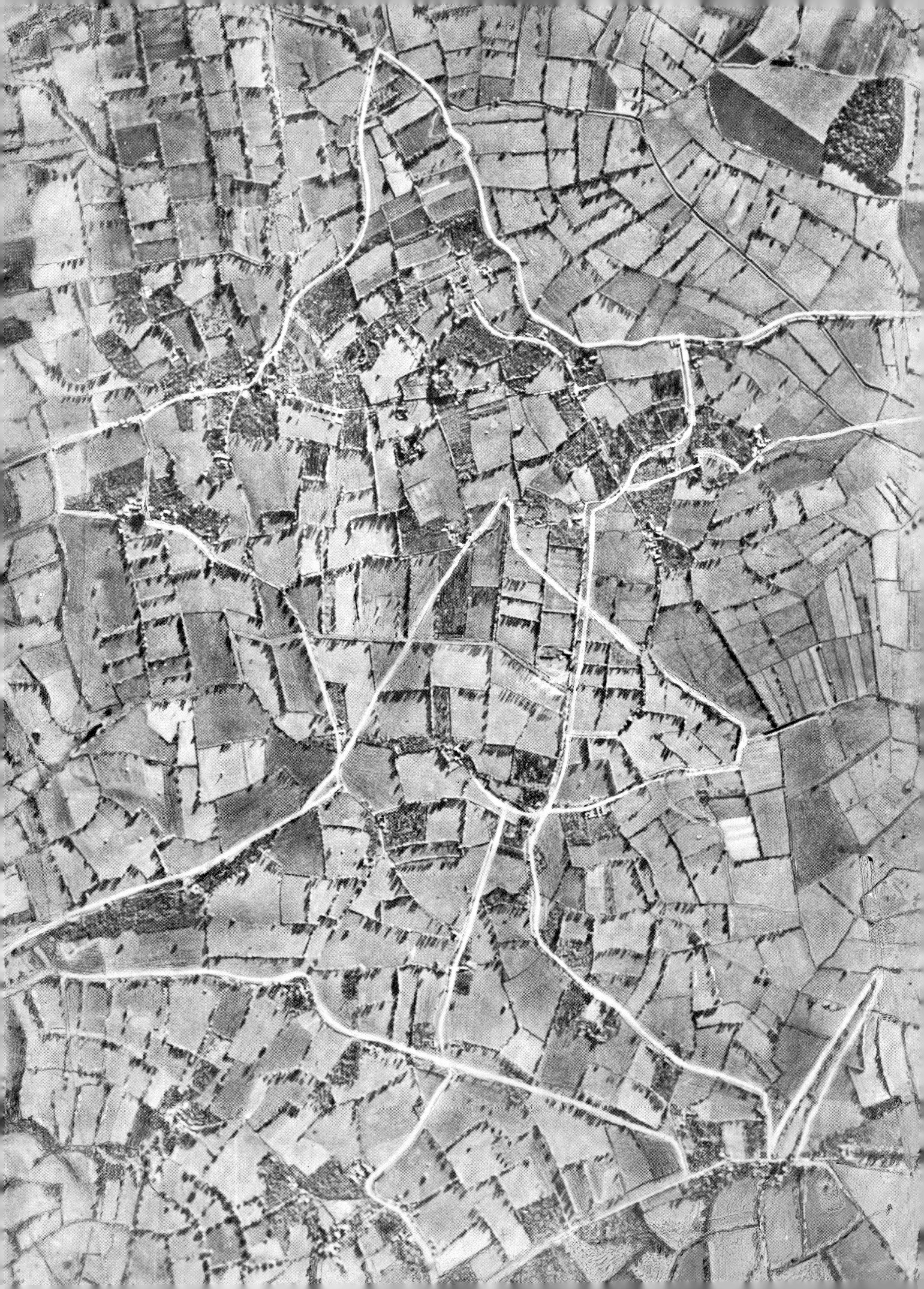

12: Sagittarius–Arthur

Here is the first Arthur of Avalon, seated at the original Round Table, a cosmic Table of Measurements—with Guinevere, Merlin and his chief knights, all corresponding to the months of the year. The Pennard Hills (*"Arddur's hill-top"*) accurately model his horse: Arthur's Bridge is by its tail. Long ages before the 6th-century-Arthur took his name, his Titanic shadow lay stretched across the Vale of Avalon. West Bradley, *"Bodelege"* in Domesday Book, seems to remember where his body lay. Is it just coincidence that Bodelege is at the junction of Arthur's leg and his horse's body?

But Arthur as a solar title stretches even further across the world. He was Ahura, Asser, to the Medes and Persians, giving his name to Assyria and indeed to the whole continent of Asia. In Egypt he was Ausar, Osiris, and his son Horus or Arueris. Horus, the Hour of the Zodiac clock. The now-extinct Guanches of the Canaries called him Ach-Ahura-Han—Han being the divine name Huan or John. The Guanches, who preserve Huan in their name, were once thought to be the last of the Atlanteans.

Osiris' myth has much in common with Arthur's; both were betrayed by sister-wife and envious nephew-son, both ferried down-river by the repentant mother-sister-wife or triple goddess; both were expected to return.

Arthur's name has passed into our language in words like Heart and Hearth, eloquent of the central place he has long occupied in our affections.

It seems that He-art and He-arth shew two of his names, for the Celtic god Hu was pronounced *"He"*. And Hu and Arthur are intertwined in myth, the adventures of one being often attributed to the other. Both dragged the Avanc or Leviathon out of the lake of Llyn Llion after the Flood, for example.

Does this tale remember the draining of Somerset's flood-prone Whale, when the channels that draw its outlines were cut to contain the river Brue? This irrigation was done by agriculturalists, and both Arthur and Hu are remembered as Ploughmen who gave this art to their people. *"Ara"* is Latin for plough; Arthur's name is more ancient, one suspects, than is generally admitted. Arthur also ploughs the *Arc* of the sky; the Zodiac is his furrow.

Baltonsborough is on our Sagittarian Arthur's head, its prefix recalling that the Phoenicians called this sun-god Baal. Bal is a frequent prefix for hills in western Britain, Scotland and Ireland.

Arthur hides in another Phoenician title—Hercules Melkarth. *"Melk"* means king, Arth of course, Arthur.

No accident then that the stars of Hercules fall on Arthur's shoulders! No indeed. For his Twelve Famous Labours are but the passage of the sun through the twelve Houses of the Zodiac. The sun has many names for he shines on all, being worshipped by all for his ardour, for his arduous labours on behalf of his creation. *"Per ardua ad astra"* should be translated *"with Arthur to the stars"*

To our ancestors, the sun was not only a sentient being, compassionate, benevolent and glorious, but a haven to which all beings whose vibrations had quickened to his point were drawn at death. We know this from an old Breton legend, worth narrating, especially as the old book, Edward Davies' *"Celtic Researches"* which translates it, has long been out of print. His source was *"Voyage dans le Finesterre"*, 1794.

"The young son of a prince of St. Pol de Leon, whilst wandering alone on the sea-shore, is overcome by a tempest. He repairs for shelter to a cavern, which proves to be inhabited by the Goddess of Nature. Her head is covered with stars; the signs of the Zodiac adorn her girdle. Her unruly sons, the winds, enter the recess. The child's limbs become rigid with a mortal cold: he is covered by water. But repose is not made for these demons.

When they rush forth, the goddess takes the amiable boy on her knees, and covers him with her robes. Nature's spoiled child, the lovely zephyr, makes his appearance. The young prince is committed to his care. He is divested of his earthly envelope", (a very Druidical concept) *"his terrestrial senses are at once refined, and he is borne aloft in the air.*

In the course of his journey, he makes discoveries of signal importance. The clouds are composed of the souls of men which have lately quitted the earth. They fly over the heads of armies, their influence inspiring courage or terror.

These are they, who in the obscurity of night and amongst silent forests, terrify mortals with long-continued howlings, with apparitions, luminous phantoms. Participating as yet of terrestrial affections, they mix themselves into the passions of men. Their agency is perceived in dreams and in panic terrors.

In vain they endeavour to soar above the atmosphere. An irresistible force—a wall of sapphire—impedes their wing towards the purer spheres, which roll in the immensity of space.

As soon as a new body is formed, they enter it with impatience, inhabit, and give it animation. Not having attained that purity which unites them to the sun, the genius of their system, they wander in the forms of the various animals which people the air, the earth, and the seas.

The prince is carried up into the vortex of the moon. Here, millions of souls traverse vast plains of ice, where they lose all perception, but that of simple existence. They forget the course of adventures in which they have been engaged, and which they are now to recommence. On long tubes of darkness, caused by an eclipse, they return to earth. They are revived by a particle of light from the sun, whose emanations quicken all earthly things. They begin anew the career of life.

Towards the disc of the sun, the young prince approaches, at first with awful dread, but presently with inconceivable rapture and delight. This glorious body is an assemblage of pure souls, swimming in an ocean of bliss. It is the abode of the blessed—of the sages—of the friends of mankind. These happy souls, when thrice purified in the sun, ascend to a succession of still higher spheres, from whence they can no more descend to traverse the circle of those globes and stars which float in a less pure atmosphere."

Such teaching, remarks Davies, is neither Gothic, nor Roman; but it corresponds exactly to that of the oldest Welsh documents, and must be Druidic. But even Christianity cannot improve on the hopeful and sublime doctrine that souls, sullied by earthly impurities, are destined to be refined by repeated changes and probations, till the last stain of evil or thick stupidity is worn away, and they are ultimately ripened for immortal bliss in ever-heightening spheres. And even Christianity has forgotten the marvellous economy of this teaching, which used all the planets and stars as stages for ever-heightening consciousness. Traces of it survive in apocryphal angelology, which identifies the angels with the planets; and in the *"seven heavens"* of the cosmic hierarchy. Sirius, it was thought once, was the sun of the sun, to which the sun was simply a planet.

Used as we are to regarding the sun as a non-sentient chemical factory, indeed ourselves as a bundle of chemical actions and reactions, such a view of the universe may startle at first. But how are mere bundles of chemicals to judge if such a teaching is true or no? This Druidic concept sweeps all matter, all electro-magnetism into one vast and meaningful complex, with point, purpose and unity—something our Behaviourist-psychology and materialistic-mechanistic view of ourselves and the universe signally fails to do.

All heroes and sun-saviours of mankind have harrowed hell to break humanity's chains, just as the sun at night passes beneath the earth, lighting those in darkness. Arthur is no exception. In our Zodiac he is dragged from his sun-horse, preparing to sail into the Underworld in his Ark or Argo in the person of his Geminian son. Arthur was said to be lowered into the underworld in a Ship of Glass—not only the translucent Moon-boat near Dundon, gleaming beneath the shallow flooding of the Severn, but a reference to the Glastonbury Mysteries. Superstition still connects the new moon with glass!

He had a double purpose; to free Gweir (Vir, Man) from his chains, and to recover the Cauldron of rebirth and inspiration from the bowels of the earth, or the dark depths of the subconscious.

Arthur is undoubtedly a sun-god. But what evidence is there to connect him with Sagittarius? The sun, after all, passes through each sign in turn; if it shews any preference it is for Leo, which it rules in summer glory. But Arthur is not the sun in glory; he is essentially the wintering sun in decline, the season of Sagittarius. His glories are all in the past, and if he or Guinevere are insulted (as not infrequently happens in the legends) he has to rely on younger knights to do battle for him. He is cuckolded too by Lancelot, final proof of his humiliating impotence — or preoccupation with higher matters!

But Ahura and Arthur are, we suspect, one, and Plunket's *"Ancient Calendars and Constellations"* finds that Ahura is Sagittarius in the primordial calendar of the Medes. Olcott's *"Star Lore of all Ages"* also identifies Sagittarius with Median Ahura, so our equation Arthur-Ahura = Sagittarius is complete.

We have already seen that this effigy is not a centaur, Arthur sits his horse with a splendid pair of buttocks of his own, happily emphasised by Breech Lane and Canters Green. His mount's neck, obscured by the rider's torso, can be seen within it, drawn by paths. The horse's head protrudes out in front, and has a willow-fringed eye.

We have already suspected that this figure, badly copied by leaving out Arthur's leg and the horse's head, may have brought the centaur to birth in Greece. For Arthur, being dragged over his mount's neck by the Piscean Whale, makes profound mythical sense, while the centaur makes no sense at all. And sense must precede nonsense, for nonsense is only half-forgotten sense.

It seems that centaurs can be added to the growing list of Greek or Middle eastern myths that only make sense in the light of their Hyperborean-British originals. Yet it is a very old mistake, for centaurs appear on Chaldean boundary-stones of the Bronze Age. It is a tragic mistake too, for it has helped to scramble the Zodiac message of man's purpose on earth. Who can recognise Evolution's peak-product, the philosopher-king so nobly symbolised by Arthur, in the degenerate centaur, boon companion of pans and satyrs? At what target will the lecherous centaur aim, with the aspirational arrow that symbolises Sagittarius' House of Higher Mind? Yet Sagittarius is a double sign, both man and animal, and can go either way; his indubitable charm opens all doors, so there is a hint of truth in the centaur too. Sagittarians take note! He is a warning to us to watch our aim, while Arthur serves still as the fount of our highest ideals.

The Greeks, however had one high-souled centaur, Chiron the four-footed philosopher and teacher of aspiring sun-heroes. He was as noble as the rest of his species were base; wounded in the heel by a poisoned arrow (always a clue to solar divinity) he voluntarily descends into Hades, restoring Prometheus to Olympus by taking his place. A true sun-god, he dies that others may live.

Both Prometheus and Chiron repeat in Greek myth their solar sacrifice, shewn in the more ancient Somerset Zodiac. Prometheus, we have seen, is Gemini, his liver eternally pecked at Liver Moor. Both sun-gods, old and young, repeat the Zodiac's message of *noblesse oblige*—the voluntary self-sacrifice of the more conscious man for the less aware, so that they too may grow in awareness, thus echoing on earth the self-sacrifice of the sun, who in Druid eyes was the abode of the highest and most conscious denizens of the solar system, united in giving their energy, life and light to its planets.

Our Sagittarian effigy has his arms outflung in the form of a cross. No accident surely, for the cross, long before Christianity, symbolised the entry of spirit into matter. Solar energy, absorbed by the world, gives life. But in so doing its vibrations are absorbed and slowed down to the point of death. The ancients said *"the king must die"*.

The Archer's arms, at right-angles to his body as if drawing the bow, run parallel to the east-west line of the Royal Cross between Aldebaran and Antares. His eye looks along it, drawing a bead on Aldebaran's Bull's-eye.

He is indeed crucified—on the Christmas-Tree of Life, whose vertical stem between Fomalhaut and Regulus once pointed out the summer and winter solstices. Arthur-Sagittarius dies and is reborn at the winter solstice.

"To crucify before the sun", says Madam Blavatsky, *"is a phrase used of initiation ... The adept who had successfully passed through all the trials, was tied on a cross in deep sleep, and left in that state for three days and three nights, during which time his spiritual Ego was said to confabulate with the gods, descend into Hades, Amenti, etc., according to the country. At a certain hour the beams of the rising sun struck full on the face of the entranced candidate, and like Hercules he was born again."*

Though Christians seem to have largely forgotten the calendrical aspect of their Mysteries, they have preserved the spiritual message of the meaning and purpose of Time, as taught by their predecessors wherever Zodiacs are found. Time for the redemption of spirit from matter, time for the emergence of consciousness from sleep, time for new energy and inspiration to shake off its bonds of inertia, for wisdom to supersede ignorance, time for the many to realise their unity in the One.

Here at Sagittarius is the original St. George of England, his arms outflung in the patronal cross. Indeed, this Zodiac explains the enigmatic patron saints of England, Scotland, Wales and Cornwall. For here too is Cornwall's patron St. Michael, both names according to Waddell brought by

Phoenicians from the Middle East, and both solar deities. Here too if Waddell is right is the first St. Andrew, or dragon-slaying Indara of the Indo-Aryans, brought to Scotland in times pre-Christian by Aryan migrants. The professor shews that prehistoric St. Andrew-type crosses are to be found all over Scotland, carved on ancient stones. And certainly there is more to St. Andrew than meets the eye, for in Syrian legend he throws off his humble fisherman's cloak to battle with a dragon and save a city. Is Andrew the androgynous man of the Mysteries? Is he too stretched on the Cosmic Cross? We have already scratched St. David of Wales and found a sun-god beneath the skin: his *"virgin-birth"* from chaste St. Nunn puts him in this select class. St. Patrick of Ireland is numbered among Glastonbury's earliest abbots, and from the incident of the thirteen idols half-buried in the earth, seems to have known of the Zodiac.

What national saint or emblem is not here? The Union Jack is made from the combined crosses of our patron saints and represents esoterically the eightfold path of spiritual development. The Prince of Wales' Feathers, like the fleur-de-lys, represent the Trinity or Godhead descending through the divine right or responsibility of kingship, the inspirational Three Bars of Light. The Summer Lion and Winter Unicorn of Capricorn support the royal arms and the whole Zodiac is Britannia's or Prytania's wheel, while she herself is Virgo, already our Mother-Goddess in Roman times.

Her wheel is the Wheel of Fortune. At the end of Malory's Morte D'Arthur occurs a tableau which perfectly describes the figure of Sagittarius-Arthur, hanging upside-down on the Zodiac wheel.

"King Arthur dreamed a wonderful dream . . . him seemed he sat upon a chaflet in a chair . . . fast to a wheel, and thereupon he sat in the richest cloth of gold that might be made; and the king thought there was under him, far from him, an hideous deep black water, and therein were all manner of serpents, and worms, and wild beasts, foul and horrible; and suddenly the king thought the wheel turned up so down, and he fell among the serpents, and every beast took him by a limb." Capricorn has him by a leg, Scorpio menaces him with claws and sting, the Whale mangles his arm at Wallyer's Bridge.

In an earlier version of this dream, the Goddess Fortuna smiles on Arthur whom she has set, sceptred and crowned, on her wheel, until at midday her mood changes; she frowns, gives the wheel a turn, and throws him down. It is the Zodiac clock! And Arthur, turning *"up so down"* has performed the first somersault. It is significant that even so late as Charles Dickens' day, the word used to be a *"somerset"*.

Our Zodiac also explains all the tales of Arthur as king of the Antipodes, lording it over misshapen monsters; or encircling with his knights a pile of gold within a cave beneath a fairy hill, sleeping until awakened by his country's need. His treasures are the Thirteen Treasures of Britain, so old

116

and so far forgotten that even the oldest accounts of them are confused. Though the lists do not tally they do however all contain a mantle of invisibility and a cauldron. Arthur's mantle of invisibility has long lain over the thirteen effigies: the cauldron is the wisdom-teaching they enshrine. And if those few initiates who dared to penetrate the cave and rifle the gold, found in the morning their pockets filled with dry leaves—well, they were the leaves of ancient books: worthless to some but to others worth a king's ransom.

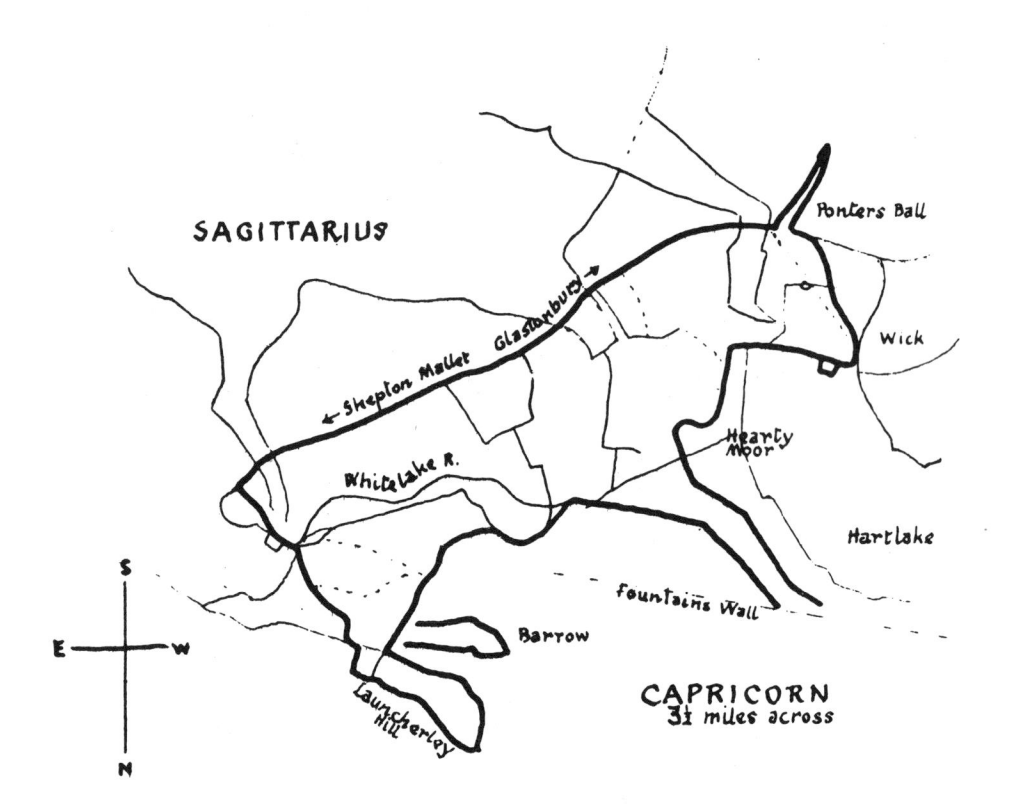

13: Capricorn

Capricorn is the northernmost figure in our Zodiac—as Norwood on his nose, North Wootton on his foot, may indicate. His back, the road from Glastonbury to Shepton Mallet, cuts through the northern end of the great earthwork known as Ponter's Ball, which has yielded Bronze and Iron Age finds. This rampart is over half a mile long and twenty feet high at the cutting, which goes by the ancient name of Havyatt. Yatt is *"gate"*, hav being the haven of Avalon, or gate to the Summerland. Somerset's Celtic name is Gwlad yr Hav.

Practically speaking, it seems to have been a barrier to deter the eastern invader, for not all who sought Glastonbury were peaceful pilgrims. But its function in our Zodiac is to model the Goat's horn. Single, long and straight, it makes a Unicorn of Capricorn, and points south-west across the circle to Somerton on the Lion's paw. We have already pointed out this ancient polarity of Lion and Unicorn expressed in this Zodiac long before they came to support the Royal Coat of Arms.

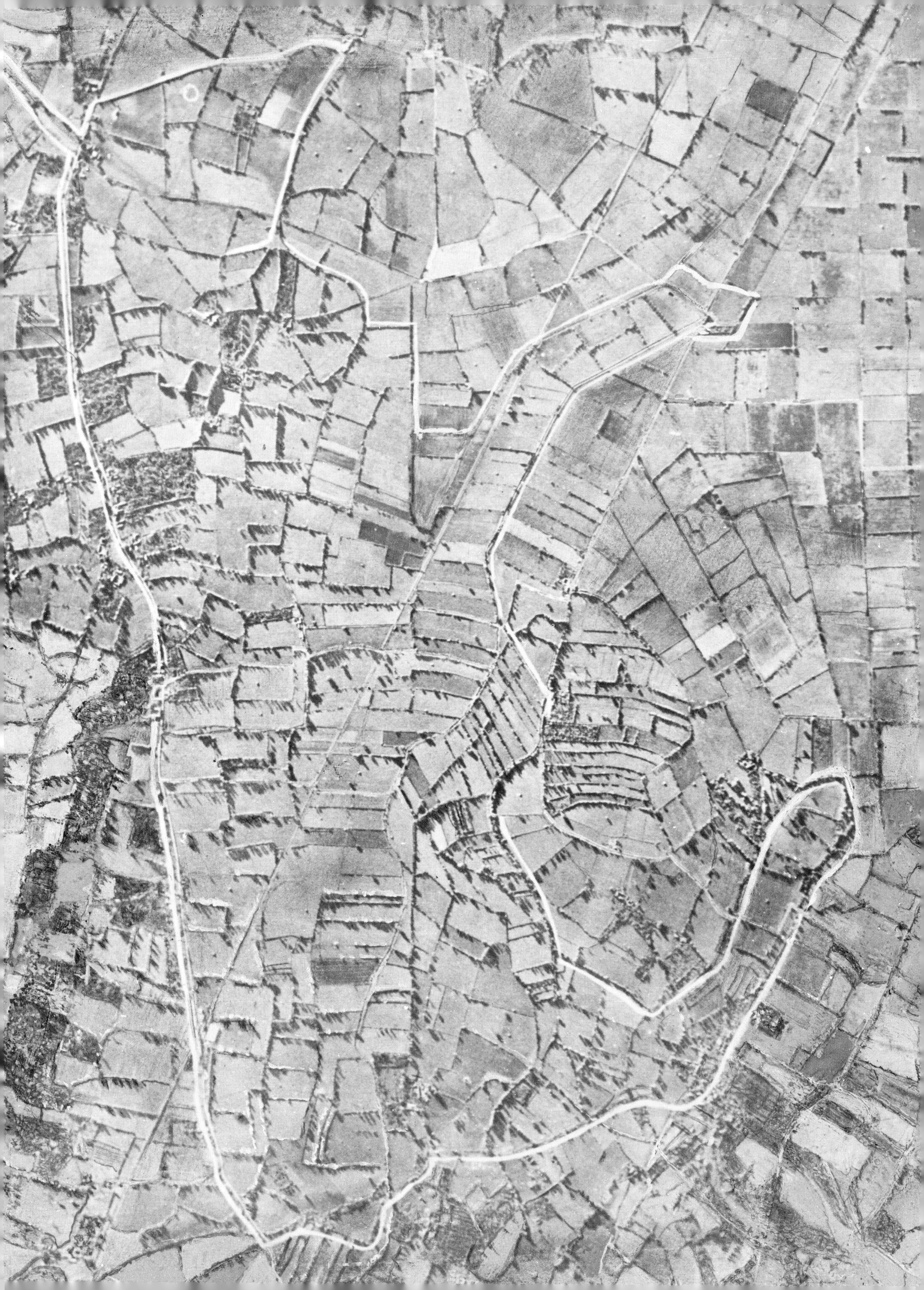

So how did they come together on the royal blazon? They were adopted by James I of England, to unite the Unicorn of Scotland with the British Lion. But how came the Unicorn to Scotland? The answer is interesting. It was brought from *Somerset* by Jane Beaufort, who married an earlier James I of Scotland. Her Plantagenet line from John of Gaunt became Earls of Somerset. John of Gaunt and the Plantagenets were deep in the British Mysteries—our royal supporters are not so accidental as they seem! They were already connected with the throne of England before the accession of James I. The poet Spenser in *"The Faery Queen"*, (1590) speaks of *"the lion and unicorn who support the throne."* Did Spenser know the ancient Secret?

Both Plantagenets and Templars were suspected of strange beliefs—a Christianity at once mystical and deviant. Arthuriana flourished under both; Plantagenet kings made pilgrimages to Glastonbury, dug up *"Arthur"* and reburied him with pomp, and named the Round Table Mound at Windsor.

Templars were known as Guardians of the Grail. The truth must be that both were well-grounded in the Mysteries of the Somerset Zodiac—their Christianity the Celtic brand, suppressed by the Church, but recognising the essential identity of the old religious teachings with the new. In fact it was this as much as anything that caused their suppression. As crusaders their understanding of their own brand of Christianity was deepened by contact with the eastern Caballa, whose philosophy mirrored the Celts'; for the ancient Mysteries whether of east or west, were based clairvoyantly on the universal subconscious, endorsed and demonstrated by Nature herself on earth and in the stars. Templar churches, like stone circles, were round—like the earth and all the heavenly bodies.

Rome had first vilified, then decimated the Druids; the Roman church did the same to Celtic Christianity, and later to the Knights Templars.

Both sets of slanders are still widely believed, alas! Can we hope that this Zodiac may heal the old unhappy breach—unifying sundered creeds by shewing the one root from which all derive?

Glastonbury, in times when its polar relation to Rome was understood, was honoured with the title *"Roma Secunda"*. Its northern free-thinking head (the Unicorn), opposed to the southern heart of faith (the Lion) created a vivid magnetic field which could erect the glory of Gothic cathedrals and unite all Europe. Zodiacs decorated the doorways of these cathedrals, the name and fame of Arthur was extolled from Britain to Italy. The flower of chivalry bloomed for a season in the Grail-vase. But the strain was too great for Rome. Under Philip the Fair of France and Edward II of England the Templars were arrested, tortured and burnt, the Order totally suppressed. *"The Lion beat the Unicorn all round the town."* The polarity collapsed, and Europe slowly fell apart, a prey to wars, plagues and witch-hunts.

The Unicorn, beaten, went to ground; to be precise, in Avalon—where Arthurian-Grail Christianity was too rooted in tradition and legend to be forgotten. Rumour was active as to his whereabouts. The whole west country was said to be the land of the Gilded Goat; the Welsh regiment still keep him as their mascot. A mysterious goat was said to haunt the Tor. His great horn at Ponter's Ball is still locally known as the Golden Coffin; not only because the leg of the sun-god has one foot in this grave, but doubtless also because the Goat himself was gilded.

The unicorn, said rumour, was notoriously difficult to catch, partly for his elusiveness (Graves' *"White Goddess"* tells us that the Unicorn means *"find the secret"*), partly because of his enormous strength. Look at Capricorn's powerful shoulders! In fact the only way to catch him was to send a pure virgin into the forest; inevitably he would come and lay his head in her lap, his ferocity tamed, he could then be netted with ease. This parable of the power of love to subdue the savage breast was popular in mediaeval art, and is probably Arthurian, or Zodiacal.

The unicorn's horn was much sought after as an antidote to poison; the story went that water however polluted, was purified when the unicorn dipped his horn in it to drink. He was not just a savage beast; there was something mysterious, mystical, otherworldly, about him.

The Virgin is Sophia, Wisdom; only wisdom can capture and bind this milk-white beast, so untameable with his clairvoyant horn, Brain-beyond-the-brain. Persecuted by the Lion of the Establishment, he becomes the symbol of Grail-Wisdom-teaching, only to be found by the pure in heart.

By the same token, Capricorn becomes the White Hart, (adopted by Plantagenet Richard II), sought through field and forest by every prince of folklore. Sometimes a crucifix could be glimpsed between his horns, these horns, annually shed and renewed, symbolised resurrection, immortality; the probing tines signify curiosity, the desire to know, which distinguishes Man from the beasts; a tool of Evolution to lead him ever further into the forest of self-knowing.

In our Zodiac Capricorn heaves his powerful shoulders up out of the marshes about the Whitelake river; he is thrusting forward, his hindquarters lost in the amoebic slime of the past; goatlike, his nose presses against the Tor, for goats must climb the mountain. He cools his weary feet in the *Hartlake*, his heart pounding from the chase at *Hearty Moor*. Place-names and legend know his hiding-place. Mrs. Maltwood's figure trails off inconclusively to his hindquarters, but I find a well-drawn back leg at North Wootton, its hoof pressed against Launcherly Hill—launching-pad for Capricorn's forward thrust? A mediaeval zodiac on the ceiling of a gateway to Merton College, Oxford, also shews a four-footed goat as Capricorn—the goat-fish is not obligatory.

Templars were undoubtedly here; Templar insignia, a bird (Aquarian eagle?) and paschal lamb with reverted head (Aries) are carved on old cottages at Wick, where Capricorn's nose touches Aquarius' wing. Though the goat is not with them he might well have been, for the Templars certainly used his symbol. Gibbon reviled them *"for being led by a goat and a goose"*. The knights are thought to have guarded the spring at *Paradise* above Wick. Was this, Mrs. Maltwood wondered, *"the cave of the rising"* or rising sun, which belonged to Capricorn in Sumeria? She says that a tunnel now fallen in penetrated the Tor at Chalice Well, and may have come out at the Paradise spring, a lovely valley sculptured by lynchets.

Traditionally the sun entered a tunnel in the west at sunset and rose from this subterranean journey at an eastern exit. *"The Babe Sun has entered a long tunnel—woe to the chief of the tents!"* sang the bards. Paradise, east of the Tor, was used by the Druids long before Templar times, witness two ancient oaks known as Gog and Magog, the last of a Druid grove. Other stumps remain, by their rings two thousand years old. It must be about that time when Capricorn's horn marked the winter solstice. Where better to celebrate the rebirth of the dying sun? Templars trod in Druid footprints.

The legend of a cavern under the Tor is one of the mysteries of Glastonbury. Christ is said to have survived the cross and come here to hide within it. And no-one who has lifted the lid of Chalice Well to hear the booming and thundering of its waters, magnified as if reverberating through vast and echoing caverns, can doubt that there *are* caves deep in the limestone. Were they once used by initiates in the Mysteries of rebirth? Did they reside, as Christ is said to have done, three days within the Tor, emerging reborn with the winter solstitial sun, in *"Paradise"*?

Earthy Capricorn is still the grave of the dying year. His horn is the Cornucopia, where seeds of the coming spring were stored. The she-goat Amalthea in Greek legend suckled the infant Zeus in her cave with the cornucopia, and, for her devotion was translated to the stars as Capricorn.

The Sagittarian sun-god enters into Capricorn at three nodal points in our Zodiac—the intuitive back of the head at Ponter's Ball, the heart, and bowels or genitals. Thus he regenerates mortal or primitive man; dying, he gives new life, a higher energy to those on earth. Profound symbol!

The name Ponter's Ball is officially interpreted as *"the wall of the bridge"*. (Pontis Vallum.) But there is no bridge here. It has been suggested by a perceptive researcher that this name may derive from the Etruscan *"Puntes Bal"*—sacrifice of Bel. This seems to make much better sense, where the dying sun-god descends into his earthy grave. But in the Zodiac the grave is not the end. In the Dionysian Mysteries the goat-stag symbolised man's immortality, its spiral-patterned horn, like the unicorn's, figuring forth the recurring round of Zodiac lives by which man slowly ascends, as on a spiral stairway, to ever-heightening awareness. The story of the Chimaera, that winged goat on which Zeus flew up to heaven, must also derive from Capricorn—it is known to be a calendar beast. It also demonstrates a mystery-teaching. Not only Capricorn benefits from the penetration of the sun-god's saving rays, but God Himself is completed, *"taken to heaven"*, on the back of his creation's efforts.

For Capricorn is Man, all men, throughout time and evolution. Thus he is equated with Pan, oldest of the gods. Horned and cleft-footed, half an animal, he has even figured as Satan, for he is ruled by Saturn. But unless we see Satan as solar energy trapped in a black coal-seam, this is unfair. Capricorn longs to be liberated, pressing his aspiring nose against the Tor—and the Tor is winged. He is trying to develop his immortal foreparts, leaving his hinder parts behind in the marsh from which he springs.

"The forest is the body, the unicorn the spirit, the deer the soul" said the hermetic tract, the Book of Lambspring. *"He that knows how to tame and master them, to lead them in and out of the forest, is a Master."*

Capricorn is also Bran, oldest of Celtic gods; his feet lost in the river like the roots of the alder, Bran's tree. Bran in the Mabinogion led an expedition to Ireland to capture the all-healing Cauldron of Wisdom. He is certainly a Nature-Giant—his head like a mountain, his eyes two lakes; he was so large no house could contain him.

But in the battle the Cauldron burst asunder, so Bran's head, no less inspirational, took its place. Directing his followers to cut it off as he was dying, he told them it would save Britain if buried under the White Mount (Tower Hill), and that it would so entertain and entrance them on the journey back that they would lose all track of time. Capricorn's inspirational horn!

Bran's head is the skull in the sacred well, that served as cup for pilgrims thirsty for the Water of Life. It was equated with the Cauldron of Inspiration, and thus with the Grail. (In the Grail procession that Perceval saw there was no Grail; instead he saw a severed head on a salver.)

Bran means brain—the words are identical in Welsh. In the human brain all the wisdom of the world is stored; man is potentially omniscient. But as we are we can use only a fraction of the brain's total capacity; the rest is stored in the unconscious, and only erupts in dreams or clairvoyant moments. Capricorn carries all the wisdom of the Cauldron in his intuitive horn—but this is as yet external to himself. He is, from his thrusting shoulders, all potential, not yet fully actualised. He presses forward up the Tor, Hill of Rebirth, Transfiguration, where men, knowing themselves fully at last, become as gods.

Our bearded goat is Merlin, the Brain of Arthur's Court who made the Round Table, the hoary Druid, inheritor of ageless wisdom and a prophet from the sea as his name implies. (For all his wisdom Merlin behaved like an old goat over the enchantress Vivien. Besotted, he told her all his spells:

tiring of him, she used these to enclose him for ever in an oak. What a warning to old philosophers! Does this tale also signify Druid wisdom locked in their sacred tree? Or the learning secreted in their tree-alphabet?)

Merlin's Chaldean counterpart was Oannes (Johannes) also a sage from the sea who instructed his people in wisdom. Capricorn is also Jonah, another sea-prophet, and watery John the Baptist, clad in goatskins. John, however hairy, is always a diviner. Taliesin knew it all when he said

"Johannes the diviner was I called, and Merddin."

As earthy or natural man he is hairy Esau, preferring an immediate meal to his divine birthright; and hairy Enkidu, the animal-man sent to overcome the Sumerian sun-hero Gilgamesh.

Capricorn is ruled by Saturn or Chronos—Old Father Time. Plutarch knew where he lay in our Zodiac, and quotes his informants, two travellers fresh from *Britain. "Moreover, there is, they said, an island in which Chronos is imprisoned, guarded by Briareus, for sleep is the bond forged for Chronos. They add that around him are many divinities, his henchmen and attendants."*

Capricorn, mortal man, appears in the High History, not surprisingly, as The King of Castle Mortal.

CADBURY CASTLE
"CAMELOT"

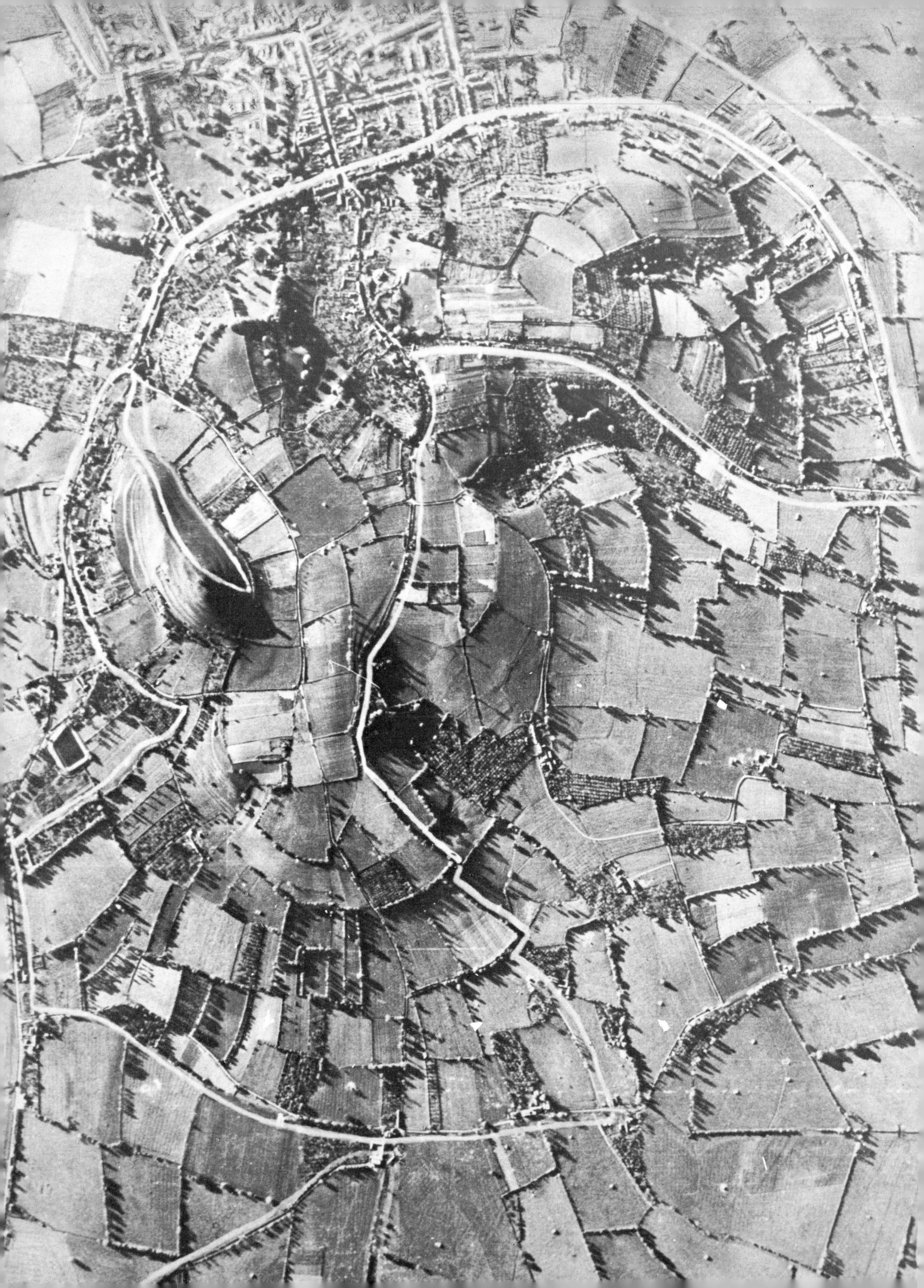

PHOENIX at AQUARIUS
1½ miles across

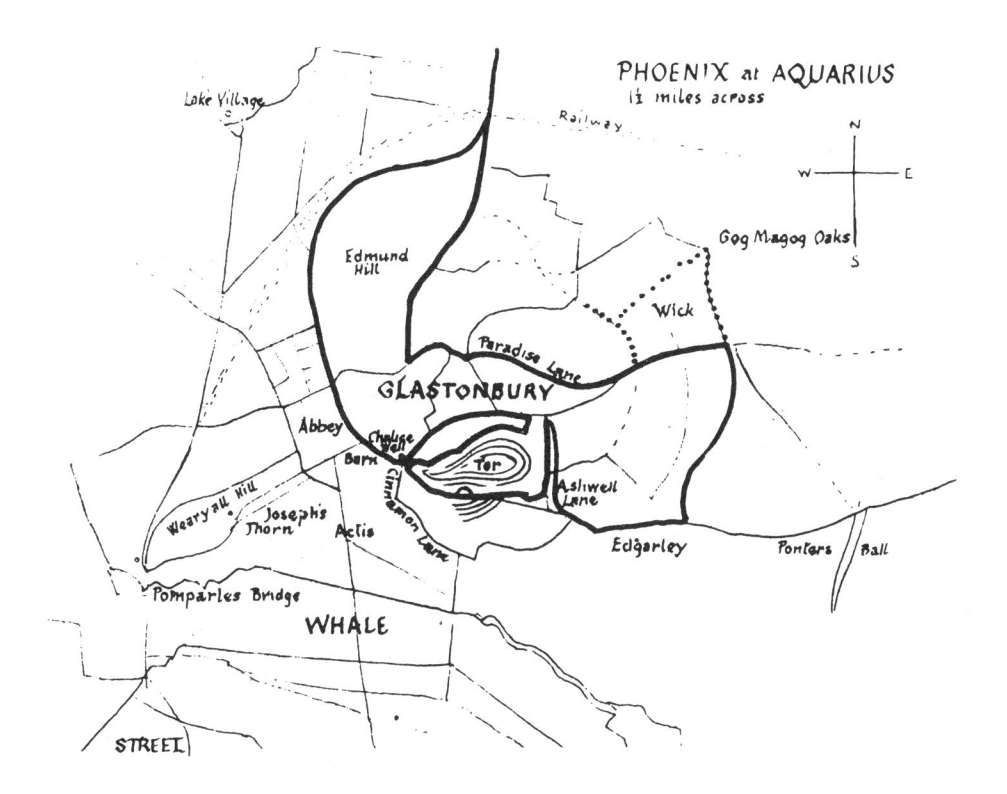

14: Aquarius

It was surely Nature herself who made this eagle or Phoenix, for the very hills themselves contour his head, body and wings. Circular in shape, the Phoenix can equally well be read as the urn of the Watercarrier, a form used for Aquarius by the early Babylonians. Other early Zodiacs preserve the original Trinity of Father, Mother and son by signing Aquarius simply as a waterpot, so it seems that the Waterman only appeared (making a fourth human figure) when this profound symbolism was forgotten.

Glastonbury Tor models his head, its lynchets ridging the folds of his neck as it turns backward towards the setting sun. Sunsets from the Tor are worth a backward glance.

Chalice Well, that famous chalybeate spring, is on the end of his beak, confirming him as a Watercarrier, and the many cures recorded here in the past shew him as conveying in a very real sense the Water of Life. Joseph of Arimathea is said to have hidden the Holy Grail in its recesses, and whether he did or not, the very tale shews an understanding of this elevated place as the home of the vessel of inspiration, healing, rejuvenation and rebirth, signed by the urn or cauldron before it became the Christian Grail. Its water-supply is unfailing; thousands of gallons a day pour from unimaginable subterranean sources even in drought. The combination of such a reliable water-supply and the pyramidal hill, rising so steeply to some five hundred feet from surrounding sea-moors slightly below sea-level, made it an irresistible holy place from earliest times, magnetising both pilgrims and legends.

Chalice Well assists the legend-making by growing clots of crimson algae in its waters, recalling the tale of Joseph's chalice that contained the blood of the Crucified. This plant, and its iron-red water that stains the path of the spring, gave the Well its other name, Blood Spring. Which came first, the legend or the plant?

The Phoenix has been a symbol of resurrection since ancient Egypt. It was said to fly into Heliopolis every five hundred years, renewing itself by burning on a self-made pyre of spices and emerging as a worm. After five days it grew into a chick and flew off once more. It was a calendar bird, its five days' gestation reconciling the days of the year with the degrees of the Zodiac circle. Actis, son of Sol the sun, an astrologer, fled his native land and founded Heliopolis. *Actis fields* are just below the Tor. So are Cinnamon Lane and Ashwell Lane, nearby; uncannily reminiscent of the Pheonix' spicy funeral-pyre. Was *this* the land that Actis left for Egypt? Is Glastonbury Tor the first pyramid—pyre amid which the Phoenix burns?

The eagle, another crested bird, has long figured as a resurrection-sign. Roman emperors had it carved on their tombstones. (A peacock served Aquarius in a Roman Zodiac, the crest signifying the emerging spirit of the new year.)

Ganymede, always associated in Greek minds with Aquarius, took off from Mount Ida's peak on eagle's wings for Olympus. He stands for the perfected man in the Mysteries. Loved by Zeus for his beauty, he was borne aloft to become cup-bearer to the gods. The Chaldean eagle Zu, linked by E. M. Plunkett's *"Ancient Calendars and Constellations"* with Aquarius, stole the tablets of fate from the sun-god Bel. Typically Aquarian, he was determined to be equal with the gods. Indian Garuda, half-man, half-eagle, burst through the ring of fire (the Zodiac) to steal the cup of immortality in its moon-goblet. Both tell the same tale. Here on the Tor we can catch both oriental thieves in the act. Like Ganymede, they are laying hold of immortality; Masters in the Mysteries, they burst through the Zodiac's ring of earthly lives and take off on eagle's wings for higher spheres.

Druids also understood these myths, as British Llew witnesses in the Mabinogion. He could only be killed at one point in the year, when he took his annual bath, which he entered by mounting a goat's back. Standing with one foot on the goat, the other on the bath, he was shot through by Gronw's treacherous spear. (Between Capricorn and the Aquarian Cauldron.) With a great cry he flew away as an eagle.

Surely the British Edda too speaks of the Aquarian Eagle in these lines—

*"There maun all afterwards live under the same laws
The golden tablets they found in the grass
These were of the olden days. From Attar's head* (the eagle)
Unsown earth were they, Waxed into tilled acres."

(Waddell's translation)

Golden tablets of the law were stolen by Zu also. But thrown down on the grass? This makes a Sinai of the Tor. It is indeed a Mount of Transfiguration, its *"Christed Man"* in the centre, flanked by Moses of the Red Sea crossing, (Pisces) and rough Elijah the desert prophet, (Capricorn).

The Aquarian eagle's head is drawn by the same road from Glastonbury to Shepton Mallet that defines Capricorn's back. South of this road are lynchets, known as *"Chapels"* that make the bird's crest. Are these the *"unsown earth, waxed into tilled acres,"* where the tablets of the law were thrown? The Edda gives another hint that the Tor is the eagle Attar; it says: *"The eagle flies over it—there Fialla* (the falcon) *hunts for fishes."* Not much of a hint, perhaps, but one Fish can certainly be seen, only a mile away; Wearyall Hill, like nothing so much as a great salmon leaping from the sea-moors that surround it. It is the only effigy readily recognisable from the ground; the only visible clue for the initiate.

Such an initiate was Perceval in Arthurian legend. From ingenuous beginnings as the second Twin within Mrs. Maltwood's Griffin, he sets out like the Fool of the Tarot card, until trial and error bring growing wisdom. He meets three hermits sitting on the sea-shore, who tell him they have twelve *chapels* nearby where lie twelve dead knights they must watch over. Joseph's twelve companions, watching over the Twelve Hides or hidden effigies of the old (dead) religion! Does the name *"Chapels"* on the crest of the eagle or phoenix, overlooking the whole Zodiac, stem from this legend? But before this he reaches a castle that burns continuously. This must be the Tor, fanned into a funeral-pyre by Phoenix-wings. A hermit tells him *"that of this castle and one other will be kindled the fire that shall burn up the world and put it to an end."* At this he departs hastily, passes three kingdoms (Pisces, Aries and Taurus) until he comes by ship (Cancer) to the island where the three hermits are sitting—Dundon Hill. *"The ship ran somewhat anigh the land".* It still does, running right up under Street.

The ever-burning Castle of the Tor makes one think. The Zodiac is a clock, to be read on all scales from the minute, hour, day, year, century, to the precessional ages. It embraces all time, and can therefore predict the end of time.

The Phoenix not only marks the end of the year and the beginning of the next, but the end of the world and its apotheosis or transfiguration into a higher state. It also indicates the nature of its end and new beginning. Is the earth destined to become a sun, as suns seem destined to become supernovae that give birth to galaxies? Can we see in Jupiter's red spots the incipient self-luminosity that will in time make it an independent solar system, its twelve moons becoming planets? So, one gathers from Gurdjieff and Ouspensky, the ancients taught. We have already seen something of this philosophy as taught by the Druid astronomers, in the Breton story of the Prince de Pol de Leon. And whether we seriously wonder about it or dismiss it as preposterous, such a view of the universe has an awe-inspiring wholeness, a creative dynamism that gathers the destiny of stars and Man in its embrace. For Man, it asserts, must aim to reach the vibratory intensity of the sun.

And certainly nothing in the universe is static, all is in a state of change, of becoming. It may even be that the earth depends for its translation to solar glory on the progress of its most conscious creatures. The gathering speed of global change and unrest today is interpreted by astrologers and clairvoyants as the beginning of an increase in the earth's vibrations, attributable to the dawning age of Aquarius, ruled by Uranus of the lightening-strike.

The High History says something very mysterious about the Grail. *"King Arthur beheld all the changes, the last whereof was the change into a chalice."* What can this mean? There were, we are told, five changes. Does this refer to the whole history of man back to the Flood, which cataclysm seems to have happened in the Age of Cancer the Ark? *Five precessional ages?*

Did Arthur from his heavenly seat watch the progress of mankind from the Geminian Age to the Aquarian? Did Joseph's two silver cruets symbolise the two fishes of the Piscean Age? The fish-shaped vase he holds in Langport church's mediaeval stained-glass window make one wonder; the legend of his arrival on Piscean Wearyall Hill early in the Piscean Age makes this explanation even more likely. The Christianity he brought, itself signed by the Fishes, was the religion of that age. When Joseph hid the Chalice in Aquarian Chalice Well, was he indicating the time and place of a new revelation for a new age?

To see the adventures of the Round Table knights as telling the time on a great clock in no way invalidates these encounters as allegories of spiritual experience. The astronomical philosophy embedded in Arthurian legend is well illustrated by the great clock of Wells cathedral, where Arthur's knights wheel round and tourney on the hour, struck by the hammer of Jack Blandifer the sun. This splendid toy is said to have been made by a monk of Glastonbury. On it is written *"This dial denotes the universe, its archetype."* The language of the Mysteries!

To the ancients, Time existed for self-perfection.

Our Phoenix, looking back to remember the Zodiac chain of lives spread out before it from its eyrie, sees the whole pattern. Hovering over Tor and town, he enfolds both in giant pinions like a guardian angel. The road to Wick traces his eastern wing round South Down Hill, two roads to Wells from Glastonbury between them draw the western wing, meeting at a point north of Tor Hill. A steep *"pilgrims' path"* marked by occasional great stones underlines his beak from Chalice Well to the Tor's summit, where the tower has long stood as a Mecca for strenuous endeavour. The first church here was destroyed by earthquake—typical of Uranus, the lightening-striker. Violent destruction, as well as sudden inspiration, are in his gift. No wonder the Abbey, sited on the Phoenix' Burning Castle, burnt down.

Here Perceval's eagle eye can indeed *"perceive all"*, *"piercing the Vale"* of Avalon, as his name ingeniously implies. Here, seeing himself reflected in its Glass Mountain and its holy well, he perceives too the depths of his own nature and sick unto death, remakes himself like the Phoenix. He is thus given the title in the High History of *"Par-lui-fet"*—he who makes himself. Those who essayed to climb the Glass Mountain had to stick needles into their own reflection so that their heels would not slip back. Self-analysis! *"Man, Know Thyself."* From a British Museum papyrus comes this revealing hymn to Ra—*"Thou everlasting sun, self-begotten, who didst give birth to thyself... Prince of Heliopolis."*

It was Heliopolis that sheltered the infant Christ at the Flight into Eygpt, said the Copts. And in Egypt it was said that *"a soul might make its transformation into the Phoenix which flew to Heliopolis"*—obviously a Mystery-teaching. *For Copt and Celtic Christian, Christ restated the ancient Mysteries.* And though the later Church suppressed this belief, the monks of Glastonbury secretly perpetuated it, witness the Bull, Lion, Man and Eagle on the four compass-points of Glastonbury's magnificent tithe barn, and the eagle carved high on the Tor's old tower, to remind pilgrims on the summit that they too may become Aquarian eagles, and *"Make their transformation into the Phoenix."*

In the High History Gawain sees many such Zodiac symbols on his Grail-Quest, but does not understand them. He asks a hermit to explain them to him.

They are all parables of the transformation of the *"old law"* into the *"new law"* of Christianity, he is told. But when Gawain asks why a clerk removed the original golden cup from a marvellous fountain in the forest and *substituted his own*, the hermit becomes cagey. *"Sir"*, he says, *"I will tell you no more thereof than you have heard, for it behoveth not to discover the secrets of the Saviour, and them also to whom they are committed behoveth keep them covertly."*

But we, aided by the Zodiac, may see the marvellous fountain as Chalice Well, source of the Water of Life; the clerk as the Aquarian Master in the

Chalice Well

Note Vesica Pisces
on the lid's ironwork.

There are two chambers,
the inner one 5-sided.
Guesses at dating
their stonework vary.

Its other name, Blood
Spring, refers to the
Legend that Joseph
hid the cup of the
Last Supper there.

It is radio-active,
& its iron content
stains its channel red.

Its flow is an unfailing
25,000 gallons a day.
Miraculous healings
have taken place here.

MARY CAINE

Mysteries, who no longer needs the official golden cup to drink from, but can provide his own cup, equally golden, from his own understanding.

Here is the fount of all myth, legend and Mysteries, not least of the Mysteries of the Arthurian Grail. But Gawain is no Master of the Mysteries. He sees the Grail in which a child appears, changing into a Suffering Saviour, and does not recall the numinous Gemini figure. He sees an eagle on top of a copper pillar, and knows nothing of the Royal Star Cross, whose northern star Fomalhaut has its earthfall on Aquarius (at Crab Tree Grove near the Wells road).

This Cross seems to be remembered in Glastonbury Abbey's arms, which bore a tree lopped and bare with horizontal arms. This tree, stricken by Aquarian thunderstorms, often appears in the Mabinogion, as standing by a marvellous fountain. Gawain, leaving his Grail-Castle exams in disgrace, is soaked to the skin by the ensuing rain-storm, and in this sorry state has to take shelter in the poverty-stricken Waste Land that his own incomprehension has created. But have we not all been Gawains, until Mrs. Maltwood rediscovered the long-lost meaning of these legends, of this otherworldly landscape, for us?

She has also replaced the crested bird of the spirit into his long-lost place in the Zodiac.

How could later Zodiacs have forgotten this bird, when world-wide legends identify him with Aquarius? Yet so it was; and her discovery was made in our own dawning Aquarian age.

PISCES
A WHALE and 2 FISHES
1" = 1 mile

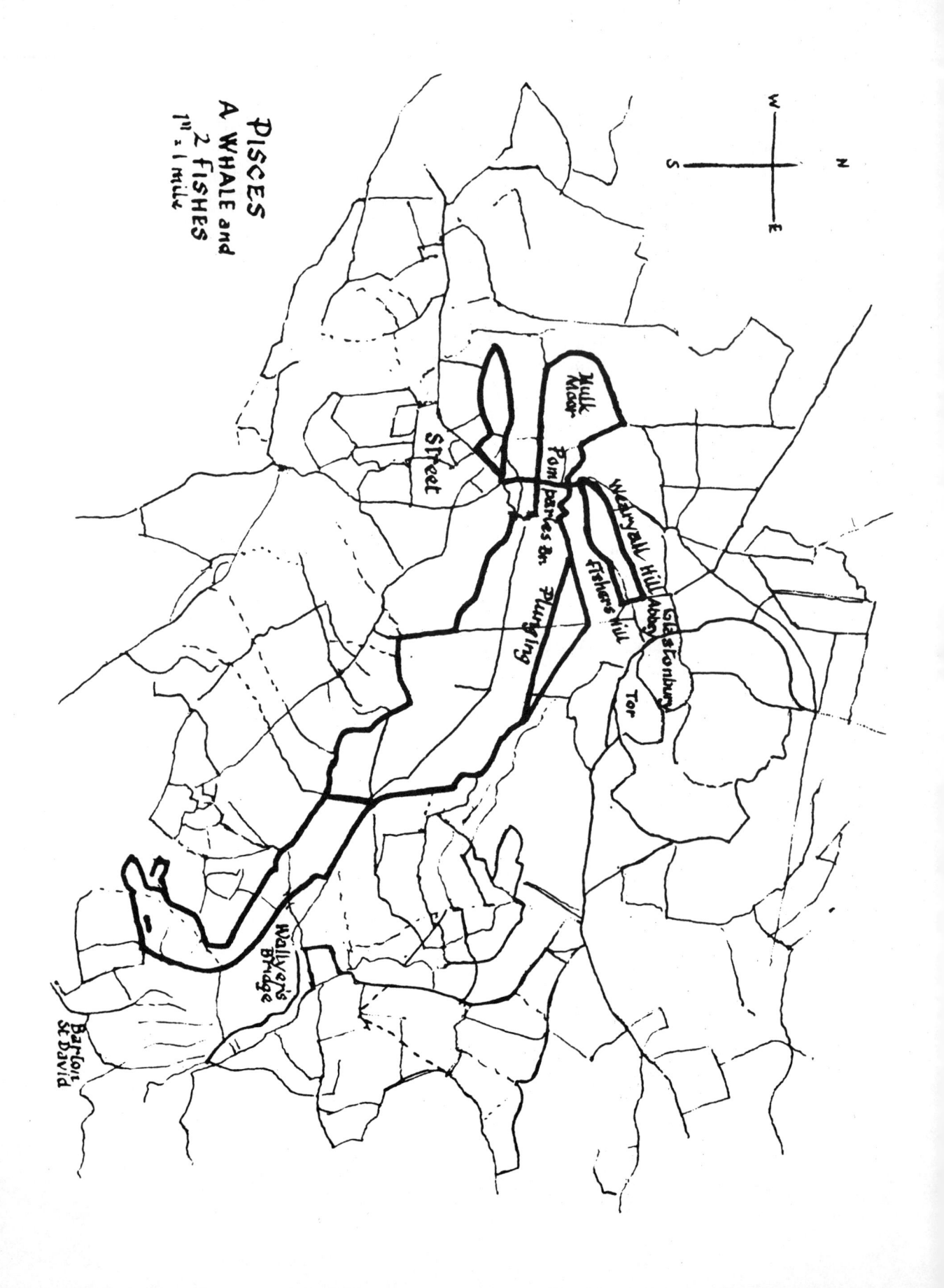

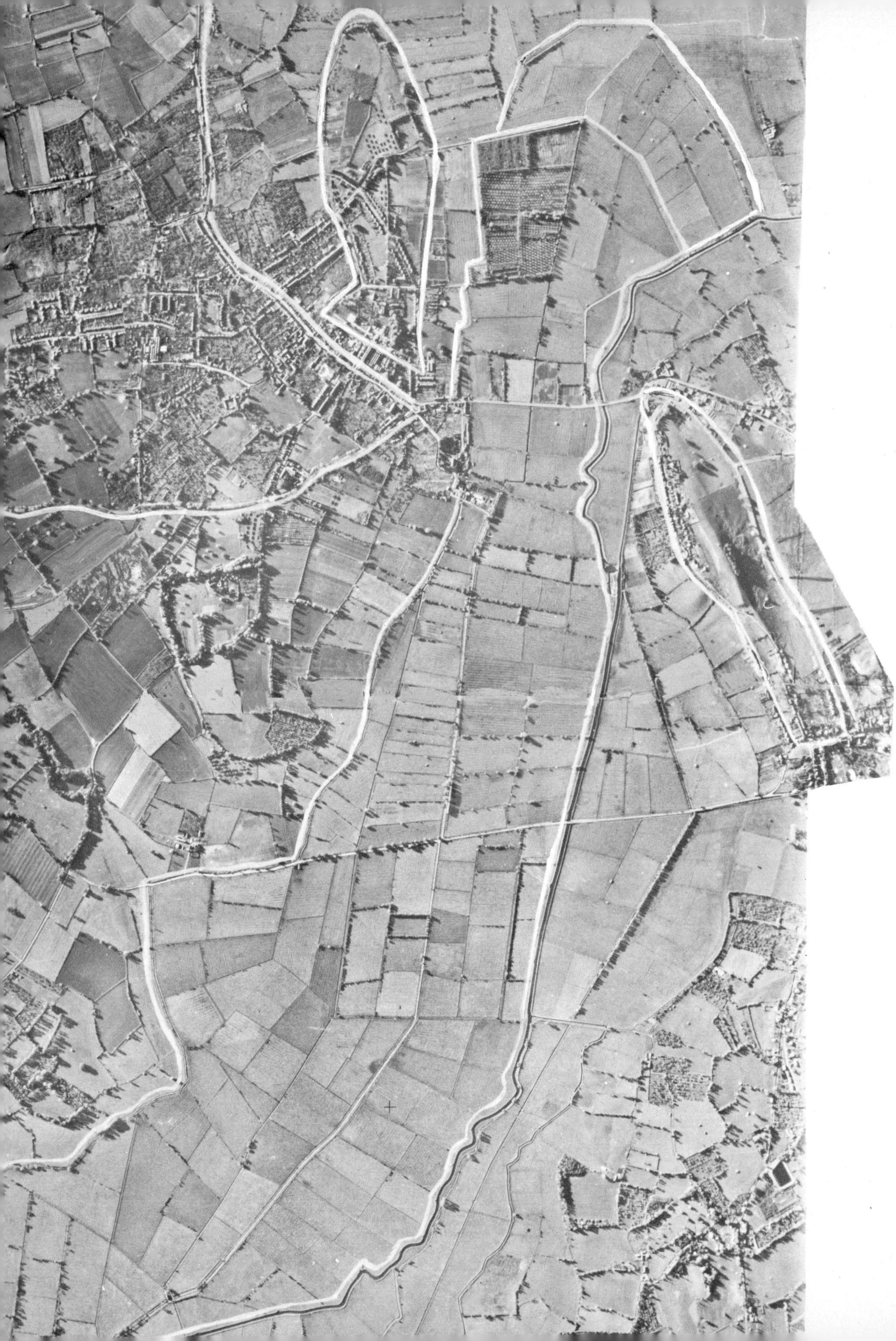

15: Pisces

Two Fish are all one expects of Pisces, but anglers in the Zodiacal waters between Glastonbury and Street will find they have netted a bonus in the form of a huge whale, tied to his two smaller companions by a cord. He is Cetus, who occupies this part of the sky, just beyond the zodiac belt. But he is no gatecrasher to the circle, having an important part to play; it is he who drags the sun-king off his horse down to his sunset in the western sea . . But his triumph is short-lived; at sunrise he must disgorge his prey. Whale's jaws hang reassuringly like a trophy on Glastonbury Abbey's gate—typical Zodiac coincidence. And the name *"Plunging"* on the Whale's back shews it was quite a tussle. It is interesting that in Chaldean myth a great fish swallows the sun—and inexplicable, when one remembers that their only sea was the Persian Gulf, *due south.* It looks as if Oannes brought the myth from somewhere where the sun appeared to set in a western sea.

In Layamon's Brut, Arthur too was swallowed by a great fish, being disgorged after three days; in western Britain this tale makes good mythological sense.

"Who brought Jonah out of the belly of Ked?" asked Taliesin.

Flanking the Whale, his two companions are dwarfed—mere map-minnows by comparison, both being less than a mile long. They are the smallest of the effigies, yet Wearyall Hill, the northernmost, is impressive enough from the ground. This hill, says Mrs. Maltwood, has for generations been believed to be the burial-place of a gigantic sacred Salmon, and to prove it, Fisher's Hill leads up to it. The Celtic Salmon of Wisdom, so wise that even to touch him and lick your fingers made you omniscient, inspired! He has not strayed far from his traditional haunt, the Severn. In the Mabinogion tale *"Kylhuch and Olwen"* he takes Kay and Bedivere on his back up this river to rescue the Mabon (the Youth) from the prison of Oeth and Anoeth, (Knowing Not-Knowing) or the Charnel-house of Bones in Gloucester. This tale surely echoes Arthur's rescue of Gweir (Man) from the Underworld, and must derive from the Mysteries of the Zodiac. Who better than the Salmon of Wisdom to save mankind from not knowing what he knows? Surely knowledge or rather wisdom lies deep in the dungeon of the unconscious; only knowledge of his own buried self can set the Mabon free. He is the self-contemplating Gemini figure, his head bowed in suffering; his upraised arm and poised fingers, as if sewing, make him the original Tailor of Gloucester (A tale, or Tailor, long before Beatrix Potter.)

Sitting in his boat, he is also the mysterious Fisher-king fishing for his own self in the depths, or, Messiah-like, fishing for the souls of men. The

Mithraic Mysteries in Britain seem to have known him, for at the Temple of Mithras at Lydney-on-Severn a figurine of the Romanised god Nodens was found, complete with rod and line, in a pointed cap, like any suburban-garden dwarf. The title is ancient and wide-spread; Babylonian Adapa the Wise was a "Wise Fisher", Buddha and Orpheus of the Orphic Mysteries are both Fishers. Fish have always been a symbol of Life, but of a mystical chaste life (from the fish's apparent chastity or lack of contact in mating). It stands for life renewed, life beyond the grave. Christ, whose Last Supper was of blood or wine as if at Aquarius' Blood Spring, *after* his resurrection prepared his disciples a meal of *fish* on the sea-shore. Fish are notoriously bloodless. He knew his zodiac, as so many gospel-incidents shew. Pisces is also the sign of enlarged consciousness, of the man of the Mysteries with no abiding city. Like the fish, or the Son of Man, he has nowhere to lay his head. The tramp and the mystic are both Pisces on different levels. (Does the enormous Whale beside the minute minnows in our Zodiac illustrate this Piscean expansion of consciousness?)

Gemini and Pisces are much connected, for the Fisher-king's castle is Weary-All Hill, while he himself, maimed in the thigh, is our Geminian Christ-figure. Some have seen him as the sun-and-seed king on whose health and strength the well-being of the land depends, like Tammuz, Attis. And there is no doubt that there is such an element in the Arthurian Fisher-king's story, for when the initiate fails to ask the Grail Question the king, already sick, grows worse, and the land with him. But no-one would suggest that the Grail-Quest is simply a question of physical potency or national economics; nor that the Question itself was about Balance of Payments. No, it is a spiritual matter, and chastity, not masculine potency, was essential for seeing the Grail. Courage was required, but it was moral courage as well as physical prowess.

The test of the three bridges that led to Grail Castle required for instance moral courage and faith. *"They were right great and right horrible to pass. And three great waters run below."* says the High History. To Gawain the first seemed a bowshot in length and only a foot wide. *"Strait seemeth the bridge and the water deep and swift and wide."* Impossible, either on foot or on horseback; but he essays it, expecting to die—and finds it broad and easy to cross. The next seemed as narrow as the first, but slippery, frail as ice, and vertiginously high above the torrent. Yet commending himself to God he presses on to find it was the richest and strongest he had ever seen. The third was no problem. He had won his way into the castle, and had only to pass a lion *"right great and horrible"* which crouched down as soon as he approached it, acknowledging Gawain's mastery.

A bridge over the Brue on the Whale's tail, called Pons Periculosus in 1415, obviously remembers these perilous bridges; it is still called Pomparles. (The Brue divides into three streams just west of this bridge; perhaps there were once three bridges.) Here, says Leland, Arthur threw Excalibur into the water. Here then Arthur parted with the sword of the spirit — another way of saying he was swallowed by the Whale; and that his spirit was returning whence it came — to Ked, the Lady of the Lake.

We have already noted that the second Fish strains westward from Aries' head at Street, and wondered at the strange coincidence that Street, on Aries and Pisces, makes shoes and sheepskin rugs. The Watercarrier as we have seen is equally famous for its Spring. And how right that the most numinous of all abbeys should lie between mystical Pisces and the Tor's sacred hill. How right that Arthur should be said to lie before the abbey's altar, between the whalebones and the devouring Whale — between the Hill of Resurrection and the Piscean Hill of life after death. The ecliptic line, i.e.— the sun's path, when transferred from the planisphere on to the map, runs through the Abbey grounds. Arthur the dying and renascent sun belongs here. He and Guinevere were said to lie under pyramids, though these have long gone. The sun manifested itself on a *pyramid* in Phoenix-form at Heliopolis. St. Patrick was also buried under a pyramid here in 472 A.D.; his day is March 17 — the end of the Babylonian year, the beginning of the Roman. Just another coincidence?

The ecliptic sun-line also runs along Wearyall Hill, where Joseph planted his staff, the Holy Thorn, and on to the sharp apex of Aries' head, where Street's old churchyard, being round, undoubtedly marks an ancient holy place. One of Pisces' stars falls there too; another falls on the second fish's tail at Abbey Grange. The monks seem to have known where the stars fell, and marked them. See Star Map on page 24.

Here on Pisces Joseph is especially remembered. Wearyall Hill, they say, is so-called because it is the spot where he and his twelve companions, wearied-all, rested after their long journey. Here he preached to Arviragus the Silurian King, and was granted the famous Twelve Hides of Glastonbury, (obviously the twelve Zodiac animal-hides, or hidden figures, that may well have originated the *"hide"* as a measurement of land). These hides envelop Glastonbury, Baltonsborough, and quite an area of the Zodiac, though not all of it. They may have served as symbols of what was really given — the old religion, placed in the hands of the new, since the Druids, decimated on Mona by the Romans, could no longer preserve it. The timing is perfect, whether the story is myth or history; for the Druids were massacred and their hegemony broken in 61 A.D. Joseph is said to have landed in Britain in 63. Resurrection on the *"third day"!*

Joseph, planting his magically flowering staff on Wearyall's Piscean sign was sticking a calendar peg into the great clock (an ancient custom) to indicate the new Piscean Age — and Christianity the new religion of that Age, signed at its inception by the Fishes. If the timing is exact, so is the siting. The Zodiac is a space-time pattern. Here is a coincidence to end all coincidences, and presents sceptics with a neat problem.

Glastonbury Abbey

MARY CAINE

Joseph is identified in Arthurian legend with the Fisher-king, regaling his followers at Grail-Castle with a mystical meal of fish. The Fisher-king's Grail-test with its Question was designed to find a worthy successor to the ailing ruler; one with courage, faith and above all an enquiring mind. (This last virtue was Druidic rather than Christian, for the later Church took care to keep its too-enquiring minds in monasteries under lock and key.) Joseph had indeed supplied Britain with such a Successor, and one of their own in blood, according to Celtic belief. Old Welsh and Cornish family trees, still extant, trace back through Arthur and his knights to Josephes, Joseph's son. Some legends marry Joseph into the British royal family of Bran or Brons, making the princess Anne his daughter; some say he married her to his brother Joachim in Palestine just before the birth of her daughter the Virgin Mary. The accounts though confused and conflicting, concur in joining the Holy Family with the royal family of Britain through Joseph the wealthy tin-trader and *"noble decurion"*. (He is very Piscean, having no abiding city; for he is equally divided in British myth at least between Britain, Palestine, and the high seas.) Equally Piscean is the way he brings all together into one meaningful whole. This, surely, is the function of the last sign of the Zodiac. And he does this even before we have decided whether his coming is legend or fact. Jupiter rules Pisces, and Jupiter's metal is tin! Joseph The Tin-man lands on Pisces.

But there is so much more to Joseph than meets the eye that he deserves a chapter to himself. In this, the growth of his legends and some teasing apocryphal Zodiac references can be examined at greater leisure, and we can explore the nature of Joseph's *"little wattle church"*, the original and enigmatic structure which the abbey was erected to protect.

To end this chapter it only remains to sail down the Brue to Wallyer's (Whale's) Bridge, where the great beast mangles Arthur's arm at the circle's centre. Perceval rows down this river in the *Castle of the Whale,* and finds as we do that there is a fearsome dragon there. This incident in the High History so clearly speaks of the Whale with a serpent's head that it provides one of the most striking clues to the Zodiac source of Arthurian legend. The Brue in fact carries on down the nose of this huge Leviathon (Hulk Moor seems to refer to its size) and continues on to the neck of the serpent I found. The stars of Draco follow the curve of its neck exactly. Mrs. Maltwood's snake-head is in the exact centre of the circle at Park Wood.

Perceval thrust his sword down its fiery gullet, extracting a red-hot key with which the prisoner of the Castle of the Whale could be released. The eqinoctial line from Taurus to Scorpio runs straight through Park Wood's serpent-head, like Perceval's sword. The Key? The key to Time and its purpose.

This gullet corresponds with the four stars of Ursa Minor, which Arabs called *"the hole in which the earth's axis found its bearings"*. Kochab, the pole-star of 2700 B.C., is one of these four stars. (Our present pole-star is not among these, being at the other end of the constellation.)

The North Somerset Mummers' play seems to remember this *"hole"* at Park Wood, for it speaks of *"the Black Prince of Paradise, born in a fiery hole."* Incredible that this star-tradition should survive so long—and that Park Wood should keep its significant shape for so many millennia!

From the four-starred enclosure grew the pole-star Tree of Life whose apples were stars. When Perceval fights this dragon he sees a king and a maiden hiding from it in a great tree. Adam and Eve, hiding guiltily when they succumbed to the temptation of the Black Prince of Paradise? Is Perceval with his key to Zodiac star-lore able to redeem the race of Adam? Adam was imperfect; Perceval, following Galahad, becomes the perfected Man.

It was these Apples of Star-wisdom that tempted not Eve alone, but Hercules and many another hero to our far western Paradise, that other Eden of the Hesperides, *"whence tin comes"*—not least among them perhaps, Joseph and Christ Himself. Such is the message of Pisces in our Zodiac.

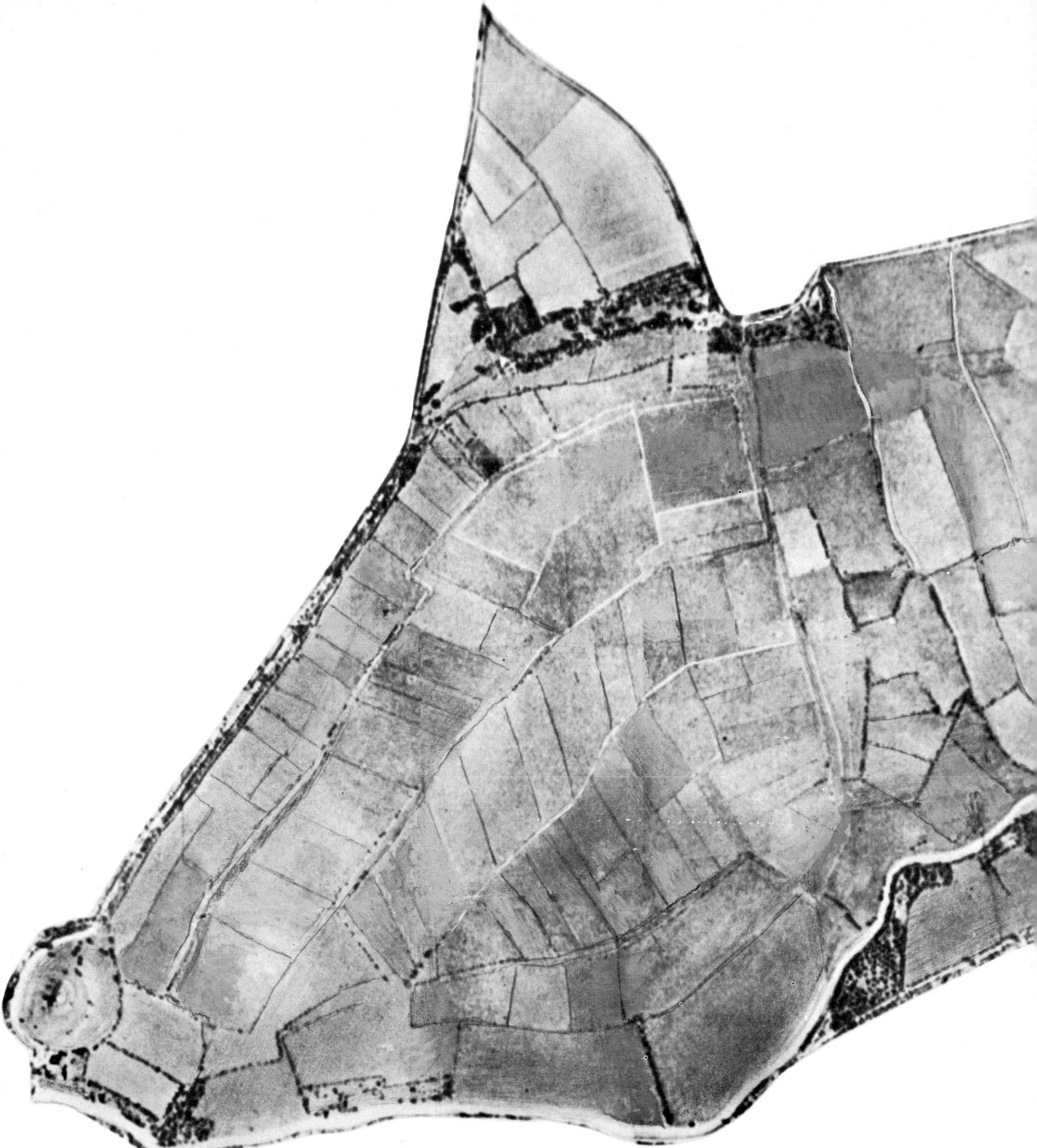

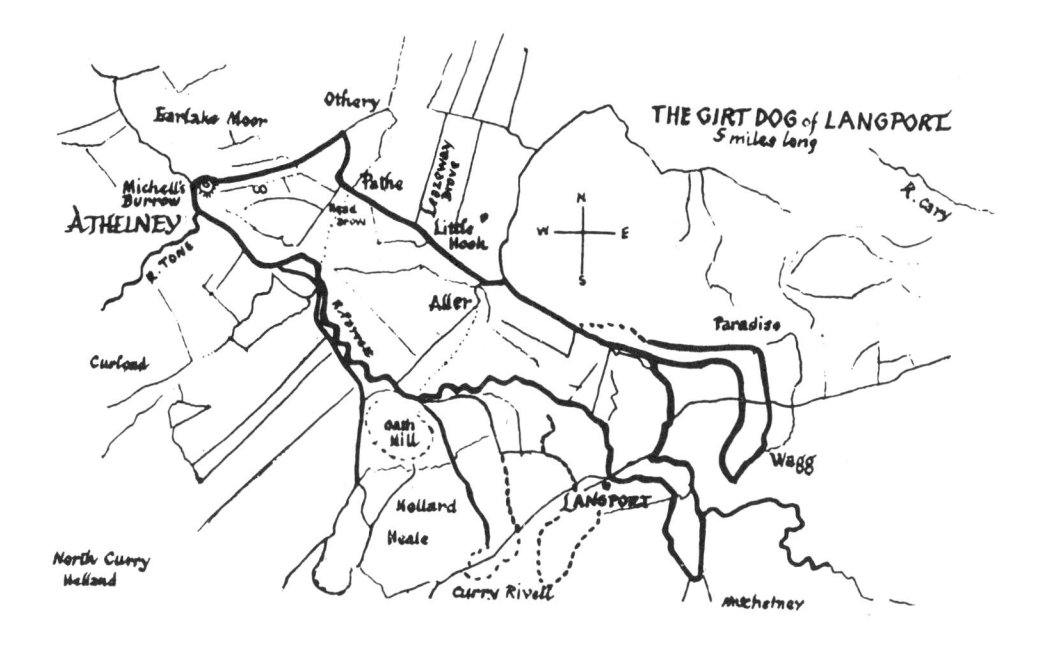

16: The Girt Dog of Langport

Here is perhaps the best-attested effigy of all, in place-names and in the old Somerset Wassail Song (Oxford Book of Carols) which says of him:

> *"The Girt Dog of Langport has burnt his long tail*
> *And this is the night we go singing wassail."*

This Cerberus of the British Mysteries, perhaps the first Cerberus of all, lying immediately south-west of the circle, is the guardian dog of the western Hades. As he is outside the circle the stars of Canis major do not correspond.

He, like the Whale and Ship, is artificially drawn by irrigation and by paths, consciously and deliberately as it would seem from his finely-drawn head. A double circle at his eye appears in the air-photo. He guards the sea-approach from the Severn Channel, his underside from his nose to his back leg delineated by the tidal Parrett river from Athelney to Langport, a distance of over five miles. The Parrett is banked high on either side to prevent flooding—a truly Sumerian feat of irrigation.

And the Parrett, says Mrs. Maltwood, has a Phoenician or Sumerian name, the *"Pharat"* or Euphrates. Hercules must have sailed up it coming to the Hesperides. He passed Hartland Point near Ilfracombe, for this promontory was the *"Heracles Akron"* of Ptolemy. Hercules was a Phoenician before he was adopted by the Greeks, and it was *Hercules who strangled Cerberus at the mouth of Hades*. It could only happen here!

"Girt" indeed in size, he is also *"girt"*—tethered—and by a lead at Leazeway Drove fastened to Little Hook on his collar. So courage, pilgrim; his tail still wags at *Wagg*.

Indeed, place-names proclaim him everywhere; there are two Head Droves and Head Rhine on his head, Earlake Moor is by his ear, as is Othery which surely stems from Greek *"otis"*, an ear. This stands on a hill, like those of several other effigies, to hear the music of the spheres; its name, Grove Hill, and Chantry Drove below, suggest he received the chanted prayers of both Druid and Christian down the ages. The river Tone is his tongue. North Curry and Curry Rivel are on his front paw; guard-dogs used to be known as curs. Curland is not far away.

An old road called Curload leads to his nose at Alfred's Burrow, Athelney. Cur-road, surely! The L is a typical Somerset substitution, as in Bristol. His head and cocked ear resemble Anubis the dog-headed janitor of Egypt's Underworld Amenti, that the Celts called Annwn. Anubis of Annwn. So the place-names Hellyar and Helland here must mean Hell's Gate and Land. Did initiates take their vows of secrecy at Oathe Hill as they sailed down the Parrett into this *"underworld"*, sighing with relief as they emerged safe and sound at Paradise on his tail?

He is Gwyn ap Nudd's dog Dormarth, whose name means Death's Door. In the Black Book of Carmarthen Gwyn says of him: *"Handsome is my dog, and round-bodied; Dormarth with the ruddy nose, ground-grazing; how you gaze on me when I mark your wanderings on cloud-mount!"*

Only a Glastonbury Giant can make sense of this; only a star-effigy can at once inhabit earth and sky. Sirius, Canis Major's bright Dog-Star, is his celestial nose, while his *"ground grazing"* nostril at Alfred's Burrow is no less ruddy—being an artificial hill of red clay, brought perhaps in prehistoric times from Red Hill, three miles away. (Or so says Collinson's History of Somerset.) This three-tiered mini-Tor, convoluting the Dog's nostril in high relief, is one of a triangle of terraced hills enclosing the Zodiac circle; both Alfred's Burrow and Cadbury Castle are just *twelve* miles from the Tor. This looks like planning on the grand scale. Nor is that all. The hill at Athelney is one of a line of hills dedicated to St. Michael that mark the great ley known as the Great Dragon line, stretching from St. Michael's Mount off Cornwall through Brent Tor, Alfred's Burrow (also called Michell's Burrow) and Glastonbury Tor with its St. Michael's church. It is said to travel right across England in a north-easterly direction, with Cornish-Phoenician Michael fighting the Dragon all the way.

Arthur too had a Dog with the interesting name of Cabal.—The Caballic Mysteries; Like Gwyn ap Nudd he was Lord of Glastonbury Tor. And Gwyn had a brother Gwythyr, whose name must be a compound of Arthur and Uther his father. So Arthur and Gwyn in early myth seem to be brothers. Gwyn and Gwythyr-Arthur were sons of Nudd or Neidd, goddess of Night and Fate like Egyptian Nut. Together they roared over the Tor on wintry nights, hunting with their Dog(s) for the souls of the dying to bring them into her underworld beneath (beneidd) the Tor. She is also Arianrhod of the Zodiac's Silver Wheel and the Tor's turning Castle: the Spiral Castle with its maze.

Arthur preserves his identity with Gwyn (Huin the wind) in the old riddle:

> "Arthur O'Bower has broken his band
> He goes roaring down the land;
> The king of Scots with all his power
> Cannot turn Arthur of the Bower."

The answer to this riddle of course is that Arthur O'Bower is the wind.

Why O'Bower? Bower is an old name for a maze, as Julian's Bower, the maze at Alkborough, shews. Gusty Arthur is Lord of the maze on the windy Tor: lord of the riddle of life and the riddle of death in its subterranean caverns below.

The moon, said the Druids, was Hell, where lost souls wait their chance to reincarnate on earth at eclipses of the sun by the moon; the sun being heaven. Our Hell-Hound's connection with the moon is emphasised; first by the tidal character of the Parrett that draws him, and second by Moon Drove on his mouth and by Full and Half Moon Plantations on his back.

As the *"Questing Beast"* it runs through Arthurian legend, appearing and disappearing like the moon, inexplicably and for no perceptible purpose; it seems that its existence was still dimly remembered, but not its geographical layout or its significance as guardian of the lost circle. Perhaps it *was* remembered, but only mentioned in such a way as to preserve the Secret. Certainly the details are significant. The Questing Beast is in fact a bitch who gives birth in the High History to twelve hounds—obviously the twelve effigies. You could hear her coming through the forest because of her rumbling stomach. In Malory's Morte D'Arthur *"the king saw coming towards him the strangest beast that ever he saw or heard of; so the beast went to the well and drank, and the noise was in the beast's belly like unto the questing of thirty couple hounds;"* The Parrett that draws this beast's belly has a tidal bore at spring tide; the noise of the swirling waters is well described!

Sir Palamedes followed this beast for fourteen years, but what he found, or whether he found anything, is not defined. He should have found

Himself, of course, for the Quest of the Questing Beast leads to the Quest of the Grail. The *"Huth Merlin"* says specifically that she appeared first in the reign of Uther Pendragon, being explained by Merlin as having to do with the Quest of the Grail. But exactly *what* she has to do with it, only the Zodiac can tell us.

Perceval in the High History encounters *"a little white beast with twelve hounds in her belly, that bayed aloud and quested within her."* As soon as they were born they slew her, but might not eat her. Her flesh and blood was gathered into two golden vessels by a knight and a damsel.

Explanations in the High History are more bewildering than the events they claim to elucidate, doubtless to allay suspicions of heresy. A hermit tells Perceval that the beast, kindly and sweet, is Christ; her matricidal pups are the *"people of the Old Law"* in fact the Jews, who tore him to pieces. Improbable though this seems one can imagine the Inquisitor, hot on the scent of Templar heresy, withdrawing, baffled, by the apparent pious orthodoxy of this exposition. But we can suspect that the flesh and blood of Christ in the two vessels refer to Joseph's two cruets, the knight being Joseph, the damsel his ward St. Anne. He appears with these cruets in an old stained-glass window in Langport church; Challis Wall is on the Dog's collar. The *"people of the Old Law"* are obviously the twelve effigies; to call them Jews is a cryptogram for the Caballistic star-lore they express. Arthur's Dog was not called Cabal for nothing. The thirty couple hounds of Malory's account must be the days and nights of the moon month whose tidal bore made the Parrett, her belly, so noisy.

Joseph of Arimathea is not the last of the long line of pilgrims who travelled up the Parrett. What was Alfred doing, skulking in Athelney, burning those famous cakes? (It was a hot time for the Dog, with the Danes burning Langport on his back leg and Alfred burning his nose.) Mrs. Maltwood propounds a startling theory. *Was Alfred preparing a "sop to Cerberus"* before entering the Mysteries as an initiate? Burning barley cakes is an ancient solar custom, and the Zodiac is solar myth. She tells us that cakes used to be fed to the Dog, but whether she meant the well-known *"sop to Cerberus"* in Greek myth, or was recollecting a local custom at Athelney is ambiguous. I have so far not traced any such local custom, and would be very interested to hear if any such tradition survives. But whether there was such a habit or not, the very fact that this odd story survives in Asser's Life of Alfred should alert us to *"double-entendres".*

But Alfred, a Saxon? What could he know or care about Britain's ancient Secret? The truth is that the West Saxons of Alfred's line stemmed from Britain. His ancestor Cerdic bears a British name; it is a variant of Caradoc, a royal name; Cerdic's forbears were Bron, Beldeg and Odin—or Bran, Belin and Gwydion—British god-kings to a man. This family was known as the Gewissae, which surely means the Knowers, Wise Ones— perhaps Gnostics. It is not surprising to find then that Merlin came from the land of the Gewissae. What was it that they knew?

The clue (as if we needed one) is found in Taliesin's poem.

> *"There is a greater secret, though known to few—*
> *The magic wand of Mathonwy, which grows in the wood*
> *With more exuberant fruit, on the bank of the river of spectres.*
> *Kynan shall obtain it when he comes to govern."*

Kynan is another royal name, both Cornish and Breton. Math son of Mathonwy was the Celtic Pluto, ruler, like Gwyn ap Nudd, of the Underworld. His magic wand or measuring-rod, the foundation of mathematics and star-measurement, was doubtless the pole-star Tree whose exuberant fruit were the starry apples of wisdom, growing on the bank of the Parrett, Cary or Brue, all rivers of Avalon's *"spectres"*. This secret was obviously passed down from royal father to son. Alfred obtained it too when he came to reign! The West Saxons under Cerdic then were not simply barbaric pirates taking advantage of Britain's weakness, but ex-patriate Britons, invading what had once been their homeland to regain their lost patrimony.

This conclusion is confirmed by Alfred's choice of Asser, a Welsh monk, for his adviser, whom the Welsh say was brother to Morgan Hen, king of south Wales. His curiously Assyrian name is that of the sun-god Asser, Ahura, equated with Arthur; the laws Alfred encouraged him to recode were the old British laws of Molmutius, deriving from the famous and enlightened laws of the Medes and Persians—our *"Trojan"* law. The picture Asser gives in his *"Life"* of thick-armed thanes tumbling over each other to gain Alfred's approval by learning their ABC is delightful. Alfred's zeal for learning, his informed religious enthusiasm, his sense of justice, are surely Druidic. He had indeed a Druid for mentor in his youth, for Swithin's name is that of the *Syweddyd* or Druids. Druids were said to be able to control the weather—surely Swithin's reputed power over the weather reflects this. He wished to be buried outside Winchester cathedral, not inside it, but they ignored this last direction. Druids worshipped in the open air—*"in the face of the sun, the eye of light"*—Swithin was undoubtedly a Druid and a Christian one. He is said to have taken Alfred as a boy to Rome. (Winchester still has Arthur's Round Table in its Law Courts.)

And where did Alfred baptise Guthrun, his defeated Danish enemy? At Winchester, his capital? At Glastonbury Abbey, already famous in his time? No—*at Aller, on the pilgrim's path that draws the Girt Dog's back.* To those who reject the Zodiac's existence this is inexplicable; it was in the middle of nowhere. Alfred generously gave his enemy the choice of having his head cut off or becoming a Christian; Guthrun very sensibly chose the pilgrim's path. It was not only a Christian baptism, but an initiation into the ancient Mysteries. As Alfred could not get rid of the Danes in the north-east of England, he was dressing Guthrun to rule the Danelaw—and seeing to it that he ruled by laws altogether more sublime.

In Asser's *"Life"* Aller is spelt Aahl. Is this not Aahlu, the Sumerian Paradise of Gilgamesh? Does not Alfred's own name contain the magical syllable? Athelney, Aller, Avalon, Arallu is I believe the royal secret that occurs in so many "*Saxon*" kings' names. They "*obtained it when they came to govern.*"

At Wedmore after the baptism, Alfred gave Guthrun "*many fine houses*". I suspect that these houses were the houses of the Zodiac, and that Alfred was repeating Arviragus' generous gift to Joseph of the Twelve Hides of Glastonbury. There is much secret history in Asser's Life of Alfred, and it is as usual the Glastonbury Zodiac that enables us to read between his lines.

Alfred, only about five feet high and afflicted with a bowel complaint throughout his life, was able to bring the Danes, twice his height and girth, into some order; in a reign torn by wars fought against impossible odds, he brought a renaissance of hope, justice, education, religion and prosperity to his country. His inspiration, as much evidence shews, was the Zodiac; his Catholic Christianity was informed by its Celtic fount. It has I believe, been the secret fount of civilisation, not only here, but in many other parts of the world, when its teachings have been understood and followed.

Drayton's Polyolbion (1612) preserves some Druid lore about the Parrett.

> "*For from the Druides' Time there was a prophecie
> That there should come a time (which now was near at hand
> By all forerunning signes)
> If Parrett stoode not firm upon the English side
> They all should be supprest.*"

Something here was worth preserving: successive heroes, Arviragus, Arthur, Alfred, fought bitterly to save it. Our ancient radio-carbon clock still keeps its measured time. When its hour strikes, can it not do again what it has so often done before?

MARY CAINERI

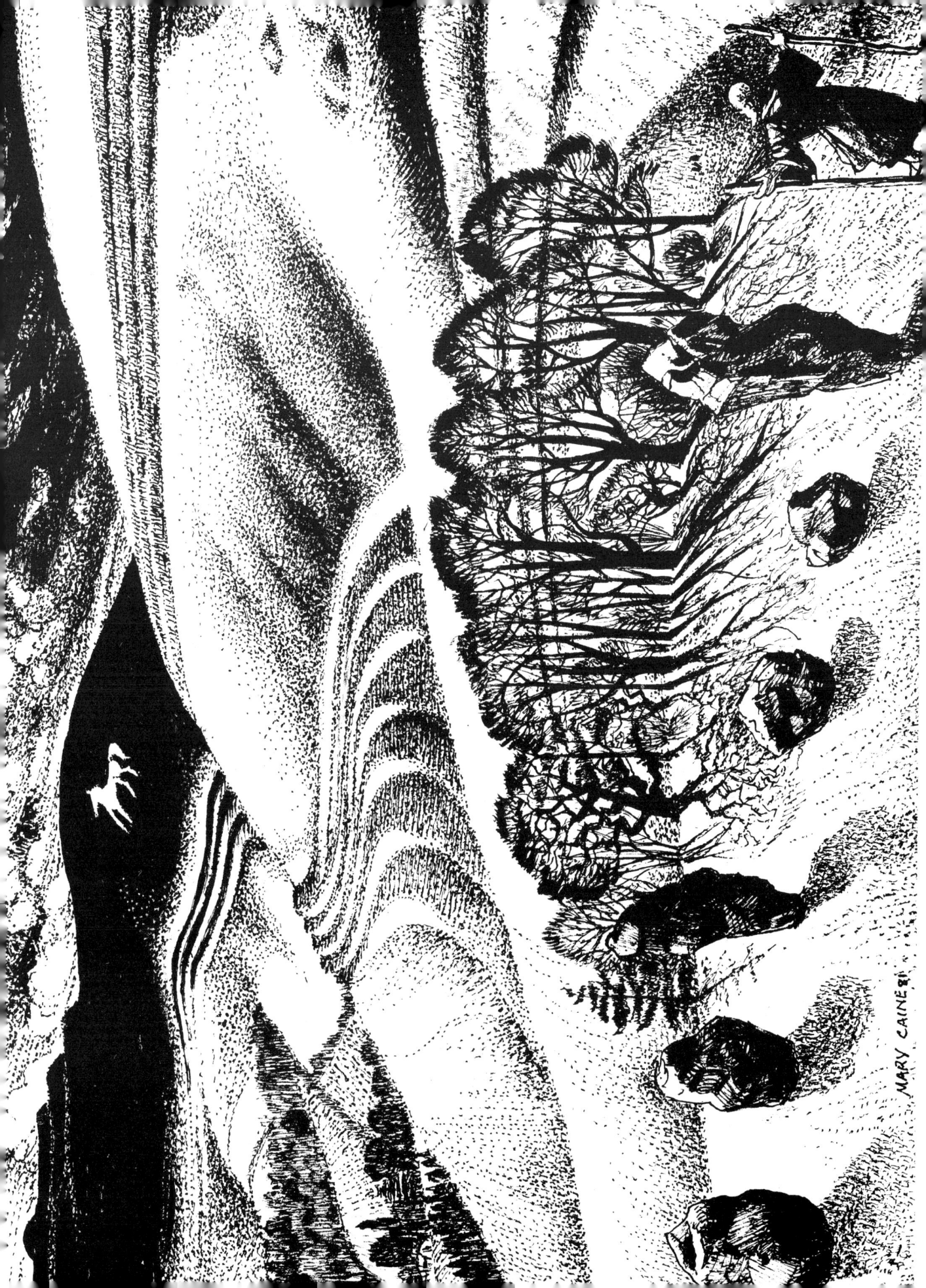

17: The Zodiac in some Sumerian Myths

The gods of Sumeria are known to us from clay tablets of 1000 B.C., found at Ashur and Nineveh, which tell stories far more ancient; the Epic of Creation contains the earliest form of the Flood legend.

Among the first gods and goddesses was Tiamat, the sea, who represented Chaos from which all life was drawn, and was pictured as a great fish. She echoes Ked the Celtic Whale. Tiamat spawned monstrous fish-men, scorpion-men, serpents and dogs—a chaotic Zodiac. It was the task of Marduk (later Bel) to draw life and form from this confusion, and in a great battle he vanquished Tiamat, *banishing her ugly brood to the Underworld.* Creating heaven and earth, he set the stars in order in the sky and beneath it made a *"microcosm in which Man was to do service to the gods".* Heaven was called E-Sharra; earth reflected it. Sarras the holy city-state attained by Perceval and Galahad when they sailed in Solomon's ship beyond the sight of men! Tiamat's ugly brood is banished to *Avalon, for the Sumerian Underworld, Aahlu or Arallu, was said to be in the far west,* Sarras means "star-city."

The old clay tablets also tell the tale of Gilgamesh or Nimrod. We need not be surprised then to find he has to come to Britain in his quest for eternal life. The island of his quest was Khassisadra—surely Britain's Tin Islands, the Cassiterides, its metals worked by the Khassi from the Caspian, and the Cimmerians who became the Cymry of Wales. We have already seen how many place-names in our Zodiac area, indeed in the whole of western Britain, proclaim this ancient connection, and how these eastern family ties are shewn in the names of old British kings, gods and goddesses. The kilted Celts of Britain and the kilted Khaldees of Chaldea are it seems akin. Both, in their figurines, display the same absurdly protuberant noses. Their chariots are similar, their harps too. The shape of Babylonian and Celtic mirrors in the British Museum are identical, and the metalwork of Luristan and European Celts shew striking similarities.

Britons called themselves Culdees; their rejuvenating Cauldron of Ceridwen echoes that of Medea, Mother of the Medes. Our ancient *"Trojan Law"* breathes the same tolerant justice as the famous Laws of the Medes and Persians.

Arthur, it seems, is Median Ahura; Babylonian Anahita, our own Black Annis. Somerset may well lay claim to be the *"Seat of the Sumers".*

Let us see what other clues to Avalon the Epic of Gilgamesh from the Sumerian city of Erech can offer.

Ishtar, jealous of Gilgamesh, makes an adversary, Enkidu, to send against him, a hairy creature, half-man, half-beast. But after wrestling to a standstill they become great friends, thus foiling her plan, and together do great things. Ishtar next tries to seduce Gilgamesh, but fails, and in revenge, she sends a long-horned bull to destroy him; this too he overcomes. She curses him and Enkidu curses her back, but is not strong enough to defy a goddess, being all too mortal, and she has him killed. Gilgamesh, grief-stricken, travels far to ask his *ancestor*, Utna-Pishtim, who dwells in the Blessed Isles in the far west, how to find the plant of eternal life to revive his friend. The divine temptress, the bull, Enkidu as both the mortal Geminian Twin and Capricorn, all point to the Zodiacal source of this myth. But there are more clues.

On his way he fights a fire-breathing dragon, and eventually after long journeying reaches a mountain chasm guarded by fierce lions. (Such a chasm lies between the head and neck of Leo on the hills above Hurcot.) Undaunted he presses on until he sees Mashi, the huge mountain of sunset, which divides the living from the dead. Its peak rises to heaven, but its root is in Arallu. The Tor? Its dark tunnel beneath is guarded by two Scorpions of such fearful aspect that he swoons, but they revive him and point the way to Utna-Pishtim through the dark cavern, which is *twelve* miles long. After *twelve double-hours* of blind groping, he emerges into the sunlight of a beautiful orchard whose apples are flashing jewels (stars?) Unlike Adam, he resists these also, and at last reaches the Shores of the Sea of Death, ruled by the sea-nymph Sabitu. (Sabrina, goddess of the Severn?) She advises him to abandon his quest and to make merry with her while he can, for all men must die—but he refuses again, and builds a ship to embark on the Sea of Death. After sailing long and encountering terrible things he at last finds his ancestor, and asks him how he became immortal. Utna-Pishtim tells him of a city on the banks of the river Parutti where the star-gods dwell (which we may be forgiven for seeing at the Parrett), and how these gods decided to extinguish the early race of men by sending a terrible flood. Utna-Pishtim's account closely follows (or rather precedes) the Deluge story of Genesis. But he, Utna-Pishtim, was spared, being warned to build an ark, and after floating on the waters, came to dwell in this Paradise for ever. If Gilgamesh wishes for immortality, he too must sit for six days and seven nights in his boat, his head bowed in sorrow. Painful self-analysis, symbolic death and rebirth, have always been the initiate's path. It is astonishing how clearly this Sumerian tale seems to remember the Gemini effigy bowed in sorrow in his boat. Gilgamesh sleeps in this posture, and feels strangely revived on waking. Utna-Pishtim completes his cure by taking him to a healing fountain (Chalice Well?) and giving him the Plant of Eternal Life. But this, alas, is stolen from him by the Lion of Earth before he reaches home. Returning, he finds his city Erech ruined; but he, now a Master Mason, rebuilds it, giving it the Mysteries of Life which he has received on his travels, "*when he beheld the world and peered into the Mysteries".* He is equated with Nimrod, who built the Tower of Babel—or Babylon.

Gilgamesh is the first recorded Quester of the Mysteries of the Far west. But Jason too in his Argo, with his Median Medea and her rejuvenating Cauldron—his Golden Arian Fleece, is thought to have reached the Baltic. Why not Britain?

The Parrett must have been navigable in ancient times, whether naturally or banked against flooding, as it is today. Saxon monks from Muchelney are credited with these works—and doubtless they kept the waterways in repair. But the persistent pictures of the hero bowed in his ship that come down to us from early myth suggest that the Parrett and the Ship were there before mediaeval times. Sumerians were famed for astronomy and irrigation. Did they cut these canals to a Zodiac pattern?

Is it not possible that the original Zodiac of the Sumerians was the Zodiac of the Summerland of Somerset—Gwlad Yr Hav, the glad haven of perpetual summer bliss in Avalon—which Mesopotamian Sumerians remembered as Aahlu, the writer of Genesis as Havilah? Is it possible that the first missionary merchant-adventurers went *east*, not *west*, naming the Euphrates or Pharat after the sacred river Parrett of Somerset, and Sumeria itself after the Summerland Paradise in the far west?

Preposterous? Such a reversal of present-day thought must seem so, at first; yet when we examine with open minds the evidence left by the earliest writers, the suspicion grows that this may have been the way of it.

From the Rev. R. W. Morgan's collection of 'Cymric Triads & Druidic Fragments' comes an account that confirms these suspicions. Briefly summarised, it tells how the Cymry in migrating to Britain were *returning* to their homeland of before the flood. The Great Ship Nevydd Nav Neivion was, it says, built in Britain at the inundation of the world, and was One of the Three Mighty Works of Britain. It preserved one man and one woman, Dwy Van and Dwy Vach, who began the world's eventual repopulation. For a long while their descendants, the Cymry, dwelt in the Summerland of Deffrobane, by the sea of Afez. (Azov?) But at last they determined under Hu Gadarn to seek their first home, returning to the White Island in the West, where their ancestor had built the Ship.

Was our Zodiac Ship not cut by these Summerland or Sumerian migrants to commemorate the Ark Nevydd Nav Neivion, and their triumphant return?

18: Was Britain Part of Atlantis?

Britain in Mesolithic times was the northern extremity of a greatly extended Continent of Europe—the English Channel was but a tributary of the Rhine. Land's End was not the end of the land, which reached to the Scillies; nor was Finisterre, for Brittany bulged many miles out into the Atlantic. Between Wales and North Devon was dry land; the Severn Estuary did not exist. Mesolithic Plymouth and the Isle of Wight were many miles from the sea, and Beachy Head was a smoothly-domed down from which you could walk across to France.

Britain still remembers its lost Arthurian land of Lyonesse; Brittany still mourns its lost land of Ys. Tales of sunken lands persist from Wales to Portugal, and legends of Atlantis still haunt Morocco, where the coast of Africa extended to the Canaries. The geological dates for the loss of this enormous area agree with Plato's date of 9400 B.C., for the sinking of Atlantis.

It is fashionable today to place the Atlantean disaster in the Mediterranean—an absurd contradiction in terms—by equating it with the volcano of Santorin which destroyed Crete. This is not only the wrong place but the wrong time; only about 8000 years too late! Plato received the tale of Atlantis from Solon, who had it from Egyptian priests, who were careful historians. Impossible that they should have confused the Atlantic with the Mediterranean, or mis-dated the Minoan holocaust (which happened practically on their doorstep and at the height of Egypt's long civilisation) by no less than 7000 years. Yet having said this, it *does* seem possible that by Plato's lifetime, about a thousand years after the sudden collapse of the Minoan culture, certain elements of the Cretan disaster may have been used to colour the infinitely more ancient memories of the downfall of Atlantis. The gold and *"orichalcum"* with which Plato's Atlantis was so liberally overlaid, the cloud-capped towers and gorgeous palaces, may by Plato's time have been borrowed from vanished Knossos to embroider the glories of Atlantis. The volcano of 1500 B.C., at Santorin may also have added its spectacular melodrama to the record of the original Flood which swept away so much of Europe's Atlantic seaboard. For the deluge of 9000 B.C., they say, was not caused by seismic eruptions but by the melting of glaciers of the last Ice Age. It was not the land that sank, but the sea-level that rose.

Could such an antediluvian culture have had metals? No-one can dogmatise about cities sunk beneath the waves, but no worked metals have so far been found that can be dated back so far in time, in adjacent areas that survived the Floods. Bronze seems to have first been smelted in Egypt about 3700 B.C., so far as present knowledge goes.

Having stripped Atlantis of much of its temporal glories, what is left to account for its persistent hold on the world's imagination?

Why, the quality of its thought, not only astronomical and mathematical but spiritual, which after its physical destruction still survived to illumine its infant colonies in the Middle East! And this numinous system of ideas emanated, as much evidence shews, *from the Temple of the Stars in Britain*. Its effigies and geographical location correspond so well with the accounts of the Atlantean gods of Sanchoniathon, Plato, Diodorus Siculus and others that it is difficult ultimately not to accept them as the origin of Atlantean philosophy, cosmology, science and religion.

This is not to say that Britain was the centre of Atlantis; cold hard facts preclude that possibility, facts as hard and cold as the last Ice Age. For its glaciers covered the northern half of this country for some 50,000 years until they began to melt at about 10,000 B.C. They covered Ireland altogether. Hibernating Ireland was well-named Hibernia, the winter-land.

Yet it is a curious fact that the glaciers never touched Avalon, though they came perilously near. The floods that created the new Severn torrent when these glaciers melted came nearer still, even submerging temporarily some of its low-lying effigies—notably the water-signs. But though much of Lyonesse disappeared for ever, Avalon's sacred circle still remains.

Surely it was these terrible floods that came to the ears of the Egyptians? For though dynastic Egypt was not to appear till some 5000 years later, Europe was well populated when the sea-level rose. Hills became islands, rivers became estuaries, settlements were engulfed, and the new sea roared up the Channel, cutting Britain off from the Continent. Europe must have been full of horrified survivors, heading south and east as fast as legs or sails could carry them, bearing awe-inspiring tales of kinsfolk drowned, whole landscapes submerged. Such tales would live long in folk-memory . . . . Some still survive, like that of Welsh Dwyvan and Menu with his ark, or King Gradlon's daughter of Brittany, who wantonly opened the sluice-gates and flooded the kingdom of Ys.

If Britain was far from the centres of Atlantean pomp and circumstance, it nevertheless seems to have had a disproportionate spiritual influence. For Atlas, king of Atlantis, and his fellow-Titans belonged to the far western land bordering the Ocean (the Atlantic) that bounded the known world. Hesiod (9th cent. B.C.) tells us that *"It is there, among impenetrable shadows and foul vapours, at the very end of the world, that the Titans, by the will of the king of heaven, are buried."* They were, he says, drowned in the Flood. He also says that the word Titan comes from a root meaning *"to stretch out"*. So here are giant divinities, buried and stretched out on the earth at the fog-bound end of the known world. To be precise with Plutarch, in Britain!

Early descriptions of this sacred isle varied enormously; not all travellers saw it as gloomy and fog-bound. Some visited it when the sun had dispersed the "foul vapours" and Avalon's orchards were ripening, for Hesiod also tells of the Golden Apples of the Blessed Isles of the West, guarded by the Hesperides, daughters of Atlas the Titan. Perhaps one of Hesiod's sailor-informants gained his impression of Britain in winter, another in summer? Or perhaps the gloomy account is far older, remembering a Britain at the turbulent end of the last ice-age, when its Titans were being buried by the rising waters of the Atlantean Flood.

The Hesperidean conditions may describe the later period from 5000 to 2000 B.C. when Britain, now an island, enjoyed a warmer climate than we have today. The Hibernian winterland had become a perpetual Hesperidean Summerland, whose fortunate inhabitants gathered two crops in a year.

We need have no doubt where the Garden of the Hesperides originally was; Solinus describes Britain as *"the very Fortunate Islands of the Bretannides"*, and Dionysius Periegetes' History says of us *"In the Hesperides whence tin comes, dwell the sons of the noble Iberes."* (The earliest Britons are known as *'Iberian'*.) Herodotus connects the Cimmerians with amber and tin; Pausanius calls the Cimmerians Celts.

Several writers (of more recent date, including Velikowsky) have seen the War of the Titans and Greeks as remembering elemental upheavals from Deluvian times. Enraged Titans, cast out from heaven, hurled rocks, diverted rivers, piled mountain upon mountain, roared like thunder and hurled lightning at their supplanters, while puny mankind cowered and fled in terror.

The Titans were the earliest gods of all, and were identical with the *"Sons of God"* in Genesis from before the Deluge, and with the *"Fallen Angels"* of the Book of Enoch. (This book's very name implies immemorial antiquity, for Enoch, great-grandfather of Noah, was a seer from before the Flood.) In the Ethiopian version of this mysterious book Enoch is whirled through the air *to the west,* where an angel shewed him one mountain of iron, one of copper, one of gold, and one of soft metal (tin or lead) where arms were made by Giants or *"Satans"*.

It must have been this record, long stored in libraries along the North African coast from Carthage to Egypt, that sent Phoenicians and Cretans of Hesiod and Homer's time scurrying back to Britain to find its Giants and their mountains of treasure. But long before this, in 9000 B.C., Pyrenean Azilians, Iberian Atlanteans, made cave-homes in Britain. Later graves of Iberian type dated to about 4000 B.C., line the Cotswold banks of the Severn and are connected with those extraordinary people who erected our megalithic monuments and mighty mounds. Perhaps we cannot yet call them Phoenicians, but they came from the same south-western quarter as the Atlantean Azilians—Iberia and Morocco—where the Phoenician city of Carthage was later built.

The Phoenicians

Was it these mysterious proto-Phoenicians who stored the seeds of Atlantean wisdom when their primaeval centres were submerged, sowing them anew in after ages not only in Neolithic Britain (remembered as the source of these ideas), but all along the Mediterranean shore as far as Troy and even Sumeria? Astronomical stone circles line this route from Britain to Persia—sure sign of a star-gazing people with that most essential tool of civilisation, a calendar.

It is a strange fact that calendars in Egypt and Sumeria begin at much the same time, and both cultures feature Zodiacs from their inception.

Egypt, it is now suspected, was colonised from north-west Africa; the Sumerians, says Berossus, were first instructed in the arts and sciences by a prophet, half-man, half-fish, who emerged from the sea, *"after which nothing further was invented".* Instant civilisation! The beginnings of Egyptian civilisation seem to have been equally sudden.

The Phoenicians, or proto-Phoenicians, were well fitted for spreading the Word. Based around north-west Africa, these intrepid maritime adventurers were within sailing distance of the surviving Mysteries in Britain, and of the colonies they were to found in the east. Their library at Carthage was said to rival that of Alexandria before the Romans dispersed it.

Herodotus begins his *"Legend of Io"* with the words—*"The Phoenicians, having migrated to the Mediterranean—".* Ancient Phoenicia in Palestine and Syria seems to have been but one of their colonies.

The Ras Shamra Tablets of c. 1350 B.C. found near Beirut, refer to their ancient and mysterious priesthood, the Cabiri, *as islanders,* sons of the sea. As by this time Phoenicians were trading here in metals, Britain must have been one of their islands. *"The Hesperides, whence tin comes"* as Diogenes Periegetes said...

They brought more than metals to the Mediterranean. The Ras Shamra Tablets' account of Adam and Eve and the Eden Garden were inscribed at least six or seven centuries before the Genesis story was written. The first Eden it seems was the Hesperides Garden by the Severn sea, whose apple-orchards bore golden apples, star-lore from the Tree of Life, containing all the Knowledge of Good and Evil. The Cabiri were masters of the Caballistic world-system portrayed, together with the Eden story and the Deluge, in the Summerland Zodiac from the dawn of time.

How apt that the Phoenicians, people of the Phoenix of rebirth, should convey these pregnant myths from the land of the Deluge to the waiting peoples of the Mediterranean! They were midwives to the new world's rebirth, and the Eden of Mesopotamia was perhaps but one of the second Gardens of Innocence planted by these seed-carriers.

Their very legends are redolent of abduction, pregnancy, rebirth. Let Herodotus finish his sentence. *"The Phoenicians, having migrated to the Mediterranean and settled in these parts, then abducted Io from Argos and took her to Egypt".* As a reprisal, Cretans landed on the Phoenician coast and abducted Europe, daughter of the king of Tyre. Next the Greeks abducted Medea from Colchis, and in the following generation the Trojans abducted Helen from Greece. Are all these rapes not symbols of the cross-fertilization of ideas that was going on in the Mediterranean? Io–I into O–is a diagram of the Divine Word penetrating the world like an arrow-shaft. Europe surely indicates where that arrow first fell to earth. And though Io named the Ionian sea, let us not forget that the peak on our own Iona is called, simply, I. Which came first?

Comyns Beaumont suggests that the Phoenicians not only traded but settled in Britain, and the first Tyre was not in Palestine, but Portland Bill, on our own south coast, connected by a long line of forts (still to be seen) with Sidon at Sidmouth and Seaton. Was it from our European Tyre that the Cretans abducted Europe?

Another girl of the same name, Europa, which must mean *"from Europe"*, was abducted by a white bull and taken to Crete, where she gave birth to Minos, founder of the Minoan civilisation. Zeus was this bull in disguise. But he had a roving eye, and also loved Io, until his jealous wife Hera turned her into a white cow and stung her with gadflies. Maddened with pain, the poor creature flung herself into the sea, thus naming it the Ionian, and swam as far as the Bosphorus, founding not only Egypt but Troy.

Zeus, king of Heaven, was seen as the active agent in this cross-fertilizing of ideas; it was regarded as the will of heaven that after the first Atlantean failure, the first Fall, Man should try again.

Swimming cows and bulls seem to have symbolised the Phoenicians. No wonder, for the Bull was sacred to Poseidon, king of Atlantis. Plato shews the Bull-Cult as central to their Mysteries; Atlantean priests, like the Druids, sacrificed white bulls, fertilizing the earth with their blood. For Taurus is the libido, the life-force in man and nature. Only if it be harnessed, only by sacrifice can Taurus become the patient builder of civilisations. But where do we find the earliest evidence of the cult of the bull? In the caves of those noble Cro-magnons of 20,000 years ago, superb artists of a stature and brain-capacity as great if not greater than our own, forerunners of Atlantis or perhaps even Atlanteans; in the caves of southern France and Spain. Spain, where the bull's blood is still ritually spilt in the ring.

Atlas

When the earth was subdivided into kingdoms, Plato tells us, Saturn gave Atlantis to Poseidon, his son. Poseidon married a mortal, Cleito, and their ten sons eventually subdivided the kingdom among themselves. Atlas and Gadir, the eldest, were twins; *Atlas ruled the north*, naming Atlantis, Gadir took the south, naming Gades or Cadiz, and Agadir. Eleven god-kings and one queen—the Zodiac! In its circle Atlas is indeed a Twin; like Atlas he supports the starry sphere on his upraised arm. His head is bowed under his burden. Perseus turned him into stone, and he is indeed turned into a mountain, or at least into two steep hills.

He is also remembered by the Atlas Mountains near Carthage, but as this reverses Plato's geography—for the Atlas range is south, not north of Cadiz—we can assume that this is a localization of the Phoenicians' gods whose original effigies were in Britain. Phoenicians worshipped the Cabiri twins—*"they who return to the light."* Their mantle later fell on Castor and Pollux, who took special care of sailors, and were much prayed to during storms at sea. Mercury, who rules Gemini and protects travellers, must have shone benignly on the Phoenicians. The Twin of our Zodiac is also at sea in his ship.

Abducting and transplanting gods and goddesses was also a favourite trick of the Greeks, taught by the Phoenicians. It is ironic that present-day Britons regard their own Titanic pantheon as having Greek origin; but perhaps it serves us right for forgetting them. There is hardly a mountain or cave in the Aegean which is not pointed out proudly by Greek guides to British tourists as the birthplace of one or another of them. Yet from these very legends, it is plain enough that heroes like Perseus, Hercules, Jason, Odysseus, had to slog or sail to the Hesperides in the far west to do business or battle with them.

Maximus of Tyre asserts that *"the Hesperides, an island in the Atlantic, was long, narrow and secret. Atlas had his statues and images there, and a hollow mountain, very lofty, within which were apple orchards with golden apples."* Where else but Britain and Avalon's Isle, with its lofty Tor of cavernous limestone, its golden apples, its giant images?

Perseus killed the terrible Gorgon there, and turned Atlas to stone by shewing him her head—a truly petrifying sight. Hercules killed Albion, a Titan surely nothing if not British. Erin, another British giant, must have been Albion's Irish wife, but she too appears in Greek myth as Erinnys, chief of the Furies (or Fairies). She is one with Hecate, queen of the Underworld, who is also called in Greek Prytania. Britannia, British Anna, our Virgo! Is she not also Shakespeare's Titania, by her very name a she-Titan? And is her consort Oberon not Albion? Did Alberich, the fearsome dwarf of the Ring of the Nibelungs, derive from Albion of the Zodiac ring?

Iberius was another *"Greek"* Titan who must have originated among the Iberians or Hibernians. Whether he came from Spain or Ireland, it is plain that he belonged to the lands beyond the Pillars of Hercules. Iberia and

Hibernia are, I suspect, but variations on the same word for the wintry Atlantic beyond Gibraltar.

The Titans then must have been the Giants of Lyonesse, famous in British folk-lore, who still haunt Cornwall, Welsh Cymry-land, and Ireland; the Giants of the Zodiac. Their roaring and bellowing echoed round the ancient world, filling all who heard it with awe. Was the Latin Avernus (Hades) not Avalon, home of gigantic and unquiet shades? Yet it was also Paradise, Eden.

We have seen that the Welsh Annwn, Hades, had the same dual and contradictory character.

Plato gives us a description of the Sacred city of Atlantis which closely resembles a maze, with concentric circles of earth and water. Here was Cleito's stronghold, built by Poseidon by mounds and deep ditches. Most ancient cities after all were built in more or less this fashion for defence, with a castle rising above spiralling terraces. But it is interesting that Geoffrey Russell has recently found that the steep terraces of Glastonbury Tor are cut in the shape of a *"Cretan"* maze. A Cretan maze that may well be older than Crete—perhaps even Atlantean.

The Celtic goddess Arianrhod also had a maze—a *"turning"* or spiral castle, and as she was Queen of Heaven this palace was the Milky Way, spiralling galactically in space. But she was a virgin who gave birth to twins, so like Cleito was undeniably Zodiacal. *"As Above"*, said the Cabiric Mysteries, *"So Below"*. Glastonbury Tor may have been the earthly residence of both queens. It was once an island, and even if it lacks the concentric rings of water the Vale of Avalon is full of canals.

Celtic Arianrhod's maze became in time Greek Ariadne's labyrinth, where lost souls wandered until saved by Theseus the Saviour from the Minotaur of their own devouring desires. But so the Druids taught, long before Greece. Their Theseus was Esus, the Divine Essence; God in Man, so clearly portrayed within the Gemini Babe in his rescue-ship or life-boat.

One clue to indicate that myths and other cultural ideas did not originally spread from east to west, as generally imagined, but from west to east, is the enigma of old Greek, Pelasgian and Etruscan letter-forms. They do not derive, as Egyptian hieroglyphics do, from recognisable drawings of the objects they indicate. Nor do they resemble the square letters of old Chaldean or Hebrew; though there are occasional borrowings. What does their sprightly form most resemble? Why, the sprigs or twigs of trees! Only the Druids of Britain had a primitive tree-alphabet from which the Greek letter-forms could have derived. The Greeks themselves acknowledged this great debt by remembering that Cadmus, the Phoenician and one of the Cabiri, had brought letters into Greece. The Runic alphabet, resembling crude Greek letters, also hints at its derivation from the original Druidic inspiration.

Atlas, Enoch, Idris, Noah

If the stories of Atlas king of the Titans stem from the Gemini Giant in our Zodiac, this explains why he was held by the ancients to be the Father of Astrology and higher magic. (Higher magic may tentatively be defined as an attempt to ascertain the will of heaven by divinatory or mystical means, with a view to aligning human will to the Will of God; it is thus identifiable with mystical or higher religion. Lower magic is quite the opposite, being the black art of invoking spirit or demonic forces to help in achieving *human* desires.)

Atlas was equated with Hermes, inventor of letters and bringer of inspiration from God to man. Of course! For Hermes is Mercury, ruler of Gemini flooded by the Three Bars of Light. But he was also identified with the patriarch Enoch from before the Flood. Enoch who *"walked with God"*. The mystical Book of Enoch, so avidly read by Gnostics and early Christians, was said to have been written by Hermes Trismegistus, *"king of Egypt after the Deluge"*.

Both Jewish and Mohammedan tradition remembers divinely inspired books written by Adam and Enoch and handed down; some said that Shem, son of Noah, transmitted these. Shem was the *"first to be called a Phoenician"*. Arabs called Enoch Idris—a name, significantly enough, both Arabic and Welsh. No wonder then that the Welsh said that those who sat overnight on the top of Cader Idris would be found in the morning either dead, mad, or inspired. Idris surely means *"the man of ideas;"* to the Greeks and Trojans that mount of Ideas was Ida. It was from Mount Ida that Ganymede, the perfected man, took off for higher spheres; Enoch also took off in like manner, for *"God took him"*.

Noah too had a book, made, so says the Jewish Encyclopedia, from sapphires, which served him as a lamp in the Ark. It was passed down to Solomon. As Solomon venerated the ark as source of his wisdom, and as the ark containing the founder of divination and astrology is a key figure in the Glastonbury Zodiac, there seems little doubt about the nature of this book. The Sapphires are the Sephiroth of the Caballistic Tree of Life, studied by Solomon.

The Book of Enoch treats likewise of astronomy and astrology, the calendar, alchemy and divination, of the Creation, the Fall, the Deluge, and the Last Judgement. It is apocalyptic, prophetic. It contains fragments of the *"Book of Noah"*, one of which is of particular interest to us. God tells Noah that he will imprison those angels who have been unrighteous and led men astray, in a burning valley in the *west, among mountains of gold, silver, iron and tin.*

This valley, burning sulphurously, would become a place of purging, a Hades, where the fallen angels and the men they had led astray were purified, physically as well as spiritually, by hot sulphur springs.

There is more than a hint here of the Vale of Avalon with its purifying mysteries, its Fallen Star-Angels or Giants (for Mars and Venus, astrologers say, do indeed lead men astray)—and the hot springs of the ancient city of Bath, so near the metal-mining Mendips and Wales. These waters, Noah was told, shall heal kings and mighty ones of the earth. They have!

Compare the Fallen Star-Angels of the Book of Enoch with the *"Sons of God"* in the Book of Genesis. Both fell to earth, married mortal women or were seduced by them, both had Giant offspring—for Genesis says that *"there were giants on the earth in those days."* In the Caballistic Zohar these same fallen angels, also fathering Giants by mortal seductresses, *were bound to earth on black mountains: here they still instruct men in all the arts and sciences.* Who are these if not our Somerset Giants?

Noah, grandson of Enoch, personified the survivors from Atlantis. Sitting like Gemini in his ark, he represents those who understood the ancient science of astrology aright, as God-inspired, life-giving, Divinely-indicated upon the earth. Those who turned its knowledge into *"black magic"* were submerged beneath the waves. All ancient books condemn the misuse of astrology, blaming these *"fallen angels"* for the Fall of Man. The Bible among them contains many strictures on astrologers, spirit-raisers and *"false prophets"*, and this had led the Churches to condemn astrology as a whole. *But did the Magi not find the Son of God by astrology?* Knowledge is power—and though power can be used for corrupt purposes, we can hardly reject a power-source for this reason. We might as well ban all further science-research because among many benefits it has produced the atom-bomb. No, we cannot turn the clock back, but we *can* learn from our past mistakes, and do better. What else is history for?

Noah, though he turned his back on doomed Atlantis, nevertheless brought its *Zodiac animals with him in his Ark*, for they contained the very essentials of future civilisations in their mathematics, astronomy and cosmological measurements. The Ark of the Hebrews was a sacred palladium constructed in miniature on Noah's original, whose measurements must never be lost, for civilisation, furthering man's true purpose, depended on it.

Josephus, the Jewish historian, equated the Genesis Giants with the western Titans. Sanchoniathon, the ancient Carthaginian, says that the Cabiri, the priestly caste of the Phoenicians, were commanded by Thoth (the Egyptian Hermes) to write down their ancient records and deliver them to Osiris, god of the Cabiri before his cult appeared in Egypt; an interesting pointer for those archaeologists who suspect that Egyptian culture came from the Libyan west. The Cabiric Mysteries were those of the Mother-goddess Hecate or Kore: Mother Carey of Britain, Virgo of the Zodiac. We have already noticed parallels between the myth of Egyptian Osiris, (Ausar) and Arthur, and that Osiris' son bears the Zodiacal name Horus (the hour). Surely the history that the Cabiri delivered to Osiris was that of Atlantis and its Star-Temple; the same that Egyptians later gave to Solon, and Solon gave to Plato.

The Deluge story was an important part of its teaching. It contained a warning against flouting Creation's Laws, indicating at the same time that these laws had been preserved in the ark for the future guidance of Man. This only appears obliquely in the Bible version as *"The Covenant"* made between God and Noah. Only those who read Noah's animals aright can guess what that Covenant consisted of. Menu the Measurer is a better name than Noah.

"Mene, mene, tekel upharsin" said the writing on the wall at Belshazzar's feast. *"Thou hast been measured in the balance and found wanting."* Atlantis, too, had been found wanting. Only those who *"walked with God"* survived. Noah had indeed a remarkable talent for survival, for he lived, so we are told, nigh on a thousand years. He came from a long-lived family; most of his patriarchal stock, including Methuselah, survived to an age that strains credulity and *"makes one gasp and stretch one's eyes."*

Some have seen the lives of these noble patriarchs as symbolising schools of the Mysteries, which lasted for thousand-year cycles, and Enoch was certainly one such. But had the author of Genesis another aim also? Did he not desire to shew that those who lived by the divine laws of Evolution achieved long life and immortality?

The Zodiac is the graphic illustration of the divine laws; its pattern secretly implied throughout the Bible, both in the Old Testament and the New; more openly taught in the Book of Enoch, the Zohar, and other books of the Mysteries.

The name of Hermes Trismegistus, reputed author of the Book of Enoch, is usually translated as Hermes Thrice-Greatest; but I detect a hint of the Three Magi in his name. The Three Kings came from the three quarters of the earth to find the fourth in the first and secret quarter. Were they too, not Grail-seekers? He lies hidden in our own secret quarter, still an infant in Evolution's womb, but of infinite potential, as his numinous effigy in Somerset makes plain.

His names are legion, for we are many; Atlas, Attis, Enoch, Idris, Noah, Esus, Jesus, Dion-ysus, Menu, Manannan, *Man*.

Atlantis and its fall is not a comforting thought. It is easier to dismiss it as fairy-tale, not history, for it implies that human evolution is not continuous or inevitable. It implies a Judgement, a periodic Test which we may not pass. We prefer Darwinism, which shews us as constantly improving on primitive cave-man beginnings and becoming every day and in every way better and better and better. The huge hiatus in time between Plato's fabled island-continent way back in 10000 B.C. or so and the known beginnings of neolithic culture in 4000 B.C. has made scepticism easy, while its vague and improbable geography, somewhere in the vast Atlantic, has strengthened disbelief.

Yet recent discoveries in the Middle East have dramatically closed the time-gap. In Jericho and some sites in Turkey (near Noah's Mount Ararat) impressive foundation-walls have been uncovered that go back to the 8th millenium B.C., great fortress-cities *beneath* primitive neolithic villages of later date. Magnificently carved stone jars and sculptured heads of high artistry have dumbfounded archaeologists. City-building, civilised men were here millenia before ancient Egypt began.

Were these the *"sons of Noah"*, only faintly remembered in recorded *"mythical"* history by the books of Enoch and Genesis?

These well-cut, well-laid stones, capable of bearing high walls and towers, yet buried so deep in time, are disturbing to our Darwinist concepts. Primitive man it seems can be the degenerate descendant of greater ancestors he cannot even remember—whose thoughts he can no longer think.

What is to stop this decline? Has it indeed always been arrested? Can man sink below the human level? For only a degree or two of consciousness separates us from the animals. Are the great apes perhaps descendants of such human failures, still around to warn us? Is the truth of this the very opposite of what we have so comfortably been taught? And if we have indeed risen from apes, can we sink back again?

It is interesting that in the Zodiac effigies the animals far outnumber the humans. Nature, it seems, is loaded against that divine spark which differentiates us from the rest of her creation. What she has given she is always trying to take back, as though she feared the consequences of her gift. Human evolution is only achieved against Nature; education must fight with overpowering biological urges; the gardener against the greater vitality of the weeds; the city-builder against the jungle; the poet and seer against society. Dali's humans wilt and are only prevented from falling on all fours by artificial crutches propping them at all points. Dali, an Iberian, perhaps remembers Atlantis.

Would it not be well, before Nature wins again and Evolution despairs of us, to renew the search for this hidden spark, this Man in ourselves we cannot find?

19: The Somerset Zodiac in Greek Myth

To do justice to all the references to Britain, the Hesperides, the Hyperboreans and their Zodiac in Greek legends would fill a large book, so a random sample must suffice, enough I hope to alert you to the entertaining game of reading classical myth with the Zodiac in mind, and making new discoveries.

The tale of Hercules simply bristles with clues. By his birth, death, general character, and of course his Twelve famous Labours, he is unquestionably a sun-god whose adventures take him through the twelve Houses of the Zodiac. His very name proclaims his heliacal nature. Musclebound extrovert though he seems on the surface, he nevertheless seeks after wisdom, and the outer passage of the sun conceals the inner self-creative labours of the Initiate in the Mysteries. Like Gilgamesh (with whom he has been identified) he is a Grail-seeker; one might say that his twelve mighty labours were the task of knowing himself through analysis of the houses of his horoscope.

But the Mysteries were celebrated in Greece, so why drag Hercules to Britain? Why, because he sails through the Straits of Gibraltar, naming them the Pillars of Hercules, and is not content until he reaches the Hesperides Garden, and finds Atlas supporting the starry firmament on his shoulders. He persuades the Titan to find the Golden Apples of Wisdom for him, while he himself assumes the burden of holding up the heavens. (Not unnaturally Atlas is reluctant to go back into harness, and has to be tricked into it.)

Having achieved Self-Knowledge through his mighty Labours, he was now fit to receive the Cabbalistic science of cosmic movement, proportion and harmony from Atlas, founder of all the sciences of Atlantis; fit to take the Cosmic slide-rule of Aaron's rod or Math's magic wand, which survived the Flood in Noah's Ark and was preserved in Hesperidean, Hyperborean Britain in the proportions of its Zodiac.

Hercules was a Phoenician one of the Cabiri, bringing the secrets of the Golden Number to found the art, architecture, modal music and intellectual vitality of Greece. His Phoenician name was Hercules Melkarth, meaning King Arthur. As if to clinch this identity, the stars of the constellation Hercules fall upon Sagittarius, the Arthur of the Glastonbury Zodiac. And only here is Sagittarius not a centaur, but a mounted warrior.

Hercules in his Twelve Labours fights most of the creatures of the Zodiac: the Nemean Lion, the Stymphalian birds, (Aquarius and Libra) a whole herd of Taurean oxen, a bull, the dragon-serpent Ladon that guarded the Golden Apples of the Hesperidean Garden (Draco), the Ceryneian Hind, (Capricorn), and Cerberus, guardian Dog of the Underworld of Hades. He also encountered Amazons, who can only be Celts, for where else in the ancient world did women fight like men? (Boadicea was heir to a long tradition: Atalanta was her ancestor.) And where else but in Britain would he encounter earth-giants like Antaeus, who could only be overcome by holding them up in the air? The Glastonbury effigies are in fact a mirrored reflection of the heavens, and only correspond to their starry counterparts when the planisphere is held above one's head.

Hercules obtained the girdle of Hippolyte, Queen of the Amazons. It appears that this was no ordinary girdle; Hera Queen of Heaven and Earth was enraged to find that it had been given away. Why? If Hippolyte was a Celt, as we suspect, we may also suspect that it contained the great Celtic secret; being a representation of the great girdle of the Glastonbury Zodiac.

Did Hercules wear this trophy, a symbol after all of the Mysteries he had travelled so far to find? It seems he did; for in Homer's description of him we learn that *"Around his breast a wondrous zone was roll'd, where woodland monsters grin in fretted gold."*

Hercules, I confidently submit, wore this trophy over one shoulder like the ribbon of the Order of the Garter—another *"girdle"* signifying the Mysteries of Britain instituted by that Arthurian devotee, Edward III.

Another Labour which seems to connect our Greek hero with Britain is the capture of the oxen of Geryon. Now Geryon is a manifestly Celtic name; Gwair ap Geirion in Welsh myth was imprisoned in Annwn or Hades, and his name means Man. Arthur attempted to rescue him when he descended into Annwn to obtain the Cauldron. He is represented in the Zodiac by Gemini, the *"Son of Man"*, with the ox of Taurus at his elbow. Greek *"Geryon"* may also be Welsh Gwron, third of the Three Primary Bards, who represent (according to Ed. Davies' *"Celtic Researches"*) Light, Harmony, and Energy. As these are the forces of the Celtic Trinity, Gwron is again Gemini, Man harnessing the energy of the earth through the ox. The *"Greek"* legend makes good sense in Welsh. Hercules the sun-god is rescuing Man.

As he descends into Hades he meets two unquestionably Hesperidean or British characters—Medusa the Gorgon, whose father Orcus (some say) named the Orkneys, and Meleager who figures in Celtic myth under almost the same name; Meleagant, abductor of Guinevere and a lord of the Zodiac's Tor. If the British Virgo were not such a hag, we might hesitate to identify the Gorgon with Guinevere, but they are both different aspects of the same earth-goddess. It is significant that she and Meleager are also found together in Greek myth.(See page 173)

While in Arcady (ostensibly in Greece) Hercules hunts a boar of such terrible aspect that all who saw it hid themselves very sensibly in bronze jars. This boar-hunt is a favourite sun-hero's exploit, both in Greek and Celtic myth, and the boar, from its white crescent-shaped tusks is the moon, pursued by the sun. Arthur also hunts the boar Twrch Trwyth (Torch of

Truth?), so here again the Celtic version has more than merely calendrical significance. Was the Torch of Truth carried from here to Mount Olympus? And was the first Arcady really in Greece? It was a region like the Hesperides Garden of other-wordly overtones, temperate climate, dreams of bliss and eternal youth. All names mean something. Was Arcady not the land of the Zodiac Arc or Ark? It was in Arcady that Hercules that great archer put centaurs to flight with his arrows, banishing them to Cape Malea. But Cape Malea of course is in Greece. Or was it? Cape of Apples! Is there not a hint here of Avalon's apple-orchards, under whose trees at least one Centaur still lurks? Cape Malea, abode of Apollo Maleatas the apple-god. But Apollo and his mother Latona were Hyperboreans, born and bred in Britain, as Hecateus the Greek historian of the 6th century B.C., plainly states. (The stars known as Apollo's Lyre are strung across Sagittarius' back, for good measure.) Apollo's Celtic name was Avallach, the Apple-god of Avalon; he figures in Arthurian myth as the Maimed King. Druids, the priests of Boreas, worshipped him at Stonehenge—and Stonehenge was old when Greece was young.

In Arcady too were the Stymphalian birds, monsters who fed on human flesh; Hercules soon picked these off with his arrows. And in our Zodiac the effigy of Sagittarius-Hercules the Archer is flanked by the enormous birds of Aquarius and Libra. No other Zodiacs have any birds at all.

No sun-hero's exploits are complete without a fight with a dragon to rescue a beautiful maiden. Hercules vanquishes several serpents, including the many-headed Hydra, and rescues Hesione the daughter of a king of Troy. She, like the Fallen Angels in Enoch, was chained to a rock. Is she not our earth-bound Virgo? And is our Sagittarius not locked in combat too with a many-headed dragon?

Hercules also killed the dragon Ladon that guarded the Golden Apples of the Hesperides, and this dragon bore the same name as the river on whose banks he captured the Ceryneian hind. Our Zodiac dragon, Draco, is drawn by a river (the Brue), and near it lurk both Aries and Capricorn; either could be the Ceryneian Hind. For this elusive prize, who evaded Hercules for a whole year, had horns of gold, and could be either the Arian Ram of the Golden Fleece, or Capricorn whose horn, a great earthwork, is still known locally as the Golden Coffin. The term of one year mentioned in Hercules' myth, probably remembers this horn which now marks the winter solstice, the year's end.

Ceryneian? The name puzzled and intrigued me until I recognised it as Kerin or St. Keyne the harvest goddess of our Zodiac, whose cornucopia or wheatsheaf at Keinton Mandeville gave the name *"Kerin"* to the whole Cornish promontory, shaped like the corn-horn of Ceres. But this cornucopia is also the golden horn of Capricorn the White Hart and Unicorn, the Golden Hind of December where Kerin's seeds are stored in winter. Virgin and Unicorn are mythically bound together in calendrical embrace.

Homer, like Hesiod, knew of the British Mysteries. Contemporary with Hesiod, (9th, 10th or 11th century B.C.), his name is curiously Phoenician. For a homer or omer was a measure, equal to ten ephahs. Was Homer too a *"Measurer"*? A Menes? Like Milton, he was reputedly blind, but this blindness gave sight to an inner eye, where myth is more real than outer reality. His metric measures gave high poetry to Greece. His picture of Hercules in the 11th Book of the Odyssey reads like an aerial view of our celestial-terrestrial Zodiac.

(Pope's translation)

*"Now I the strength of Hercules behold
A towering spectre of gigantic mould"* (intuitive punning by Pope?)
*"A shadowy form! For high in heaven's abodes
Himself resides, a God among the Gods...
Here hovering ghosts like fowl his shade surround
And clang their pinions with terrific sound,"* (Dove and Phoenix)
*"Gloomy as night he stands, in act to throw
The aerial arrow from the twanging bow.
Around his breast a wondrous zone is rolled
Where woodland monsters grin in fretted gold."*

And are these not the Titans of the west, also sung by Hesiod?—

*"More fierce than Giants, more than Giants strong,
The earth, o'er-burdened, groaned beneath their weight.
None but Orion e'er surpassed their height.
His shafts Apollo aimed; at once they sound
And stretch the giant Monsters on the ground."*

And there they lie to this day, like Tityus the Titan.

*"There Tityus large and long, in fetters bound
O'erspreads nine acres of infernal ground."*

These Gargantuan creatures were seen by Odysseus, another Grail-seeker to the west. But the secret is that such questers are not simply viewing something outside themselves, but also *seeing themselves reflected*. Like the Arthurian knights, they are themselves the effigies. *Odysseus, Ulysses*—the very name gives him away. The one he has come to find is his true self, his *"essence"*, hidden in the Babe Esse of *Lyonesse* in his boat. Like a true Phoenician, he tried to make his pilgrimage pay its way, for he returns with *"vessels laden with a plenteous store of brass, of vestures, and resplendent ore."* The resplendent ore might be tin from Cornwall, or Welsh and Irish gold. The vestures? Tartan plaids and kilts coloured with woad and other dyes.

In the fifth Book of the Odyssey, Zeus promises our sailor that he shall return from Ogygia to Corcira in the Mediterranean in *"twice ten days' sail"*. By no means an impossible time for a voyage from *Ireland, which Plutarch says is Ogygia*. Homer tells us that Ogygia lay in remote parts, and unknown seas; its king, Gyges, was a Titan.

Ulysses also visited Wales—and didn't like it much:

> *"When lo! We reached old Ocean's utmost bounds*
> *Where rocks control his waves with ever-during mounds.*
> *There in a lonely land, and gloomy cells*
> *The dusky nation of Cimmeria dwells.*
> *The sun ne'er views the uncomfortable seats*
> *When radiant he advances, or retreats:*
> *Unhappy race! Whom endless night invades*
> *Clouds the dull air, and wraps them round in shades."*

He was of course, used to the Mediterranean, and by 1000 B.C. things weren't what they had been in the Hesperides of earlier times. We must mournfully admit that this description fits Welsh Cymry-land better than the original home of the Cimmerians in the Caucasus. Besides, Odysseus could only have reached the Black sea by sailing through the Dardanelles, where the smoking ruins of Troy would remind him of the cause of all his misfortunes. Yet he never mentions them. Can we imagine Homer—or Odysseus—missing such an elegiac opportunity? We must remember too, that he was going to the courts of Dis, in the far west, like Gilgamesh to consult the dead.

The description of this awe-inspiring place is an interesting one for Zodiac students—

> *"The ship we moor on these obscure abodes,*
> *Disbark the ship, an offering to the gods:*
> *And hellward bending, o'er the beach descry*
> *The doleful passage to the infernal sky."*

In the land of the Cimmerians this forbidding underworld is also described as the *"nether sky"*. Now what can such enigmatic phrases mean, if not our Zodiac, the sky reflected on earth? Homer, like Hesiod, knew the Secret of Britain.

Scholars have long sought to confine the voyaging Ulysses to the Mediterranean; but which is more likely to inspire an Odyssey—tame coastal trips round well-charted seas, or this wild adventure through the Pillars of Hercules and up the treacherous Atlantic seaboard, the Bay of Biscay—the turbulent rocks of the Cornish coast?

Ulysses, Odysseus, bears all the marks of an initiate in the Mysteries. Indeed, he becomes a Master, for he learns to master not only his circumstances, but himself. He outwits the Cyclops, those one-eyed Giants who can only be our Zodiac effigies (one-eyed because they are drawn in profile). A master in the Mysteries, he learns to sublimate the Zodiacal nature-impulses in himself, though many of his crew are devoured by them. Knowing his weakness when tempted by the seductive sirens, he has himself bound to the mast when they sing, while his crew hurl themselves overboard into their fatal embrace. He alone remains a Man, upright before Circe's deadly charms, while his crew literally make pigs of themselves at her festive board, and are driven squealing into her sty. He overcomes every disaster, (and he has many) by a mixture of courage and cunning, being not only a bold man but sly. The Mysteries had little room for *"stupid saints"*; holding intelligence a quality dear to Evolution's purpose. He is a King among men, a Man among beasts, and saves his crew from many a tight corner, even from their own folly, when he can. And he is true to his Penelope, despite a little dallying here and there—as she is true to him, though she too has every temptation, from infidelity to despair. Homer has been called amoral, ethically primitive. This I cannot understand. He saw life itself as the School of the Mysteries—remarkably clear seeing for a blind man.

But before Hercules and Odysseus, Perseus, Hercules' grandfather, made the passage to the far west. He certainly saw the seamy side of the Hesperides Garden when he encountered the three Graeae (hags who owned but one eye and one tooth between them, and had to pass them round when they wanted to see or chew). One feels the Phoenician-Cretan sailors exaggerated their reports of our Virgoan hag somewhat, but it is true she has only one eye, and was regarded as a triple goddess. The Greeks said that all Cretans were liars, but it would be kinder to say that they were imaginative, for we can now see that they built their lurid tales on a substratum of truth.

In the same lovely garden Perseus met and vanquished the Gorgon Medusa, with snakes in her hair and tusks where her canines should be (an unhappy trait inherited from her father Phorcys or Orcus, lord of the Underworld in Perseus' day). His name meant the Boar—the beast whose tusks symbolised the crescent moon; he was thus lord of the Zodiac's calendar, and indeed fathered all its *"monstrous brood"*, not only the Gorgons and the Graeae, but the dragon Ladon. Because his fame was brought to Greece by mariners, or because his kingdom bordered the Atlantic, he was known as the Old Man of the Sea. The ocean is after all a special sort of underworld.

The Graeae were called the Phoreides, the Fates, the Parcae—one might almost say the Porcae. The Gorgon Medusa's tusks remind us that the Celtic goddess Ceredwen (our Virgo again) was very fond of turning into a sow, and her Druid priests called themselves Syweddyd (Swine) in her honour. Perhaps as the fecund mother-goddess she needed as many breasts as a sow; perhaps the Druids saw themselves burrowing for truth in these terrestrial effigies, as pigs dig for truffles in the earth.

One more reason why the earth-goddess took such lowly form. Sows eat almost anything, including their own young; the earth-mother, prolific and a voracious eater, consumes us all at death.

Perseus stole the eye and tooth from the gibbering Graeae (or Fates) thus bending Fate to his will, as a true initiate should, and blackmailed them into revealing Medusa's whereabouts. As Virgo, she was standing right there all the time! It wasn't her tusks so much that bothered him, but her basilisk glare that turned all who encountered it to stone. This snake-goddess—a medium or *"pythoness"*, had hypnotic powers; so he looked instead on her reflection in his polished shield and decapitated her. It was all done by mirrors! So the initiate must look at life's adventures and temptations; the shield of the Mysteries can break their hypnotic power. He is no longer a rabbit before a snake, but a Man who recognises them as tests of character set by Higher Powers, hoping he will pass with distinction and thus deserve promotion up the evolutionary ladder.

Many Greek legends are connected with Britain's pantheon by the telltale names of their gods and goddesses, even though the scene of their adventures seems to be specifically Aegean.

Take for example the myth of Atalanta. This Amazon (who should be the patron saint of Women's Lib.), was suckled by a *bear* and became as strong and fleet of foot as any forest creature. She wrestled with Peleus and beat him, killed centaurs who attempted to ravish her, and declaring that she would only marry the man who could catch her, outran them all until they dropped dead. She was at last wooed and won by Melanion, who dropped golden apples as he ran, knowing that no Hesperidean could resist stopping to pick them up.

I suspect that Melanion is much the same person as Meleager, another of her suitors who organised a boar hunt involving all the heroes of Greece. The fierce Boar of Calydon was sent to ravage the kingdom because Meleager's father, when sacrificing to the twelve gods of Olympus, quite forgot Artemis the Moon-huntress. It was of course her moon-boar. Atalanta was the first to wound it, Meleager finished it off—but not before it had killed and maimed most of the flower of Greece. After she and Meleager-Melanion were married they were turned into lions for some misdemeanour or other. Virgo into Leo is surely Zodiacal myth. Atalanta was suckled by a bear. Was she a daughter of Arthur whose name in Welsh means Bear—the Great Bear? Meleager too sounds uncannily like Celtic Meleagant, a lord of Glastonbury Tor who in Arthurian tales abducts Guinevere the chaste and much-chased.

Virgo changes into Leo the lion, in the precession of the equinoxes. It is the Riddle of the Sphinx. How old is this myth? Is Atalanta an Atlantean? The *"Greek"* story begins to look very like Hyperborean calendar myth. *"Hyperborean"* means *"under the Great Bear"*—just where Atalanta was suckled at birth.

The myth of Atalanta only makes sense in Britain!

Those Greek nymphs, the Horae, now take on deeper significance, for their name means the Hours.

One of the Horae, Carpo, drowned herself in the river for love of Camillus, son of the river-god Meander—and Zeus in compassion turned her into fruit—which is what her name means anyway. What an inconsequential tale. Would the love-lorn maiden not have been better off in her new element as a fish—a carp, perhaps?

But translate Carpo to Somerset, where her love Camillus becomes the Celtic sky-god Camulos (giving his name to the river Cam and the Camel villages)—drown her before his very eyes as he watches from his stronghold, Cadbury Castle or Camelot, and she becomes fruitful indeed—Mother Carey the harvest-goddess, drowned and drawn by the river Cary.

Camulos or Camillus is also Kasmilu, one of the Phoenician Cabiri, whose Mysteries I suspect were taken from our Zodiac to the Mediterranean.

As Jason has already figured in earlier chapters we should also give a brief account of his quest of the Golden Fleece.

This fleece was first a flying Ram, sent by Zeus to rescue the twins Phryxus and Helle from their cruel stepmother. Helle fell off its back into the Hellespont, but Phryxus reached Colchis on the Tigris, gratefully sacrificed the ram to Zeus and hung its fleece in the temple of Ares or Mars, setting a dragon to guard it. The Ram is obviously Aries, his fleece, guarded by Draco, symbolising the Zodiac Mysteries. The twins, mortal and immortal, are Man, rescued by Zeus from bondage to earth, their cruel stepmother, by giving them the knowledge of their high purpose enshrined in the stars. Chaldean wisdom on the Tigris!

Jason, seeking this Golden Fleece, gathers the Argonauts, among them Theseus, Orpheus, Hercules, the twins Castor and Pollux—a distinguished crew—and with the magic of the terrible Medea vanquished the dragon and won the Fleece.

Pursued by its owner, Medea's father, the king of Colchis, Medea cuts up the body of her brother and throws him in bits into the sea, effectively delaying the sorrowing father, who picks up the pieces. They cross the Danube, the Mediterranean, and evade the Symplegades, rocks that move in to crush passing ships, (Sym = Together, Gades = Cadiz). These are thus *the Straits of Gibraltar.*—They come to the Ocean—the Atlantic. There can be little doubt that Jason's voyage, like that of Odysseus, is based on the Cretan-Phoenician trade with Britain, and that his adventures are Zodiacal. His paramour Medea with her rejuvenating cauldron, the fate of her brother, scattered in pieces like Osiris, the death of Jason himself, crushed by the Argo while sleeping—are all redolent of the Mysteries.

Jason's Argo sported a bough from the prophetic oak of Dodona; strong hint of Gaulish druidism. The rumours he picked up in Chaldea's Colchis only whetted his appetite for seeking this knowledge at its western source, like many another fabled hero. Like them, he had to travel the world to find —Himself.

Theseus was not just one of Jason's crew. His tale also needs to be told, for it concerns Minos, Ariadne and the labyrinth, all elements in British myth.

The Athenians had killed Minos' son Androgeus—the androgyne or Perfected Man in the Mysteries. All-powerful Minos in revenge demanded seven youths and maidens yearly to feed his monstrous Minotaur, half-bull, half-man, kept in his labyrinth in Crete. Animal-men consigned to the animal-man. (Minos, to ensure that none should find the way out of this maze, had walled up its architect, Daedalus and his son Icarus, within it. But Daedalus, resourceful man, made wings from feathers dropped from passing birds, so both flew free. Icarus flew too near the sun which melted the wax of his artificial wings, and fell to earth. Whence had Daedalus obtained this wax? No doubt from passing bees.)

Theseus, prince of Athens, determined to join the hostages and end this servitude. He promised king Aegius, his weeping father, that if he succeeded in killing the Minotaur he would change the black sails of the sacrificial ship for white ones—a signal of victory which could be seen from afar. (Tristram of Lyonesse has a similar *"black sails"* episode.)

Once in Crete, he gained the love of Minos' daughter Ariadne, who gave him a ribbon to unwind when he entered the maze, so that he could find his way out again. He killed the Minotaur, saving his people, and taking Ariadne with him embarked in such haste that he forgot to change the sails. Thus his father, watching from afar, thought Theseus dead and threw himself into the Aegean sea. The-seus (the god Zeus? Jesus?) is a Saviour who seems to die but survives death. He overcomes the Minotaur (his animal passions) by Ariadne's thread of memory—he remembers who he is and whence he came. Greek Ariadne, as we have seen, is Celtic Arianrhod, her maze on the Tor a spiral or Turning Castle that reflects the revolving stars. Minos has already been equated with Menu or Noah, who brought these Atlantean myths from Britain. (He was one of the sages who entered the Ark.) Only in Britain does this *"Greek"* tale reveal itself as star-myth. Man lost in Life's maze, finding his way out through experience, memory—increasing self-knowledge—consciousness.

These are but a few of the *"Greek"* myths which can be traced back to the Zodiac, and not just any Zodiac, but specifically to the British circle of sleeping Titans. There are many more. Of such stuff was the wisdom of the Hyperboreans, which so awed the Greeks.

Scholars' long-maintained vagueness about the whereabouts of the land of the Hyperboreans can only be described as perverse. Greek Hecateus, c. 400 B.C., knew where it was. Here is his account, quoted by Diodorus of Sicily.

"Opposite to the coast of Celtic Gaul, there is an island in the ocean, not smaller than Sicily, lying to the north, which is inhabited by the Hyperboreans, who are so named because they dwell beyond the north wind. This island is of a happy temperature, rich in soil, and fruitful in everything, yielding its produce twice in the year.

Tradition says that Latona (Apollo's mother) was born there, and for that reason the inhabitants venerate Apollo more than any other god. They are, in a manner, his priests, for they daily celebrate him with abundant honours.

In this island, there is a magnificent grove of Apollo, and a remarkable temple, of a round form, adorned with many consecrated gifts. There is also a city sacred to the same God, most of whose inhabitants are harpers, who continually play upon their harps in the temple, and sing hymns to the God, extolling his actions.

The Hyperboreans use a peculiar dialect, and have a remarkable attachment to the Greeks, especially to the Athenians and the Delians, deducing their friendship from remote periods. It is related that some Greeks formerly visited the Hyperboreans, with whom they left consecrated gifts, and also that in ancient times, Abaris, coming from the Hyperboreans, into Greece, renewed their friendship (family intercourse) with the Delians.

It is also said that, in this island, the moon appears very near to the earth, that certain eminences, of a terrestrial form, are plainly seen in it; that the God visits the island once in the course of nineteen years, in which period the stars complete their revolutions, and that for this reason, the Greeks distinguish the cycle of nineteen years, by the name of the great year.

During the season of his appearance, the God plays upon the harp, and dances every night, from the vernal equinox to the rising of the Pleiades, pleased with his own successes.

The supreme authority in that city and sacred precinct is vested in those who are called Boreadae, being the descendants of Boreas, and their governments have been uninterruptedly transmitted in this line."

Where can this be but Britain, opposite the coast of Gaul? Diodorus Siculos clinches it by referring elsewhere to Britain as similar in shape to Sicily.

Clearly Hecateus credits Britain with being the source of important discoveries in Greek astronomy; clearly Apollo's mother was a Somerset lass, and thus Apollo himself had British origins. His name gives him away; he is Avallach, god of Avalon's apple orchards.

The *"remarkable round temple"* of Hecateus' account may be our Zodiac, or Stonehenge—perhaps both. Amesbury is listed in the Celtic Triads as one of the Perpetual Choirs of Britain, where bards like Hecateus' harpers played and sang continuously. But Gwyn ap Nudd, lord of Glastonbury Tor, was one of the *"Three Happy Astronomers of Britain"*, so his astronomical circle may also have been meant.

Did the Hyperboreans have telescopes? If not, why should the moon be seen here so large and clear? Glastonbury glass is known from the Lake villages of the 3rd. century B.C.—perhaps the Druids knew the secret of it earlier still. They were famous astronomers, and a Triad enumerating the **Secrets of Britain** includes *"the speculum of the son of pervading glance."* The Phoenicians, they say, invented glass.

There was more intercourse between East and West than is generally assumed. The inhabitants of Babylon, says Antoninus Liberalis, often visited the temple of Apollo in the land of the Hyperboreans. Hercules went from Greece to the Hyperboreans by way of Illyria and the river Po, says Apollodorus. From Greece this is a bee-line for Britain. He also visited the Hesperides, lured by its Apples of wisdom, as we have seen. The land of the Hyperboreans and the Garden of the Hesperides are one and the same. The wisdom for which both were famed inspired Pythagoras, and must therefore have had a profound influence on classical Greece. Herodotus and other writers say Abaris the Hyperborean travelled to Greece by means of his arrow or wheatstraw (the first compasses were so made) to converse with Pythagoras, then visited Egypt with him. Abaris must have been a Druid from Avebury—both names mean *"the holy one"*.

20: Brutus of Troy and Gogmagog

One indication of an ancient "*Hyperborean*" civilisation here is that there was in Britain a comprehensive road-system long before the Romans came; the Roman armies did not make them, they simply metalled them. The Watling Street and the Fosse Way already traversed the land in opposed diagonals like a St. Andrew's cross; a third track from the Hampshire coast at Christchurch northward to Avebury proclaims its pre-Roman pedigree in no uncertain terms, for the *"ring"* of Ringwood, Old Sarum, Stonehenge, Casterley camp and the vanished circle of Marden are strung upon it like beads. Place a ruler along these places—it becomes clear that the Romans were not the first to draw straight lines on the grand scale. The London to Bath road is also clearly pre-Roman, witness Silbury Hill and Merlin's Mound at Marlborough. A study of the mounds, ponds, fords and hill-notches that mark these ancient leys leaves one staggered by their number and design; the work that Watkins did for the country round Hereford in his book *"The Old Straight Track"* could be repeated in any other shire. The astonishing grid-system he has revealed acquires further complexity in the work of Sir Norman Lockyer, who maintains that these roads were not simply means of going from place to place, but were carefully aligned on important stars at their rising or setting points, or to mark summer and winter solstice positions of the sun. E. O. Gordon in *"Prehistoric London"* has shown many such alignments in the straight roads in and round London which she claims were viewed from the city's ancient mounds.

If all Britain was indeed laid out on an astronomical system, as the stone circles certainly seem to have been, the concept of an earth-Zodiac seems at once to change from an *"inherently improbable"* one to an inevitability. We may even expect to find others at nodal points. In fact the position of the Glastonbury Zodiac—a circle contained within the angle of two ancient tracks, (the Shepton Mallet—Glastonbury road and the Fosse Way) is repeated exactly in another Zodiac I have found at Kingston on-Thames. Here the two tracks are the London-Epsom Stane Street and the London-Staines road, both regarded as *"Roman"* roads. A remarkably similar arrangement occurs at a third possible Zodiac centred on Nuthampstead, found by Nigel Pennick.

Can it be coincidence that all three sites preserve memories of Gog and Magog near the angle at which the roads containing these Zodiacs meet? The GogMagog Hills of Cambridge are just north-east of the Nuthampstead circle; the two famous Guildhall giants are north-east of the Kingston Zodiac; two ancient oaks, Gog and Magog, are to be found just north-east of Glastonbury Tor. No, it is surely no accident; for T. C. Lethbridge, who found strange turf-cut figures on the GogMagog Hills, identified them with the sun and moon, chief deities in the old solar cult, whose path through the heavens is the Zodiac.

The sun and moon must have been known and worshipped under these titles all over Britain in very early times, for the name Goemagot's Leap remembers the giant who was pushed over a cliff near Plymouth by Brutus' lieutenant Corineus in 1100 B.C. (Two giants were cut in the rock of Plymouth Hoe in prehistoric times and only disappeared about four centuries ago.) From east to west, ancient Britons were very conscious of the cynosure of these *"goggling"* heavenly eyes watching them by day and night; we can see how they felt about them when we look at the *"spectacles"* of the Cerne Abbas Giant and Lethbridge's Mother Goddess on the Cambridge Hills.

But Magog in Genesis was the son of Japhet and grandson of Noah. Gog prince of the land of Magog also appears in Ezekial as a powerful military threat to Israel from the north. The incidence of these strange names in Britain and the Biblical East constitutes a mystery, which used to be explained by assuming that Bible-reading Britons transferred the fascinating syllables to their hills, hoary oaks, processional giants, or anything else that took their fancy. Is it not far more likely that Gog and Magog were names for the sun and moon in the old universal religion of both east and west? Is it not more probable that the grandson of Noah took his name from the earth and moon-mother, and that Ezekial's Gog of the land of Magog took his title from the sun, as so many kings have done?

Universal though the early sun and star religion may have been, the names by which these luminaries were known varied enormously with time and distance; Gog and Magog, bestriding the world from east to west like a giant rainbow, would seem to imply a single human agency—like a migrating tribe—to keep their names intact over such an arc.

Strabo uses the word *"Gogarene"* to describe Armenia, the traditional resting-place of Noah's ark, and the Magog of Genesis has some interesting brothers; Madai for instance, eponymous ancestor of the Medes, Javan, progenitor of the Ionians—but above all, Gomer of the Gomerians who became the wandering Cimmerians and at last the Cymry of Wales. Great historians, the Welsh, with a sense of their past only comparable with that of the Jews. The county of *Montgomery* still remembers their founding father; who then if not this people, brought Gog and Magog to Britain?

If the relationship between Asia Minor and Britain be so well attested back in these early times, need we any longer regard the coming of Brutus, grandson of Aeneas of Troy, to these shores as *"legendary"*? It looks as if the tale may have a basis in fact, and deserves to regain the place in history books it enjoyed in Shakespeare's time. It is recorded as early as 800 A.D. by the historian Nennius, who in turn quoted from *"ancient books of our ancestors"*, now alas no longer extant.

Brutus it seems landed at Totnes about 1100 B.C., rather more than a century after the fall of Troy, having embarked from Italy, where his grandfather Aeneas had become king. At Totnes they will still shew you the Brutus Stone in the main street, and quote you Brutus' delightful couplet delivered on his arrival—*"Yer I be and yer I rest, and this yer place shall be called Totnes!"*

Whether there ever was such a person as Brutus, whether he was the first crowned king of Britain, is of course debatable. But as a personification of early migrations from the Dardanelles and even further east, he is more than probable; the name Brutus certainly occurs in the Trojan or Etruscan noble families of Rome. Scottish kings kept it too, in forms like Prwt and Bruce. In essence he existed, if not in cold fact.

Geoffrey of Monmouth set down his advent in his *"History of the Kings of Britain"* with such corroborative detail that he might have been an eye-witness, and for this he has been castigated as a liar by modern historians. Is this judgement not flat-footed pedantry? The English, unable to follow the arched flight of bardic style, have always called the Welsh liars—Teutonic Greeks called the Cretans liars for the same reason. Homer was just such a *"liar"*; nobody took the existence of Troy as history a century ago—until Schliemann embarrassed them all by digging it up. But Schliemann loved Homer; (a copy of the Iliad was always in his pocket). Without love nothing can be found, and to read Geoffrey of Monmouth with contempt is fruitless. Is is not more constructive to regard him as the Homer of British prehistory? He is a superb stylist, far more readable than most modern historians, and if read with understanding will unearth for us many a rare pearl of true tradition.

One of these pearls—a jewel indeed to Zodiac students—is the prophecy which he records as directing Brutus to Britain, uttered by the Sybil of Cumae.

> *"Brute,—past the realms of Gaul, beneath the sunset*
> *Lieth an Island, girt about by ocean,*
> *Guarded by ocean—erst the haunt of giants,*
> *Desert of late, and meet for this thy people.*
> *Seek it. For there is thine abode for ever;*
> *There by thy sons shall Troy again be builded;*
> *There of thy blood shall Kings be born, hereafter*
> *Sovran in every land the wide world over."*

Milton (who knew a great deal about ancient Britain) said of this poem *"The verses, originally Greek, were put in Latin (saith Virunnius) by Gildas, a British poet; and him to have liv'd under Claudius."*

When Brutus reached Britain however, it was not entirely free of giants; according to Geoffrey he had to overcome many of them. Their leader,

Goemagot, was finally thrown over that cliff which is called to this day Goemagot's leap near Plymouth.

But Goemagot can only be GogMagog, the giant or giants always associated as we have seen with a terrestrial Zodiac; if this poem was originally Greek as Milton asserts, it certainly seems that the Giants of the British Zodiac were known to the oracle who inspired Brutus. It was a true inspiration in other ways; Troy *was* builded here, for the old name for London was Trinovantes—New Troy—and its inhabitants bore the tribal name of Trinobantes. The kings born of this Trojan blood have indeed been *"sovran in every land, the wide world over."*

Troy is said to have been built in concentric rings; is it not interesting then to find so many of our ancient mazes are called *"Troy-Towns"*? One at Somerton, Oxfordshire is on a site said to have been founded by Brutus' wise men or magi; a Sumer-town indeed. Here, according to tradition, was the origin of Oxford University, later refounded a little further down-river by the Pheryllt, a Druidic order of metal-working alchemists. The river, be it noted, bore the holy name of Tam-Isis, mother-goddess of the Mysteries—and it is surely no coincidence that Oxford has one of the few carved Zodiacs in England (in Merton College). The seat of learning was founded here because it was the centre of the country; well-founded, for it is still the first university in the world.

Troy was known poetically as Holy Ilium; the ilium or ileum is part of the pelvis, upon which man stands erect. Ilium was the pelvis or cradle of subsequent civilizations, the port from which the new world set out. The sack of Troy was the Phoenix-pyre of the old world from whose flames the new world was reborn; the Phoenicians, sailing to found new civilisations, were not named so for nothing. Troy was not only history—it was more; it was myth. Not myth in the debased modern sense, but in the sense in which the *ancient* used the word—eternal truth. If the Phoenicians were conscious of their role as Olympic runners, bearing civilization's torch to the ends of the earth, so no less was Brutus. Geoffrey of Monmouth wrote the ancient *myth of Britain—more important, more conscious, than the mere facts of history*; nor did he invent it, for it was here millenia before his time. His great contribution was to show ourselves to ourselves—to externalise and express the subliminal—and all England rose to acclaim him.

Brutus then was the Rod of Jesse, the spine of homo erectus growing from the evolutionary womb of Holy Ilium; but if Brutus was the shoot, Arthur and his Round Table Chivalry was the Flower, the Head. Under Bishop Geoffrey's careful nursing, that flower, long folded in the stem, budded and bloomed—filling all Europe with its scent.

Indeed, all Europe claimed to descend from one or other of the sons of Troy. Romans regarded Aeneas as their ancestor; the Parisii who founded Paris remembered Priam's son; (the city still exhibits Paris's weakness for

Helen). Troyes, further up the Seine, was founded by the Tricassi—surely the Cassi from Troy?

To keep *troth* with Troy, vanished city of *truth,* was the aim of all the old western bards who kept the myth alive. Trojan Law was True Law, Troy Weight (only used for precious metals) True Measure, the foundation of trust between Celt and eastern metal-trader, and a reminder of their essential relationship. Troy-towns, mazes built on the legendary pattern of Troy, enshrined True Philosophy, being built all over Europe to remind man of his true origins and encourage him to thread the maze of life (and the maze of his own unconscious) like a Trojan if he would find Truth.

So entrenched was the Maze-habit that the Christian Church adopted it and enjoined the threading of the labyrinthine paths as a Lenten penance; even laying out mazes on cathedral floors, as at Lucca and Chartres.

Though they were often laid out on flat village greens, the first mazes (like the great maze in the terracing of Glastonbury Tor) were designed on hills, thus serving both religion and military defence. *"Home"* was thus on the hill-top, a place of illumination and safety.

True Law must be inspired, and therefore had to be received (and given forth to men) from a mount; a mountain is the outward symbol of that state of objective detachment from human affairs necessary for true judgement. The moral laws we still live by, from both Old Testament and New, were given from a mount.

Where ancient settlements lacked a natural hill an artificial one was piled up; our country is full of these *"tons"*—literally tons of earth. The word *"town"* derives from them, for they not only marked the crossings of ancient leys or roads, but were used for assembly, free speech, eisteddfod, law-giving. Often law-courts or old prison cells are still found beneath them, as at Oxford and Cambridge. Many Norman motte-and-bailey castles were built upon these far more ancient Mottes or meeting-places, thus effectively depriving the citizens of their ancient right of free-speech upon them, and seizing the seat of law.

Alas for inspiration! For this was the essential quality invoked in all such ancient assemblies, hence the names Whit, Wych and Wick so often found on or near them. The name Week, another variation, remembers the Phoenician festival of Pentecost, or Weeks. (Seven days—seven steps up the mound to perfection.) Often there is a Plough or Seven Stars inn at their base, as at Totnes, Newton Abbot and Whitechapel, London. For to the ancients these seven stars of the Plough signified the Seven Days or Words of Creation—the Logos at work. (It is no accident that these seven Plough-stars fall on the Logos-Dove of our Zodiac at Barton St. David.) A beautifully drawn Dove also encircles Newton Abbot's High Weeke, outlined by roads, and by this and other signs visible on the map I suspect another Zodiac here. But that is another story . . .

Kevin Kingsland, founder of the Community who published this book, was born on the crest of Newton Abbot's High Week! These Whit-mounds once quickened bards to prophecy; *"Trojan"* seership was a valued way of keeping in line with the true path of evolution.

Pwyll in the Maginogion ascended the Mound of Arberth to find a wonder, and was not disappointed; he who spends a night on Cader Idris will be found in the morning either dead, mad, or inspired. A risky business!

"There are certain persons in Cambria," says 12th century Geraldus Cambrensis, *"whom you will find nowhere else, called Awenyddion, or people inspired; when asked about any doubtful event they roar out violently, becoming as it were possessed by a spirit. They do not answer connectedly, but a skilful observer can discover the answer in spite of their incoherence. They must then be roused from their ecstasy as from a deep sleep, and compelled by violence to return to their senses; they do not recover until violently shaken by other people, nor can they remember the replies they gave . . . They invoke in their prophecies the true and living God and the Holy Trinity, praying that their sins may not prevent them from finding the truth. These prophets are found only among those Britons who are descended from the Trojans."*

The *"Awenyddion"* are the people inspired by the Awen, or Holy Spirit. If we are asked then how such a huge and invisible design as the Zodiac was discovered, may we not reasonably answer *"By clairvoyance"?*

Nor has this prophetic strain died out.

'OWL-FACES' AND CHALK-CUT FIGURES

T. C. LETHBRIDGE found the Moon Goddess Magog on the Gogmagog Hills, Cambridge. She rides a horse who is drawing a chariot. Compare her 'spectacles' with the decorated stone (below) of c. 6000 B.C. from the Marne Valley and the outlined horse with the White Horse of Uffington (top right). Is she Arianrhod with her "toilsome chair" (see p. 94) or chariot, and Turning Wheel? Is the chariot the square of Ursa Minor. And is the hen-headed horse she rides Ceridwen 'night-mare'? And the 'Brood Hen'?

TROY TOWN MAZE

21: The Zodiac in Celtic Poetry

Do not expect to find the words Glastonbury Zodiac writ large and clear across Celtic poetry and myth. The Mysteries were always kept secret. This was not due entirely to the jealous priesthood who guarded them, but partly due to the abstract and abstruse nature of such studies, which appealed to few. Those who seek them can always find, now as of yore.

Religious persecution gave another pressing reason for secrecy; Rome against the Druids, Rome against early Christians, the Roman Church against the British Celtic Church, compelled caution. But a secret can be kept too close; in times of invasion, carnage, mass-migration, it could easily be lost for ever. It had to be preserved and passed down in cryptic utterances which would be dismissed by those not in the know as gibberish. And there *are* many allusions to the Zodiac of this nature in Celtic myth and poetry which have floored successive oppressors, and even Celtic scholars up to our own day, which can only be illumined in the light of Katharine Maltwood's discovery of the Avalon Zodiac.

Heresy was to become an increasingly dangerous word—yet it was not in the Druid's vocabulary. Such a concept was foreign to a philosophy which valued the fruits of the Awen so highly. The authoritative dogma of Roman Christians was an intolerable strait-jacket to the bard whose Christianity was a re-statement of the older Mysteries; he could be racked for seeing Jesus as Dionysus, though both were said to be born at the winter solstice, both instituted a similar ritual meal of bread and wine, both rose from the dead. The Virgin, he was forcibly told, had nothing to do with Isis or Ceridwen. Yet Christian bards still dared to extol her Cauldron in the 1200's; *"Flowing is my bardic lay . . . a smoothness produced from the Cauldron of the Awen"* sang Elidyr Sais; his contemporary Llewarch ap Llewellyn agreed: *"Duw Dovydd gives me a ray of melodious song from the Cauldron of Ceridwen."*

Beaten and disbanded, they had their beautiful revenge; from the Cauldron they made the Chalice and Grail Christianity.

Taliesin as we have already seen made many cryptic allusions to the Giants. He even identified himself with the Gemini Babe in his boat; but to understand this or make Zodiacal sense of his poetry we must re-examine his story, already briefly told, at greater length.

The Tale of Taliesin

Ceridwen, the great Celtic Nature-Goddess, gave birth to a child so ill-favoured that she called him Avagddu—Black-Wings, Night, or Chaos. Wishing to compensate him for this misfortune she decided that if he couldn't have beauty, he should at least have brains. She therefore determined, so says the Book of Taliesin, *"agreeably to the Mysteries of the Pheryllt, to prepare for her son a cauldron of water of inspiration and knowledge. In the meantime Ceridwen, with due attention to the books of astronomy, and to the hours of the planets, employed herself daily in collecting plants of every species which preserved any rare virtue"*—and while she was botanising set little Gwion, son of the blacksmith of Llanfair Caereinion, to stir the potent brew for a year and a day, while blind Morda fed the fire.

But the essence of this concoction flew out as three drops, scalding little Gwion's finger. He promptly licked it—and was at once inspired. All the virtue of the brew was contained in these three drops; the rest was deadly poison, only fit to be thrown away. Gwion, who now knew all things, realised that he like Jacob had stolen the blessing intended for the eldest son, and that Ceridwen would be revenged. Indeed, she soon pursued him, first striking out Morda's only eye.

He fled through three elements, becoming by his new-found arts a hare, a fish, a bird; but she chased him as a greyhound, an otter, a hawk. At last in desperation he took the form of a grain of wheat, one of thousands on a threshing-floor; unwisely—for the harvest-goddess knew every grain. Turning herself into a great black crested hen she unerringly picked him out (in the older poem quoted earlier she became a mare and a ship). Either way she swallowed him. And that, you might think, was that. Not a bit of it. Nine months later she bore him, her second son. This was the moment she had been waiting for; the helpless babe was completely at her mercy. But when she looked upon him, such was his beauty that she hadn't the heart to strangle him, so packing him into a leather bag, (some versions say a coracle) she threw him into the sea.

Floating to the weir of Gwyddno Garanhir on May-Day, he was fished up like an old boot by Gwyddno's son Elphin, a prince marked by ill-fortune. Poor Elphin was being tested by fishing here, for the May-Day catch at the weir was known to be plentiful—if he couldn't catch a fish then, he couldn't catch anything. It looked as if the ill-starred prince had failed once more. Nevertheless, he ceremoniously named him Taliesin, and despite the jeers, took him home with him.

The babe rewarded him with a long poem from the saddle-bow, promising him luck. *"I have been loquacious before being gifted with speech"* as Taliesin says of himself.

(Chaldea had a similar Creation-myth in which the primaeval mother-goddess produced an ugly son Mummu *"Chaos"*. However, from Mummu came forth Lakhmu, *"Light"* or the *"Logos"* who corresponds to little Gwion or Taliesin Radiant-Brow.)

Gwion, at first sight of humble origins, was not such a nobody as all that. His father the blacksmith was obviously one of the Pheryllt, a Druidic order of metal-working alchemists from whose divine recipe Ceridwen made her inspirational brew.

So what does this myth mean? Is it just an ancient Creation-story, brought by Phoenicians from Chaldea? Or taken from Britain to Mesopotamia? Whichever way it was, it has complex meanings which repay meditation.

It is obviously also an Initiation-myth, witness the candidate's three births before he could become the Master-Bard Taliesin—a feat he achieved in the teeth of the vengeful Nature-Mother Ceridwen; his hazardous births repeated by three hair-breadth escapes from pursuit.

"The Cauldron will not boil food for a coward," says Taliesin.

As all this, we are told, took place *"in the time of Arthur's Round Table"* we may confidently assume that it took place within it—that is, in our Zodiac—an assumption strengthened by the blind man Morda (Mordred the Death-Scorpion?) whose one eye Ceridwen struck out. The effigies are one-eyed, being drawn in profile. Was Morda's task not to feed the flames of knowledge? The cauldron burst after the three inspirational drops flew out and its contents flowed into the weir of Gwyddno, poisoning his horses. It was from this same weir that Taliesin was fished out. Is this not a hint that mere knowledge, unlit by inspiration and imagination, is more dangerous than ignorance?

As a Creation-Myth, it may also indicate that all created things have failed their purpose unless they can generate the three divine drops of Consciousness. These Three drops drip from the Lance in the Grail procession too.

But Taliesin's tale is not finished. True to his infantile prophecy, he changed Elphin's fortunes by making his court famous for bardism. But Elphin (who must have been the elfin prince of fairyland) boasted of his bards and was imprisoned by the jealous king of North Wales, with a silver chain about his feet like Gwair, till he could make good his boast. Taliesin then proposed a contest between the North Welsh bards and himself, with Elphin as prize.

He made a poem of the Zodiac, which confounded his opponents and has never been understood since, until Mrs. Maltwood discovered its source. The poem identifies him with the Geminian Babe in the Coracle, shewing the Zodiac as the source of all myths across the ancient world. His very name shews its universality: *"Tal"* means *"tall, high place"*, in Wales and Syria. Medea killed Talus the sun-god just as Ceridwen *"killed"* Taliesin.

Here, with suggested interpretation, is the poem, the *"Hanes Taliesin"*, which secured Elphin's release.

Primary chief bard am I to Elphin, and my original country is the land of the summer stars. (Or *"land of the Cherubim".* Somerset's summerland, Gemini being in the summer stars)
Johannes the Diviner I was called by Merddin (Merlin = the rough forerunner = Capricorn natural, unregenerate man)
Now every king shall call me Taliesin. (Thrice-reborn, perfected man—Jesus)
Nine months was I in the belly of the hag Ceridwen
At first I was little Gwion—at length I am Taliesin.
I was with my Lord in the highest sphere (Gemini rises as Scorpio sets)
On the fall of Lucifer into the depths of Hell.
I have borne a banner before Alexander (A for Alexander, who, says Herodotus, saw this A (Alpha or Awen) on the breastplate of the High Priest who foretold his conquests. It was thus his *"banner".*)
I know the names of the stars from north to south (Idris, "One of the Three Happy Astronomers" is also Gemini)
I have been on the Galaxy at the throne of the Distributor;
I was in Canaan when Absolom was slain, (Gemini in Sol's Ship. Absolom, "son of the Sun", also hung on a tree)
I conveyed the Awen down to the Vale of Hebron
I was in the court of Don before the birth of Gwydion. (Dundon—Fort of Wisdom)
I was instructor to Eli and Enoch (Our Zodiac, there before the Flood, inspiring seers)
I have been winged by the splendid genius of the crozier. (Dove of St. David Celtic Bishop of Wales)
I have been loquacious before I was gifted with speech; (The babe Taliesin)
I was at the place of crucifixion of the merciful Son of God. (Gemini's Jesus)
I have been three periods in the prison of Arianrhod, (Initiate's three deaths)
I have been chief director of the work of the tower of Nimrod (Tower of Babel, Nimrod, Gilgamesh the Master-mason)
I am a wonder whose origin is not known. (Our Zodiac)
I have been in Asia with Noah in the Ark (Welsh Menu, Egyptian Menes, Cretan Minos)
I have witnessed the destruction of Sodom and Gomorrah (Lot, whose name in Celtic meant Light-god, disperser of evil)
I have been in India when Rome was built; (Alexander? Or a reference to the Trojan Cymry from "Deffrobane", which some thought was Ceylon?)
I am now come here to the remnant of Troy. (Trojans in Britain)
I have been with my Lord in the Manger of the Ass (Asella and Manger stars in Cancer, the boat)
I have strengthened Moses through the waters of Jordan; (Taurus. Moses was called "Two-Horned". He too was a Babe in a Boat)
I have been in the firmament with Mary Magdalen (The three Marys, Virgo's triple star-goddess)

I have obtained the Muse from the Cauldron of Ceredwen;
I have been Bard of the harp to Lleon of Lochlin (Loch Lleon, sunken Lyonesse?)
I have been on the White Hill, in the court of Cynvelyn (Cymbeline's Tower Hill, London, where Bran's inspirational head was buried; it replaced the cauldron)
I have suffered hunger for the Son of the Virgin, (The Mabon, son of Modron the Mother, was also imprisoned)
I have been fostered in the land of the Deity (Britain's star-land, holy land before the Holy Land)
I have been teacher to all intelligences (Awen or Logos, streaming from the
I am able to instruct the whole universe Dove's beak down the ship's masts as three bars of light or broad arrow)
I shall be until the day of doom on the face of the earth,
And it is not known whether my body is flesh or fish (Turtle-dove or turtle?)

I was for nine months in the belly of the hag Ceredwen
I was first little Gwion — now at last I am Taliesin

There is more to say than these brief notes on almost every line of this extraordinary and abstruse riddle. But the most frequently recurring answer certainly seems to be the enigmatic Gemini Babe in his boat—Taliesin himself in his coracle, inspired by the Awen and thus able to *"instruct the whole universe"*. On the vexed question of whether his body was flesh or fish, the turtle-dove is not the only solution, for Gemini inspired the Arthurian story of the Fisher-King, not only a Fisher of Men, but fishing in his own unconscious depths for the Salmon of Wisdom.

Well might Taliesin ask whether the knowledge he brings out of these sea-depths is fish or flesh. It was *himself* that was fished from the weir of Gwyddno at his third rebirth; was he then flesh or fish?

His second rebirth from the belly of Ceredwen is also in a sense from the sea, for elsewhere Taliesin asks *"Who drew Jonas out of the belly of Cedd?"* Cedd or Ceredwen's cauldron is often seen as the deep. Jonah in the whale was according to Taliesin demonstrating the same idea: Idea diving into sceptical ignorant matter, to bring it to form and life, and suffering derision and even death for its pains.

The *"waters of Jordan"* also represent this sea of death and rebirth, through which the Israelites passed to the promised land. It was Joshua (Hebrew for Jesus) who led them through, not Moses, as Taliesin well knew. Moses, whose Taurean strength, faith and patience had led his people to its brink, was not allowed to pass through its waters, but like Taurus, had to remain on the hill above.

Taliesin shews that in the poetic language of the Zodiac, the *"language of correspondences"*, his own Geminian sign pictorially represents the birth, baptism, death and rebirth of the Christian's God, and that this pattern is also demonstrated in preceding events, historical or mythological. And, because it *is* a pattern, it applies equally to his own life and to that of all initiates who walk in the path set for Man by Evolution.

There are two versions of the Hanes Taliesin in Graves' *"White Goddess"*, and it is useful to compare them, as they are mutually illuminating. The other version ends—

> *"I have been instructed in the whole system of the universe;*
> *I shall be till the day of judgement on the face of the earth.*
> *I have been in an uneasy chair above Caer Sidin*
> *Whirling round without motion between three elements.*
> *Is it not a wonder that cannot be discovered?"*

Where is this mysterious castle, where one may whirl round without motion, eternally imbibing omniscient wisdom?

Where but our Zodiac, whirling with the earth yet apparently still, where one may hover between earth air and water, one's head among the stars of heaven, one's feet on the conical Tor of the Temple of the Stars, absorbing the whole system of the universe there offered?

Edward Davies, writing before this Zodiac was discovered, affirms that *"Caer Sidi implied in the first place the ark; secondly, the circle of the Zodiac in which the luminous emblems of sun, moon and planets revolved; and thirdly, the sanctuary of the British Ceres, which represented both ark and Zodiac."* It was called *Cylch bid*—the earthy circle, also *Cylch balch Nevwy*—The magnificent celestial circle.

It was at once the starry world of spirits and an earthy prison, its reflection, in which Man, lost and imprisoned in its fleshly maze, must work out his salvation, helped by the sun-Saviour who descends at great cost to Himself to nourish him with wisdom from Ceridwen's Cauldron.

This is the theme of Taliesin's next poem, *"Preiddu Annwn"*. Here Arthur acts the Saviour lowered in his glass ship Prydwen into Annwn to rescue both Gweir (Man) and the Cauldron. But as Gwyr means "truth" we can also see Arthur as the initiate, plumbing his own depths and finding the truth in the Cauldron of the Unconscious. A tale of the Harrowing of Hell (Annwn), it must remember the pre-Christian Cabiric Mysteries of Avalon. Arthur here plays Taliesin's part, Gweir or Gwair the part of Elphin, also in chains. Then as now, few indeed return from this adventure unscathed.

Preiddu Annwn

Praise to the Lord, Supreme Ruler of the high region,
Who hath extended his dominion to the shore of the world.
Complete was the prison of Gweir in Caer Sidi.   (Man in the Universe)
Through the permission of Pwyll and Pryderi   (Lords of the Underworld)
No-one before him went into it:
A heavy blue chain firmly held the youth   (earth's atmosphere?)
And for the spoils of Annwn gloomily he sighs
And till doom shall he continue his lay
Thrice the fullness of Prydwen we went into it   (Arthur's ship)
Except seven, none returned from Caer Sidi.

Am I not a candidate for fame, to be heard in the song,
In Caer Pedryvan four times revolving!   (Castle of four quarters—the earth)
It will be my first word from the cauldron when it expresses,
By the breath of nine damsels it is gently warmed   (Nine Muses)
Is it not the cauldron of the chief of Annwn in its fashion?
— With a ridge round its edge of pearls!
It will not boil the food of a coward
A sword bright-flashing to him will be brought
And left in the hand of Lleminawg.   (Lew the sun-god, later Lancelot)
And before the portals of Hell, the horns of light shall be burning,
And when we went with Arthur in his splendid labours,
Except seven, none returned from Caer Vediwid.   (Castle of the perfected)

Am I not a candidate for fame, to be heard in the song,
In the quadrangular enclosure, in the island of the strong door,
Where the twilight and the jet of night moved together
Bright wine was the beverage of the host —
Three times the fullness of Prydwen, we went on sea:
Except seven, none returned from Caer Rigor.   (The Death-king's Castle)

I will not have merit with the multitude in relating the hero's deeds,
Beyond Caer Wydr they beheld not the progress of Arthur   (Glass castle, Tor)
Three times twenty-hundred men stood on the wall,
It was difficult to converse with their sentinel.
Three times the fullness of Prydwen, we went with Arthur,
Except seven, none returned from Caer Colur.   (Twilight or gloomy castle where night and day divide—rebirth)

I will not have merit from the multitude with trailing shields,
They know not on what day, or who caused it,
Nor what hour in the splendid day Cwy was born,   (Kay? A sun-god like Arthur)
Nor who prevented him from going to the valleys of Devwy   (They were too deep for the sun to penetrate)
They know not the brindled ox, with his thick headband,

And seven-score knobs on his collar.   (Taurus garlanded with the Pleiades)
And when we went with Arthur of mournful memory,
Except seven, none returned from Caer Vandwy.   (Castle of the God-man)

I will not have merit from men of drooping courage   (Cowards who dare
                                        not be initiated into calendar mysteries)
They know not on what day the chief arose
Nor what hour in the splendid day he who owns all was born   (Winter
                                                                         Solstice)
What animal they keep of silver head;   (White Bull, Taurus, led the year)
Except seven, none returned from Caer Ochren. (Steep-sided Castle—the Tor)
Monks pack together like dogs in the choir
From their meetings with their witches;
Is there but one course to the wind, one to the water of the sea
Is there but one spark to the fire of the unbounded tumult?
Monks pack together like wolves,
From their meetings with their witches.
They know not when the twilight and the dawn divide,
Nor what the course of the wind, nor who agitates it,
In what place it dies, on what region it roars.
The grave of the saint is vanishing from the foot of the altar.
I will pray to the Lord, the great Supreme,
That I be not wretched—may Christ be my portion.

    What saint lay forgotten at the foot of the altar? Undoubtedly Arthur, whose tomb in front of Glastonbury Abbey's altar is still to be seen. But it is apparent that this Arthur is not a historical character, being in the poem identified with Christ and other god-like Saviours of the Mysteries such as Theseus, Dionysus, Orpheus, Hercules, Osiris, or the Irish Cuchulain, who harrow Hell. Such an Arthur could never be pent in an earthy grave, as Taliesin well knew, though like the sun, he may seem to die. Did not the ancient Celtic *"Song of the Graves"* say mysteriously *"Unwise the thought, a grave for Arthur"*? Arthur O'Bower in Scotland is also the wind *"roaring up the land"*.

    But the sun-hero or god-man's *ritual* death and rebirth is the burden of the whole poem. It is this *"death"* that causes the twilight and the dawn to divide, the rebirth at the winter solstice that caused the *"splendid day"* of rejoicing and the calendar feast of May-day with its Taurean bull crowned with silver May, that the poet is remembering. He taunts the monks of his day with culpable ignorance about the very origins and meaning of their religion, lamenting its divorce from scientific knowledge. Prophetically he foresees that their literal, historical understanding of the Christian Mysteries will rob religion of the support of natural science, and of all other myths not specifically Christian, to the impoverishment of both, and that henceforth science will be forced into separate and secular paths. Did he foresee the dangers to civilization from such a course, dangers to which we are now heir?

Our next poem, the *"Cad Goddeu"* or Battle of the Trees, is a long catalogue of the Druidic tree-alphabet, and, Davies remarks, must record a great battle not with weapons but with words. *"A grievous combat at the root of the tongue"*, Taliesin calls it. This long, rambling and curiously jumbled effusion is given, and expounded, in Graves' *"White Goddess"*, so I shall only quote here one or two fragments which have bearing on the Zodiac. It was undoubtedly for the possession of its secret that this *"battle"* was fought, for every now and then Taliesin breaks off his seedsmen's catalogue to drop a hint about the nature of the secret.

> *"Better are three in unison*
> *And enjoying themselves in a circle*
> *And one of them relating*
> *The story of the Deluge*
> *And of the cross of Christ*
> *And of the Day of Judgement near at hand."*

If this is not the Trinity of our circle, with the emphasis as always on the Gemini figure, then what else can it be? If there were any doubt, Taliesin ends his riddle with the same theme.

> *"Learned Druids,*
> *Prophesy ye of Arthur?*
> *Or is it me they celebrate,*
> *And the crucifixion of Christ,*
> *And the Day of Judgement near at hand,*
> *And one relating the history of the Deluge?"*

Without the Glastonbury Zodiac and its babe in his boat who is at once Christ, Noah and Taliesin, these verses are incomprehensible. With it, they become crystal clear. Mrs. Maltwood has solved the age-long riddle of the bards, about which so many scholars have scratched their learned heads in vain. *"Many an attitude undergoes the form of his body, in reading the trees"*, as the bard Gwilym Ddu delightfully puts it.

Celtic poetry is not easy reading, but its rewards are rich. It is salutary to remember the words of William Blake, another British Bard.

"You say that I want somebody to elucidate my Ideas. But you ought to know that what is Grand is necessarily obscure to Weak Men. That which can be made explicit to the Idiot is not worth my care. The wisest of the Ancients consider'd what is not too Explicit as the fittest for Instruction, because it rouzes the Faculties to act."

Another poem of Taliesin's shows that Druid knowledge concerned itself with such questions as:

"At what time, and to what extent, will land be productive?"   (Agriculture, ecology)

"What is the extent and diameter of the earth?"	(Geo-physics)
"Who is the Regulator between Heaven and Earth?"	(Cosmology)
"What brings forth the clear gem from the stone-workings?"	(Geology)
"Where do the cuckoos which visit us in summer, retire in the winter?"	
	(Ornithology)

(A Druid, wandering in the cornfields of today, would be shocked to find the 20th century answer to this question—namely that cuckoos are lucky to fly away at all, and are more likely to be found dying in convulsions in the hedgerow, from being sprayed or eating poisoned seed.)

And though it contains no reference to our Zodiac, I am tempted to add the *"Little Song of the World"* also by Taliesin.

Though I have sung already, I will sing of the world one day more;
Much will I reason and meditate.
I will demand of the Bards of the world,
Why will they not answer me!
What upholds the world, that it falls not,
Destitute of support? Or if it were to fall,
Which way would it go? Who would sustain it?
How great a wanderer is the world!
While it glides on, without resting, it is still
Within its hollow orbit. How wonderful its frame,
That it does not fall off in one direction;
How strange, that it is not disturbed
By the multitude of tramplings!

No nonsense here, please note, about the earth being flat, or static while the stars moved round it. It moves through space in orbit—ideas for which Galileo was persecuted ten centuries later!

Taurus as the leader of the year and Gemini on Dundon Hill feature in the following poem of Taliesin, called *"Buarth Beirdd"*—the *"Ox-Pen of the Bards"*. Such an ox-pen can only be our Zodiac.

Gliding rapidly were my thoughts
Over the vain poetic art of the Bards of Britain
Who, labouring to make a show at the solemn gathering
With great care hammer out a song.
I need a staff at one with Bardic lore.
As for him who knows not the Ox-Pen of the Bards   (The Zodiac)
May fifteen thousand overpower him at once!

I am a skilful composer: I am a clear singer:
I am a tower: I am a Druid: (A tower connects heaven and earth; a column
I am an architect: I am a prophet: like Columba the dove, heaven's messenger.
I am a serpent: I am Love: Libra's Venus turns the sex-serpent on the Dove's
In the social banquet will I indulge.   wing into a serpent of Wisdom)
A Bard am I, not doting on superfluous trifles;

When a master sings, his songs will be close to the subject,
He will search for remote wonders.
Shall I admit these, like men suing for a garment   (mentally impoverished)
Without a hand to receive them (or Gemini's Little Tailor, *sewing* a garment)
Like men toiling on a lake without a ship (A taunt at their ignorance of the
                                        Cancerian ship, which often disappeared beneath the floods)
Boldly swells the stream to its high limit.
Let the thigh be pierced with blood;   (Gemini's thigh has a red gash on
                                Lollover Hill on which grass never grows)
Let the rock beyond the billow be set in order   (Dundon Hill, where
                             Gemini's Christ-like head can still be seen)
At dawn, displaying the countenance
Of him, who receives the exile into his sanctuary —
The rock of the Supreme Proprietor,
The chief place of tranquillity!

Then let the giver of the mead-feast cause to be proclaimed —
"I am the cell; I am the opening chasm;   (The place of Initiation, rebirth)
I am the Bull, Beer Lled   (Hebrew term, says Davies, meaning both bull and
I am the repository of the Mystery;   dawn)
I am the place of re-animation."

I love the tips of trees, with the points well-connected   (Druid tree-letters)
And the Bard who composes without meriting reproof;
But him I love not, who delights not in debate.
He who misleads the adept shall not enjoy the mead.
It is time to hasten to the banquet, where the skilful ones
Are employed in their Mysteries   (Sprig-alphabet in order spells sun-god's
With the hundred knots, the custom of our countrymen.   Life and death)
The shepherds of the plains   (Ignorant bards. But secretly Gemini's Good
The supporters of the gates   Shepherd at Somerton Door, the Mysteries'
                                                  western gate)
Are like men marching to battle without their clan.   (Rejected through
I am the Bard of the Hall, I am the stock that supports the chair. ignorance)
I shall succeed in impeding the progress of idly chattering bards.

Some may tire of Taliesin's boasting and sarcasm to his Bardic opponents—I never do. After all, he knew a great and life-giving secret which he could not give out. Awake amid sleepers, how else could he rouse them?

Another poem of Taliesin undoubtedly refers to the flooding of our Zodiac Ark—a disaster which must often have occurred, and reminded Celtic bards of the first Deluge and its reasons.

"May the Heavenly God protect us from a general overflowing.
The first surging billow has rolled beyond the sea-beach.

A greater than he, Daronwy, there has not been   (Dundon Hill, Fort of Don,
To afford us a sanctuary, round the Proud Celestial Circle.   Genius)
There is a greater secret — the dawn of the men of Goronwy
Though known to few — the magic wand of Mathonwy,
Which grows in the wood
With more exuberant fruit, on the bank of the river of spectres.
Kynan shall obtain it when he comes to govern."

(Math's Secret was passed to Gwyddion, one of *"the three Happy Astronomers".*)

Here is a royal secret, to be passed to the young king on his accession. It involves our spectral giants, also an area liable to flood, a holy hill safe from the waters, and a *"Celestial Circle"*. The sanctuary belongs to Daronwy, or Don. It is the same as *"the rock beyond the billow, to be set in order at dawn, displaying the countenance of Him, who receives the exile into his sanctuary"*—or *Dundon* Hill, of the previous poem, *"Buarth Beirdd".*

The *"greater secret, the dawn of the men of Goronwy"*, confirms this, for it is astronomical. Gwron or Goronwy being the third person in the Druid Trinity of Plenydd (Belin), Alawn and Gwron—or Light, Harmony and Energy. Though known as the Three Primary Bards of Britain, they were not ancestors but forces: being the Three Bars of Light or broad arrow quickening the world. As Gwron was Energy, the secret the men of Goronwy had to find and preserve must have been the season of the solstices, when the sun begins to lose or gain energy; or perhaps the precession of the equinoxes, also determined at dawn. As this is regulated by the wobbling earth's axis, was the magic wand of Mathonwy that grew in the wood, the imaginary pole growing from *Park Wood* at our circle's centre towards the pole-star? Bolster Lane nearby hints that it was.

Math or Mathonwy was the Great Mathematician who orders all things; his magic wand a measuring-rod. He must have been a Phoenician who taught both Greeks and Celts from the Somerset Zodiac: the *"Amathites"* mentioned in Genesis were Canaanites. Doubtless they venerated the cosmic measurements of the Ark.

Amaeth in Welsh means *"ploughman"*. Celtic Amaethon, nephew of Math or Mathonwy, king of the Celts' Underworld, must have ploughed the Zodiac furrow, like Arthur. Arianrhod of the Silver Wheel was his sister. They were Children of Don, the Pelasgian Tuath de Danaan who came to Britain in the Bronze Age and named many constellations in Celtic lore.

Math's magic wand seems to be a tree—the pole-star Tree of Life.

The Battle of the Trees was fought, says the *"Myvyrian Archaeology"*, on account of a Lapwing, a White Roebuck and a Whelp from Annwn— three animals from our Zodiac—the bird, (Phoenix or Dove), the White Hart of Capricorn, and the guardian Dog of Langport.

Robert Graves' *"White Goddess"* shews why these three creatures were selected to account for the battle; *they are all symbols of a secret.* The lapwing is notorious for luring nest-robbers away from its eggs by trailing its wing and limping in the wrong direction as if it were crippled and thus an easy prey; the white hart lures the hunter into the depths of the forest until he is hopelessly lost; the Dog Cerberus guards the Mysteries.

Taliesin is an ambivalent lapwing; while leading us all round the mulberry-bush with his interminable tree-lore, he can't help half giving-away the secret by sudden outbursts which have nothing (apparently) to do with trees.

"I know the star-lore of stars before the earth was made;
Whence I was born, how many worlds there are—"

It is like the game of hunt-the-thimble—he keeps crying "Warmer, warmer" because he really wants us to discover the secret.

Druids hid their Mysteries in their tree-alphabet.

Here is a poem by Merddin, a bard ranked with Taliesin, which describes the Zodiac as a tree. It is called *"Avallenau"*—apple-trees—a title which to those in the know gives away the location as well. Merddin, a refugee in Caledonia, has fled from invasion, civil strife and ecclesiastical persecution, taking his precious *"tree"* with him to plant on Clyde-bank. He was the 6th century Merlin who has become the famous adviser of Arthur in all the legends, and is historical enough, however shadowy or mythical his royal master may be. But he too probably acquired the mantle of the more ancient and legendary sage, like Taliesin.

MERDDIN'S AVALLENAU — APPLE ORCHARD. 6th cent.

Beginning Stanzas

To no-one has been shewn at the hour of dawn, what was shewn to Merddin, before he grew old; namely seven score and seven delicious apple trees, of equal age, height, length and size, which sprung from the bosom of Mercy. One bending veil covers them over. They are guarded by one maid, with crisped locks; her name is Olwedd, of the luminous teeth. (The British Proserpine—Davies. Also moon.)

The delicious apple tree, with blossoms of pure white and wide-spreading branches, produces sweet apples, for those who can digest them. And they have always grown in the wood, which grows apart. The nymph who appears and disappears, prophesies words which will come to pass.

Stanza 4

The sweet apple has pure white sprigs which grow as a portion for food. I had rather encounter the king's wrath than permit rustics in raven's hue (monks?) to ascend its branches. The lady of commanding aspect is splendidly endowed; nor am I destitute of talent.

Stanza 5

The fair apple tree grows upon the border of the vale; its yellow apples and its leaves are desirable; even I have been beloved by my priestesses and my wolf; but now my complexion is faded by long weeping; I am neglected by my former friends, and wander amongst spectres who know me not.

Thou sweet and beneficent tree! Not scanty is the fruit with which thou art loaded; but upon thy account, I am terrified and anxious, lest the woodcutters should come, those profaners of the wood, to dig up thy root and corrupt thy seed, that not an apple may ever grow upon thee more.

Stanza 6

I am become a wild distracted object, no longer greeted by the brethren of my order, nor covered with my habit. Upon me Gwenddoleu freely bestowed these precious gifts; but he is, this day, as if he had never been.

Stanza 7

The proper place for this delicate tree is within a shelter of great renown, but princes devise false pretences with lying, gluttonous and vicious monks, and pert youngsters, rash in their designs—these are the aspiring men who will triumph in their course.

Stanza 8

Now, alas, the tree which avoids rumour, grows on the confluence of streams, without the raised circle. (Uprooted and transplanted to Clydebank?).

This sweet apple tree abounds with small shoots; but the multitude cannot taste its yellow fruit. I have been in company with select men to cultivate and cherish its trunk—and when Dyvnant shall be named the city of the stones the bard shall receive his reward.

Stanza 10

Incorruptible is the tree which grows in the spot, set apart under its wide envelope. For four hundred years may it remain in peace. But its root is more often surrounded by the violating wolf than by the youth who can enjoy its fruit.

Stanza 11

This tree they would fain expose to public view; so drops of water would fain wet the duck's feather.

Stanza 13

The fair tree grows in the glade of the wood. (Grove) *Its hiding place has no skilful protector from the chiefs of Rhydderch, who trample on its roots, whilst the multitude compass it around.* The energetic figures are viewed with grief and envy. *The Lady of the Day loves me not, nor will she greet me. I am hated by the minister of Rhydderch's authority—his son and daughter have I ruined. Death who removes all, why will he not visit me? After the loss of Gwenddolen, the lady of the white bow* (References to moon cult), *by no nymph am I respected. No soother assuages my grief; by no mistress am I visited. Yet in the conflict of Arderydd I wore the gold collar* (prince's torc). *O that I were precious this day with those who have the hue of the swan.* (White-robed Druids.)

Stanza 14

The tree with delicate blossoms grows in concealment amongst the forests. A report is heard at dawn that the minister has expressed indignation against the authority of the small sprigs (Druidic tree-alphabet used also for divining by lots) *twice, thrice, nay four times in one day.*

Stanza 15

The fair tree grows on the river-bank. A provost cannot thrive on the splendid fruit I enjoyed from its trunk, while my reason was entire, in company with Bun, the Maid, elegantly pleasing, delicate and most beautiful. But now, for fifty years have my splendid treasures been outlawed, whilst I have been wandering amongst ghosts, after having enjoyed abundant wealth, and the pleasant society of the tuneful tribe. (Bun, Ban the Banshee, must be Virgo.)

Stanza 16

The sweet apple tree, with delicate blossoms, grows upon the earth, amongst the trees; and the half-appearing maid predicts words which will come to pass. Mental designs shall cover as with a vessel the green assemblies, from the princes, in the tempestuous hour. The Ray-darter shall vanquish the profane man. Before the Child of the Sun, bold in his course, Saxons shall be eradicated; Bards shall flourish.

The blooming tree grows in Hidlock, in the Caledonian wood. Attempts to discover it by its seeds will be in vain till Cadwalladyr, supreme ruler of battle (in exile in France, last king of Wales) *comes to the conference of Cadvaon, with the eagle of Towy and Teivi—till ranks be formed of the white ones of the lofty mount* (Eryrie, Snowdon, where the Pheryllt Druids had a fort) *and the wearers of long hair be divided into the gentle and fierce.*

Stanza 19

The sweet fruits of this tree are prisoners of words.—The Ass will arise, to remove men from office; but this I know, an eagle from the sky will play with his men, and bitter will be the sound of Ywein's arms. A veil covers the tree with green branches—and I will foretell the harvest when the green corn shall be cropped—when the he-eagle and the she-eagle shall arrive from France.

Stanza 20

The sweet apple-tree is like the Bardic mount of Assembly; the dogs of the wood (Both priests of the grove and the Great and little dogs, Procyon and Cerberus?) *will protect the circle of its roots.*

Stanza 21

Sweet are its branches, budding luxuriant, shooting forth renowned scions.

Stanza 22

The sweet apple tree, producing the most delicious fruit, grows in concealment in the Calydonian wood. In vain will it be sought upon the banks of its stream, till Cadwalladyr comes to the conference of Rhyd Rheon, with Kynan, opposing the tumult of the Saxons. Then the Cymru shall prevail. Her chief shall be splendid. All shall have their just reward. Britons shall rejoice. The horn of joy shall sound, the song of peace and serenity.

Alas for Merddin and the Britons! Cadwalldyr, last of their kings, fled to Brittany and never came back, ending his days in Rome. He left the field to Cerdic and the Saxons, under whom England, Angel-Land, was reborn. And though these Saxons had not the British gift of prophecy, they brought something to our blood which the early Britons notably lacked—the quality of loyalty and steadiness which in after ages made it possible for the kings of Alfred's line to unite the whole kingdom under one head. Nor did this conquest extinguish the individualistic inspiration of the aboriginals, as our continuous line of poets bears witness; rather it cooled it to the pitch that made order and government possible. Under the phlegmatic Anglo-British exterior the bubbling cauldron of Ceredwen still seethes.

Merlin's prophecies (of which more may be read in Geoffrey of Monmouth's History of the Kings of Britain) seem to have been progressed horoscopes, if we judge by the frequent allusions to dragons, eagles, lions and other Zodiac animals, and by his constant allusions to the passage, appearance, half-appearance and disappearance of his moon-goddess. On the face of it, his prediction that Cadwalladyr and Kynan should return to discomfit the Saxons and bring joy to Britons hardly seems to have been fulfilled; but was he so far out? "Saxon" Cerdic, founder of Alfred's dynasty, bore a British name, Caradoc. And Alfred, if not Kynan, certainly seems to have obtained the Mysteries in his turn.

Celtic poetry in fact swarms with references to our Zodiac, as I hope this incomplete review has shewn; there is no lack, either, of hints as to its Somerset location. When more material is translated from the Welsh no doubt many more clues will come to light. An urgent task for present-day Bards! There is however much already translated, that space alone forbids me to include, still waiting to be opened with the Zodiac key.

I will end this chapter with extracts from a poem of Taliesin's which Mrs. Maltwood quotes as a reference to Leo.

If ye are primitive bards, according to the ancient disciplines
Relate the great secrets of the world we inhabit.
There is a formidable animal from the city of Satanas   (Saturn, Chronos's
Which has made an inroad between the deep and the shallows. Zodiac clock)
His mouth is as wide as the mountains of Mynnau;   (Snowdonia)
Neither death can vanquish him, nor hand, nor sword.
There is a load of nine hundred rocks between his two paws   (Somerton.
There is one eye in his head, vivid as the blue ice.   Only Leo has paws)
Three fountains there are in his receptacles,
One is the increase of salt water
When it mounts aloft over the fluctuating seas, to replenish the streams.
The second is that which innocently descends upon us
When it rains through the boundless atmosphere.
The third is that which springs through the veins of the mountains,
As a banquet from the flinty rocks furnished by the king of kings.

"This poem," says Edward Davies, "*is a select piece of Bardic lore.*"

Taliesin is not only shewing-off his knowledge of the water-cycle of condensation and precipitation; he sees it as an allegory of reincarnation—a cycle of precipitation into flesh and back again into spirit-vapour—as demonstrated in the Zodiac.

22: The Zodiac in the Mabinogion

On first entering the twilight zone of the Celtic gods and heroes everything seems vague, impalpable. The unfamiliar shadows enlarge to giant proportions, shrink to dwarfs, and are never still long enough for us to make them out before they undergo Protean changes of character and form, become inextricably intertwined, dissolve and re-form elsewhere. To read Celtic myth for the first time is like trying to decipher the dynamic maze of ornament on a weatherbeaten Celtic cross in an overgrown thicket after sundown.

But when the eyes have grown used to the half-light certain features begin to clarify; the original extravagance, the restless shape-shifting, resolves itself into the orderly Dance of the Hours, the ritual motion of the sun through the houses of the Zodiac.

Only then can we hope to reduce this formidable rout to order; first to the twelve aspects of the sun in his daily and yearly path, then to the ubiquitous Trinity of Father, Mother and Son. True, each of these has a bewildering number of names, but this we must blame on Time itself, for the history of the Celts is as long as that of the Jews.

But the Jews at least preserved their ancient tongue, which Britain (in the main) has not; Anglo-Saxons have long excluded the unpronounceable heroes of their predecessors from the familiarity of nursery-tales round English firesides. Sole survivors of the Celtic pantheon in popular circulation are Arthur and his knights of the Round Table—yet even they fled abroad during the Saxon invasions, and have only returned to us (their manners and armour polished almost beyond recognition) through Breton minstrels in the train of the Normans. (The Iolo MS asserts that the Round Table was brought back to Britain from Brittany by Rhys ap Tewdwr. For this he well deserved to father the later Tudor dynasty.)

Arthur has been regarded as a comparative new-comer to the ancient Celtic pantheon—though why, I cannot tell. He appears in the earliest poetic fragment we possess, with Kay and Bedivere, and in the oldest tale of the Mabinogion, *"Kylhwch and Olwen"*. Under various forms like Arch, Arthgallo, Arthur of the Gaels, and the memorable Art the Melancholy, he appears in British royal family trees going back to Brutus. True, he does not figure in the first four Branches (chapters) of the Mabinogion, but as these were written down a hundred years later than *"Kylhwch and Olwen"* where he does appear, this proves nothing. All five tales incorporate myths of ageless antiquity and are a treasure-house of long-lost British god-heroes.

The Arthur of later legend has a way of gathering them about his Round Table, like a powerful luminary magnetising burnt-out suns into his orbit.

Perhaps British minstrels in Brittany were brought up on his version. At any rate, it was he who returned from exile in France, not Bran Llew or Math, to rise to undying fame. France too has her Avalon, and here his legends fired the imagination of all Europe, setting off the atomic bomb known as the Age of Chivalry. His name is ancient enough to name the greatest of all constellations, for he is Arth the Bear, and Arddwr the Ploughman.

We owe much to Lady Charlotte Guest, who first translated the Mabinogion into English and gave this country back its lost pantheon, its forgotten lore.

"Mabinogion" means Tales of the Youth, Mabon, son of Modron. Strangely, he only appears in one tale, and in brackets at that—behind bars, in fact; he is always a prisoner. He is of course Man, son of Mother Earth (Modron the Matron) imprisoned in flesh, who can only be rescued by the Salmon of Wisdom.

But many other heroic youths struggle through these pages to work out his salvation for him; his mantle falls upon them all.

But let us begin at the beginning.

The First Branch — Pwyll Prince of Dyfed

Pwyll, a mortal, steals a stag from another hunter's dogs, and finds the offended huntsman to be Arawn, fairy king of Annwn. (Is Ar-awn Arthur? Annwn is certainly Avalon.) To ingratiate himself he offers to fight Arawn's enemy, Hafgan. (Summer king.) As a reward Arawn offers him his wife and kingdom for a year, and they exchange forms and kingdoms so successfully that Arawn's wife thinks Pwyll is her husband. But Pwyll is unswervingly chaste despite her charms. He governs generously and well, and at the year's end meets his adversary Hafgan, disabling him with the single stroke which is all he is allowed by the rules of the sun-game. Hafgan (like Arthur) is borne away, sick unto death, but notably not dead, for sun-kings like old soldiers never die. Pwyll in fact is an initiate who passes all his tests, chastity, wise administration and personal courage, with flying colours. King for a year is king for a day, and the origin of this strange old custom becomes clear. Arawn's heart warms toward this paragon of men, unites the two kingdoms and gives Pwyll the title of Head of Annwn.   (Master of the Mysteries.)

Pwyll goes to sit on the mound of Arberth, whence none return without receiving wounds or seeing a wonder, (like Cader Idris) and sees a fair damsel ride slowly by on a white horse. He spurs after her, but cannot catch her, though her stately pace never alters. He tries again, but the fleetest horse cannot overtake the dawdling damsel. (We are left to guess that she is the moon. Even her name, Rhiannon—"*Great Goddess*", no more than hints at it.)

At last Pwyll realises what any poet could have told him—that the way to woo the moon is not to go galloping after her, but to stand still and address her. This proves so effective that in no time they fall in love. But she is betrothed already, against her will, to Gwawl, a youth of royal mien. Together they persuade Gwawl to step into a bag, (shades of Taliesin's leather bag here), tie him up and pummel him almost—but not quite—to death, after which Gwawl loses all taste for Rhiannon, not surprisingly, and she and Pwyll are free to marry. "*And then was Badger in the Bag first played...*"

Soon their son Pryderi is born at Arberth (Arthur's birth?) and our Zodiac Trinity is complete. But he is snatched mysteriously away, and Rhiannon's attendants, terrified, smear the sleeping queen with blood and accuse her of murdering him. All demand her death for such a hideous crime, and Rhiannon, outnumbered by false witnesses, keeps nobly silent. But Pwyll cannot condemn her, and ordains a penance; she must carry all strangers into his palace on her back if they will let her, and confess her crime to each.

Meanwhile, Teyrnon lord of Gwent keeps losing foals, and on May Eve keeps watch for the thief. An enormous claw comes through the stable window to snatch the newly-born foal, and Teyrnon cuts it off. There is a frightful scream and a commotion, and a child is found in the straw. It is of course Pryderi, freed from death's Scorpionic claw, and born as a good sun-king should be, in a stable.

His brocaded silk garment gives him away, but Teyrnon fosters him for some time before returning him to the palace. All admit his resemblance to Pwyll, and Rhiannon is vindicated. She is delivered, she says, from all her care, and thus gives Pryderi his name, which means Thought or Care. *He is undoubtedly our pensive Gemini.*

He turns out to be all that is desired in a prince, and after his father's death (for Pwyll is after all only half-divine) rules Dyfed wisely and well. He maries Cigfa, "*one of the high-born ones of this Island*", and turns up again in the Third Branch with more adventures, where, leaving aside the Second Branch, we will pursue him forthwith.

The Third Branch — Manawydan Son of Llyr

Pryderi befriends Manawydan son of Llyr, a dispossessed prince whose cousin Caswallawn (Cassivelaunus) had supplanted him as king of Britain. Pryderi offers him the seven cantrefs of Dyfed and his Mother Rhiannon to wife, and pays him the compliment of calling him "*One of the Three Ungrasping Chieftains*". (Manawydan and Rhiannon are well suited—for he must be Menu the Measurer and she the Moon by which he measures.)

On the miraculous mound of Arberth the four of them, Pryderi and Cigfa his wife, Manawydan and Rhiannon his wife, experience another wonder. There is a peal of thunder and a dense mist. When the mist disperses they realise they are alone in the world, for wherever they look *"neither house nor beast nor smoke nor fire nor man nor dwelling"* was left. It is the Waste Land, utterly depopulated.

They go to Lloegr (England) to earn their bread as saddle-makers in Hereford. So excellent are their wares that the other saddle-makers conspire to slay them. Pryderi, young and hot-blooded, is for fight, but Manawydan, older and wiser, persuades him to take another trade elsewhere. So they become in turn shield-makers and cobblers, but everywhere are pursued by jealousy. (One suspects that these episodes reflect the stitching posture of the Babe in the boat, from which both Manawydan-Menu and Pryderi the semi-divine sun-god originated. Pryderi stitched, while Manawydan sewed gold buckles on the shoes. He was thus called *"One of the Three Gold Shoemakers"*, and must be identical Twin to the little Tailor of Gloucester.

Always losing to evil, yet always rising indomitably again, they return to Dyved and see another wonder. They turn huntsmen and are lured by a boar (whose half-moon tusks are a lunar symbol) to a mysterious castle on a mound. Boar and dogs disappear within, and impetuous Pryderi follows, despite Manawydan's warning.

It is the Grail-Castle of Avalon, because it contains a marble fountain with a golden bowl suspended from heavenly chains. Pryderi and Rhiannon lay hold of the bowl and are stuck fast. (Here is a Celtic prototype of the unprepared Grail-quester who is dumb-founded by the Mysteries, and can neither move nor speak.) The castle vanishes, and they with it, leaving Manawydan and Cigfa bereft. Manawydan, chivalrous centuries before the Age of Chivalry, assures the frightened Cigfa that she is safe with him. He turns farmer and sows three fields of corn to maintain them, but just before harvesting it is eaten by mice. He catches one of them, larger and slower than the rest, and is about to hang it for a thief when three men appear, one after another (in this depopulated land!) and offer to buy it. A clerk offers one pound, a priest three, a bishop steps up the offer to a whole train of pack-horses and their baggage, but Manawydan, realising that at last the game is in his hand, will settle for nothing less than the lifting of all enchantment from Dyved, the freedom of his friends and a promise that no further harm shall befall them. The mouse turns out to be the wife of the *"bishop"*, who is really a kinsman of Gwawl, the battered *"Badger in the Bag"*, bent on vengeance. The kingdom and its king are restored, and Pryderi owes all to Manawydan, who with wisdom, perseverance, tolerance, patience and cunning worthy of Ulysses, has won the day. Thus he repays his young friend's generosity!

The Fourth Branch

Alas for Pryderi! He is no longer the hero here; even his decline and fall are of secondary interest in the following tales, which see things from the side of his tricky enemies. Gwydion and Gilfaethwy. He deserves his eclipse, for his solar glory has waned to the point where his judgement is affected, and he becomes first the dupe of Gwydion, the rising sun—and finally his victim. He is like Arthur without his Merlin, for in this Branch Pryderi's wise Manawydan had disappeared.

The story opens with a strange picture which I suspect reflects once more our Gemini Babe in his boat. *Math, son of Mathonwy, lord of North Wales, is never happy unless he has his feet tucked into the folds of a maiden's lap.*

Mathonwy his father is Amaethon, whose name means *"Ploughman"*, like Arthur's; his son then is surely our Gemini figure whose feet are tucked under him in Cancer's maternal moon-and-womb-boat. The maiden Goewin is his foot-holder, and her name recalls Goemagot or Gogmagog, the goggling sun-and-moon Giant(s), so we can call her *"White-shining Moon-Maiden"*. Math, reclining in this significant posture, leaves the admin problems of his kingdom to his cunning nephews Gwydion and Gilfaethwy, who are mortal—indeed all too human. Gilfaethwy pines with longing for Goewin, and Gwydion thinks nothing of plunging all Wales into civil war in order to get Math's feet disentangled from her lap and out of the way so that Gilfaethwy may rape her. What a pair! Yet these scoundrels are also the two Gemini twins, in their role as aspiring human initiates to the Mysteries. To obtain these heavenly treasures in fact one must be tortured with overwhelming desire and learn all the cunning of Ulysses.

To stir up trouble Gwydion goes to demand Pryderi's pigs, given him by Arawn of Annwn. (The effigies, half-buried in the earth, can only be found by the Syweddyd, or Swine-Druids, rooting for the precious truffles of truth in Avalon's Annwn.) Pryderi will not let them go until they have doubled their number, but Gwydion makes from toadstools twelve stallions in golden harness and twelve gold-collared greyhounds, and dazzles Pryderi by apparently *"doubling the number"*.

For Pryderi, a master in the solar Mysteries, to have been tricked into exchanging things of such evanescent value shews he was slipping into dotage. When his new treasures turn back into toadstools he pursues the Gemini thieves with his army, but they hide in Harlech until Math, mustering all his forces, goes to fight Pryderi. Gilfaethwy then slips into Math's palace and takes Goewin by force. They have obtained the Houses of the Zodiac and the Moon-girl whose passage through them is the Key to the astrological and calendar Mysteries, a key-measurement, as we have seen, hidden in Math's boat.

Things go badly for Pryderi, and he has to yield twenty-four hostages—in fact he *"yields the day"*. But he challenges Gwydion, cause of all this uproar, to single combat; Gwydion does not lack valour, and slays him. So ends Pryderi's life-cycle, at least in one sense; but he has a way of surviving, like the sun, despite apparent deaths, and revives later in the Mabinogion as Peredur, and in Arthurian legend as Perceval.

Meanwhile, back at the palace . . . Goewin confesses to Math that he must find another maiden, for she is maid no longer. His vengeance is interesting. He hauls the skulking brothers before him and turns them into beasts; the first year they must be coupling hinds, the second hogs, the third wolves. Each year to their shame they produce young after their kind, and are hunted and scorned by men. One might say they are questing spirits condemned to material or fleshly form, but also initiates on the painful path of discovering their own animal nature, coming to grips with it and mastering it. This period of self-discovery is not unfruitful, and Math blesses their increase.

(We are reminded here that Math is Noah, sending the animals forth two by two and bidding them increase. The Mathematician bids them multiply.) Their three animal-forms also recall little Gwion's flight from the avenging Goddess before becoming Taliesin Radiant-Brow . The Zodiac is the fount and origin of all these tales.

When their penance is done Math receives them back into his court, forgives and restores them to true human shape. They are now Druids, and he pays them the compliment of asking their advice on his marriage. They easily pass this test, recommending none but Arianrhod, Goddess of Caer Sidi, Spiral Star-Castle, and the Silver Zodiac Wheel.

Math, to test her virginity, makes her step over his magic wand, but before she can escape through the door she gives birth to twins. Instant motherhood! Well might Taliesin describe Math's wand as having *"more exuberant fruits"*.

No doubt this is splendid phallic symbolism, but is also more. As the star-goddess steps over Math's measuring-rod it marks an hour of destiny, for Lleu the Mabinogion's next sun-god is born. As usual, he is one of twins, and as his birth must be at the winter solstice we are hardly surprised when his twin Dylan slips at once into the sea of Pisces, so quickly that Math only just has time to baptise him.

Lleu's father is unknown, so his mysterious birth is established in this delightful episode. Gwydion whips the waif up from the floor, pops him in a chest and apparently forgets him until one day he hears a faint cry from within. (The sun-hero abandoned in cradle ark or chest.) Gwydion gives him to be fostered by *"a woman with breasts,"* and at two years old he is big enough to come to court by himself. (The Giant Gemini Babe.) He goes to Arianrhod's Castle to see his mother, and she refuses to give him a name, but the wily Gwydion is equal to her. He takes the boy *in a boat*, and pretending to be *shoemakers* they again visit Arianrhod in disguise. She unwarily compliments the boy on his deft hand (those delicate Geminian fingers) and Gwydion triumphantly exclaims *"Now he has a name! Lleu Llaw Gyffes"*— the fair one with a deft hand. Gwydion like Manawydan was one of the *"Three Gold Shoemakers"*.

Arianrhod is equally reluctant to grant her son arms, but Gwydion again tricks her into it. However, when it comes to giving him a wife, she is adamant. Gwydion therefore complains of her to Math, and together they fashion a wife for Lleu out of flowers, the fairest maiden ever, and baptise her Blodeuwedd, *"Flower-face"*. They rule their kingdom together and all are content. But not for long enough to bore us, for with a horn-blast appears Lleu's dark rival, Gronu Pebr. He arrives while Lleu is away visiting Math in the Underworld and steals Blodeuwedd's heart. In the period of Lleu's decline his earth-wife plays him false, as inevitably as the earth turns from the setting sun.

Together they plot Lleu's death. This is no easy matter, for in only one way can he be killed, namely, by a spear that must be a year in the making, and only fashioned when all good folk are at church. Also, it must be hurled at him at one moment only, when he takes his annual bath, with one foot on its rim and the other on a goat's back. This information Blodeuwedd wormed out of Lleu with a show of love; information which is valuable to us as well, for it shews the sun at the winter solstice of that time between the *"bath"* of the Aquarian Cauldron or water-pot, and Capricorn the goat. Just to clinch matters, when the fatal spear is hurled. Lleu with a great cry flies upwards in the form of an *eagle*. He reflects the earth-pattern in all his forms—in spring he is identical twin to Dylan the Fish, in summer he comes into his own name, Lleu or Leo, in autumn he goes missing like the elusive Scorpion and is cuckolded like Arthur (Sagittarius), in winter he dies and resurrects as the Aquarian Eagle.

Flying to a distant oak he perches, while rotting flesh falls from him and is devoured by a sow. This must be the earth-mother Ceredwen, for whatever we may think of her dietary habits, his body belongs to her. Math however finds him and nurses him back to health in his Underworld, and Lleu in due time kills his rival Gronu Pebr with the same *single blow* of the lance with which he himself was pierced.

Gronu's heart fails him at the last, and he prevails upon the generous Lleu to place a stone between them; but Lleu's lance pierces both stone and rival, *"and there"*, concludes the tale, *"the stone is, on the bank of the Cynfael river in Ardudwy, and the hole through it"*.

Blodeuwedd was turned into an owl, to be pecked at by all right-thinking birds, for her dark deed. But was her lover so dark? Can we not identify Gronu with Gwron, Energy, Light—the new sun who supplants the dying orb of night and winter? The pierced stone by the Cynfael river is (or was) a helestone holed for the sun's shaft to penetrate, and connects the tale with megalithic beginnings. The Christian details are, we may be sure, a sop to the Church of the time when these tales were written down.

Now let us return to the Second Branch.

The Second Branch — Bran and Branwen

I have re-arranged the branches of this ancient tree in order to make a through passage for Pryderi, but in the Druidic tree-alphabet it is risky for the ignorant to re-group the sprigs; who knows what spelling howlers I may have committed? Or what sacred word I may have jumbled beyond recognition? If however it be carefully noted that this branch is out of place, no great harm will be done. You may put it back.

The Second Branch introduces king Bran of Britain and his sister Branwen, and its action ranges between Ireland and London. The Cauldron makes its appearance in a sequence we can identify with the hazardous expedition in Taliesin's *"Preiddeu Annwn"*, from which only seven returned.

Matholwch king of Ireland comes to woo Branwen, sister of Bendigeidfran, or Bran the Blessed, king of all Britain. His seat is London, but the wedding takes place in Wales. Bran's brother is the wise Manawydan, and both are sons of Lyr — king Lear.

While all are feasting merrily, Branwen's half-brother Efnisien (a born mischief-maker) cuts off the lips, ears and tails of Matholwch's horses, furious that he was not consulted about the match.

Matholwch departs in high dudgeon, but Bran offers him full compensation and throws in the cauldron of rebirth for good measure. It was in any case originally Irish, says Bran, having been given him by a monstrous Irish giant. Matholwch confirms this, remembering him as Llasar Llaes Gyfnewid who had escaped from the Iron House when the Irish attempted to kill him and his wife by piling charcoal round the house, firing it and blowing it with bellows until it was white-hot. Realising that they were not popular, they then emigrated to Britain with their cauldon.

But Bran and Matholwch were both wrong — or rather let us blame the bards who wrote these stories down in the twelve and thirteen-hundreds, after long centuries of oral transmission. The Cauldron did not come from Ireland, though its fame was celebrated there, as indeed it was in ancient Greece. How then did mediaeval Welsh bards come to think of it as Irish?

By their period Avalon had been over-run by Romans, Angles, Saxons and Normans, and the shame of losing their prime sacred area to foreign invaders produced a sort of amnesia. The provenance of most of the Mabinogion tales of Avalon became Welsh; Britons, driven into Wales, took their sacred geography with them. While they had lived all over Britain, this sacred circle was known to be in the west; when they were pressed into Wales, the Neverland retreated still further west, to Ireland. Informed Bards like Taliesin and Merddin knew better, as we have seen, preferring the conscious agony of loss to the uneasy comfort of forgetting.

Ireland kept its Druidic organisation intact long after Druids had been dispersed in Roman Britian; many British Druids fled there, and Irish myth repeats the Avalon Mysteries faithfully, often only substituting Gaelic forms for the original heroes' names. And though some Irish myths place the Otherworld even further west in the Atlantic, others remember the Fairy-land of Fand, to the east of Ireland.

However, the ancient tale of Bran and Branwen at least remembers that the Cauldron belonged to Giants. The sadistic tale of the white-hot Iron House may well recall Iron Age or even Bronze Age furnaces and the Giants or Satans who smelted ore; or it may refer to the perpetual fires of Brigit the White and triple Goddess. But these too may have smelted ore; the Druidic Pheryllt were metal-working alchemists.

> *"Perfect is my chair in Caer Sidi*
> *Plague and age hurt him not who's in it —*
> *They know, Manawydan and Pryderi.*
> *Three organs round a fire sing before it*
> *And round its points are ocean's streams*
> *And the abundant well above it —*
> *Sweeter than white wine the drink in it,"*   sang Taliesin.

For *"organs"* round the fire read *"Bellows"* used both for organ-blowing and smelting, and we can take our pick, as Taliesin doubtless intended. Either way the Iron House is the Pheryllt Cauldron of the Mysteries, *"warmed by the breath of nine Muses"*, as Taliesin tells us in his *"Preiddeu Annwn"*.

The *"abundant well"* above this crucible of self-regeneration must be Chalice Well, itself the Aquarian Cauldron.

The insult to their king rankled with the Irish, and they vented their spite on poor Branwen, degrading her from queen to cook, and ordering the butcher to give her a daily box on the ear. Ireland closed its traffic with Britain, that this scandal should not be known there.

But Branwen sent a starling with a message to Bran, and before long terrified observers saw a forest approaching them by sea. This was his fleet, and beside it a moving mountain with a great ridge and two lakes on either side. This was Bran's face, for the giant (who could never be contained in a house) was wading towards them. After a treacherous parley during which Branwen's young son Gwern was thrown in the fire (a recurring fate for young Celtic kings), battle was joined. To give the cauldron of rebirth to the Irish was ill-advised, for the Irish popped their dead and wounded in it so that they emerged as good as new. (Except that they were dumb—were they ghosts, or was this the effect the cauldron, or Grail, always has upon the unprepared?) Efnisien, seeing that Bran must be defeated, and tortured with remorse for the slaughter his mischief-making has caused, threw himself into the cauldron and burst it in four pieces with a last mighty effort, bursting his heart also.

Thus such victory as there was came to the British. But of them all, only seven returned... Among them there were Pryderi, Manawydan and Taliesin. Bran himself, mortally wounded in the heel (a typical fate for sun-kings) commands that his head be struck off and taken to London to be buried on Tower Hill. Here, facing France, it will repel all invaders. (Unfortunately, Arthur dug it up later, and thus let in the Saxons, Angles and Danes. This was One of the Three Doleful Uncoverings.)

Branwen too broke her heart, appalled that two good islands should have been laid waste on her account, and died in Ireland. But the head was magical, and entertained its bearers so well that they forgot their sorrows, even forgot the time—and though they spent over eighty years on the homeward journey, it seemed but a short time.

Some have seen Bran's Singing Head as the Cauldron renewed, its power of enchantment unimpaired. But the Cauldron *was* lost, and remained so for many centuries until Mrs. Maltwood rediscovered it. Bran's Head however still sings wherever the lays of ancient Britain are repeated; its power of enchantment undimmed. Taliesin has seen to that, for he was one of its original bearers. For Bran or Capricorn is Man through the ages, and in his head is stored all the memories of our long and half-forgotten past.

After the Four Branches of the Mabinogion's Tree of Life come Four Independent Native Tales; the Dream of Macsen Wledig, Llud and Llefelys, Culhwch and Olwen, and the Dream of Rhonabwy.

Prince Macsen need not detain us long, for although his dream was of Britain's secrets, most of the tale deals with his wooing of the British princess Elen in Snowdonia, his seven years' enchantment there, the consequent loss of his Roman Empire, and the splendid part played by Britons in recovering it for him. A comforting tale for Roman-dominated Britain! It is history, or semi-history (for in the 380s AD, Magnus Clemens Maximus, a Roman soldier in western Britain, *did* take Rome with the help of British forces, thereby denuding Britain of all defence against barbarian invasion—and he *did* ally himself by marriage with the British Silurian royal family.) But it is the inner meaning of his story that most concerns us. He is transported in his dream by a mysterious boat of enormous size to Britain, and as it had two deck-planks, one of gold, the other of silver, this can be no other than the Cancerian boat of our Zodiac whose deck conceals sun and moon-measurements. His love-affair then was not to be taken on the literal level alone, but was an affair with the British Mysteries. But he was one of those adventurers who bring doom in their train; he left Britain defenceless, and under his short reign as Roman Emperor Christianity took a turn towards intolerance which has left long scars.

Macsen's Dream however contains one more reference to the Zodiac which is so oblique that it is only recognisable by repetition in other contexts. It is described as a game of chess played by kings. When Macsen reaches the palace of Elen's father Eudaf or Octavius in Snowdonia he finds two princelings (the Gemini Twins) playing the game of *gwyddbwyll* (draughts or chess) with a golden board and golden pieces. On an ivory throne sits a hoary king carving more golden pieces, and though his name in the tale is Eudaf, we may suspect that this venerable lord is Arthur, who as Sagittarius plays the part of God the Father in the Zodiac's Trinity.

The Creator then is making little men for his human chess-game, which is played by his sons, half-human, half-divine, on the golden chequerboard of the Zodiac, the world. His daughter-wife, Elen-Guinevere, is Virgo, mother of all. Even kings are only pawns; even pawns are made of gold! It is an eternal symbol of human life activated by unseen forces, a view taken by all astrological Mysteries. Lewis Carroll the initiate shews the progress of Alice from pawn to queen through the squared fields of Looking-Glass Land. One suspects that he knew the whereabouts of the original Glass Castle, by intuition or otherwise; he certainly understood that the object of the game of Life was not merely to amuse a bored Creator but to make us from unconscious pawns into kings and queens indeed.

The next tale, that of *Llud and Llefelys*, tells how Llud king of Britain and his brother Llefelys overcame the three Plagues of Britain. The first plague was the invading tribe of the Coranieid, the second was a scream which went up from every hearth on May-Eve, causing terror in men, miscarriage in women and flocks.

The third plague was the mysterious disappearance of all the king's provisions. Three parables of the Waste Land.

Wise Llefelys, now king of France, solves Lludd's problems; the hostile Coranieid can be overcome by certain insects which will leave the earlier Britons unharmed. The scream came from the British dragon, almost vanquished by the dragon of the foreigners; the fighting could be stopped by digging a pit in the very centre of Britain, namely at Oxford, filling it with mead and covering it over with silk. The fighting dragons would fall into the pit, drink the mead and turn into harmless pigs, when they could be safely gathered up in the silk and buried deep in the earth. The third plague was caused by a mighty giant who stole the king's food by night while all were asleep.

To overcome him Lludd must watch all night, (staying awake by dipping himself when necessary in a cauldron of cold water), catch him red-handed and fight him single-handed.

How are we to understand all this?

The Coranieid were historical enough, or pre-historical. They were an Iron-Age group of Goidelic Celts whose warlike invasions shook the earlier settlers to the core. But we can hardly interpret the insects who demolished them in the same literal way. The first recorded use of *"germ-warfare"*? Hardly. No, there is *double-entendre* here.

Davies' chapter on the Coranieid in his *'Celtic Researches'* also contains a possible solution to the insect problem. He quotes Himilco the Carthaginian's name for Britain as the *Oestrymnides—"Gadfly Islands"*—a title bestowed in 420 BC. But in Celtic both Gadfly and Druid teacher were signified by the word *cler*—a useful pun for Druid *"Clerks"* whose aim was to sting themselves and their students into self-awareness. Swine, gadflies— Druids revelled in such self-deprecating nicknames, which concealed their lore from the ignorant and revealed it to the wise.

Lludd's cure for Coranieitis may thus have been a dose of Druid teaching which had power to tame these brigands into respectable citizens. Thus they were absorbed, not decimated, for Davies counts such famous tribes as the Brigantes and the Iceni among the Coranieid.

The second plague seems to say the same thing in another way. The fighting Cymric and Coranieid dragons, reconciled and gloriously drunk in the mead-pit, became "domesticated" swine, indistinguishable from one another; that is, Syweddyd, Druid brethren at the ritual mead-feast. Llud gathered them up in the silken covering and buried them deep in the mountains of Snowdon, all the way from Oxford.

Why? Is there any connection between Oxford and Snowdon? There is indeed. Ancient traditions insist that the Druid Pheryllt, the brotherhood of the Cauldron Mysteries, founded Oxford as a place of learning; doubtless it was another *"Ox-pen of the Bards"*. (There should be a Zodiac there.) Their stronghold was Dinas Affaraon in Eryri—Snowdonia.

Neither brigands nor pigs are often afforded silken shrouds; such a garment surely clothed the contestants in a new gentility.

The thieving giant of the third plague may also refer to the taming of the Coranieid, for *Cor* or *Cawr* means *"giant"*. Lludd vanquishes him after a terrible battle, but nobly spares his life, and his formidable enemy becomes his faithful liege-man. The Waste Land becomes peaceful and prosperous once more.

In *"Llud and Llefelys"* we are obviously among the Mysteries of pre-Christian Britain. Is the giant then also Lludd the initiate's own dark side, whose *"giant state"* must be faced and overcome by frequent immersion in the bracing water of the Cauldron—by self-analysis?

The cure for the Waste Land in each case is a dose of the Mystery-teaching, which inculcates magnamimous values and civilizes hostile barbarians.

The next tale, "*Culhwch and Olwen*" simply bristles with Zodiac clues. By its style, syntax and vocabulary, it seems to have been written down at least a hundred years earlier than any of the other tales, in the tenth century AD., though in common with all the earliest part of the Mabinogion, this is no guide to its true antiquity.

I hope my brief precis will not deter you from the joy of reading this extravagantly imaginative legend, for no resume can possibly convey the enchanting humour, conscious and unconscious, the ebullience, the direct force and unexpectedness of the rip-roaring adventures of Culhwch in his quest for the beautiful Olwen. You must personally meet Clust son of Clustfeinad (Ear son of Hearer) who though he were buried seven fathoms below ground, would hear an ant fifty miles off when it stirred from its couch in the morning; or Gilla Stag-Shank who cleared three hundred acres at a single leap; or Gwefyl, who on the day he was sad would let one lip down to his navel and put the other over his head for a cowl; or Uchdryd Crossbeard, who would throw the bristling red beard he had on him across fifty rafters of King Arthur's hall. You must shake hands with Glewlwyd Mighty-Grasp, and Isberyr Cat-Claw, and Lluch Windy-hand, nod to Gwrfan Wild-Hair, chat to Samson Dry-Lip, play Boomps-a-daisy with Echel Big-Hip —Zodiac Giants all.

We are alerted to the Mysteries by the very name of the hero, for "*hwch*" means hog, while "*Cul*" or "*Cu*" is a sun-title. Culhwch's origins are a thorough muddle, as usual with fatherless sun-kings; his mother went mad and wandered off from the palace, so that he was born in a pig-sty— which Zodiac students will recognise as less lowly than it seems. He is, significantly, first cousin to Arthur. He is fostered out and "lost" while his royal mother dies and the king his father takes another wife. But an old crone tells her of Culhwch's existence (a variation on the prophesied sun-king's birth), and his step-mother has him brought to court and offers him her daughter in marriage. He protests that he is not ready for marriage (reasonably enough, for he is only seven), and she—a type of wicked step-mother, Arianrhod, or Morgan-le-Faye—curses him with the words "*Thy side shall never strike against woman till thou win Olwen, daughter of Ysbaddaden chief Giant.*" This is tantamount to a death-sentence, for beauteous Olwen is closely guarded by Ysbaddaden—as his name, "*Hawthorn*" implies. She is in fact the original Sleeping Beauty of folklore, behind the thorn-hedge.

Here must be the original of Joseph of Arimathea's Holy Thorn of Glastonbury.

Ysbaddaden is undoubtedly the tired old sun-king; his eyelids have to be propped up by two forks so that he can see to hurl things at Culhwch, his young supplanter. (Balor, the Irish giant whose name betrays his solar character, also needs eye-forks.) Ysbaddaden's failing eyes may account for the strange similarity of his name to the Gnostic Abaddon, Prince of Darkness. Was it carried by the Cabiri in the dawn of time to the Middle East?

Culhwch enlists the aid of Arthur and his men to find and win Olwen; but no-one knows where Ysbaddaden's castle is, though it is thought to be somewhere in Arthur's kingdom, not far from Severn's banks.

Yet when they eventually come upon it, it stands up high from a great plain, and can be seen for miles—like Glastonbury Tor.

On the way they find a shepherd on a mound, with a huge dog as big as a stallion. (Gemini, that is, the Good Shepherd Orion, and Sirius or Cerberus the great dog of Langport.) His wife, a giantess, complains that Ysbaddaden has slain twenty-three of her sons, and produces the last of them from a chest where she keeps him hidden. It is clear that Ysbaddaden's *"last hour"* is here. The boy goes with the company to wreak vengeance on the old giant, and is obviously the first Jack of the Beanstalk and a Giant-killer. His mother, the giantess Virgo, though affectionately inclined, does not know her own strength, and Cei saves himself from her fatal bear-hug by thrusting a stake between her hands. (Is this the straight line of the Fosse Way, which runs through her hand?) The giantess breaks the stake, just as Jack's mother hacks down the beanstalk. The Fosse Way is also broken in Virgo's hand.

Ysbaddaden's welcome when they reach his fortress on the Tor is to hurl poisoned spears at them; but they catch them and hurl them back, piercing his knee, his back and his eye; yet he is no more than seriously inconvenienced, and realising that their fielding is a match for him, temporises by setting Culhwch some forty tasks, each more impossible than the last. Culhwch with the help of Arthur and his weird men achieve about twelve of them, which is quite enough for any Grail-Quest; the rest are simply duplications of the original number—variations sprung from the oft-told theme. The Cauldron appears under several guises, there are at least six oxen, as many fierce dogs, two Chief Boars and their young, Cors Hundred-Claws who, although he is listed as yet another hound, must be Scorpio, a Virgoan Maiden or two and the Black Witch daughter of the White Witch from the head of the Valley of Grief in the uplands of Hell. This redoubtable hag gives them as much trouble as Twyrch Trwyth Chief Boar himself, until Arthur *"struck her across the middle until she was as two tubs"*. No bad description of our Virgoan Witch's figure! Add the rescue of the Mabon, the Salmon of Wisdom, the wise-counselling Stag of Rhedinfre, three equally wise old birds of unimaginable antiquity, two giants with the significant names of Wrnach and Diurnach (Urn-Giants), and our Zodiac requirements are fully met.

Our heroes return triumphantly to Ysbaddaden, shave his beard as requested (an operation which includes cropping both ears, scalping him and finally making a job of it by beheading him) while Culhwch gets his girl, who we may see as Sophia, the wisdom of the Mysteries.

The *Dream of Rhonabwy*, the last of this group of Independent Native Tales, reads at first glance like an interminable catalogue from a theatrical costumier. Every fringe and button on the tunics of the hosts who assemble in the glittering pageant of Rhonabwy's dream is noted with loving care; the bard who tells the tale admits that no-one can tell it without a book *"by reason of the number of colours that were on the horses, and all that variety of colours both on the arms and their trappings, and on the precious mantles, and the magic stones."*

But all this froth and bubble is I believe intended to divert us from perceiving the strong-flowing river of time and history beneath. The Dream of Rhonabwy is a lament for the lost Mysteries of a greater past.

The dreamer, caught up in one of those endemic Celtic feuds of succession, falls asleep on a flea-bitten ox-hide in a ruinous hall. This setting is designed to contrast with the royal splendour of his vision, and to point the poverty-stricken misery of present reality compared with the magnificence of his country's past. For he dreams of Arthur's noble retinue. When Rhonabwy and his companions appear before the great king, he laughs, and asks where such little fellows were found? *"Lord"*, says his servant, *"at what art thou laughing?" "I am not laughing"* says Arthur, *"But rather I feel sad that men as mean as these keep this Island, after men as fine as those that kept if of yore."*

The hosts gather, company by company, each in its own minutely described livery, at a ford on the Severn; the Battle of Badon is imminent. Yet it never quite happens, and though there is much to-ing and fro-ing, it has all the inconclusiveness of a dream. Arthur seats himself on a great throne, wrapped in a mantle that renders him invisible, yet able to see all. He plays an interminable game of *gwyddbwyll* with his knight Owein, using gold pieces on a silver board, which we recognise as the chess-game of fate. Here once more is the Zodiac's Father-God, manipulating armies and human affairs on the chessboard of the world. Britain's history is being played, and as the games are lost and won, so the men of one side or another are picked off and devoured by black ravens.

At last Arthur, wearied of all this senseless destruction, crushes the chessmen and the board, and summons bards to sing to him. *"But never a man was there might understand that song . . . save that it was in praise of Arthur."* Rhonabwy is lamenting that no one understands or remembers the Glastonbury Giants, whose philosophy had once inspired his land to greatness.

Sleeping on an ox-skin was a well-tried method of inducing clairvoyant dreams; Trojan Brutus dreamt of Britain on such a couch. The Dream of Rhonabwy was that of an initiate in the *"Ox-pen of the Bards"*, and as its locale suggests, took place in Avalon.

The last three tales are romances of later date, and though Zodiac clues are no less in evidence, the characters and adventures have lost the original Celtic exuberance. One misses the wit and guile of the earlier tales, the savagery of the carnivorous sow, the delicious deformities of Big-Hip and Bow-Back, the mind-boggling men who could hear an ant at its morning toilet a hundred miles off, or run along tree-tops as fast as the wind. Caers blossom into turreted keeps, pig-stealing gives way to tournaments and the noble Quest of the Grail, and all is heavy brocade and polished armour.

However, though minstrels tailored their lays to suit the new Norman nobility, the ancient theme of the Mysteries was still the burden of their song.

The Lady of the Fountain, first of this last group of romances, begins with a tale of woe from a failed initiate, Cynan.

Cynan, a visitor at Arthur's court, tells his most extraordinary adventure. He was young, high-spirited and arrogant when he began it, but has ended up a sadder, humbler man. He found the fairest vale in the world, with trees *"of equal height"* (which at once alert us to Merddin's Avallenau.) In a great plain was a shining castle near the sea, with four-and-twenty maidens, all lovelier than Guinevere at her best. (Where can he be but in Avalon's Zodiac-Clock?)

He is directed to seek a big black man on a mound with one foot and one eye, armed with a club. (This must be the Giant Orion on Gemini's Dundon Hill, surrounded, as Cynan saw, by animals.) All these creatures, lions, stags, serpents, bow down to him just as the Zodiac menagerie does to the Gemini Giant, and "are as numerous as the *stars in the firmament"*. The Giant is doubtless black because he is the dying sun-god, already embarked in his moon-boat for his nightly journey beneath the earth. One remembers too the *"fallen angels"* of Enoch, chained to *"black mountains in the far west"*.

From here Cynan is directed to a hill beneath which is a fountain with a golden bowl. If he spills its water on the ground, the Giant tells him, he will get all the adventures he wants, and more than he bargains for. Cynan finds the fountain, spills the water, and with an earth-quaking thunder-clap comes a hailstorm which kills every living thing. Cynan, almost killed too, next encounters an outraged Black Knight whose land he has unwittingly devastated. Ignominiously beaten, he returns humiliated to Arthur's court.

"God knows," he says, recounting the tale to Owein, *"no man ever confessed against himself to a story of greater failure than this. And yet, how*

strange that I have never heard tell, before or since, of anyone who might know aught concerning this adventure, save as much as I have told, and how the root of this tale is in the dominions of the emperor Arthur without its being hit upon."

"Why, sirs," said Owein, *"were it not well to go and seek to hit upon that place?"*

He sets out, finds the vale, its castle and its twenty-four maidens, the Black Giant and the fountain beneath the hill. He spills the water from the golden bowl on the ground, provoking the storm that spreads devastation and strips the leaves from the trees. (We may know that this happened at Chalice Well, because the arms of Glastonbury Abbey bore a tree, lopped, stripped and bare.)

It is the same golden bowl that once held Rhiannon and Pryderi prisoner; they (like many today who first hear of the Zodiac's inspirational philosophy) are dumbfounded and unable to react to it.

Owein symbolises another common reaction by spilling its water—outright rejection. In both cases the Waste Land inevitably follows.

But in the later romance of Owein, the spilling of the water has become an inexplicable ritual necessary at the outset of his adventure, while the punishment of the Waste Land in which the original initiates wandered for so long is compressed into a sharp hailstorm and the conventional duel with the Black Knight, whom Owein, improving on Cynan's performance, defeats. We need to remember the earlier myth of Manawydan if we are to recognise the Waste Land episode here.

(When Rhiannon and Pryderi stick fast to the golden bowl, everything disappears, and Manawydan and Cigfa are left alone to build up civilisation from scratch by becoming hunters, craftsmen and farmers. But their progress is dishearteningly slow, for everything they attempt is brought down or snatched away by the rampant forces of chaos. At last Manawydan, stripped bare of all but his native cunning, outwits them and restores his friends, and his world, to order and sanity. Manawydan the Wise is Man; the history of Mankind.)

But Owein's Waste Land is still ahead of him. He marries the widow of the knight he has slain (or in other words, embraces the Mysteries) and becomes the doughty champion of the Fountain. But after a blissful honeymoon period, a longing comes upon him for the life at Arthur's court, and promising to return in three months, he deserts the Lady of the Fountain for three years. Incensed, she returns his ring, and he, stricken with remorse, rushes off into the wilderness and lives with the animals until his clothes drop off and he grows hair all over his body. (The honeymoon period followed by the growing horror of self-knowledge is well-known to students of the Mysteries. Is he traversing the state of Capricorn, the hairy animal-man?)

At last he has seen and suffered enough, and is found more dead than alive and anointed with precious ointment by a compassionate damsel, so that his hair falls away in scaly tufts and he slowly comes to himself again. (Is she Virgo, or has he returned to the healing of Aquarian Chalice Well?) He repays her by defeating her oppressor, and politely declining her offer of marriage goes on his way, for he is now able to resist such extra-marital adventures.

He next saves a lion from a serpent (Leo and Hydra are inter-twined in Avalon's Zodiac, both being drawn by the river Cary), and the lion becomes his constant companion and guardian, helping him to defeat all wrong-doers. While sharing a tasty roebuck with him, Owein hears a maiden moaning from within an urn; it is Luned, his lost wife's moon-maiden, who procured his marriage to the Lady of the Fountain and is now about to be burnt for his faithlessness. But before he can rescue her he has to encounter a savage monster and save two boys, (Gemini) with the lion's help. Just in time he returns to Luned to find two more handsome youths about to burn her, slays them, returns with her in triumph to his wife, and they all go to live happily at Arthur's court. He has learned to live *with* the Mysteries and *by* them. But he has one last adventure with the Black Oppressor, whose hall is strewn with corpses. He must be Scorpio, the House of Death.

Owein conquers but does not slay him—for who can slay Death?—and liberates *twenty-four* widows from durance. He has harrowed Hell and freed its captives, in true sun-king style, at the same time redeeming his own wasted hours, his misspent youth. For what else are these *"Houris"* but the Hours of the Zodiac Clock?

Peredur Son of Efrawg, the hero of the next romance, is also on this Pilgrim's Progress, as his name, "Round about the hard way", implies. Peredur stands half-way between Celtic Pryderi ("Searcher for the beauty of the natural order") and the Grail knight Perceval—"Pierce the veil". These three heroes are obviously connected by name, character and adventures, and are in the mainstream of the flow of the ancient Mysteries from Druidic to Templar times. All are honest simpletons who make good.

Peredur, seventh son of an earl, his father and six brothers all killed in battle, is hidden by his mother in rustic obscurity, away from the hazards of chivalry. But Fate sends three armed knights jingling past him in a glade. *"They are angels"*, says his mother when he eagerly asks what they are. *"I too will be an angel!"* replies the boy stoutly, and making a saddle of withies he rides off to Arthur's court on a bony nag, armed only with holly-darts. He leaves poor mother fainting, and unknown to him she dies heart-broken.

On his first brash adventure he siezes meat and drink from a whimsical lady who gives him all he asks, including a ring—surely the Zodiac circle. He little knows what he has bound upon himself. Arrived at Arthur's court he is prophetically hailed as a deliverer by two dwarfs. Cei kicks them flying, and sneers at Peredur's ridiculous get-up, suggesting that he wins his spurs by avenging Guinevere on a knight who has just thrown wine in her face. No knight has dared this adventure, but Peredur fatally pierces his eye through the narrow slit in the visor with a well-aimed holly-dart, and helped by Owein, dons his victim's armour, something which in his ignorance he cannot do unaided. A holly-dart in the eye is a winter sun-hero's death, and Peredur, his successor, takes his enemy's horse on further adventures, swearing to avenge the dwarfs on Cei.

He leaves Arthur at Caerleon (surely royal Somerton on Leo of Lyonesse) and rides to Gemini, where he sees two boys fishing on a lake, and accepts a venerable lame man as his guru. (Who but the Fisher-King of the later Perceval legend, who is both Menu the Sage and Pryderi's wise Manawydan? Here Peredur defeats two Geminian youths at sword-play, and is sent to the Grail-Castle, (though it is not named), being warned to ask no questions or betray astonishment at what he may see there. So when a strange variant of the Grail-procession passes by, he can hardly be blamed for his silence. It is a horrifying charade—a lance dripping with blood and instead of the covered Grail a decapitated head upon a silver salver. Peredur continues his conversation as though nothing had happened, doubtless hoping that if he takes no notice it will go away.

The tale of Peredur has been described as a Grail legend without the Grail—but is this not Bran's inspirational head which replaced the Celtic Cauldron of Wisdom? And was the Cauldron not the earliest form of the Grail? The Mystic Vessel is here all right, but disguised.

If the Grail is not easily recognisable in this tale, neither is the Waste Land, which should follow Peredur's dumb-founded silence. Yet it too happens off-stage, for later on in the tale a loathsomely ugly girl upbraids Peredur for not asking about the procession, attributing her deformities and many other evils to his silence or lack of concern. (She is of course Perceval's Loathly Damsel.)

Peredur's adventures at this stage symbolise youthful thoughtlessness; he thrusts through happily oblivious of the damage he leaves in his wake. This is emphasised in the next encounter.

He defeats a knight who has just slain another, and forces him to marry the dead man's wailing widow. The widow curses him as the cause of his mother's death—the first he knows of this—and later in the tale reappears to curse him for her enforced and loveless union.

Poor Peredur! He tries hard, but can't get it right yet, and has fallen into the trap of trying to right all wrongs by force majeur, without much vision or psychology.

He is both fair-minded and chaste, however, as he proves when his next adventure leads him to a besieged castle, where nineteen brothers offer him the lion's share of the meagre rations and their unwilling sister into the bargain, to induce the young champion to help their cause. But Peredur insists on fair shares for all, politely declines the maiden, and defeats all their enemies without reward.

His growing stature makes him a target for sorcery, but he is proof against its power, and banging nine witches on the head, he forces them to teach him all they know. Our simpleton is learning fast.

Many students of the occult get no further than the witches' Court, but Peredur is not content with black magic. Significantly, his next meeting is with a hermit. He lodges the night, and falls into a meditative trance. True, we are told that he is dreaming of his lady-love; but ladies in chivalry frequently denote a more mystical attraction, and in the context of the hermit's cell we may reasonably take it thus. From this trance Peredur is not to be diverted, though no less a person than Arthur desires to see him. Knights who summon him brusquely are absent-mindedly overthrown while our hero continues his meditation; scornful Cei is left half-dead; churlish and aging sun-king that he is, he suffers here his long-promised coup-de-grace. But charm, we are to understand, can turn the strong where bullying fails; and in response to Gwalchmai's courteous entreaty Peredur consents to come to and meet the great Arthur. Gone is the simpleton, the boy from the backwoods; gone the brash adventurer. Peredur is now worthy of the Order of Chivalry; he has shewn that his first allegiance is to the King of Kings, and now even the Round Table's king eagerly seeks his friendship.

But there are qualities he must still acquire, impulses he must learn to subdue. At Caer Llion he meets the beauty Angharad, is rejected, and swears a vow of silence until she accepts him. This is one of the initiate's hardest ordeals, and recurs in Arthurian legend, involving the hero in calumny and injury without self-justification or explanation. Sad, silent and alone he wanders into the wilderness of self-analysis.

His first battle is with a lion, which he throws into a deep pit filled with Leo's victims. The geography here resembles the craggy quarries and ravines of Leo's head—and as he next meets two she-giants, one young, one old, who explain that he is in the Round Valley where all are Giants—we can recognise Leo and Two-faced Virgo in the Zodiac's Round Table. He next kills a serpent and takes its gold ring, (Draco); is wounded in the thigh (Gemini) by Scorpionic Cei, and is even attacked by Arthur himself who fails to recognise him, so wasted and wan has he become. Arthur is undoubtedly the effigy of Sagittarius, for though he charges Peredur *he does not budge from the spot*. It is another duel between the young and old sun-kings of gigantic proportions, for everyone goes to the tops of their houses and hills and high places to watch. Arthur (as in the Zodiac) is unhorsed. Angharad falls for the wan unknown victor—she is one who obviously prefers her men pale and interesting—and Peredur, released from his silence, makes himself known and returns in triumph to Arthur's Court with his girl.

And that, one might think, is the happy ending. Not a bit of it—there are still pages of adventures in store for our knight errant. One wishes, indeed, that the tale *would* end there, for thereafter Peredur's encounters tend to repeat not only themselves, but almost every other Arthurian adventure his conteur can remember. One gets the impression that Peredur's story-teller, caught in the golden ring of the Zodiac, will go round and round for ever. But as even these repetitious variations contain pearls for Zodiac students, we must follow them until the raconteur drops dead from very exhaustion.

A stag-hunt leads Peredur to the court of a big one-eyed black man, known as the Black Oppressor. (Scorpio?) Before ridding the world of this plague, Peredur learns that he lost his eye attempting to wrest from a Worm a stone that turned all to gold. This our hero must have, but on his way he comes to the court of the Sons of the King of Suffering, surely Gemini's stricken and Messianic effigy. They are killed each day by an "Addanc", a fearsome monster we recognise as the Avanc or Whale—but are revived by immersion in a tub (the Cauldron, here signed by the Ship that cradles Gemini).

The ancient Celtic name of this monster makes one pause.

As Peredur's uncles own the Zodiac Castles or Houses of his adventures, the word *"Avanc"* must derive from the same root as the Latin *"avunculus"*.

This suspicion is confirmed by the later Perceval, whose father and eleven uncles owned all Avalon. The wicked uncles were Scorpio and Capricorn, and the owner of the *Castle of the Whale*. (Joseph of Arimathea, too, in British legend was the great-uncle of Jesus—planting his flowering Thorn on Piscean Weary-All Hill, just above our Avanc-Whale.)

Undeterred by the sight of these dead Sons of the King of Suffering, Peredur presses on to tangle with the Addanc, though lovely maidens clutch at him and warn him he will not be revived if he is killed. He is even offered two paths to comfort and safety, but stoutly chooses the third which leads him to the monster's cave, and is given a stone of invisibility by a mysterious damsel in return for pledging his love.

This, forgetting all about Angharad, he gladly gives. (Is Peredur merely unfaithful, or is this a later hero who knows nothing of Angharad, whose adventures are variations on the original theme and then added to it? Or are his ladies ideals, unattainable until attained, then inevitably replaced by higher ones?)

"Where shall I seek for thee?" he asks. *"In the direction of India"* she answers enigmatically and disappears.

The Addanc has a nasty habit of striking his challengers with a poisoned spear from behind a pillar at his cave-mouth. This pillar must be the North

Pole, stretching from the Dragon's head at Butleigh, the Zodiac's centre, to the Pole Star. And is the Pole-Star not the alchemical stone in Draco's tail? I suspect indeed that all the stones that change hands in these tales are important stars in the Zodiac's astro-philosophy, for after killing the wily Addanc with superior guile, Peredur gives the stone of invisibility to Edlym Red-Sword, his trusty (if temporary) follower. Is "Edlym" Red-Eyed Taurus, whose red star Aldebaran connects with the star Antares in Scorpio to form the Zodiac's equinoctial line? Yes, Edlym *is* Taurus, ruled by Venus; for Peredur rewards him with a stray countess he does not need, and the Bull, well contented with this countess-cow, promptly drops out of the story.

Peredur now comes to Aries, for at this point he sees a flock of black and white sheep, and a burning bush, recognisable to Zodiac students as the sign of Taurus-Moses, the "two-horned" leader.

After this he reaches a river-valley, a veritable forest of water-mills, all busily grinding corn to feed a great gathering, met to joust for the hand of the Empress of Constantinople. Recognising her as the Lady from India, he falls into one of his trances, gazing upon her for three days while the tournament proceeds without him. Meanwhile he lodges with the miller and borrows money from him for maintenance. The practical miller's wife, realising that trance-states pay no bills, goads her husband into waking Peredur with a great clout from an axe-haft. Smiling, Peredur comes to and proceeds to business, overthrowing hundreds at the tournament and deluging both Empress and miller with booty. As victor, he is acclaimed Knight of the Mill, and wins fourteen happy years with the Empress. (One suspects that Cervantes owed Don Quixote's famous mill-episode to Peredur.)

But who is this seductive Empress? Is she not Sophia, symbol of Constantinople's Gnostic Wisdom? For the Cymry came from *"Deffrobane"*, said variously to be Constantinople and Ceylon.

While they "converse graciously" together, three huge men give her goblets, challenging her to give them to any champion who dares fight. Peredur accepts all three, tosses down the wine, and slays them one by one. He has dared to drink of the cup his Saviour drank, and withstood the worst the three "wicked uncles"—Scorpio, Capricorn and Pisces, could do to him. He is master of Wisdom, of Circumstance, of Fate.

But isn't this where we came in? Is this not the insulted Guinevere once more? As if to underline this, the Loathly Damsel here makes a belated appearance. She should have appeared when he failed to shew concern at the anguished Grail procession—but better late than never, for her description will make the most nondescript of us feel better. *"Blacker were her face and hands than the blackest iron steeped in pitch; but it was not her colour that was ugliest, but her shape: high cheeks and hanging baggy-fleshed face, and a stub wide-nostrilled nose; one eye mottled green, most piercing, the other jet black, deep-set in her head. Long yellow teeth, yellower than flowers of broom, and her belly swelling from her breastbone higher than her chin. Her backbone was shaped like a crutch; her hips broad, but everything narrow thence downwards, save that her feet and knees were clumped."*

She is, like Peer Gynt's natural son, a symbol of the ruin caused by his youthful folly, and like Peer Gynt's son she curses him. Because he did not shew concern at the macabre emblems of the bloody lance and head, the kingdom fell into strife; injustice and oppression stalked the land.

Peredur, faced with his past self, is stricken with horror. He is fired with a desire to understand, and sets out for the Castle of Wonders. A priest reproves him for riding, for it is Good Friday—a time for dying to the old self. Humbly he walks to a castle, where he is imprisoned unjustly for three days by its king. Secretly freed by the king's daughter, he fights his jailor's enemies and returns nightly to voluntary imprisonment again, until the king recognises his champion, frees him and loads him with honours. It is a variation of the sun-hero's *Harrowing of Hell.* Only when the initiate sees himself is he able to forgive his enemies and do good to those who hate him. Agreeing profoundly with his severest critics, his only desire is to make reparation for his past blindness. It is the Easter of Rebirth.

But he is *too* impatient to put things right. At the Castle of Wonders he sees chessmen playing themselves, and when the wrong side wins he throws the pieces and the board into the lake. The Loathly Damsel once more reproves him; this is the Empress's chessboard, and he must recover it. I take this as a reproof against impatience at the slow process of historical Evolution. Peredur despairs that right will ever triumph. He has yet to see that evil is necessary if we are to exercise free-will; that without it we cannot learn to choose. (Where would he, or we, be without it? The polarity of Good and Evil is like the polarity of the north and south pole, essential for the electromagnetic field which we call life and consciousness. Only while this field exists can we gain experience; only while the chessboard is there can the pieces play. This, surely, is the meaning of the recurring symbol of *gwyddbwyll* in Celtic and Arthurian legend. No mean philosophers, the Druids! They had an answer to a problem over which twentieth century churchmen still scratch their heads.)

To recover the board however is not just a matter of diving into the lake, the Ugly Maiden tells Peredur—he must fight and overcome the Black Man of the Castle of Ysbidinongle. (Ysbidinongle is readily recognised as a jumbled—or jingled—version of the giant Ysbaddaden in *"Culhwch and Olwen";* but in this context he is obviously Giant Despair, for when Peredur ditched the chessboard he was committing the deadliest sin of all.)

He kills the giant, only to find that he must also slay an enormous one-horned stag who is laying waste the forest. Here Capricorn makes its belated entry into the tale. Ruled by Saturn, planet of limitation, hard work and frustration, this seems to indicate that Peredur, having conquered despair, next settles down to a period of unrewarding struggle. He must now develop perseverance (particularly hard for this glamorous victor of tournaments,) and listen humbly to the advice of that most deformed and despised of God's creatures, the Loathly Damsel. What a change from the brash young tornado who swept all in his path to perdition! Following her instructions to the letter he kills the one-horned monster, but gets small thanks from the Empress who is enamoured of it. (Ladies of Legend have a soft spot for unicorns and minotaurs.) There is however a way to win back her friendship: Peredur must joust three times with a man beside a bush and a stone slab.

By this time the raconteur is exhausted; there is no golden bowl, no fountain, no thunderstorm—but for all that we have been here before. It is Chalice Well, and the knight who guards it rises from under the stone slab as from a grave; he is huge, with rusty armour and a huge bony horse. Every time Peredur unhorses him he leaps back into the saddle—exactly describing Sagittarius' effigy, half out of the saddle, his leg descending into the "grave" of Ponter's Ball. The encounter is inconclusive, for as Peredur, tired of this Jack-in-the-boxing, dismounts and draws his sword, the knight disappears taking Peredur's horse with him.

Our hero must perforce walk to the next castle, where he finds the lame uncle of his earlier adventures, his early mentor. Here all is "explained", though as usual in Arthurian myth we ourselves must try to explain the "explanation".

A youth beside the old lame king claims to be at the back of it all; he was the Ugly Damsel in disguise, the Black Man of Ysbidinongle (Ysbaddaden-uncle?), the youth bearing the bloody Grail-spear, and so on; the decapitated head substituting for the Grail was his cousin's, slain by the witches of Caer Loyw. The youth tells Peredur that they also are cousins.

All these consanguineous relatives are a clue to Grail and Zodiac seekers. The *"Sangreal"* has itself been interpreted as Sang-Real—Royal Blood. The youth, the uncles, the cousins, *are Peredur himself—we ourselves;* of Blood Royal, though half-animal, we are also half-divine, bought, as the Christian Mystery obscurely puts it, by the Blood of Christ.

Peredur has been fighting—himself! All the evils, apparently outward and circumstantial, that he has slowly overcome, were the animal in himself. In losing his horse and walking ignominiously to this Castle of self-knowing, he has lost his original motive-power, his egocentric ambition. But here he finds his horse safely stabled, ready, reconstituted as it were, for use; and able now to carry him in the service of a greater than himself, as he himself is now the Christed Man.

Finally with Arthur and his knights he slays the witches of Caer Loyw whose enchantments caused many men to lose their heads—that is, to be witless and enslaved, unable to see themselves as they truly are.

In *Gereint Son of Erbin* we come to the last of the Mabinogion tales. Its hero, already familiar to readers of Tennyson's poem *"Gereint and Enid"*, is a cousin of Arthur—a pedigree which qualifies him for the Mysteries. He begins gallantly enough at Arthur's court, but is soon stripped of his finery by a cunning device of the story-teller and reduced like Peredur to the status of *"Outlandish Knight"*.

Caught unarmed while hunting with Guinevere, he enquires the name of an aloof and mysterious knight. For answer the knight's dwarf slashes both Gereint and a damsel of Guinevere's across the face with a whip. Honour demands vengeance, and Gereint, disdaining to punish the dwarf, follows the knight until he disappears into his castle. Gereint, needing armour, finds nearby a knight fallen on evil days, dispossessed by Gereint's aloof enemy, who lends him rusty old-fashioned mail and his tattered but beautiful daughter; thus equipped Gereint enters the lists of the knight's tournament and brings him low. For this he finds himself a hero when he reaches Arthur's court, for his arrogant enemy proves to be no less a person than Edern ap Nudd.

But who, you may well ask, is he? Besides being related to the shadowy Gwyn, we hardly know; his legends are all but lost in the Celtic mists of Avalon. But his kinship to Gwyn ap Nudd make him loom like one of Glastonbury's Giants, and this suspicion is deepened by the one remaining memory of his exploits: he is credited with slaying *"three most atrocious Giants"* at Brent Knoll near Athelney. It is the first hint of the Zodiac in the romance of Gereint.

But we have another clue to Edern's identity in Chretien de Troyes, whose tale *"Erec"* reproduces *"Gereint and Enid"*. In *"Erec"* Edern becomes Ider son of Nud. But Ider is Idris, the Geminian Noah in his boat! There seems then little doubt that Gwyn ap Nudd and Edern were either the Gemini brothers, or Arthur-Sagittarius and his young son. Gereint's adventures too are those of the Zodiac's Round Table, and if its details have become blurred this is because the old Welsh story has come back to us from France heavily coated with that country's ancient preoccupation—the love of Paris for Helen. Not for nothing is its capital so named!

Gereint, reigning in Cornwall happily with his bride, becomes soft, and being reproached for this by Enid, drives her angrily before him, determined to prove to her that he is as brave as ever. He takes her gentle reproach as evidence of infidelity—he can't be in the wrong, so it must be she—and though she warns him of every danger, his morose jealously increases until he goes mad. (It is interesting to find that he defeats *twelve* robber-knights on the journey, even so.)

At last he tackles three enormous giants at once, is overcome and left for dead. Enid's shriek of despair brings help and he is carried to an earl's court, where the earl loses no time in propositioning Enid. At her faithful refusal he boxes her ungallantly on the ear, and her scream brings Gereint's "corpse" to life; weak as he is, he cleaves the earl in two. They ride off on one horse, a delightful symbol of their reconciliation. They meet the Little King, or the king of Zodiac Fairyland (whose castle sounds very like Glastonbury Tor) who tells Gereint that in the valley below there is a hedge of mist, within which enchanted games are played—dangerous games from which no adventurer has returned. They are in the dominion of earl Ywein—surely Owein, Arthur's gwyddbwyll-partner. It is not chess that is played this time, but something more sinister; for though the hedge is of mist reaching right into the sky, it somehow manages to have thorns, and each thorn spikes a human head.

Undeterred, Gereint enters alone into the mist and finds a great orchard (where can this be but Avalon?) with a horn hung on an apple-tree beside a pavilion. Within is a maiden, and beside her an empty chair, obviously the Siege Perilous of Arthurian legend. Gereint boldly seats himself upon it and at once is confronted with its scandalised owner, a ferocious mounted knight. The battle is long and hard, but after breaking several lances Gereint defeats him, and blowing the horn from the apple-tree, forever disperses the mists and enchantments of the place. On this fanfare the Mabinogion ends.

But Gereint was not so successful as his tale implies; the enchantment lingers still; nor are the mists of Avalon so easily dispersed.

Gereint was Earl of Cornwall, and near Looe there still exists an earthwork known as the "Giants' Hedge". A local legend tells how Giants caused this to grow in order to protect *"an old man and a boy"* from their pursuers. The Rev. H. A. Lewis, in his little booklet *"Did Christ Come to Cornwall?"* takes the legend as a reference to Christ and Joseph of Arimathea; but can we separate these from the Holy Boy of Somerset's Gemini and his Zodiacal *"uncle"*?

The Giant Ysbaddaden's thorn-hedge is still palpably with us as Joseph's magically-flowering thorn at Weary-All Hill and Glastonbury. What is legend, what is fact? Celts wisely refused to separate the two, seeing the facts of history as the working-out of the eternal pattern of Myth on the revolving stage of Time...

Are not the eleven *"Branches"* of the Mabinogion a clue to this? Are they not the eleven branches of the Caballistic and eternal Tree of Life, still rooted in Avalon's first Eden, its apples leaning down low to refresh us with their wisdom as we penetrate the hedge of mist which surrounds us?

23: Joseph of Arimathea

Did Joseph come to Britain or didn't he?

If we admit the possibility that he may have been a Phoenician, his journey, at first sight so improbable, becomes much less so. But however much evidence we collect (and there is much) it is never entirely conclusive; acceptance or rejection of his legends seems in the last analysis to depend on subjective factors—our type, or level of understanding—even among those who have troubled to inform themselves on the matter.

But the struggle to arrive at a conclusion leaves us greatly enriched; even if we never arrive, the journey is vastly rewarding, making many things clear that were hidden from our eyes. Joseph in other words belongs like Arthur to the world of myth, whose function is to heighten understanding. This is not to say that Joseph is not historical—rather that his historicity is less important than the truths his legends conceal.

He symbolises Gnostic, Johannine *Zodiac* Christianity, brought to Britain in Phoenician-Roman times, reviving Druidic teaching in a new form just when that ancient organisation had collapsed. The Druids were finally massacred in Mona in 61 AD; Joseph, legend tells, arrived in 63, accepting the Twelve Hides of Glastonbury for maintenance of his party—the Zodiac Mysteries. (If they were to nourish *him*, we may suspect that he in turn was to preserve *them*.)

The *"primitive Christianity"* he brought to Britain differed from the later Roman brand in tonsure, rubric, feast-dates and above all in emphasis. This last reflected a deep difference of outlook—the difference between the literal, factual mind and the poetic and mystical.

Celt, Armenian and Copt favoured several imaginative and allegorical writings which were soon banned by Rome, (now called the New Testament Apocrypha) ascribed to various apostles and abounding in miracles, Gnostic allusions to the Mysteries, Pythagorean numerology and angelic hierarchies. The Cauldron revives the dead as in Greek and Celtic myth, and the Grail (though not under that name) plays an important part as the Cup of the last Supper, the cup by which an angel ministered to Christ in the Agony in the Garden, and the cup offered to the Virgin Mary at the Annunciation.

The idea of the Grail as a cup indeed stems from these Apocryphal books, though even there its growth from the more ancient Cauldron can be traced. St. John for instance was immersed in a boiling cauldron, surviving unhurt. It was the Cauldron of the Mysteries, for he was guardian of the Virgin, herself the *"Chosen Vessel"*, being identified with the mystical Cup like Ceres with the cornucopia. *"Christ, Son of Mary, my Cauldron of pure descent"* sang the 12th century bard Daffyd Benfras, punning on Mair and Pair, Welsh for Cauldron.

The cult of Mary was only adopted by Rome under popular pressure from the eastern and western churches; but Joseph and the Grail was too much—the line had to be drawn somewhere. Both breathed the earlier Mysteries, from which Roman Christianity was anxious to cut itself loose; its Christ was to be literal, historical, new—not a re-statement of eternal verities long held under various guises all over the world.

Something of forceful, practical St. Peter pervades the church he is said to have founded; something of the mysterious St. John clings to the Johannine churches of Celt and Asian. Simple Simon Peter, providing for his dependants by fishing, made up for his somewhat dim understanding of the divine teaching by ardent devotion to his master; St. John *"the Divine"*, celibate and seer, withdrawn on Patmos out of time, comprehended Alpha and Omega and the purpose of it all in an apocalyptic flash. Peter, charged to *"Feed My sheep"*, was to provide spiritual nourishment at ground-level—the Church in the world. Obviously feeling that this was not the whole story he pointed to John and said *"And what of this man, Lord?"* The enigmatic answer came *"If it is My will that he should/wait until I come, what is that to thee?"*

Off-beat Christians have thus seen John as the vehicle of the Church of the Future, destined at last to supersede the Petrine Rock; one whose enlightenment would eclipse the blind faith of Peter's. Others have seen the two as co-existent, Peter's church as the triumphant Lion, John's as the elusive Unicorn. The rare moments when the two have co-existed in amity, they argue, have produced high points of civilisation; our royal arms supporters are an idealistic symbol, not often operational. Prester (Presbyter) John's kingdom was a secret place, much sought, seldom found. But there are signs that in these apocalyptic days the secret understanding, the clairvoyant perception of the Johannine vision is coming into its own. The sceptical, questioning man of the dawning Aquarian Age needs to *know*, whether by normal or paranormal means, what it is all about; the blind unquestioning faith of the Piscean age is no longer adequate. Is the day of the Church of John almost here?

The "Acts of Pilate" or Gospel of Nicodemus

In the New Testament Apocrypha Joseph of Arimathea has an importance not accorded him in the canonical Gospels. But these gospels were selected by the *Roman* church from a vast amount of early Christian writings. Gnostic books fared badly in this early 11+ selection; though John was included, as the disciple Jesus loved, those who thought like him got short shrift. John's Book of Revelations was already on the lunatic fringe. Enough was enough.

Joseph was one of the casualties, the writings attributed to him excluded. The Gospels say nothing about his doings after the crucifixion; he does not appear in the Acts. As far as the faithful knew, he might have died after the Entombment.

The 4th century Acts of Pilate has a different story to tell, one of great consequence for Grail legend. Joseph, it asserts, was arrested and imprisoned on suspicion of faking the Resurrection by taking Jesus' body from his tomb, but the risen Lord, lifting up the jail bodily, allowed him to creep out from under it and return home to Arimathea, so that when they came to stone him to death they found the seals unbroken, but the captive fled.

Summoned once more before the Sanhedrin to explain himself, he silenced them with his erudition and sincerity, demonstrating how the Resurrection was foretold in the Law and the Prophets. Faced with evidence from their own sacred books they became uneasy and demanded further witnesses. Nicodemus came forward to corroborate Joseph's words, also two souls recently in Hell but released by Christ's Harrowing. Witnesses indeed!

(Christians owe their belief in His descent to this account—an element in the earlier Mysteries.)

The names of these two witnesses, Leucius and Charinus, or Kerin, are intriguing: Kerin means Cornish, and Leucius is the same name as that of the British king who c. 170 AD officially declared our country Christian. *Did Joseph call two Cornish-Phoenician tin-traders to witness to the real existence of the Western Hades?* Confirmation of this wild theory appears in the "Questions of Bartholomew", another Apocryphal book we shall quote.

Difficult as it is for chauvinist Britons to admit that even two of their compatriots went to Hell, nevertheless if the horrid thought be entertained for a minute some interesting ideas arise. The name Charinus or Kerin is surely that of Charon, who in Greek myth ferried the souls of the dead across the Styx to the Underworld. We know that the ancients thought this to be in Britain, and this is confirmed by Procopius, the 6th century Byzantine historian who records a rumour that Breton sailors were excused all taxes by the Franks because they had to ferry dead souls across the Channel to Britain at night—an unenviable task.

The Acts of Pilate tells how the Sanhedrin tested Leucius and Kerin by making them write their account of Christ's Harrowing of Hell in separate cells and that their testimony agreed to the letter. (Their texts agree with the Zodiac too, for in their Hades were the Archangel Michael, Adam and Eve, Enoch, and the two Crucifixion robbers.)

All this came to Pilate's ear, and he bade the Jews search their prophecies. What chiefly disturbed them in their research were the *measurements of the Ark*. Its length, they read, was two and a half cubits, its height and breadth one and a half—a total of five and a half cubits. By a process I can only describe as *"Arimathean Arithmetic"* they reluctantly concluded that this represented five and a half thousand years from the first Adam to the second, and that the man they had crucified was indeed their promised Messiah.

Though these calculations will hardly impress us as deeply as it affected Pilate, they do nonetheless shew that the Ark was thought to contain a timescale by which the past and future could be read, events of great moment recognised.

Such mathematics are worthy of Math son of Mathonwy, Lord of the British Zodiac or Hades; or of Enoch who preserved them through the Flood in his Ark. Yes, Joseph of Arimathea knew what he was doing when he brought two Cornish sailors to testify to the truth of his incredible story. Were they fresh from Hell, or Britain? It amounts to the same thing.

So it is consoling to remember that Celts regarded Hell and Heaven as the same place, and that the Greek Underworld was also the delectable Hesperides Garden. Only our Zodiac resolves this contradiction. To those who could master its planetary impulses it was Paradise; to those enslaved by them it was Hell. Or so the Hyperborean Druids taught, capturing the imagination of the ancient world.

Today we are taught to deride the study of astrology as irrelevant to our course; but what mariner ever came safe to port without a knowledge of winds, weather, tides, currents, and above all the stars? The earliest Christians knew better, and Joseph of Arimathea was a master-mariner.

The Questions of Bartholomew

The early Christians were well aware of the British Zodiac, as this Apocryphal writing shews. Here the apostles beg the resurrected Christ to shew them Hell. Reluctantly, he gives in. "Beckoning to the *angels of the West*" he transports them to a place called Cherubim, or Tartarus, *the place of truth*. Here Christ dares the terrified Bartholomew to stand on the neck of Beliar, a *huge giant 1900 cubits long*, and ask his name. This, Bartholomew learns, is not only Beliar but Satanas, *"the angel who keeps Hell"*. (We are in Taliesin's *"land of the Cherubim"*, with its *"formidable animal of the city of Satanas, whose mouth was as wide as the mountains of Mynnau"*, Beliar's mouth too *"was as the gulf of a precipice"*. Bartholomew, finding courage, *presses him half into the earth*, reminding us of Cornish St. Padarn, who pressed Arthur himself into the earth up to his head.

Beliar, under this pressure, says he was the first angel made when God

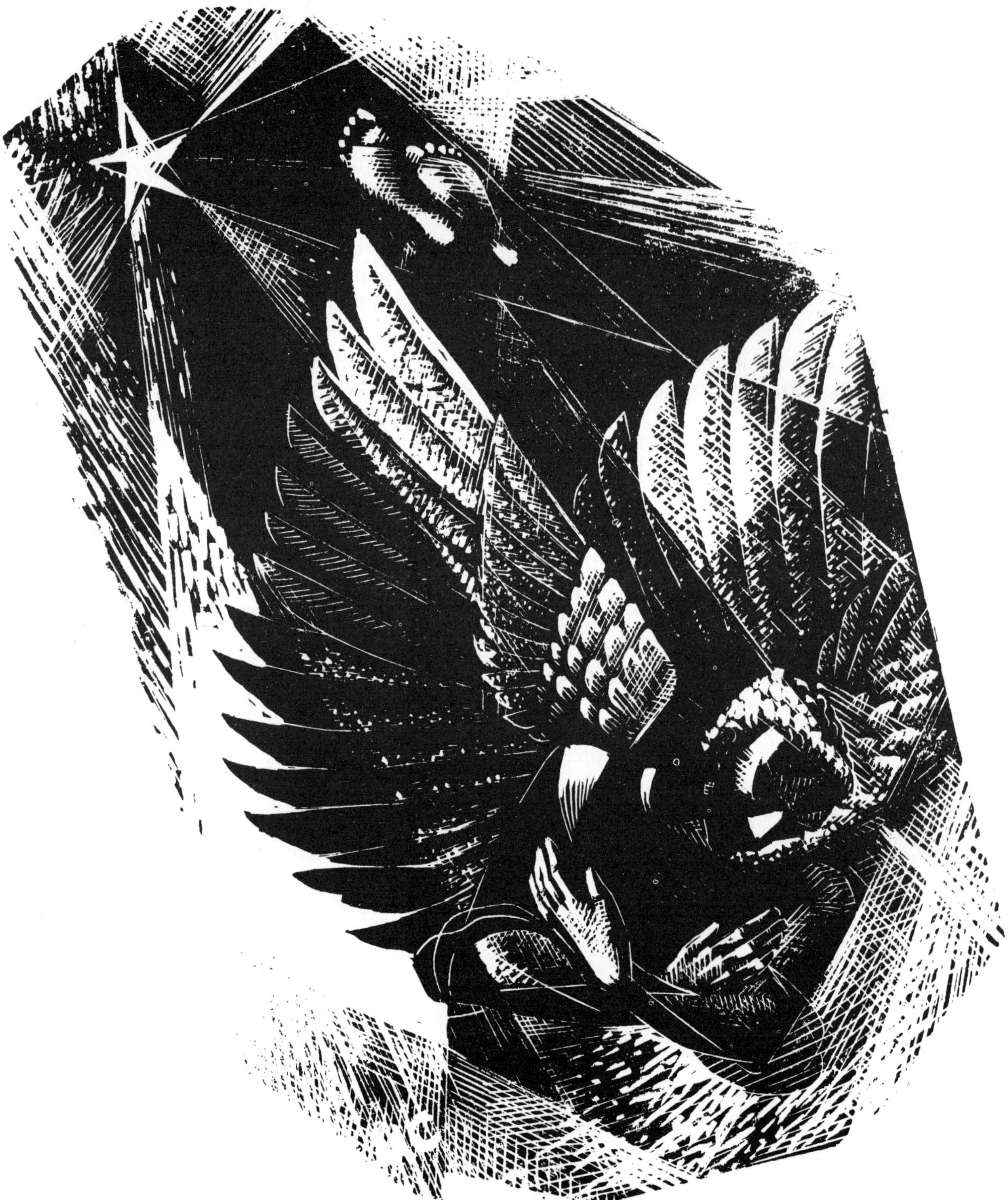

made the heavens, followed by Michael, Gabriel, Raphael, etc. They are obviously stars.

When Satanas fell to earth with the rebel angels he fell into Tartarus, (which Hesiod says was the abode of the fallen rebel Titans. Tartessus, said the Greeks, was on the Atlantic coast.) Tar-tar, says Graves, means "far, far, west".

Beliar tells how he traps men into the seven deadly sins, and these, we have seen, were enslavement to the planetary impulses.

The mystic cup so reminiscent of the Grail also appears in the *"Questions of Bartholomew"*. An angel conjures it from the air with a loaf of bread to nourish the Virgin at the Annunciation, thus consecrating her the Chosen Vessel to bear the Son of God.

The Story of Joseph of Arimathea, which purports to be told by himself, is the next Apocryphal fragment to be reviewed. It is perhaps disappointing that it does not mention the Grail at all. But it does betray knowledge of the Zodiac. It contrasts the two robbers of the Crucifixion in such a way that we can hardly fail to recognise them as the Gemini Twins—one all too mortal, the other received in heaven with honours worthy of the Christed Man. Mercury, god of thieves, rules Gemini; a fact well-known to the Gnostic author of this tale.

One robber, Gestas, was beyond redemption, stripping wayfarers, hanging up women by the feet and cutting off their breasts, and drinking the blood of babes. The crimes of the other, Demas, were more excusable; like Robin Hood he robbed the rich to give to the poor. He also stole the Law from the Temple, seizing the *mystic deposit of Solomon*—(the ark?)—and stripping the priestess, Caiaphas' daughter, intriguingly named Sarra. She obviously guarded the Mysteries of Sarras, goal of all Grail-seekers. The robber who stole the Ark and stripped its priestess of her *sari* was aiming high; had he not penetrated her mysteries and laid them bare? He was the Good Thief who stole spiritual treasures from the priestly dogs-in-the-manger, to give to those who needed them. This interpretation is borne out by the exceptional honour shewn him; Christ at the Crucifixion sends him straight to paradise, *"where no man else is able to dwell."* Shining, his spirit appears to John, who falls down as before *"a king in great might"*, and asks Jesus who he can be. Jesus answers *"Seekest thou to know hidden things? Art thou wholly without understanding? Perceivest thou not the fragrance of paradise filling the place? Knewest thou not who it was? The thief that was on the cross is become heir of Paradise; verily verily I say unto you, it is his alone till the great day come."* This mysterious identity can only be explained by our Zodiac, where one Geminian twin, or Robber, has become the *"Christed"* Man.—As all must become when Evolution finally achieves its purpose.

The Story of Obed

This tale explains how Joseph of Arimathea obtained the Cup of the Last Supper. The disciples, instructed to follow a man with a Waterpot on his shoulder, were led to the house of Obed. (The Watercarrier survives in Luke's Gospel too). Obed, an old man, told them how a bodiless hand had set a richly jewelled cup on his table in preparation for the Supper. After it was over sly Judas returned to steal it, but as his unworthy hand touched it he suddenly realised the baseness of his betrayal, and despair seized him. Wild-eyed, dishevelled, he thrust the cup into the hand of Simon the Leper, telling him to take it to Pilate. The sacred vessel affected Pilate in the same way, and when Joseph came to beg the body of Jesus, the distracted Roman implored him to take the cup away. As Joseph held it he received a vision of himself bearing it to far-off lands. The cup also appeared luminously to Obed as he died shortly afterwards.

This tale appears in Dr. Francis Rolt-Wheeler's *"Mystic Gleams from the Holy Grail"*, but without reference; I have so far been unable to trace its source, and would be grateful for information. The preceding tales can be found in Montague James' *"The Apocryphal New Testament"*.

The Healing of Tiberius

This tale, with several interesting variations, is known from manuscripts of the 8th century. It is probably older.

Briefly, Tiberius, sorely diseased, hears of Jesus' healings, and sends for him, only to find he has just been crucified. He banishes Pilate for his part in this, and Veronica, a Phoenician woman, heals him with her handerchief on which the face of Jesus has been imprinted.

In a version called *"The Vengenace of the Saviour"*, it is Titus, king of Aquitaine under Tiberius, who is healed by the handerchief of cancer of the nose. In gratitude he goes with Vespasian to sack Jerusalem, crucifying many Jews and selling others at thirty a penny—to teach them not to sell their Healer for thirty pieces of silver.

In yet another version from the *"Golden Legend"*, Vespasian is the sufferer. From childhood he had been troubled with a wasp's nest in his nose (his name, which sounds like a sneeze, derived, we are solemnly told, from this affliction.) He demands of one Albanus *"from the land of the wise"* that he should cure him, and Albanus, though unable to do this, tells him that the very name of Jesus will work wonders. Vespasian believes, and at once the tenacious wasp's nest falls away. His gratitude takes a similar form; with Tiberius he sacks Jerusalem. There Josephus the Jewish historian saves himself by predicting that Tiberius will be made Roman Emperor. They find and release Joseph of Arimathea, walled up for years by the Jews and sustained solely by the Lord, who had instructed him in secret teachings and fed him with the Cup.

This is all very interesting to Grail-questers. The mention of Veronica and secret teachings makes one suspect a Phoenician source, as does the king of Aquitaine. Joseph's fame has spread westward before Joseph himself. And Robert de Borron, earliest redactor of Grail legends, came from Aquitaine. Albanus must come from Albion, the Hyperborean *"land of the wise"*. He was expected to heal Vespasian because the Druids were famed as doctors. Caesar's doctor was Divitiacus, a Druid, not a Roman.

In the **Acts of Magdalen**, another old legend from the south of France, Joseph begins his westward trek. According to this account, Joseph, Lazarus, Mary Magdalen, Martha her sister and Maximin the rich young man of the Gospels, were all set adrift by the Jews in a ship without sails or oars, in an attempt to rid Palestine of several key witnesses to the Resurrection.

But Providence guided them safely to Marseilles, where Martha and Mary founded missions and ended their days, and Lazarus and Maximin became bishops. But no version of the tale tries to retain Joseph in the south of France; according to an old manuscript in the Vatican, cited by Cardinal Baronius, he and his company crossed into Britain and remained there.

The legend of Mary Magdalen is as dear to the French as Joseph's is to western Britain, and if neither are literally true, the tales at least are ancient —far more so than recent scholarship will admit. The 2nd century *"Recognitions of Clement"* records that all these persons were with St. Philip at Caesarea, a port from which they could have sailed to Marseilles. Perhaps the ship sans sails or oars is a little fanciful, but the Chronicon of pseudo-Dexter (392 AD) confirms that Joseph had to flee Palestine in 48 AD and was received in Marseilles. And it is interesting that none of these refugees, so prominent in the Gospels, appears again in the Acts. Though the Bethany family owed everything to Jesus' healing (Lazarus saved from death and Mary from "worse than death") they are not among the organisers of the early church in Palestine and seem to have disappeared completely.

Freculphus, 9th century bishop of Lisieux, says that *Joseph and his party were received in Marseilles by Druids,* who passed them on to the parent grove in Wales. He cites one Josephus as his source for this fascinating information: doubtless that Josephus who *"by annunciation of the voice of an angel"* wrote the lost original of the High History in 720 or so. Other Grail romances also acknowledge him as their source. But even this mysterious hermit was only drawing on more ancient apocryphal accounts, as we can see.

The *"Ecclesiastical Antiquities of the Cymry"* insists that many Silurian Druids adopted Christianity during this first mission, being made bishops. *"Bran, son of Llyr Llediath, first brought the faith of Christ to the Cymry from Rome, where he had been seven years a hostage for his son Caradoc, whom the Romans imprisoned"*, say the Triads. Bran appears in earliest Grail romance as Bron, brother-in-law of Joseph. He catches a mystical fish to feed the brethren—obviously the Celtic Salmon of Wisdom.

Dr. J. W. Taylor in his book *"The Coming of the Saints"* has traced the rumours of Joseph's journey from Palestine through Cyprus to Provence, then up the Rhone to Morlaix in Brittany, (where they still revere St. Drennalus as a follower of Joseph) and across the Channel, where they are met by corresponding folk-tales in Somerset and Cornwall. Both counties supplied metals to the Phoenicians, and the places that remember Joseph the tin-merchant are mining centres or ports. Taylor makes the penetrating comment that Phoenician trading-posts and colonies were always the first to receive Christian missionaries; not only Antioch and Tyre, but Marseilles, Alexandria, Spain and Cornwall.

Critics of these legends often accuse the mediaeval monks of Glastonbury of inventing them to attract pilgrims and revenue to their abbey; from the foregoing evidence we can clearly acquit them of this charge. The *"Acts of Magdalen"* has also been dismissed as late apocryphal fiction, perhaps 8th century. But popes and kings were already visiting her cave at St. Beaume in 500 AD, and the cave-church of St. Lazarus at Marseilles is even earlier, perhaps 1st century. Joseph was counted among their party; if his legends are fiction, at least they were not invented in Britain.

At Fecamp in Brittany they remember a fig-tree log, washed miraculously ashore. It contained two cruets holding the blood and sweat of the Crucified, and was set afloat, not by Joseph, but by his colleague Nicodemus in Palestine. An early reference to Joseph from Glastonbury Abbey (to be quoted) shews him as bringing not the Grail-Cup but these cruets to Avalon. As the Fecamp legend is earlier than the popular cult of Joseph at Glastonbury, English monks have of course been accused of annexing the cruets for Joseph, thus going one better than Fecamp. But it seems more likely that both legends have a common source.

For there *was* a founder of Christianity in Britain in the 1st century, and whether it was Joseph or another, he brought an eastern, not Roman brand of the faith. Celtic missionaries, amazingly enough, were already converting Europe from Britain at that time. Beatus, a Briton, founded the Helvetian Church, dying about 100 AD; his cell is still shewn at Unterseen on Lake Thun. Mansuetus or Mansuy, an Irishman, his contemporary, became bishop of Toul in Lorraine. Marcellus, an early British martyr-bishop of Tongre and Trier, died in 166; St. Cadval (Cadwallader) founded Tarento cathedral in 170.

In 190 Tertullian of Carthage wrote "The extremities of Spain, the various parts of Gaul, *the regions of Britain never penetrated by Roman arms,* have received the religion of Christ." Sabellius the heretic said in 230 AD "Christianity was privately expressed elsewhere, but the first nation that proclaimed it as their religion was Britain". Origen (185-254) Greek founding-father of the early church, said "The power of the Lord is with those in Britain". In 300 Dorotheus bishop of Tyre, said that the Aristobulus of St. Paul's epistle was bishop here—a statement confirmed by Greek martyrology and by old Welsh records who knew him as Arwystli.

These early statements all come from "Johannine" Christians, suspected and sometimes banished by the Roman church. They had no reason to lie, but there was good reason from Rome's point of view why their voice should be suppressed. The Church of the next two thousand years was to be Peter's, not John's; Roman, not Asian or Celtic.

But though these eminent theologians confirm the very early, even apostolic mission to Britain, none of them mentions Joseph. This is odd, if he did come, for in their much-read Apocrypha he figured large. It is one reason for regarding *"Joseph"* as a symbolic rather than a literal British missionary. There is another, as we shall see later on.

Yet he is an excellent symbol, for whoever came here brought an Asian, Gnostic brand of the faith; he used the Phoenician trade-route and was probably employed by the Romans when they annexed British metal-mines, and was on friendly business terms, perhaps even related to, the British Silurian royal family who worked them, and who certainly had Phoenician ties of blood.

Joseph, the wealthy man of the Gospels, may well have been a Phoenician tin-trader. He may well have been the *"noble decurion"* as Jerome calls him—an officer, we are told, often put in charge of mines. As an officer essential to Roman economy he could dare to beg from Pilate the body of Jesus, the most controversial condemned criminal of his day. This right was reserved for relatives, if they dared to ask; Joseph, in Syrian and Cornish tradition, was Jesus' great-uncle. He passes with tact and diplomacy between all warring factions, fulfilling all required conditions for the Founder of Christianity in Britain. He is the perfect symbol; like God, if he did not exist it would have been necessary to invent him.

The earliest Grail legends were written down by Robert de Borron of Aquitaine in the 1190's. He did not invent them, but used Apocryphal sources already current there and grafted them on to the Arthurian lays he must have heard from Bledheri the famed Welsh bard, at Duke William's court. It was no shotgun marriage; the two were made for each other—for the Glastonbury Zodiac was the original inspiration for both.

His unfinished trilogy, *"Joseph of Arimathea"*, *"Merlin"* and *"Perceval"* were taken up and embroidered by others until all Europe was ringing with the *"Matter of Britain"*. At the same time Chretien de Troyes wrote down a more purely Celtic version of the Grail legend, *"Perceval le Gallois"*, from hearing the British minstrels' *"Peredur"*. The Cauldron in exile was preparing under French chefs its most potent brew, one that was to put all Christendom in a ferment of Chivalry. The Plantagenets and Templars were drunk with it. This moment of glory was made possible by the Angevin Empire which united France and England under Henry II. The part played by Eleanor of Aquitaine, daughter of Duke William, in all this has I feel been underestimated; she was Queen of France before becoming Queen of England; it was during her lifetime that all the early Grail romances were written down. *"Arthur's grave"* was opened at Glastonbury beneath her gaze.

Henry's motives were not purely spiritual, they say. He needed Grail Christianity as a lever against the Pope. But Arthur as a once and future king was no good to him. It bolstered the rebellious Welsh nationalistic hopes too much. A very dead Arthur would dampen their independent spirit. He fostered the Joseph cult, they say, for the same reason; for the Welsh clung to their patronal St. David as the Grail-Bearer to Britain.

Their tale goes like this: St. David, a pilgrim to Jerusalem, was made Archbishop of Wales by the Patriarch of the Holy City. He also gave David "a consecrated Altar in which the body of Our Lord once lay". Transport was no problem; it was wafted through the sky to Wales. Like Joseph's Grail-Ark, a Voice would speak from it, and it performed miracles. But on David's death, c. 600 A.D., it was hidden *in skins*—surely *Hides*?—and no man afterwards could tell its form, shape, colour, general appearance, or its whereabouts. Was this not our Zodiac, or even more specifically, its ship in which the Gemini Jesus lies? It was known to both Celtic and Eastern Christians. If it was, this would explain the veritable fleet of stone altars on which Celtic saints sailed blithely on their missions overseas. The 'altar' could 'alter' with the level of their hearers' understanding. They brought the Mass wherever they went; the Lord's body lay consecrated on the altar and in their ships. His blood was contained at once in the Grail-Cup and in their vessels. (Gemini's Christ fits his Vessel as an acorn fits its cup.) Celts spoke in pun and parable so that only those with ears could hear.

Robert de Borron's *"Joseph"* relates how the *"Vessel in which Jesus performed his Sacrament"* was taken by Simon the leper to Pilate, who gave it to Joseph when he came to beg the body of Jesus in return for years of military service. At the burial Christ's blood flowed into it, and the relic remained in Joseph's house. The Jews then imprisoned him in a tall tower for forty years, but Christ nourished him with the Vessel and with secret instruction until Vespasian released him. He began his westward journey with his followers, but settled and cultivated the land. All prospered till some of the party fell into sin, and the land became waste. Hungered, they invoked the Vessel, and a divine voice told his companion Brons to catch a fish. This fed the faithful but left the sinners hungry; they could not even see the Grail, placed in full view on the table, and finally left the company in shame. One Moses, falsely pretending penitence, was reinstated at the table in a vacant seat between Joseph and Brons—a Siege Perilous—and was swallowed into an abyss which opened beneath him. The company proceeded westward, instructed by Christ from the Grail.

In Robert de Borron's tale, Joseph does not reach Britain, though Petrus, one of his party, sets off for the "Vaux D'Avaron"—surely the Vale of Avalon.

But Joseph entrusts the Grail to Brons (known as the Rich Fisher by virtue of his single catch) and his grandson Alain. It is left to other romances to bring Joseph, or at least his son Josephes, to this country.

(The name Alain has continuous connections with Glastonbury. Avalon, says the "High History", first belonged to one Alain and his clan. A splendid mediaeval tomb in Glastonbury parish church belongs to John Alleyn. Bligh Bond discovered many lost foundation-walls in the Abbey through the automatic writing of his friend, another John Alleyn, who received messages from a departed monk of the Abbey.)

De Borron's Grail-vessel is nebulous. It could be a dish, bowl or chalice. It could equally be a secret description of the Ark of the Zodiac, in which *"Christ makes his sacrament"* also, for this is a "vessel" too. Many passages in other Grail romances support this idea. The Rich Fisher, common to his and Chretien's Grail stories, is otherwise unaccountable; but in our Zodiac his vessel does indeed receive the blood from his wounded thigh at *Redlands*. De Borron's "Merlin" shews that he knew the Grail and the Round Table were connected in Britain. His Merlin indeed goes there from Brittany to set up this Third Table with its Siege Perilous, in continuity with Joseph's Second Table with Brons' Fish, or Salmon of Wisdom. Robert knew the secret of the Grail, but could not speak it openly. His description *allowed* the Church to see it as the Cup of the Last Supper, ostensibly orthodox; it was sufficiently teasing however, with its Secret Words, to allow those who would to see further into the Mysteries. For those, his *"Perceval"* frankly pursues the Quest in Britain.

The concept of this hidden body of inspirational, life-enhancing knowledge has been derided and forgotten. The ark has become a children's plaything; its high purpose as stimulator of civilisations quite lost. Yet the ancient world knew they owed their cultures to its measurements, exoteric and esoteric; the Deluge story was at once a treasure and a warning not only for Chaldeans, Jews and Greeks, but for the Druids. Edward Davies has been derided for insisting that the Ark was fundamental to their teaching, but the Zodiac with its Ark-animals shews that he was right. Arthur ploughed the Zodiac furrow across the *arc* of the sky. In the Plantagenet and Templar revival, the Gothic *arch* soared as the Ark's Mysteries sailed once more into view, slowly sinking again when the perennial Vessel disappeared below the horizon of civilisation's conscious mind. For Ark and arch are one word. Noah, bearing the seeds of civilisation from his sunken world to their second Eden-garden, took the arched rainbow as a divine promise that Evolution was willing to try again.

The *"Grand Saint Graal"* attributed by some to Walter Map, Henry II's chaplain and archdeacon of Oxford, understood all this. In its prolific pages Josephes, son of the Arimathean, took the Grail *in an ark* to Britain. Though small enough to be carried, this Vessel could expand, like Dr. Who's police-box, to the size of a cathedral, and Christ Himself would appear in it, sometimes as a babe, sometimes as the crucified. This metamorphosis of course exactly reflects the Gemini figure in our Zodiac: Josephes, significantly, made his portable ark in Bethany, "place of a boat". In this cathedral-ark a mysteriously different mass was celebrated with Secret Words, and Josephes was consecrated Pontiff of the Inner Church. Dangerously heretical!

There seems no doubt about those Secret Words. They were Zodiac teachings, based not on blind faith but on natural and cosmic laws, facts and measurements; the purpose of man in evolution as demonstrated by Nature herself in the Grail-bowl of the Vale of Avalon. Indeed, though the Grand Saint Graal's geography is deliberately vague, it mentions the "abbey of Glays", which can hardly be other than Glastonbury. The author is led to a "Great Book", the source of his information, by a huge beast compounded of Dog, Lion, Wolf and Lamb; obviously our Girt Dog or Questing Beast.

We are introduced to two enigmatic characters, Evelake and Nasciens his son-in-law. Evelake was originally a humble cobbler of the city of Sarras in Egypt but through his sagacity was made a general by Ptolemy. Joseph of Arimathea, passing through Sarras on his westering way, helps Evelake by making a Red Cross shield which routs his enemies, and the grateful cobbler-general, hitherto a Saracen, is baptised, taking the Christian name of Mordrains. Converting his fellow-Saracens he becomes a saintly visionary. Later on his visions shew him Joseph's son imprisoned in north Wales with his Grail-Ark; he sets out at once, decimates the heathen Welsh, and rescues him.

But one night, sleeping near the Ark, he desires to see the Grail. A voice from a cloud warns him away, but he looks within—and is at once smitten, blind and paralysed, to the ground. Yet stricken as he was, he burst into ecstatic praise, declaring that he had seen *"the Marvel of marvels, the Wisdom beyond all wisdom, and the King of kings"*. He became known as the Maimed King, and lived for centuries sustained only by the Grail-mass, until the coming of Galahad the perfect knight. Meanwhile Britain lay enchanted under *"the times adventurous of the kingdom of Logres"*, and Merlin initiated the Round Table and the Quest of the Grail. *The cobbler Evelake is Avallach, Gemini, the Maimed King of Avalon*—smitten while bowed in sleep

His son-in-law Nasciens is also Gemini—perhaps the other Twin; his first name was Seraphe, his battle-axe a fiery serpent, Caballistic symbol of the Seraphim. He is clearly one of the Fallen Angels, and being descended from Solomon, belongs in his Ship. He too was baptised by Joseph, his Christian name Nasciens suggesting many meanings—*"Bearing"*, *"Reborn"*, *"Not knowing"* perhaps *"the Unknown One"*—all suggestive of the Babe in the Boat. He too was maimed, smitten for daring to draw the Grail-Sword of David which only Galahad his descendant would be worthy to unsheathe.

Our Gemini Babe has often been baptised before, as we have seen. Taliesin, another babe baptised in Gwyddno's weir and like Nasciens, reborn, also had his original home in the *"land of the Cherubim"*, or summer stars; the Cherubim and Seraphim of Ezekial's vision, all eyes and turning wheels, were the galaxies and Zodiac stars. But before Ezekial our Zodiac was known to Jewry, from the Phoenician Book of Enoch and the Ras Shamra Tablets' Eden.

Seraphe-Nasciens like Evelake became a seer and was lifted by a mighty hand and placed on the Turning Island, an inchoate mass of magma whirling among the stars. Terrified, he implored his Saviour's help, and Solomon's Ship came to rescue him. This Ship, we remember, enshrined cosmic knowledge, being made to last *"four thousand years till Galahad should come"*. Nasciens, Lancelot and his son Galahad all descended from Solomon.

Taliesin too had been ecstatically whirled to this Turning Island *"between three elements"*; in this elevated state of consciousness he was *"able to instruct the whole universe"*. Turning Islands, like Solomon's Ship and the city of Sarras, belong to the starry universe—but they are reflected by Glastonbury Tor, the Ship of Sedgemoor and the Somerset Zodiac, long known both in the ancient east and west. So why place Sarras in Egypt? Partly to put Rome off the scent, partly because its Saracens, a tribe long before Mahomet, worshipped the sun, moon and stars, partly because many Apocryphal books stem from there, and partly because Moses and Jesus, both identified by Taliesin with the Babe in the Boat, were cradled there, one in the Nile, the other at Heliopolis city of the Sun.

Such, with many variations, is the fantastic theme of the Grand Saint Graal. (In one of these Josephes crosses the Channel on his shirt.) It is a trap for the literal-minded, an arched bridge of high parable for the initiate. Well might the flat-footed pedant wonder how such a fandango could put all Europe in turmoil! But for the Zodiac student there is substance beneath the froth, reality in the author's claim that his source-book contains the Great Secret of the World.

To reject such *"fairy-tales"* is adolescent. The child understands them in one way, the true adult in another. Joseph (or whoever) *did* come, *"in nothing but his shirt"*—a missionary risking cannibals, utterly dependant on his British host's goodwill. His "ark" did indeed grow, not into one cathedral but many, the proportions of their "naves" reflecting the cosmic measurements of Argo Navis, the cosmic arc, as Charpentier and others have shewn. Arthur drawing the sword from the stone, Celtic saints floating on stone altars from port to port, symbolise the dauntless spirit overcoming mere inert matter. To such spirits matter *does* yield, the impossible becomes fact, miracles and signs *do* happen. The opposite attitude dries up the springs of inspiration and invention, denies hope to all who need it, and narrows the bright horizon to a hard grey line from which the angels have regretfully withdrawn. Such a narrowing of human potential makes Evolution despair, and then men sink slowly into monkeys once more.

Melkin's Prophecy

This fascinating fragment, unhappily known only to us from John of Glastonbury's copy of the late 1300's, is attributed to one Melkin, *"a seer of the Britons before Merlin"*. The antique style of writing, the Middle eastern names, breathing the old Apocryphal and bardic spirit, do however incline scholars to believe that John could not have invented it. It may well be an old Culdee prophecy. Leland claims to have seen the original shortly before the Abbey's dissolution. Here it is, with all its Zodiacal overtones.

"The Isle of Avalon, eager for the death of pagans, for the burial of them all, adorned before all other places in the world by foretelling spheres of prophecy, forever will be honoured by those who praise the Highest. Abbadare, mighty in Saphat, most noble of pagans, with one hundred and four thousand, hath there found rest. Among whom, Joseph from the sea, from Arimathea, has found perpetual sleep; and he lies in a bifurcate line near the southern angle of an oratory made of wattles above a mighty Virgin, worthy to be adored by the aforementioned *spheres, thirteen in number,* dwellers in that place. Joseph truly has with him in his sarcophagus two vessels, white and silver, filled with the blood of the prophet Jesus. When his sarcophagus shall be found, whole and entire, it shall be seen in time to come, and shall be open to all the world. From that time forth neither water nor dew from heaven shall fail the dwellers in that famous isle. For a long while before the Day of Judgement in Josaphat these things will be revealed and declared to the living."

Some think that Melkin was Maelgwyn, uncle of David of Wales and abbot of Glastonbury c. 450. Others believe the lost Liber Melkini was written by "Melkites", royalist Copts, before the Arab conquest of Egypt in 641. Both could be right, for 3rd century Coptic hermits settled in Ireland, and Glastonbury's recently-excavated hermit-huts bear the same stamp. The *"prophet Jesus"* has a Saracen ring to it; certainly none but very early or eastern Christians would describe their Founder in such terms. Saphat and Josaphat are Phoenician or Jewish names meaning "judgement", perhaps in this context, "judgement-seat". It seems to be the same place occupied by the *"thirteen foretelling spheres"*, and these are surely the twelve Zodiac effigies and their guard-dog in the British Hades. Here is further evidence that this great Circle was known in the Middle East, and that Joseph was identified with Avalon at a very early date.

And who is Abbadare, noblest of pagans, with his 104,000, also buried there? This is the number of Man the Microcosmos in the Greek Gematria—Man in God's image. "Abu Adar" is both Adam and Arthur, according to Waddell's *"Phoenician Origin of the Britons"*. He is in fact Avalon's Sagittarius—Man in the image of God. Adam was one of those released by Christ from Hell in the *"Acts of Pilate"*. Arthur in Celtic Myth releases Man from the Underworld. It is all shewn in our Zodiac.

And who is meant by the *"mighty Virgin"*? Surely the effigy of Virgo, to whom as Earth-Mother the whole Zodiac belonged. Though the gentle, compassionate Virgin Mary succeeded to many of her titles, "mighty" was not one of them. She indeed became Queen of Earth and Heaven, but always remained lowly and accessible to the faithful.

And where is Joseph's elusive sarcophagus? Some said it was in the *"little wattle Oratory"* he built, the site now covered by Joseph's chapel at the western end of Glastonbury Abbey. But is this *"little wattle church"* a code-name for the whole circle in Avalon's low-lying wattle-beds? Was this seen as an osierbed in which Moses and Christ Himself were cradled?

Gildas the Wise, 546 AD., and Nennius, 750

Before examining this wattle church in William of Malmesbury's account, let us see what our earliest historians say about the founding-date of Christianity in Britain. Like the early fathers already quoted, they do not mention Joseph, though Gildas does at least give a compatible date. After mentioning Boadicea's revolt, his Liber Querulus (Complaining Book) goes on to say:

Meanwhile these islands, stiff with cold and frost, and in a distant region of the world remote from the visible sun, received the beams of light, that is, the holy precepts of Christ the True Sun, shewing to the whole world his splendour . . . at the latter part, as we know, of the reign of Tiberius Caesar.

Tiberius died in 37 AD, an uncomfortably short time for the enlightenment of such *"a distant region"* after the Resurrection. Boadicea's date, 61, is nearer that generally accepted by literal adherents of Joseph's coming in 63.

Gildas is unpardonably vague. He mentions neither Joseph nor Arthur (who if we take him literally) was his contemporary. This is astonishing, as Gildas was long connected with Glastonbury Abbey. However, the details we need may have appeared in another book of his, *"The Acts of the Illustrious King Arthur"*, now lost. John of Glastonbury gives an excerpt, already quoted in Leo's chapter, about the Great Lion with chains about his neck. It ends, *"Joseph of Arimathea, a noble decurio, with his son Joseph and several others came into greater Britain which is now called England, and there finished his life."*

England was still called Britain in 546, so this passage is unlikely to date back to Gildas. Maybe a later author signed himself by his name.

Our next historian, Nennius, writing his *"History of the Britons"* about 750, does not mention Joseph either, nor even a 1st century mission. He says *"After the birth of Christ, 167 years, king Leucius, with all the chiefs of the British people, received baptism, in consequence of a legation sent by the Roman emperor and pope."*

William of Malmesbury, writing in 1129, states that two papal legates, called Fagan and Deruvian, built the old church at Glastonbury. Then he corrects this with another tradition that they *restored*, but did not build it. (We have already noted that in 1000 AD before William's time, Dunstan's biographer knew of the Glastonbury church *'not built with human hands"*.) **William, a t**rusty scribe still respected today, wrote in his *"Acts of the Kings of England";* *"There are documents of no small credit which have been discovered in certain places to the following effect: "No other hands than those of the disciples of Christ erected the church of Glastonbury.""*

So William, at least in his earlier book, does not mention Joseph either. In his later *"Antiquities of Glastonbury"* the legend at last appears, but is thought to have been added by his copyist, for our earliest manuscript only dates from about a hundred years after William's death in 1143. It is this general silence about Joseph until the 1200's that has caused scholars to doubt his coming; but they should remember there were political and religious reasons for this. Joseph's Christianity was Gnostic, Johannine; it was connected with the Celt's most closely guarded Secret. Though they converted many in Europe, British Celts would not impart their religion to invaders. The Saxons had to wait for Augustine in 600 AD, and when he brought Roman Christianity it soon suppressed the Celtic church. The Normans under William the Conqueror were faithfully papal too, and dissident Celts had to keep quiet. The silence about Arthur in these centuries stems from the same reasons. Europe knew more about both than England, from emigré bards; it was not until the heterodox Plantagenets succeeded to England's throne that the climate allowed these myths to flourish once more in their own soil.

But it is time to hear what William of Malmesbury (or his copyist) has to say about the mysterious Old Church in his *"Antiquities of Glastonbury"*,

"St. Philip . . . coming into the country of the Franks to preach . . . chose twelve from among his disciples, and sent them into Britain. Their leader, it is said, was Philip's dearest friend, Joseph of Arimathea, who buried the Lord. Coming therefore into Britain 63 years from the Assumption of Blessed Mary, they began faithfully to preach the faith of Christ. But the barbaric king and his people, hearing such novel and unaccustomed things, absolutely refused to consent to their preaching, neither did he wish to change the traditions of their ancestors; yet because they came from afar . . . at their request he granted them a certain island called Ynis Wytrin . . . Later on, two successive kings, although pagans, observing their pious mode of life, presented to each of them a portion of land . . . It is believed that the Twelve Hides get their name from them to this day.

Thereupon the said twelve saints residing in this desert, were in a short time warned by a vision of the angel Gabriel to build a church in honour of the Holy Mother of God . . . in a place shewn to them from heaven, and they, quick to obey the divine precepts, completed a certain chapel according to what had been shewn them, fashioning its walls below, *circularwise,* of twisted twigs . . . A chapel, it is true, of uncouth form, but to God richly adorned with virtue . . . The said saints continued to live in the same hermitage for many years, and were at last liberated from the prison of the flesh. *The place then began to be a covert for wild beasts* . . . until the Blessed Virgin was pleased to recall her house of prayer to the memory of the faithful."

Was their vision a map of the Zodiac shewn them by Apocryphal Gabriel? It was a circular plan they saw. The "wild beasts" and the Twelve Hides make me suspect that the whole passage is in code. Avalon has long been haunted by a great Lion, a Salmon of Wisdom, a Goat that climbs the Tor, Giants and a Dragon at Butleigh.

The floor of Joseph's church points the same way. "In the pavement may be remarked on every side, stones designedly laid in triangles and squares, and sealed with lead, under which if I believe some sacred mystery to be contained, I do no injustice to religion." Squares and triangles, or triplicities and quadruplicities, belong to the Zodiac mysteries. The floor William saw pictured the Zodiac, as many cathedral floors still do, as at Rochester and Chichester, though a fearful and forgetful church usually carpets them over to avoid detection today. It cannot believe with William that *"it does no injustice to religion".*

It is interesting that the design was encased in lead—for that is how Joseph's *"Ealde Kirche"* was said to be encased to preserve it. A circular wattle structure covered in lead within the later cathedral? The mind boggles. Besides, lead would not preserve osiers from woodworm. No, the floor described the real "wattle" or Natural Temple all about the abbey. This was the "arcanum sacrum", the arcane secret set down by William. He is preoccupied by it.

"The very floor, inlaid with polished stones" Or, "At night, scarcely anyone presumes to keep vigil there, or by day to spit upon *its floor* . .

Is he laying clues? Further passages suggest this. "No-one ever brought hawk or horse within the confines of the cemetery who did not depart injured in them or himself". (Arthur and his Sagittarian horse, and the

Aquarian eagle are near neighbours of the Abbey; both are injured, indeed suffer death and rebirth.) It is William of Malmesbury who called Avalon *"a heavenly sanctuary upon earth"*, and dubbed Glastonbury *"Roma Secunda"*. There seems no doubt that he was in the Secret.

No survey of Joseph's legends should neglect our own local folklore, but as this has been collected and published by others I need only summarise it here. *"Joseph of Arimathea at Glastonbury"* by the Rev. Smithett Lewis, one-time vicar of Glastonbury, *"Did Our Lord Visit Britain?"* by the Rev. C. Dobson, *"Christ in Cornwall"* by the Rev. H. A. Lewis, can all be bought at Glastonbury Abbey's bookstall. *"The Child Christ at Llamana"* by the last-named author is now out of print. The Rev. R. L. Morgan's *"St. Paul in Britain"* is still available, an illuminating study of the origins of of the Celtic Church. We owe a debt to these scholarly parsons; it is surely no accident that they are preponderantly Welsh.

Joseph in British Folk Lore

We are now familiar with the Glastonbury legends—the Flowering Holy Thorn on Wearyall Hill, the Twelve Hides granted by Arviragus, Marius and Coel; the twelve hermit-huts round the Old Church, or alternatively round Chalice Well where Joseph hid the Grail so that its waters ran red with the precious Blood; the two silver cruets as a variation on the Grail.

The coming of Jesus, both as Boy and Man, with his uncle Joseph, was suppressed to a whisper in the Abbey's important ecclesiastical centre; but it was long repeated in less sophisticated parts like Cornwall and the Mendips. Cornishmen used to shout *"Joseph was a tin-man!"* as they flashed the tin, and sang *"I saw three ships come sailing by"* in which were *"Joseph and his fair lady"*.

A Somerset tale that Jesus came in a ship from Tyre as ship's carpenter, and was storm-bound there through the winter was echoed in Upper Galilee. Joseph and Jesus legends have been collected from some twenty places in the west such as Jesus Well Padstow, Ding-Dong Mine, Penzance, St. Michael's Mount, Creeg Brawse, Carnon Downs, Polperro, St. Just and Falmouth, Looe, and from Burnham, Pilton and Priddy. The Looe memories are of Cornish St. Anne, mother of the Virgin, echoed by those of the Breton Duchesse Anne de la Palude. But Looe island was once divided into Parlooe and Portlooe. Is Palude Parlooe? Looe has a St. Anna's Well, (the church at nearby Hessenford was once dedicated to her) and a chapel on old Looe Bridge. Essa's Bed, a rock off Llamana or Looe Island, and Hessenford surely recall Yesse or Esus her grandson. Jesus in the Breton legend visits St. Anne in Cornouaille's Bay of Palue, where she returned from Palestine to end her days in her native land. Though Llamana once belonged to Glastonbury Abbey, the form Essa for Jesus is Celtic, not mediaeval, and breathes Phoenician-Apocryphal overtones.

Looe's ancient earthwork, known as the *"Giants' Hedge"*, was built, or so they said here, by the pixies to protect an old man and a Boy who landed here.

Fact or fiction, Joseph is strangely connected with Giants. He lands on one, burying his Chalice in another. For Zodiac pilgrims, he and his Divine Nephew may well *be* Glastonbury Giants, as were Manawyddan and his nephew Pryderi, Gwydion and his nephew Llew, Bran and his nephew Gwern, Ysbadadden (Thorn-Hedge) and his young supplanter Culhwch. Celts saw Jesus as re-enacting their more ancient sun-myth.

Penardin, St. Anna's daughter (sister to the Virgin in Celtic-Christian tales) points out this grafting process. In older Celtic myth Penardun was the daughter of Don who united the two great pantheons of Don and Llyr by marrying Llyr. (Both houses boasted twelve gods each, and were obviously derived from our Zodiac). Penardin's last act was to fuse the new Christianity on to the old Celtic pantheon. Joseph's *"twelve companions"* are variations on the same theme, for Bran, son of Llyr, becomes Joseph's chief ally Brons, *"the Rich Fisherman"*, a title clearly deriving from the Zodiac Fisher in his Boat. He well deserved to be Joseph's lieutenant; had he not battled for the Cauldron before it became the Grail—his decapitated singing head a substitute for the lost Vessel?

But Zodiac students should keep an open mind on Joseph's and Jesus' coming, overlaid though it undoubtedly is with older myths; they, more than most, can see reasons why the Phoenician tin-merchant should—and could— have brought his Nephew to see Himself and study His role in Britain's first Open University.

Myth, because it reflects the eternal pattern, is continually re-enacted on one level or another in history. The Gnostic Apocrypha was well aware of this.

The Priddy Legend is interesting and revealing. This remote hamlet in the Mendips seems on the face of it an unlikely place to attract the Lord. Yet a story persists that he visited it with Joseph. There is no local monastery which could have disseminated a mediaeval legend; Priddy is a *"ghost-town"* now, surviving from ancient days. Attempts to demolish the legend as the invention of a local school-mistress who wrote a *"Joseph and Jesus"* play some fifty years ago for her school, brought letters protesting that she only used traditions already there. Had the critics not heard the famous phrase *"As sure as the Lord was at Priddy?"*

A closer look at Priddy's past reveals reasons, both business and doctrinal, for such a Visit. Here cluster ancient copper and lead mines, barrows both long and round, *"hermits' caves"*, the famous Priddy Swallet and four large prehistoric earth-circles in a row, of ritual significance, for they are too many and too large for pounds, their walls too low and their siting too flat for defence. From the air appear fainter circles intersecting them, as if the existing row replaced others of even greater age. What were they all for?

Here was obviously an ancient mining centre, with, one suspects, its own Druid school of philosophy. For the Druids visualised all Creation in four circles; the first was Annwn, the Cauldron, or bubbling chaotic abyss from which all life was drawn into the second, Abred, the world of form and flesh. Here all slowly fitted themselves through painful experience, trial and error, for the third circle, Gwynfed or heaven. The fourth, Ceugant, was the Creator's alone.

The abyss or Cauldron was also graphically symbolised by Priddy's Swallet, a deep pot-hole beloved of climbers today, where the marsh-waters drain into the bowels of the earth, forming the river Axe and flowing underground for four miles south-east to emerge in a splendid cascade from Wookey Hole.

Such parable-material would hardly be ignored by the Druids, who saw this world as a reflection of a higher, and demonstrated their teaching by Nature-parallels. Here the divine Essence descended as dew and rain into the earth's womb, to be reborn from a cave, giving life to all. The Mother-goddess herself presides over her cavern as a great stalagmite shaped like a woman. Nature has formed her own uncanny likeness, drip by drop, century by century. Like Tar-Annis, she is blackened by pitch; the Witch of Wookey has often been burnt in ritual. By the sunless shore of these dark waters a little boat is moored, like Charon's own, waiting to carry dead souls to who knows what shadowy halls; from these, only reached by swimming underwater, reverberating booms will shake the chambers from unimaginable depths. Surely this is the Styx, not the Axe?

The river-name Axe also occurs at the site of Phoenician Carthage, where Annis was known as Tanit, her son Esus as Eshmun or Iesu-munu. He was also Asclepins The healer, killed by Zeus for raising the dead to life!

Wookey means Witch. This stalagmite is not Wookey's only witch. The skeleton of an old woman was found near the cave-mouth with a crystal ball of stalagmite and the bones of two tethered goats who must have starved when she died. These remains are in Wells Museum, together with many shards and neolithic flints, shewing that her cult was only the degenerate end of far older rituals.

Here is "the black witch, daughter of the White Witch, from the head of the Valley of Grief in the uplands of Hell" whom Arthur slaughtered in the Mabinogion, "striking her across the middle until she was as two tubs." The Mendips are the uplands of Avalon's Hell. No doubt Cheddar Gorge and caves were part of the Mysteries of Chedd or Ceridwen also.

What does the name Priddy mean? "Earth", or "earthen hut", say flat-footed place-name books, missing the point and poetry as usual.

"Pryd" says the Welsh scholar Morien Morgan, means *"the beauty of Natural Order"*; thus *"a system demonstrating a cosmic order through observation of Nature."* As Above, So Below.

The name of Pryderi, lord of Annwn or Hades in the Mabinogion, confirms the supposition that Pridd did not merely mean *"earth"* in the sense of *"soil"* but rather *"the world"* as part of a cosmic system demonstrated by the earth itself; a world moreover which included Heaven and Hell, Time and Eternity.

Priddy was perhaps so named because it was a place where men penetrated *beneath* the earth to discover its secrets, both through the Swallet and the lead-mines—like Arthur in his ship Prydwen, because it was a centre for the earth-goddess Ceridwen's Nature Mysteries.

An interesting description of one of these rites is given by Morien Morgan in *"The Winged Son of Avebury"*.

"The solar drama appears to have been annually performed in many localities in Wales, and doubtless also in many other places in Great Britain and Ireland, until the time the Druids lost their hold of England, Scotland and Ireland. The Druids spoke the Welsh language, and in that tongue preserved their sacred dramas, called Mabyn Ogion, or Adherents of the Babe Sun; which are now too often in fragmentary condition.

In these fragments which have come down to us, we find clear allusions to three noted localities in Wales, celebrated as places where to the last days of Druidism as a religion, the said dramas were annually performed. These were Pontypridd, Bala, and Borth, Cardigan Bay. In the last-named, that portion of the drama dealing with the descent of the sun into the underworld of Hud and Lledrith, Annwn and Gwenydva or Hades and Elysium, was annually performed between Borth and Arkle, Ireland. The luna-crescent coracle, called Arthur's barge and Coroogl Gwydrin, or the Coracle of the Water-buffetings, contained the image of the sun as old Taliesin or Arthur.

But the return journey of the barge to Borth contained a new body, that of a Babe, supposed to be made for him in the coracle by Cariadwen the consort of Celu. It was understood that this renewal took place while passing through the underworld, to the south-east of the horizon."

There are several points to note in this passage.

First, is the similarity of the name Pontypridd to Priddy merely fortuitous, or does it hint in both cases at the earth-Mysteries?

Second, is Borth not *Birth*? Is Arkle not the lunar-crescent *Ark*?

Third, note the identity of Arthur, Taliesin and Gwyddyr, sun-gods all. Gwyddyr is more familiar as Uther, Arthur's father, once a sky-god.

Fourth, the confirmation from an old Welsh scholar that the Druids featured in this ritual a Babe in a Boat, as in the Glastonbury Zodiac, although in Morgan's day this Zodiac had not yet been re-discovered.

Did Joseph witness such a ritual at Glastonbury Tor and Priddy? Did he bring "Christ the True Sun" as Gildas calls Him, in his ship as a babe, boy and youth to learn His role in this great "open university" of the Druids? If he did, they were both enacting the Myth. For in a very real sense Joseph's ship was the Ark of Solomon—Sol the sun. It bore the seed of Solomon, the Flower of the Rod of Jesse, of David's line.

The fact that Joseph and Solomon's Ship figure in the Grail legends shew that *this was understood when they were written.*

Why worry then, whether the coming of Joseph and Jesus are Myth or History? For Myth illumines and makes sense of history. More, it creates history, giving it at the same time an upward twist. No-one, for example, can deny the civilising influence of Joseph's Grail and Arthurian legend upon emergent Europe.

Glastonbury's Glass Castle reflects more clearly than most mirrors, though it is not without some distortion; but at least if one stands in the right position one may catch a glimpse of eternity and Evolution's purpose.

Speaking mythically, One who fulfilled Evolution's expectations for Man was brought to see Himself reflected in Glastonbury's Glass. (The double image presented, both Child and Man, is reflected in the legends of His coming, which are undecided whether He came as Babe, Boy or Man, and incline towards several British visits at different ages.)

Historically, it was possible; almost one might say, it was *made* possible. *But did it happen? Did* those feet in ancient time walk upon England's mountains green?

Which brings us to the enigma of William Blake, the last of the bards. How did he, a Londoner, know of these obscure Cornish and Somerset legends? Mona Wilson's Life of the poet provides an answer. He was descended from the family of Admiral Blake, whose birthplace was Bridgwater, *near the Somerset Zodiac.* William's forbears doubtless moved to London in the train of the admiral. There are Blakes also round Looe (in my own family) also tracing their descent from the admiral, who had a house at St. Erney— its garden path still called *"the Admiral's quarter-deck"* His arms are in the ancient church opposite. If the poet's family came from here, they could hardly fail to know Looe's legends. And William (born 1757 just a hundred years after the admiral's death in 1657) seems to have heard them at his mother's knee; his first engraving at fourteen years old was of "Joseph of Arimathea landing on the rocks of Albion". His interest in Druidism, so marked in his work, apparently led him to become Chosen Chief of the London Order of Druids for some years until his death. He appears as such upon their Rolls.

JOSEPH OF ARIMATHEA among the rocks of Albion' by William Blake at the age of 16.

MARY CAINE

It was at meetings of this Order, curiously enough, that I first heard of the Glastonbury Zodiac in 1961—just at the time of Mrs. Maltwood's death!

The name Blake means "black". I have read somewhere that they were black because they were Phoenicians whose task was to blaze the ancient tin-tracks with beacon-fires. Perhaps too they were bronzed Phoenicians, black-faced miners. Joseph of Arimathea also lit a beacon on such a track, according to:

The Legend of Crewkerne

This, by E. J. Watson, tells how Joseph and his companions were led to a straight track, an ancient Phoenician metal-route, marked by small grassy mounds (barrows?) and passed through an earthwork named Cunnygar. (King's garth or caer.) They rested every five miles, planting one of their staves to mark and sanctify the way. (Leys are marked by trees as well as barrows and forts.) Only Joseph's staff was left when they reached Wearyall, its blossoming taken as a sign of the Old Teaching flowering again in the New. On one hill Joseph found a standing stone, set the Grail upon it, and its light blazed out, illuminating the woodlands around. (Was this Gemini's pineal beacon on Dundon Hill?)

Crewkerne, whose church preserves Joseph's stone seat, is on an old track to Somerton and the Mendips from Axemouth and the south-west. This passes near Hamden Hill and Montacute, where there was a mediaeval legend of Joseph's burial. Joseph was a ley-hunter!

His myths, inconsistent though they are, have an extraordinary way of knitting all together into one significant pattern. He makes sense and significance out of history; he can do the same, it seems, for geography. His Secret is surely the Space-time Pattern, which he must have learnt from the Divine Instruction in his Apocryphal tower. Vespasian freed him from this tower, and Vespasian is said to have invested Montacute's Hamden Hill while conquering Britain. In myth at least, they meet both here and at Jerusalem! What does this mean? We know of their first meeting through the Apocrypha. This early Christianity was taken round the known world by Phoenicians, to whom it was a restatement of their ancient Cabiric Mysteries, themselves based from diluvial times on our Zodiac. Joseph-and-Jesus legends are found only in Phoenician-frequented parts of Britain, and did not emanate from Roman-Christian monastic houses. Indeed, where they adopted them, as at Glastonbury and Crewkerne, they did so reluctantly and late.

Melkin's description of Joseph the wanderer's burial on a bifurcated line was my first clue; was this a branching ley-line? Crewkerne's legend deepened suspicion; **Montacute's Legend**, though it does not deal with Joseph, does spring from his reputed burial-place; and because it tells of ley-lines, brings suspicion near conviction.

Briefly, Canute's standard-bearer, Tovi, found a buried flint cross here: under it another made of wood. He harnessed twelve black and twelve white oxen to draw it wherever they would, vowing to build a shrine to house the cross where they rested. They dragged it right across Britain to Waltham. There in Tovi's shrine the cross performed miraculous cures. It was called the Leodgaresburg Cross—perhaps "Leodgar" was Hamden Hill camp, guarding Leo six miles north? (Leo appears carved on Stoke-sub-Hamden Church, as we have seen.)

King Harold was cured of paralysis and a blind eye by the holy relic and gratefully enlarged the shrine into Waltham Abbey. It is not insignificant that the abbey sports a Zodiac the length of the nave on its ceiling; Tovi's 24 oxen, black and white, sound like the hours of the day.

At Hastings Harold's battle-cry was *"Holy Cross! Holy Cross"!* Alas, it did not avail him; he was blinded once more, and stricken with the final paralysis of death. There are overtones of solar myth about this kingly death.

The flint cross is odd, too. No flint nodule can produce a cross large enough to need 24 oxen to draw it. And why the wooden cross beneath? Was it a flint *cross-road*, "metalled" by Romans, with an even older corduroy road beneath? These, made by wooden balks laid criss-cross, are neolithic; many have been found in Somerset. And were these cross-roads Joseph's burial-site—the "bifurcated line"? Montacute's conical hill, terraced and towered like the Tor, suggests a natural ley-mark, leading to Hamden's ancient and important camp.

Tovi's 24 oxen hint not only at a connecting link between leys and Zodiacs—they also indicate the natural origin of ancient roads. The ley-theory holds that they are formed by electro-magnetic lines of force, sensed and followed by migrating animals and birds. Founding-myths like Waltham Abbey's are so common that one can only suppose that animals were set to find nodal sites of powerful vibrations. Glastonbury is said to have been founded where Glaesting's wandering sow at last settled down and littered. Cuthbert, they say, followed a dun cow to found Durham cathedral; Dun Cow lane runs beside it. St. David followed his dove until it perched on Menevia (Old Bush), where he built St. David's cathedral. (Tovi also means Dove, like David.) Friston church in Sussex was built in cruciform style because four cows lay down in a cross upon the site. These lines, the theory goes, are marked by subterranean water-courses; and what mediaeval cathedral has not a well beneath the altar in its crypt?

Water is essential for all life, animal or human; no settlement, monastic or secular, could be founded without it. The Druids were famous water-diviners—but so are animals; no doubt Druids used animals when their own "magical" powers failed.

What the Druid-astronomers knew, and we have forgotten, is that the subterranean water-pattern was only part of the pattern of the universe, a kaleidoscope whose shapes and movement could be observed and calculated in the stars, sun, moon and earth and all upon it, not least in the life and character of men and civilisations.

If Montacute's crossed leys are meant by Joseph's sarcophagus, well might Melkin say that when it is found neither dew nor rain shall fail the dwellers in our isle.

"Joseph" symbolises the secret transmission of this Space-Time Pattern. Landing on the Zodiac, he lets us know where it is to be seen. Choosing the Fishes, he shews that he can tell its time: his silver cruets (these same fishes) held the blood of the Saviour of the Piscean Age. He hides the Grail in Aquarian Chalice Well, where it is found in the dawn of the Aquarian Age.

If the equinoctial Ages fit the Zodiac effigies so well, let us look at these in detail. Then trying another time-scale, see how English History opens to the Zodiac key.

The Zodiac and Precessional Ages

Every 2150 years or so the sun rises in the spring equinox against a different Zodiac sign, the whole cycle taking nearly 26000 years. This movement is due to the slow wobble of the earth's axis, its pole pointing in succession to a circle of seven different pole-stars. (Hence Draco, the circumpolar constellation, was said to have seven heads.)

The sun now rises in spring against the cusp of Pisces and Aquarius, though the exact date for the beginning of the Aquarian Age is debatable.

Some say it has already begun, some that it will begin in 2300 AD; so we may take the round figure of 2000 AD to start our time-table.

AQUARIAN AGE BEGINS	2000 AD	
PISCEAN AGE BEGAN	150 BC	
ARIAN AGE BEGAN	2300 BC	Great migrations & invasions
TAUREAN AGE BEGAN	4450 BC	Megaliths pyramids, lynchets
GEMINIAN AGE BEGAN	6600 BC	Merchant culture-bringers
CANCERIAN AGE BEGAN	8750 BC	The Flood and its Ark
LEO'S AGE BEGAN	10900 BC	("Golden Age" of Atlantis)

All remembered history is contained in five ages. The Grail had five changes, the last being into the Aquarian Chalice. Previously it was signed by two silver cruets or Piscean Fishes. Before that, I submit, it was the vase of Aries' horns ♈ and earlier still the bowl of Taurus' horns. ♉ The Geminian Pillars of Hercules ♊ are all that remains of the Three Bars of Light,

Gemini's true sign. This, typifying Ideas, the Alphabet, was transmitted by the Geminian Phoenicians, sailing in the Cancerian ark to found new cultures in Egypt, Chaldea, Crete, from Atlantis, sinking in the Cancerian Age of the Flood. The "wise Men of Gotham", who went to sea in a bowl". Their bowl was the Cauldron, the original form of the Grail—Cancer's Ship.

The settled Taurean Age produced megaliths, mighty earthworks, the pyramids, the slowly-built splendours of Egypt and Chaldea, split and spread by the mass-migrations from east to west of the roving, battle-scarred Arian Age. The Piscean Age was typically one of religion and religious wars, of empires founded by sea. Water-power turned to steam-power and electricity under Uranus, ruler of approaching Aquarius. In its air-sign we take to the air. Under Aquarius, sign of the Brotherhood of Man, new visions of social and racial equality and justice struggle (not without revolution and constant upheavals) to come to birth.

24: English History Fits the Zodiac

(Time-scale: 1 Year to 1 Degree. 30 years = 1 Zodiacal Sign or House)

CANCER 780-810 Danes in long-boats begin to raid, at Dorset and Lindisfarne 793. Cancer the Ship.

LEO 810-840 Ecgbert (802-39) The Lion, made Bretwalda of all England. Danes cease raids till 837.

VIRGO 840-870 Ecgbert's sons split England into Virgoan details. Incessant Danish raids.

LIBRA 870-900 Libra produces great generals. Alfred and Ethelbert, as becomes a dual sign, fight the Danes. **Alfred the Great, 871-900**, restores Government, Law, Education and the Church. A fair, wise and accessible king all characteristic of Libra. A typical Libran compromise was to divide England with Guthran the Dane. Another Libran duality.

SCORPIO 900-930 Edward the Elder, 901-24. Scorpionic reign entirely devoted to subduing aggressive Danelaw. A strong man for a Martial period. Athelstan, succeeding him, beats the Scots, Irish and Danes.

SAGITTARIUS 930-960 Athelstan and Edmund's two splendid reigns. Athelstan 925-40, Edmund 940-46. England united and allied by marriage to the Franks. Edmund "the Deed-Doer" escapes death on horseback at Cheddar Gorge and enacts Sagittarius' Dying Sun-King by his assassination when only 25. Edred, 946-55 and Edgar, 958-75, continued in splendour (despite the "regrettable" Edwy's short three-year reign) and this period of great kings was much beholden to St. Dunstan, the gay, witty, high-minded courtier and adviser. Very Sagittarian!

CAPRICORN 960-990 Dunstan turns Capricornian, being made Archbishop of Canterbury 960. Till now his rises and falls from power have given him a rough ride, like Sagittarius. Now, under Edgar he assumes the Capricornian mantle of Merlin the mage and sage, under Saturn. His wise and venerable rule staves off the impending evils of Capricorn until the murder of Edward the Martyr in 978, and the disastrous reign of Ethelred the Unready 978-1016. Dunstan and Ethelred effectively shew the good and bad aspects of Capricorn.

AQUARIUS 990-1020 The great Wessex dynasty ends in a whimper and the new Danish one (Canute) begins, echoing the renascent sun of Aquarius. More than one dynasty takes over in Aquarius, as will be seen.

PISCES 1020-1050 Canute, 1016-35, and the Piscean Waves! Hardi**canute** his son was a Piscean sot, and after two years' reign England **was** drowned in faction over the succession. Eventually the Wessex "Fish" overcame the Danish, and Edward the Confessor, devout and unworldly (typically Piscean) became king 1042-66, but left government to Earl Godwin. He rebuilt Westminster Abbey. On his accession he *sailed* over to England from Normandy. Harold, Godwin's son, signed over any chance of being King after Edward's death by incomprehensibly *sailing* to Normandy, being captured by Duke William, and apparently, from this position of weakness, swearing the English throne away to William; making this oath "upon the bones of saints". His fleet was dispersed by gales; his brother Tostig sided with William. The waves of Pisces, the sign's duality, the capture, the betrayal, are all typically Piscean.

ARIES 1050-1080 Not only Harold's wars, but the Battle of Hastings characterise this Martial time. England is said to be ruled by Aries the Pioneer. Nothing more symbolic of Aries, ruled by Mars, can be imagined than *William the Conqueror* 1066-1087.

TAURUS 1080-1110 William Rufus, 1087-1100, typifies Taurus' worst side. He was fleshy, licentious, and bad-tempered and violent. In death he was the target or "Bull's-eye" for an arrow.

GEMINI 1110-1140 (The brothers.) Henry I, 1100-35, was Rufus' brother. Henry lost his son in the White Ship. How Geminian! The Boy in the Boat. Also in this dual period come the alternating reigns of Stephen and Matilda. The influence of Matilda begins to dominate in

CANCER 1140-1170 The maternal sign. Matilda, daughter of Henry I invaded England in 1139! The barons had elected her cousin Stephen king, as she was a woman. Matilda crowned queen 1141, but civil war ensued. Cancer's female influence however founds dynasties, and Matilda's son Henry II *sailed* from France to found the Plantagenets. Female influence was still strong, for his wife Eleanor of Aquitaine enlarged his Angevin Empire. Under her encouragement *Arthurian chivalry was also re-founded from overseas.*

LEO 1170-1200 Though Henry II, 1154-89, owed much of his reign to Cancer, he became a Leonine king. (He established his Leonine dominance over Rome by murdering Thomas a Becket in 1170!) And what could be more Leonine than his son Richard *Lion-Heart*, 1189-99? Much solar myth attaches to Richard. His rescue by a bard from prison and his death by an archer, are typical—as is his liaison with Robin Hood, the Green Man or shadow-sun-king. John, his treacherous brother, also fits the myth. William, also called the Lion, was king of Scotland from 1165 to 1214.

VIRGO 1200-1230 John, 1199-1216, shews a typically Virgoan decline in England's fortunes. Virgo (with the brilliant exception of Elizabeth the Virgin Queen) is not a good sign for kings, for Virgo is the sign of the efficient subordinate, not the leader. John *did* have an efficient and reliable subordinate, William the Marshal. John's subordinates indeed overcame him when Magna Carta was signed. Though this piece of "Libran Law" was worked out in detail under Virgo in 1215, it did not become effective until

LIBRA 1230-1260 Henry III and his opponent Simon de Montfort, "Founder of Parliament". (It should be noted that Eleanor, imprisoned by her husband Henry II, came into power again under John's Virgoan reign—until her death in 1204.) Women flourish under Virgo. Henry III, in this Libran period, suffered from the sign's duality. (1207-72). He was crowned in 1227, when the barons and the crown were *equally balanced* in power. A typical Libran compromise with Simon de Montfort was eventually arrived at, and English liberties and Law established, though not without much Libran generalship on both sides. Magna Carta and Parliament echo Alfred's Libran Laws.

SCORPIO 1260-1290 Edward I. "The Hammer of the Scots", used the Scorpion's claw to draw Scotland and Wales, resisting fiercely, into a united England. His reign, 1272-1307, reaches into Sagittarius. The claws of the "hammer" did their work, and his later reign was that of

SAGITTARIUS 1290-1320 Truly a Sun-king. But his homosexual son Edward II, though inheriting his father's glory, soon undid himself and England's fortunes. He reigned from 1307-27, into

CAPRICORN 1320-1350 and in this period of Saturnine influence lost his wife and life. A horrible death in Berkeley Castle, anally pierced by a red-hot poker, shews the worst of Scorpio and Capricorn!

AQUARIUS 1350-1380 Edward III, 1327-77 though his early life was shadowed by his frustrated mother's liaison with Roger Mortimer, king in fact if not in name, outgrew this Saturnine influence to become indeed a king. (Aquarius reflects Leo's royal sign.) His character averted the change of dynasty threatened by Mortimer, and he re-founded the glories of Arthur in the Windsor Round Table and the Order of the Garter. Both Edward and his son the Black Prince achieved glory by Uranian lightening-strikes, typical of Aquarius. The Black Prince did not outlive his father, and his son Richard II succeeded in a position of Piscean weakness, as a mere boy. Before the Piscean shadow became reality however, Richard bravely faced Wat Tyler's rebels, saying "I will be your leader". To lead the common man is an Aquarian ideal.

PISCES 1380-1410 Richard II, 1377-99, did not fulfil this promise. Fitful, erratic, wilful and weak by turns, he shewed both Aquarian and Piscean faults, and died a Piscean death, being murdered in captivity. His rival, Bolingbroke, banished *overseas*, returned to depose him. Pisces favours poets; *Chaucer flourished under Richard's artistic reign.*

ARIES 1410-1440 Henry IV 1399-1413 (Bolingbroke) invaded under Pisces, but conquered in Arian style, arresting the Piscean decline. Aries produces rebels, in this case Glendower and Hotspur. Also heroes. Where but in Aries should we find *Henry V*, 1413-22? Or *Agincourt?* (1415). Aries rules the head; when afflicted producing madness. *Henry VI inherited madness* from his French line. *The heroine Joan of Arc was burnt during this fire-sign.* (1431)

TAURUS 1440-70 Taurus is the sign of the foster-father, and the Duke of Bedford, Henry's uncle, was the real ruler, faithful like good Taurus to his trust. The burning of Joan was the only blot on his escutcheon. But events were already working towards Gemini...

GEMINI 1470-1500 The Wars of the Roses, or *brothers and cousins* all descended from Edward III. Richard Crookback, 1483-5, succeeds his *brother* Edward IV. Caxton's press set up—Mercury, Gemini's ruler, favours intelligence, learning, communication. *And where if not under Gemini, shall we find the murdered Little Princes in the Tower?* Malory wrote Morte D'Arthur in 1470.

CANCER 1500-1530 (Which changes dynasties through the female line, or from overseas) put an end to the fratricidal Wars of the Roses. Henry Tudor sails in from Brittany in 1485, claiming the throne through his mother Margaret Beaufort. A Lancastrian from John of Gaunt, he strengthened his claim and united the two warring Houses by *marriage* to Elizabeth of York. Two women thus secured his crown. Maternal Cancer! Henry's son, named Arthur, hints at a British revival echoing that of Cancerian Eleanor of Aquitaine. Cancer seeks security—a home with abundance. Henry, 1485-1509, amassed wealth, which Henry VIII spent lavishly as the Leonine Sun-King. At first Henry VIII's court was indeed a home for all the scholars of Europe. His marriage to Katharine of Aragon seemed stable, lasting for some 20 years.

LEO 1530-1560 Henry VIII, 1509-47, a Sun Cancerian, anticipates the Leo epoch by 10 years at the "Field of the Cloth of Gold", 1520—the dawning sun. Leo's effect is clear. Henry, like Henry II under Leo, asserted his dominance by repudiating Rome and becoming head of the English Church. Leo is a great womaniser, but has few children. Henry, about 1530, rejects Katharine for Anne Boleyn, anxious for a male heir. Six wives; three children, one a sickly boy who died before manhood! Edward VI, 1547-53, only reigned six years. The roaring lion went out with a whimper. But this fire-sign was characterised by burnings which flamed into a threatening, lurid sunset under Mary Tudor's holocaust of martyrs. A ravening Lioness! 1553-1558.

VIRGO 1560-1590 Elizabeth I was another (1558-1603) but of a different mould. Her reign tempered by temperate Virgo. *Where but in Virgo should we expect to find the Virgin-Queen?* And is not the Triple Goddess herself served by three queens in this period? Four, counting Lady Jane Grey. But Virgo favoured among this group only the one who was cautious, temperate, chaste; raging Bloody Mary was struck down at its onset, uncontrollably romantic Mary Queen of Scots was forcibly controlled in prison throughout its period, and as Libra's warlike aspect began to loom up, she was executed in 1587. The Armada (1588) was beaten too.

LIBRA 1590-1620 If Elizabeth's admirals shew Libran generalship, her policies, both secular and religious, are a triumph of Libran compromise and justice; she aimed at peace, but ably defended her realm when she had to. She was adored as the Goddess she symbolised. 1603-25 James I was a Libran man-woman, a sex-balance which favours women, weakens men. Bisexual and mystical—even superstitious, he alienated the country by his favourites, his witch-hunts; broad churchmen by his High Church views, parliament by his belief in the Divine Right of Kings. (Proud Scorpio beginning to shew.)

SCORPIO 1620-1650 Charles I (1625-49) paid tragically for this pride by public execution in Scorpio's Death-Sign. Where else but in *Scorpio should the Dying and Divine Sun-King die?* He brought it on himself, as Scorpios do, listening to his father's and wife's absolutism, ignoring growing popular demand for shared government. Scorpio is not a sign that shares government. It produced Cromwell whose reign, 1649-58, was more successfully absolute than Charles', though elected by popular pressure. It is the sign (when not afflicted) of the Dictator, holding down dissidence by force. (Edward the Elder subdued the Danes, Edward I., the Scots and Welsh, under Scorpio.) Order restored by strength and force under Scorpio produces the expansive and creative reign of

SAGITTARIUS 1650-1680 the Sun-King in glory. (Each sign is paired in character, though not identically.) Sagittarius, the popular sun-king, was shared by Cromwell and Charles II. Charles II's early life had been shadowed by Scorpio's secrecy, in hiding. This secrecy persisted through the Sagittarian period, lurking in the Cabal and the Treaty of Dover. In appearance, Charles II is an interesting mixture of swarthy Scorpio and humorous, whimsical Sagittarius. (1660-85) Charles II in hiding is Scorpionic, so is his secret Catholicism, his secret Cabal, his Secret Treaty of Dover. His gay, libertine court, his encouragement of science (Newton) archaeology, (Aubrey, Stukeley) and the Restoration Theatre, even his mistresses, are Sagittarian. For this is the sign of Higher Mind, though with animal's legs! Henry VIII, too involved, executed his cast-offs; Charles humorously paid them off and kept cool. Wise, detached, amused, he learnt from his early sufferings to become a true Sagittarian Sun-King.

CAPRICORN 1680-1710 Though prolific, he had no legitimate heir. A slow death (he apologised for "being an unconscionable time a-dying") was Capricornian, as was his unpopular successor, his bigoted Catholic brother James II, who abdicated in 4 years. The seven Bishops' aquittal undid him; Capricorn favours the Church. William III of Orange 168 -1702, was never popular but was dour, patient, plodding and dutiful—and childless. Very Capricornian! Mary's sister Anne, 1702-14, though not a strong character, inherited Capricornian respect for the crown recovered by William. It endured, and even became popular again under

AQUARIUS 1710-1740 A popular sign! It reflects Leo's glories, but can change or renew dynasties. Thus the Stuarts' sunset blazed in glory under Anne, and the Hanoverians took over. Aquarius is friendly, and Anne's friends the Churchills and Abigail Hill were influential, even overbearing. (Aquarius likes to dominate like Leo, but masks this under a cloak of democracy.) Under Anne, a confirmed Tory, Whigs and Tories equalised in power, broadening parliament's base. Aquarians are great talkers. Marlborough's battles, Blenheim, Oudenarde, Malplaquet, secured England's glory. Anne's death by a stroke, her children all stricken down, shews Uranus' lightening-strike ruler of Aquarius. The succession, in trouble again, passed to George I who though vaguely Stuart by descent was a foreigner, speaking no English, from Hanover. Shades of Canute, and of the Black Prince who did not live to succeed. Succession problems! The old Pretender (1715). But Aquarius likes reason, not romance, and preferred prosaic Protestant George to Catholic Stuarts. George reigned under strict conditions and Prime Ministers like Walpole first appeared. Aquarius is secular. Commerce and corruption flourished, religion wilted.

Wood's Hell-Fire Club flourished under Aquarius. Yet a *people's religion was* reborn in the Wesleys, to flower under Pisces' mystical ray. Colonial trade shews Aquarius' expansive influence, and stocks and shares begin to increase the people's (not the monarchy's) wealth. Wilkes the reforming radical and rake, was elected despite Parliament's rejection, by the people under Aquarius, sign of the Common Man. George II, 1727-60, hardly more English than his father, also faces the new "people's power".

PISCES 1740-1770 He reigns in Piscean weakness, dominated by Pitt, Earl of Chatham (what a Piscean name and title!) who stirs England by his mystical patriotic speeches, sweeping the French out of India and Canada by *command of the seas.* Pisces' mystical poetry produces Blake and Nelson (both rebels under Aries, remembering Nelson's blind eye!) Also Admiral Hood. English landscape painting begins under Gainsborough and under Reynolds the Royal Academy was founded, 1768. Music flourished under Handel, architecture and manners under Beau Nash, furniture under Chippendale, letters under Johnson, Goldsmith, Fielding, Gray, etc. The Young Pretender, 1745, is unlucky like his father, and both peter out in Piscean despair (the Old) and debauchery (the Young) as the Hanoverian star ascends. The Piscean poor get poorer as Enclosures drive them into towns, but *water-power and canals* stimulate industry.

ARIES 1770-1800 Water-power becomes steam-power under Aries fire-sign and Watt's genius. The Industrial Revolution begins under Aries' martial star! Aries the pioneer infuses new energy. Blast furnaces, coal and iron, typically appear here, as do inventions in weaving Arian wool. Piscean William Blake is not alone in being fired by the French Revolution – America becomes rebellious too (War of Independence 1775) through George III's Arian pig-headedness.

1760-1820 George III was the first Hanoverian who could say he "gloried in the name of Britain". He was afflicted (under Aries) in the head, suffering like Henry VI under the same sign, from madness. Nelson, who joined the Navy in 1770, lost an eye. Admiral Hood (note the Arian head-name!) and the Iron Duke of Wellington (born 1769) are also outstanding Martial figures.

TAURUS 1800-1830 Though Nelson's Battle of the Nile (1798) was fought just within Aries' martial sign, Trafalgar (1805) and Wellington's Waterloo (1815) overlap into Taurus. They can be seen as the culmination of Britain's long fight for supremacy. Taurus consolidates, builds. Britain built both herself and her empire under these 30 years. Industry began to put on weight, and as Taurus gives wealth many became rich, though the bulk of the poor toiled like oxen for little reward. "Alas, noble Bull, how art thou oppressed!" as Taliesin sang. Robert Owen the pioneering philanthropist mill-owner was an exception. Born under Aries' period in 1771, he pioneered co-operative schemes under Taurus' benevolent Venusian ray. This ray also favours the arts—witness a galaxy of poets, writers, artists and architects—Tennyson, Keats, Shelley (born under rebellious Aries) Ruskin, Watts, Turner, Constable; the Adam brothers and Nash made a golden age of architecture. George III's Arian madness reflects Henry VI's; both were incapacitated for the last 10 years of their reigns, needing regents. Henry's were Bedford and Warwick the King-maker, George's was his son. Taurus the Protector! George III lived at Kew, whose Gardens are the fruits of nature-loving Taurus. Farmer George! John Bull! Castlereagh, born at the beginning of Aries' 30 years (1769-1822) suppressed the Irish rebellion, fought a duel with Canning, and under Taurus went mad and cut his own throat. (Taurus rules the throat.) George IV reigned after his father's death from 1820-30, thus neatly ending the Taurean period. Taurus' earthy Venus affected him strongly; he was profligate both with money and women; (who but a Taurean would pay his vast debts by marrying money when already morganatically married?) his love of art gave us Brighton Pavilion's fairy palace. Taurus the Builder.

GEMINI 1830-1860 Farmer George's son William IV was known as the Sailor Prince. Gemini's boat! Gemini successions are always brothers. William IV (1765-1837) was George IV's brother. On William's accession (1830 precisely) Taurean romps give way to Geminian ideas of the Brotherhood of Man. William aided overdue reforms. It is in this *Geminian period that child labour* was first restricted and factory exploitation recognised and curbed. The Chartists agitated for universal suffrage and equality from 1838-50. Gemini's Mercury prompts the 1st Public Education Act (1838). Trade Unions are formed. Mercury also speeds communication by the invention of the telegraph and the Penny Post. Alexander Graham Bell was born in 1847, though his telephone came in 1876. The Brotherhood sign gave slaves their freedom through Wilberforce in 1833. He was born under the Piscean period (1759); Pisces is the slave's and prisoner's friend. Dickens, a Sun-Piscean, also creates sympathy for the underdog and by his humanity stimulates the Brotherhood ideal. Sisters too seem aided by Gemini's Mercury, viz. the Brontes. The Brownings were another equal partnership. Mercury certainly brought out a galaxy of writers. Queen Victoria (1837-1901) possessed youthful charm and produced nine children under Gemini.

CANCER 1860-90 This lunar sign sent her into eclipse on her husband's death in 1861, but she at last emerged to rule her empire, becoming *the Mother of millions, the very embodiment of Cancer's maternal water-sign, even to her plump figure.* The mature, settled, somewhat bourgeois image of this prosperous period is very Cancerian. Wars occurred, but *overseas*. The Gemini brothers fought (under the pained but strictly neutral eye of the Motherland) the American Civil War, Indian fought Indian in the Mutiny until Mother England unified them under her wing and by responsible administration made India prosperous; the Crimean War, typically a struggle for control of the (Mediterranean) *sea*, produced that Cancerian heroine Florence Nightingale. "Gunboat diplomacy"—the China incident and the "Alabama", emphasise Cancer's Ship, as did the lowering of tariffs and Free Trade. Tennyson fished ancient Arthurian ideals out of Cancer's inspirational Cauldron, Darwin plumbed its Womb of Life for the Origin of Species—and rocked the Establishment boat. The Pre-Raphaelites and Pugin also sought for lost origins, Newman revived the Mother Church of Catholicism, and Victorian Gothic tried to re-enter the womb of the past. Remarkable *women*, Blavatsky and Annie Besant, founded mystical Theosophy here. 1870 Emmeline Parkhurst womens S.P.U. 1903.

LEO 1890-1920 Queen Victoria's last years blazed with Leonine royal glory. The Empress of an Empire on which the sun never set! Englishmen acquired a certain arrogance under the British Lion, and such pride, breeding competition, bears the seeds of its own downfall—in this case the period ends after the 1st World War, engendered by German Imperialist competitiveness. The European lions divided Africa's carcass between them and South Africa, snatched from the Boers, became British.

Edward VII, 1901-10, though a sun-Scorpion, seems more typical of his epoch. Personally royal and benevolent, he was politically constitutional, astute and conciliatory. His success abroad got him called the Peacemaker. He enhanced the monarchy's status as the focal point of the Empire. A Leonine time of Pomp and Circumstance, aided by Kipling! Edward's many loves are also Leonine; (Scorpio is passionate too.) Leo's epochs are apt to end unfortunately (Richard I., Bloody Mary) and this time, Germany, also demanding "a place in the sun", challenged British supremacy in trade and on the seas and the Great War began. Though Britain won, it was a sorry lion who returned home to lick its wounds. Leo's sun was setting in blood.

VIRGO 1920-1950 George V (1910-36) was fated to preside over this holocaust and to reign mostly in Virgo's epoch—never, except for Elizabeth I—a favourable sign in our history. By 1920 it appeared that the "world fit for heroes to live in" was an illusion. So many men had died that there were indeed many spinsters who had to earn their living. Virgo is a career-woman, unlike Cancer's wife and mother, and women demanded the vote. The cost of war produced world-slumps and jobs were short, poverty and unemployment rife. Virgo is a critic, and thus produced the arch-critic Bernard Shaw. Socialism, the right to work, flourished under hard-working Virgo, and social reforms under Beveridge and Bevan's Health Service are notably Virgoan. Virgo scrapes and saves and is pernickety about her health. Mrs. Pankhurst, a lioness, won in Virgo real emancipation for women, and in this period it is not surprising that Queen Mary's character seems to overshadow the king's. If labour troubles overshadow both, Virgo's lighter side is shewn by the era of skittish debutantes—"flappers". Virgoan hysteria follows Leo's heroism. But the dislocation and hysteria was greater in Germany, and produced Hitler. George V, who had earlier shewn the dominating Leonine quality of his father, became known under Virgo for his sense of duty—a Virgoan virtue. This was paramount in his son George VI, (1936-52) whose other characteristics, a stammering shyness and diffident reluctance to lead, were equally Virgoan. But the times favoured this nervous, conscientious man, and Virgo herself at her most seductive eclipsed his elder brother Edward VIII, sympathetic, popular and charming though he was. Like Paris, he chose love, and Aphrodite gave him the Bahamas in which to enjoy it, cruelly testing his love for the poor of his kingdom against his love for Mrs. Simpson, and setting him aside, while George VI endured the bombing of the 2nd World War with his people, earning their love and respect. The 2nd World War was forced upon us though like George VI, we felt ill-equipped to lead. Like Virgo, pacifistically inclined, we were unarmed and weak. But it was Right against Might, and duty called. Our weakness, largely due to the long interwar struggle for social justice internally, touched America, and the Virgoan Statue of Liberty herself came to our aid. But it was a barren victory. Virgo is a barren sign. But she is not idle, and in this epoch by mass-production, invention and machine-precision everyday life was transformed. For Virgo is clever; it was the age of atom-splitting and Einstein. Nor is she always a blue-stocking; she can shew unearthly beauty. Thus Garbo reigned over an age of film-stars, Freud and daughter Anna brought psycho-analysis here in 1938; Virgo is introspective. Labour (predictably) had a landslide into power in Virgo (1945). This majority shrank till in

LIBRA 1950-80 it was defeated in 1951. Since then Conservative and Labour have been evenly balanced. Libra's Scales of Justice attempted for the first time a code of world-laws—the Atlantic Charter—and a code of world-justice in the United Nations. True, like Magna Carta, both began in Virgo's Mercurial brain, but became effective in Libra. The Balance can be seen everywhere; in power between USSR and USA, between the sexes, social classes, capital and labour—even in the recent preoccupation with the Balance of Payments. The social tensions can end in a tug-of-war, with one side winning and punishing the other with Scorpio's venom—or they can be resolved amicably (Libra's

Spirit-Dove) with justice illumined with mercy. If we can do this the threatening Scorpion of 1980 can resume its ancient form of the eagle.

Any theory which assigns Alfred's Laws, letters and generalship to Libra, Simon de Montfort's first Parliament to the same sign; William the Conqueror and conquering Henry V to Aries; Henry II, Richard Lionheart, Henry VIII and Edward VII to Leo; Elizabeth to Virgo, the Little Princes in the Tower to Gemini, Charles I's death and even the legendary Arthur's (538) to the cusp of Scorpio and Sagittarius the dying sun-king—to instance but a few— is surely worth investigation by those with a history book and a smattering of astrology.

Some may argue that one may select from the multifarious facts of history those which support the theory, rejecting those which do not.

I did not however see this pattern first in recent history, where there is so much information that biassed selection is indeed a temptation. It was in fact the Tudor-Stuart sequence of kings and queens from Henry VII to Charles II that so strongly corresponded with the Zodiac from Cancer to Sagittarius, that first struck me. I went *backwards* in time to Alfred before continuing on from Charles II to the present day. Indeed, the amount of material in the last three centuries is so great that it would be impossible to see a pattern at all without projecting the rigid time-scale forward from the past. One couldn't see the wood for the trees. But going back in time, I found the scarcer facts became unquestionably more characteristic of the Zodiac period assigned to them, and was encouraged. The first entry in this list is typical: Cancer the Ship symbolises raiding Danes in their long-boats.

I also found that legends had a remarkable way of fitting the signs; Alfred and the cakes suits the Libran equality of the sexes—Canute and the waves fits Pisces to a nicety. Projecting further back it was fascinating to find that the "legendary" visits of Jesus and Joseph to Britain came in Gemini's Messiah-sign and Cancer's Ship respectively.

The latter legends fit even better when 1485 is taken as the founding-date for Cancer's Tudor dynasty. This adjustment also brings Magna Carta into Libra's Law-sign, and researchers may prefer this reading to the one given here. There is a difference of 15 years, or half a sign. Both readings have their advantages. This pattern can of course be projected into the future. No doubt such seers as Merlin and Nostradamus based their prophecies upon it.

The foregoing is of course only the briefest outline of a subject that could fill volumes. It does however serve to shew the Zodiac character-sequence at work on time-scales other than those normally dealt with by astrology—or so I hope. Some such exposition is necessary to support the assertion that the Zodiac demonstrates a Space-Time Pattern.

The implications for history alone are vast—and raise many questions. Do the histories of other countries betray the same sequence of influences at the same time, or is there a time-slip for different latitudes and longitudes?

And if history reveals such a pattern, what other subjects in the spectrum of human knowledge may not be similarly illuminated by it? For all are subject to the laws of space and time in differing proportions. Geography is one such field of research, as Mrs. Maltwood's work shews. And if geography, why not geology, which is geography throughout Time? Archaeology and ethnology, we have seen, are involved in the first Time-Scale demonstrated; that of the equinoctial ages. Modern medicine owes far more than it readily admits to homeopathy, or traditional medicine based on Zodiacal correspondences; psychology since Jung has begun to acknowledge the importance of Mythology to the human psyche, and mythology as we have seen is based entirely on the Zodiac pattern. (Jung studied Indian psychology, a far older and more sophisticated science than ours, which has never forgotten its Zodiacal roots.) Religion and theology has everything to gain by a return to its Zodiacal origins; the prospects for the sciences must be dazzling, as writers like Rodney Collin and Lyall Watson have already hinted. For the Zodiac is nothing if not creative. Pythagorean cosmology, rediscovered and applied, began the Renaissance in Europe. The Zodiac could once more open the doors on a new Renaissance.

We have 30 years of Scorpio to endure, if this historical reckoning is right. Can we learn from the past to avoid for Charles III the fate of Charles I, and the miseries of the ensuing Cromwellian dictatorship?

Scorpio, ruled by Mars and Pluto, must be a time of great energy and stress, of secret and underground activity. At its lowest level, it can be destructive in the extreme. But we can by awareness use this energy on a higher level, for reforms, and for penetrating (as only Scorpio can) the hidden secrets of the universe.—So that when this period ends, the knowledge and self-criticism it has given may find us prepared for the Aquarian Age, a Renaissance unsurpassed in human history.

GLASTONBURY ZODIAC

BIBLIOGRAPHY

Anglo-Saxon Chronicle		ed Gaumonsway 1953
Anderson, Lady Flavia	The Ancient Secret	Gollancz 1953
Ashe, Geoffrey	From Caesar to Arthur	Collins 1960
	King Arthur's Avalon	Fontana/Collins 1973
	The Ancient Wisdom	Macmillan 1977
Asser.	Life of Alfred	ed. Giles. Bell & Sons 1900
Bacon	Vanished Civilisations	Thames & Hudson 1963
Beaumont, Comyns	The Riddle of Prehistoric Britain	Rider
	Britain, Key to World History	Rider 1949
The Bible		
Blavatsky, H. P.	The Secret Doctrine	Theosophical Univ. Press 1970
Bond, Bligh	The Company of Avalon	Blackwell
	The Hill of Vision	Constable 1919
	Gematria	Rilko 1977
Book of Enoch	trans. R. H. Charles	SPCK, London 1960
Brown, Robert, Jun.	Primitive Constellations	Williams & Norgate
Bulleid, A	The Lake Villages of Somerset	Folk Press, London
Caesar, Julius	The Conquest of Gaul	trans. Handford. Penguin Books
Chadwick, Nora	The Druids	Univ. of Wales Press 1966
Chardin, Pierre Teilhard de.	The Future of Man	Collins
	The Phenomenon of Man	Collins
Charpentier, L.	The Mysteries of Chartres	Rilko
	Les Geants	J'ai Lu, Paris
Chretien de Troyes	Arthurian Romances	trans. Comfort. Everyman. Dent
Collin, Rodney	The Theory of Celestial Influence	Routledge & Kegan Paul
Daniel, Sir J.	Philosophy of Ancient Britain	Williams & Norgate 1927
Daniken, E. von	Chariots of the Gods	Corgi Books 1973
Davies, Ed.	Celtic Researches	Booth 1804
	Mythology and Rites of British Druids	Booth 1809
Doble, G. H.	The Saints of Cornwall	Printed for Truro Cathedral
Dobson, Rev. C. C.	Did Our Lord Visit Cornwall? (Booklet)	Covenant Publ. Co.
Donelly, Ignatius	Atlantis	Sidgewick & Jackson, London 1960
Eckwall, E.	Oxford Dictionary of Place-Names	Clarendon Press
Elder, I. H.	Celt Druid and Culdee	Covenant Publ. Co.
Eliot T. S.	The Waste Land	Faber & Faber
	The Cocktail Party	Faber & Faber
Encyclopaedia Britannica		
Evans, Sebastian	The High History of the Holy Grail	Dent's Everyman
Fagan, C.	Zodiacs Old and New	Anscombe
Folklore and Legends of Britain		Reader's Digest
Foerster, Werner	A Selection of Gnostic Texts	Clarendon, Oxford 1972
Fortune, Dion	The Mystical Qabalah	Benn
	The Cosmic Doctrine	Helios

Gildas Liber Querulam —	Old English Chronicles	ed. Giles Bell & Sons 1900
Geoffrey of Monmouth	History of the Kings of Britain	ed. Giles Bell & Sons 1900
Gordon, E. O.	Prehistoric London	Covenant Press London
Gospel According to Thomas (Apoc.)		Collins 1959
Graves, R.	The White Goddess	Faber & Faber 1948
Gray, E.	The Tarot Revealed	Bell, New York
Gregory of Tours	History of the Franks	trans. O. M. Dalton, London 1927
Grinsell, L.	Archaeology of Wessex	Methuen
	White Horse Hill	St. Catherine Press
Hartley, C.	The Western Mystery Tradition	Aquarian Pub. Co.
Hawkes, J. and C.	Prehistoric Britain	Pelican 1942
Hawkins, G.	Stonehenge Decoded	Souvenir Press
Heard, G.	The Source of Civilisation	Jonathan Cape
Herodotus	The Histories	Penguin Classics
Hesiod	Theogony, Works and Days	Penguin 1973
Homer	Odyssey and Iliad	Pope's trans.
Hunt, R.	Popular Romances of the West of England	Chatto & Windus
James, M.	New Testament Apocrypha	Clarendon, Oxford 1924
Jones, Owen	Myfyrian Archaeology	1801
Jowett	The Lost Disciples	Covenant Press, London
Jung, Carl	Psychology of the Unconscious	Routledge & Kegan Paul
Kendrick, Sir T. D.	The Druids	Methuen 1927
Larousse Encyclopedia of Mythology		Batchworth Press
Lewis, H. A.	Christ in Cornwall (Booklet)	J. H. Lake, Falmouth
Lewis, Rev. Smithett	St. Joseph of Arimathea at Glastonbury	James Clark
Libra, C. Aq.	Astrology (trans. fr. Dutch)	Veen, Amersfoort
Lockyer, Sir N.	Stonehenge & Other British Stone Monuments	Macmillan 1906
Loomis, R. S.	Wales and the Arthurian Legend	Univ. of Wales Press 1956
	The Development of Arthurian Romance	Hutchinson 1963
Mabinogion	Trans. by G. Jones & T. Jones	Everyman/Dent
Mackenzie, D.	Myths of Babylonia and Assyria	Gresham
Malory, Sir T.	Morte d'Arthur	Macmillan
MALTWOOD, Katharine	Glastonbury's Temple of the Stars	James Clark, London
	Enchantments of Britain	
	Aerial Supplement to Temple of the Stars	Watkins 1937
Merezhkovsky, Dmitri	Atlantis/Europe	USA Steiner Publications
Massingham, H.	Downland Man	Jonathan Cape 1926
Michell, J.	View over Atlantis	Sphere/Abacus
	City of Revelation	Sphere/Abacus
	Old Stones of Landsend	Garnstone Press
Moncrieff	Romance and Legend of Chivalry	Gresham
Morgan, Owen (called Morien)	The Royal Winged Son of Stonehenge	Whittaker
Reprinted as	The Mabyn of The Mabinogion	Thomsons 1984
Morgan, Rev. R. W.	St. Paul in Britain	Covenant Press
Moscati, S.	The World of the Phoenicians	Cardinal 1973
Murray, Margaret	The God of the Witches	Background Books
	The Divine King in England	Faber
	Egypt & Grail Romance (paper)	1916

Nennius	History of the Britons (Six Old English Chronicles, ed. Giles)	Bell & Son
Nostradamus' Prophecies	Ed. Erika Cheetham	Spearman 1973
Ouspensky, P. D.	In Search of the Miraculous	Routledge & Kegan Paul
	The Psychology of Man's Possible Evolution	H & S
O'Brien	The Round Towers of Ireland	
Pauwells and Bergier	The Morning of the Magicians	Mayflower 1971
Phillips E. D.	The Royal Hordes, People of the Steppes	Thames & Hudson
Plato	The Republic, Critias, Timaeus	Penguin Classics
Piggott, S.	The Druids	Thames & Hudson
Pillot, G.	The Secret Code of the Odyssey. trans. E. Albert	Abelard Schumann
Raine, K.	William Blake	British Council, Longmans 1951
Roberts, Antony	Atlantean Traditions in Ancient Briton	Unicorn Bookshop
Robinson, Joseph Armitage	Two Glastonbury Legends (King Arthur & Joseph of Arimathea)	Cambridge Univ. Press 1926
Rolleston	Myths & Legends of the Celtic Race	Harrap 1911
Schure, Ed.	Pythagoras	Rider 1923
Sephariol	Manual of Astrology	
Sir Gawain and the Green Knight		Everyman/Dent
Spence, Lewis	Occult Sciences in Atlantis	Aquarian Pub. Co.
	History & Origins of British Druidism	Aquarian Pub. Co.
	Mysteries of Britain	Aquarian Pub. Co.
Squire, D.	Celtic Myth and Legend	Gresham
Taylor, J. W.	The Coming of the Saints	Covenant Publ. Co. 1969
Thom, Alexander	Megalithic Sites in Britain	Oxford Univ. Press 1967
Tomas, A.	We Are Not the First	Sphere & Sovereign Press
Triads of the Isle of Britain		British Museum Collection
Treharne	Glastonbury Legends	Cresset 1967
Velikovsky, E.	Worlds in Collision	Gollancz
Virgil	Aeneid	Pan Books 1968
Wace's and Layamon's "Brut" Arthurian Chronicles		Dent
Waddell, L.	Phoenician Origin of the Britons, Scots & Anglo-Saxons	Williams & Norgate
Waite, A.	The Holy Grail	University Books, New York
Watkins, A.	The Old Straight Track	Garnstone 1970
Watson, Lyall,	Supernature	Coronet/Hodder & Stoughton
Weil, Simone	Intimations of Christianity Among the Ancient Greeks	Routledge & Kegan Paul
Weston, Jessie	From Ritual to Romance	Doubleday Anchor Books
	The Quest of the Holy Grail	Cass 1964
Wild, T. N.	Glastonbury Legends (Booklet)	Helliker, Street, Somerset
Wilson, Mona	Life of William Blake	Hart Davis (Nonesuch Press)
Wolframm von Eschenbach	Parzifal	Vintage Books

Index

Aahlu 152, 153-155
Abaddon 214-215
Abaris the Hyperborean 176, 177
Abbadare 242
Abbe, Chauve-Bertrand 83
Abbey's Arms 135
Abbot 58
Abel 39, 68
Actis 130
Acts of Magdalen 235
Acts of Pilate 229-231
Adam (also see Adam & Eve) 78, 106, 144, 243
Adam & Eve) 39, 78, 88, 159, 163, 230,
Adapa, Wise Fisher 140
Adonis 57
Aeneas 180
Aerial Supplement 33
Ages, Precessional 253
Ahura 76, 11, 114, 151
Ai 78
Alain 239
Alban Arthan 74
Albanus 235
Alchemy 86
Aldebaran 51, 115, 223
Alexandria's Library 159
Alford 101, 105
Alfred 20, 150, 151, 152, 255
Alfred's Burrow 21, 148
Aller 151, 153
Alleyn 239
All Saints 104
All Souls 104
Alpha & Omega 75, 229
Altarnun 95
Amaethon 196, 200
Amalthea 123
Amazon 69, 167
America 97
Anhíta 154
Ancient Turkish Cities 166
Androgeus (Androgyne Man) 175
Aneurin 51
Angels as Planets 113, 233
Angharad 221
Anna 62, 143
Annis 248
Annis Hill 85
Annunciation 38, 83, 92 (Dove of The –) 92
Annunciation Cup 228
Annwn 19, 22, 23, 46, 64, (Anu of) 85, 148, 190, 248, 249
Antaeus (Giant) 167
Antares 102, 115, 223
'Antiquities of Glastonbury' 76
Anubis of Annwn 148
Anu 85 (Paps of) 85
Apples, Golden, 161, 173
Apples of Wisdom 144, 167, 227
Apple Orchard 169
Apple Tree 197
Apocalypse 75
Apocrypha (N.T.) 228, 237

Apollo (Avallach) 169
Apollo's Lyre (Stars) 169
Aquarian Age 229, 253, 255, 257, 260
Aquarian & Piscean Age 253
Aquarius 25, 39, 75, 77, 83, 91, 123, **129-135**,
Arawn (The Fairy King of Annwn) 46, 203
Arcady 168, 169
Aries (Mars) 44
Argo 59, 68, 91, 160
Argo Navis 64, 241
Argonauts 155, 175
Ariadne 94, 175
Arianrhod 94, 149, 162, 196
Aries 43–46, 77, 123, 141, 223
Arian Age 253
Ark 39, 50, 68, 69, 78, 92, 164, 231, 239, 249
Arkle, Ireland 249
Arthur 20, 22, 44, 51, 69, 74, 75, 78, 83, 91, 102, 104, 106, 117, 121, 139, 141, 149, 151, 190, 191, 202, 212, 219, 221, 241, 242, his Arms 74, his Barge 249, as the Bear 173, his Boat 64, 104, his Bridge 104, 111, his Chariot 93, his Dog 150, the Fisher King 45, 61, 140, his Grave 22, 191, his Helmet 74, as Hu 51, his Knights 88, as Sagittarius 91, 111, his Well 21
Arviragus 20, 62, 141, 152
Asella 39, 61
Ashwell Lane 130
Asser (Welsh Monk) 111, 150, 151, 152
Assyria 111
Astrology 25, 26, 83, 163-4
Astrology and the Church 82, 266
Atalanta 69, 173
Athelney 21, 147, 148, 152
Atlanteans 35, 64, –Last of the, 111
Atlantic Ocean 158
Atlantis 59, 162, 69, 93, 157, 160, 162, 164, 165, 167
Atlas, Atlantis' King 59, 69, 104, 157, 160, 161, 163, 165
Atlas Mountains 161
Attis 140
Attar (Eagle) 131
Augury 35
Avalon 19, 20, 22, 23, 25, 32, 78, 102, 104, 111, 118, 122, 151, 152, 153, 157, 158, 161, 162, 163, 217, 222, 242, 245
Avallach 169, 240
Avanc, Addanc 50, 113, 221, 222
Avebury 177
Avernus 162
Avon 97
Awen 92, 97, 185
Awenyddion, The 183
Axe River 88, 248
Azilians 158

Bab 84
Baal (also see Bel) 88, 92, 111
Babcary 83, 84
Babe 39, 59, 61, 250
Babe in Boat 103, 249
Babe Sun 83, 249

Babylon 74, 129, 140, Tower of 155
Baldur 101
Balor 215
Baltonsborough 111, 141
Baltonsborough Flights 91
Ban, Bun, The Maid 201
Baptism in Jordan 61, 91
Bard 93, 96, 193
Barrington, Mrs 32
Barton St. David 83, 87, 88, 92, 93, 94, 97
Battle of Camlann 103
Battle of the Trees (Cad Goddeu) 193, 196
Beck, Adams 32
Beckery 85
Bedd 61
Bedivere 139, 202
Beheading Test 45-46
Bel 38, 52, 57, 101, 130
Beldeg 150
Beliar 231, 233
Belin 150, 196
Belinus (The Sun-God) 62
Bel Marduk 154
Belshazzar's Feast 165
Beltane 52
Benjamin 53
Berossus 159
Bethabara 61
Bethania 61
Bethlehem 53, 61
Bible 164
Black Annis 85
Black Book of Carmarthen 148
Black Oppressor 219, 222
Black Prince of Paradise 144
Black Sea 74
Blake (Admiral) 250
Blake (William) 19, 57, 101, 193, 250, 277
Blessed Isles 152, 158
Bligh Bond 239
Blodduwedd (Flower Face) 208
Bloody Lance 91, 220
Blood Spring 130
Boadicea 86, 167, 243
Boar of Calydon
Boat 64, 68
Book of Enoch 163, 165, 166, 241
Book of Noah 163, 164
Boreas 176
Borth 249
Bowed One of the Mound of Dundon 58, 69
Boy on Dolphin 96
Bradley Hill 63
Bran 22, 124, 143, 150, 209, 247
Branwen 209, 210
Brechan, King of Brecon 85
Briareus 125
Bridgwater 250

Brigit, Bride 20, Brigit's Perpetual Fires 210
Britain 22, 62
Britain Atlantis 156-166
Britain's Pre-Roman Roads 178
Britain's Conversion Date 237
Britannia 23, 117, 161
British Family Trees 62
Brittany 106, 200, 202, 203, 258
Bron 150
Bron's Fish (Rich Fisher) 236, 239, 247
Broad Arrow 33
Bronze 114, Age 118
Brood Hen 93
Brue (The River) 79, 91, 94, 101, 104, 106, 140, 151
Brut, The 106
Brutus (1st King of Britain) 74, 106, 179-181
Buddha 140
Bull's Eye 102
Bull Fighting 51
Bulls 49,
Bun 199
Burning Castle 132
Butleigh 94, 245
Butleigh Cross 94, 245

Cabal (Arthur's Dog) 149, 150
Caballa 121
Cabiri 159, 161, 162, 164
Cabiri Mysteries 164, 215
Cadbury (Camelot) 21, 88, 174
Cadbury (Castle) 88, 103, 148, 174
Cad Goddeu 193
Cader Idris 183
Cadiz 161
Cadmillus 88
Cadmus 162
Caduceus 105
Cadwalladyr 200, 236
Caer Llion 221
Caer Sidi 22, 93, 190, 201
Cain and Abel 39
Calendar 59, Calendar Myth 79, Calendar Peg 141
Callixtus 106
Camelford 103
Camelot 88, 103, 174
Camel Villages 88
Camillus 174
Camulos 88
Canada 32, 33
Canals (Rhynes 37, 50, 59, 147, 148
Cancer (Ship) 25, 59, 61, 64-70, 75, 94, 255, 256, 258, 262
Canis Minor (Little Dog Star) 63, 79
Canis Major Stars 147, 148
Capricorn 37, 75, 102, 116, 118-125, 130, 222, 223, 255, 257, 260
Caradoc 20, 62, 150, 200

Carmel (Mount —) 88
Carpo 174
Carthage 158, 159
Cary Fitzpaine 87
Cary of Kerin 85
Cary (River) 32, 63, 79, 80, 85, 94, 151. See also Mother Cary
Caspian 74
Cassiterides (The Tin Islands) 74
Cassiterides 69
Cassi (Catti) 74
Cassivelannus 74, 204
Castle Cary 80, 85
Castle of the Trial
Castle of the Whale 143
Castor & Pollux 59, 161, 174
Cathedrals 245
Cath Palug 74
Catti — see Cassi
Cauldron 22, 23, 64 (Annwn of) 67, 70, 75, 85, 91, 113, 117, 124, 130, 185, 190, 215, 228, 247, 248
Cauldron Grail Severed Head 124
Cedars of Lebanon 69
Cei (Sir Kay) 215, 219
Celtic 25, 61, 62 (— Underworld) 95, 101, 121, 143
Celts 94, — Underworld 196
Celtic Missionaries, 1st cent. 236, 244
Celtic Oath 51
Celtic Pantheons of Don & Llyr 246-247
Celtic Poetry 185-202
Celtic v Roman 62, 185
Centaur 114
Cerberus 23, 147, 150, 167, 197, 215
Cerdic 150, 151, 200
Cerne Abbas Giant 179
Ceridwen (Ceredwen) 22, 23, 67, 68, 85, 87, 91, 93, 185, 186, 189
Ceryneian 169
Ceres 68, 85, 87, 169
Cetti 68
Cetus (See Whale) 25, 68, 94, 139
Chabrick Millstream 78
Chaldea 174
Chaldeans 25, 92, 93-114 — Oannes 96, 125, 139, 162
Chalice Well 20, 38, 84, 123, 129, 130, 132, 133, 154, 210, 225, 246, 253
Chapels 131, 245
Charlton Adam 78
Charlton Mackrell 76
Charon 105, 230, 248
Cheddar Gorge 248, 255
Cherubim 231
Chilton Priory 44
Chimaera 123
Chiron 115

Chivalry 117, 119, 238
Chretien De Troyes 45, 238
Christ 38, 58, 61, 81, 83, 94, 104, 123, 133, 140, 144, 150, 233, 244
Christed Man 233
Christians' Cross 76
Christians (Early) 163
Christianity 20, 228, 243
Christmas 101
Chronos (See also Saturn) 125
Cigfa 205
Cimmerians 69, 74, 158 — Celts 171
Cinnamon Lane 130
Circe 171
Clairvoyance 85, 183
Clas Merddin 22
Cleito 160, 162
Coincidence 76
Collard Hill 50
Columba 95, 97, —the Dove, 97
Columbus 97
Column 97
Compton Dundon 47
Conchobar 51
Copley Woods 76
Copts 133, 242
Coracle 249
Coraneid 213
'Corduroy' Roads 252
Corn Dollies 84
Cornish Legend 36, 62, 67, 85, 143, 246
Cornish St. Padarn 233
Cornovii 85
Cornucopia 85
Cornwall (Earl of) 227, 246
Covenant (Ark, of the) 68, 70, 165
Crab 64 (See also Cancer)
Crater (The Cup) 87
Creation 92, 93, 95, 153, 248
Cretans 59, 67, 158, 160
Crete 69, 93, 94, 175
Crewkerne's Legend 251-253
Cro-Magnons 160
Cromm Cruach 58, (See also Bowed One of the Mound)
Cromwell 84
Cross 93
Crucifixion 20, 61, 233
Cruets 132
Crusaders 119
Culdees 153, 242
Culhwch (and Olwen) 211, 214, 215, 247
Cuneiform 58, 61
Cuthbert's Dun Cow 252
Cyclops 171
Cymry 69, 155
Cynan (Failed Initiate) 217
Cynddelw, Bard 93

Daedalus 175
Daffodil 96
Danes 20, 151, 255
Danu 85
Daronwy (See also Don) 68, 196
Davey Jones or Davy 23, 83, 96
David 95, 96
David's Chariot 93
Davies, Edward 113, 114
Dead Sea Scrolls 62
Dervish Dance 93
Diana 59
Dionysus 38, 52, 57, 123
Dioscuri 59
Dis (Court of –) 171
Ditcheat 104
Diva 94
Dive 94
Divitiacus Caesar's Doctor, 235
Dog of Langport (See Great Dog) 23, 33
Dog's Place Names 148
Domesday Book 83
Don 68, 196, 247
Don, Fort of, 58
Dormarth 148
Dove (See also Libra) 37, 75, 97, 252
Draco 78, 94 (Seven Heads) 95, 143, 223
Dragon 245
Drayton's Polyolbion 153
Dream of Rhonabwy 211
Druids 61, 91, 93, 96, 102, 115, 121, ·124, 125, 130, 132, 141, 160, 185. – Trinity 196, 235, 249, 250, 252
Druid Bishops 235, 236
Druid Grove 63, 123
Druid Swine 206, 213
Druids London Order 250
Druids in Ireland 210
Druids on Mona 230
Druid Teachings 61, 62, 68, 113, 143, 151, 162, 193, 247, 248
Dundon 33, 52, 68
Dundon Beacon 63
Dundon Camp 58, 61
Dundon Hill 38, 43, 50, 58, 131, 196, 251
Dunball 44
Duw Dovydd 95
Dwyvan 157
Dyke 101, 102
Dying Sun-God 207, 217, 255
Dylan, The Fish 207

Eagle 58, 135, 208
Earthworks 247, 248, 250
Ecclesiastical Antiquities of the Cymry 236
Ecliptic 35
Ecliptic Line 50, 59, 78, 141
Ector 53, 106

Edda 131
Eden 78, 88, 94, 144. – of Mesopotamia 159
Edern Ap Nudd 226
Edlym (Taurus) 223
Edward II 257
Effigies 167
Efnisien 209
Egypt 94, 130, 133, 148, 158, 159, 160, 163
Egyptians 64, 91, 157
Einstein 264
Eleanor (Queen) 83, 107, 238, (–of Aquitaine) 256, 258
Elen (Princess) 211, 212
Elijah 131
Elphin (Prince) 93, 186, 190
Emblett Lane 59
Enchantments of Britain 33
English History Fits the Zodiac 255-266
Enid 226
Enkidu 125, 154
Enoch 158, 163, 164, 165, 231
Entry into Jerusalem 61, 62
Epic of Creation 153
Epic of Gilgamesh 153-155
Equinoctial Line 102
Erech 154
Erin & Erinnys 161
Eryri (Snowdonia) 213
Esau 125
Esharra 153
Eshmun 248
Esse (of Lyonesse) 62
Esus 62, 78, 162, 246
Essenes 61, 62
Etruscans 58, 88, 162
Europa 69, 93, 160
Europe 93
Evans, Sebastian 22
Eve (See Adam & Eve) 68, 88
Evelake (Mordrains) 240
Evolution 39, (Darwin) 165, 240
Evolution and Intelligence 172
Evolution's Aim 36, 58
Evolution's Laws 165
Evolution's Path 191
Evolution's Purpose 165, 250
Excalibur 141

Fallen Angels 158, 164, 232, 233, 240
Fall of Man 163
Fand 209
Fecamp Legend 236
Fire Signs 77
Fish 139 (See Pisces) 253
Fish (Second) 141
Fisher King 45, 61, 62, 139, 143, 189
Fish Symbolism 140
Fleur De Lys 116

Flint Cross 252
Flints 252
Flood 39, 62, 132, 152, 157, 158
Flood Legend 62, 68, 157
Fomalhaut 115, 135
Foretelling Spheres of Prophecy 242
Fortunate Isles 158, – Goddess 116
Fosse Way 84, 104, 215
Fountain 133, 154
Fountain and Bowl 205, 217
Four Foot 102
Free Will 36, 225

Gadfly Islands (Oestrymnides) 213
Gadir 161
Galahad 63, 68, 79, 106, 144, 153, 241
Ganymede 130, 163 (The Perfected Man)
Gaul 95
Garuda 130 (Man Eagle)
Gawain 44, 45, 63, 133, 135, 140
Gemini 50, 57-63, 64, 68, 75, 79, 91, 139, 140, 161, 215, 222, 233, 240
Genesis 78, 158, 159
Geoffrey De Mandeville 86
Geoffrey of Monmouth 180
Geometer 61
Gereint Son of Erbin 226
Geryon's Oxen 168
Gewissae 150
Giant 79, 148
Giants 23, 74, 106, 162, 164, 206, 214, 247
Giant's Hedge 247
Gifl 88
Gibraltar (Straits of) 167, 174
Gildas 170, – The Wise 243-244
Gilded Goat 120
Gilgamesh 69, 125, 153, 154, 155, 167
Girdle of Hyppolyte 167
Girt Dog (See Great Dog) 24
Glaesting's Sow 252
Glass Ship 22, 70, 113, 190
Glass Mountain 23, 133
Glastonbury 20, 22, (Tor) 23, 35, 50, 95, 113, 118, 122, 124, 129, 131, 133, 148, 162, Lord of – 173
Glastonbury Abbey 20, 21, 133, 135, 139, 141
Glastonbury Castle 131
Glastonbury Glass 177
Glastonbury, Glass Castle 212, 250
Gloucester 79
Gnosticism 223
Gnostics 150
Gnostic St. John 75
Goemagot 179, 181, 206
Gogarene Armenia 179
Goggles 179
Gog and Magog 23, 123, 178
Gog Magog Oaks & Hills 178, 179

Goidelic Celts 84, 213, Goidels 88

Golden Age 70
Golden Age of Atlantis 253
Golden Coffin 120
Golden Fleece 44, 174
Golden Legend 235
Gomer 179
Good Thief 233
Gosling St. 92
Gorgon 161
Gradlon's Daughter 157 (King)
Graeae 172, 173
Grail 22, 23, 53, 63, 83, 122, 130, 135, 140, 238, 240, 251, – Changes, 253
Grail Castle 97, 140, 143, 205, 220
Grail Christianity 83, 228, 238
Grail Cup 20, 45, 76, 78, 124, 228, 238, 246
Grail Procession 45, 61, 91, 97, 124, 220
Grail Question 45, 140, 143
Grail (What Was It?) 238, 239
Great Bear 93
Great Dog 147-152
Great Dog of Langport 23, 215
Great Dog Place Names 148
Great Dog Questing Beast 240
Greeks 22, 25, 59, 94, 114, 115, 130, 148, 172, 176, – Underworld 231
Green Knight 45
Green Man 107
Grey Huntsman 46
Griffon 58, 63, 77, 131
Gronw Pebyr 130, 208
Grove Lane 63
Guanches of Teneriffe 111
Guenevere 74, 87, 103, 111, 114, 141, 168, 220
Guthrun The Dane 20, 151, 152
Guy Fawkes 104
Gwawl 204
Gweir. Man 22, 70, 113, 139, 190
Gwion 67, 91, 185
Gwlad Yr Hav 118
Gwron 196
Gwyddbwyll (Chess) 212, 216, 224
Gwyddno's Weir 186, 241
Gwydion (& Gilfaethwy) 150, 196, 206, 247
Gwyn Ap Nudd (Lord of Glastonbury Tor) 19, 20, 46, 148, 149, 150, 176-7, 226
Gwythyr 149
Gyges, A Titan 171 (King of Ogygia)

Hades 19, 23, 75, 115, 147, 148, 162, 163, 168, British – 242, 248
Hafgan (Summer King) 46, 203
Halley 7
Hallows 74, 97
Hamden Hill 251 252
'Hanes Taliesin' 187

Harold (King) 251
Harp 61
Harrowing of Hell 175, 182
Hartlake 122
Hatch Hill 37, 50
Havyatt 118
Hawthorn 166
Healing of Tiberius 185
Hearty Moor 122
'Heavenly Sanctuary' 22, 153
Hecate 164
Hecateus 175, 176
Hector of Troy 53
Hedge of Mist 178
Helen of Troy 160
Heliopolis 130, 133, 141
Hell Ditch 102
Hell in the West 231
Henry II 83, 238, 256
Henry II and Eleanor 107, 238
Hera 160, 167
Hercules 79, 104, 115, 144, 161, 167, 174
Hercules (At Hartland Point) 148
Hercules (Melkarth) 111, 167
Hermes 163
Hermes Trismegistus 163, 165
Herod 103
Herodotus 158, 159, 160
Heresy 185
Hesiod 157, 158
Hesione 169
Hesperides 95, 144, 148, 158, 167, 169
Hesperides Garden 59, 159, 159, 172, 231
Hesperides in Britain 158
Hesus 62
Hibernia — see Ireland
High Ham 33
'High History of Holy Grail' 32, 33, 44, 52, 63, 76, 78, 106, 125, 132, 140, 143, 149, 239
Hiram of Tyre 69
Hobby Horse 67, 68
Holy Ilium (Or Ileum) 181
Holy Land 88
Holy Thorn 141, 214
Homer 170, 171
Hood Monument 46, 51
Horae (The) 173
Hornblotton 101, 105
Horns 59, 111, 165
Horse Boat 67, 68
Horus 49,
Hu 50, 51, 61, 76, 111
Hwyll 95
Hydra (Seven Headed Dragon) 94, 169
Hyperboreans 69, 114, 167, (The Land of the 175, 176
Hyperborean Britain 22, 231

Ia 61
Iberians 158, 161
Icarus 175
Ice Age 157, 158
Ida (Mount) 130
Idris (Cader) 163
Idris (Ider) 220, 163
Ilchester 88
Ilminster 88
Incest 103
Indara 116
India 32, Lady From — 222, 223
Initiate 61
Initiation Myth 187
Inn Signs 78
Io 159, 160
Iona 95, 96
Ionian 95, 160
Ionian, Javan 179
Ireland (Hibernia) 74, 84, 85, 95, 97, 124, 157, 161, 209
Irish Myth 209
Iron Age 68, 118
Iron Age Celts 212
Iron House 209
Isis 102, 185
Ishtar 154
Ivel 88
Ivythorn Lane 44

Jack 23 92
Jack and the Beanstalk 23, 215
Jack the Giant Killer 23, 215
James 119
Jason 44, 51, 59, 69, 155, 161, — & The Golden Fleece 174
Jericho 166
Jerusalem 238
Jesse's Rod 62, 250
Jesus 19, 20, 62, 75, 78, 83, 95, 102, 103, 106, 185 as Dionysus, 230, 242, 246, 250
Jesus at Priddy 247
Jesus in Britain 36, 61, 242
Jesus' Two Commandments 95
Jewish Legend 20, 75, 97, 231
Joachim 62, 143
Johannine Christianity 196, 228, 229
Johannine Church 75, 228, 237
John 111
John of Gaunt 78, 121, 258
John of Glastonbury 74, 242, 243
John the Baptist 39, 61, 62, 125
Jonah 68, 96, 125, 139
Joseph of Arimathea 19, 20, 22, 36, 44, 53, 61, 62, 105, 129, 141, 143, 144, 150, 214, 228-254
Joseph's Two Cruets 242
Joseph the Tin Trader 61, 246
Josephes 143

Josephus 164
Josephus Hermit 241
Joshua Son of Nun 95, 189
Judas 102, 234
Jung 26, 266
Jung's Synchronicity 76-77
Jupiter 132

Kay 53, 139, 202
Ked 68, 94, 139, 141, 153
Kedwy 68
Keinton Mandeville 86, 94
Kepler 26
Kerin (Cary of –) 85
Kerin, Keyne, Cornwall 169
Kerinus & Lucius 230
Keynsham 86
Khassi 74
Khassisadra 69, 153
Kilted Celts 153
Kingdom of Logres 88
King Gradlon's Daughter 157
King of Castle Mortal 125
King Seint 95
Kingsley, Charles, Water Babies 83
Kit See Ked 68
Kit's Coty House 68
Knight of the Mill
Knights of the Round Table 23, 44
Knossos 156
Kore 68
Krishna 38, 57
Kundalini 106
Kynan 151, 200

Labours 167-170
Labyrinth 93, 94, 175
Ladon 169
Lady of the Fountain 218
Lady of the Lake 141
Lady Springs (Seven) 80
Lamb & Flag 43
Lamed God 52, 61
Lance 91
Lance of Longinus 61
Lancelot 44, 45, 63, (Lance of Light) 74, 79, 88, 102, 103, 114
Land of the Cherubim 233, 241
Langport Church 132
Langport (See also Great Dog) 147, 150, 215
'Language of Correspondences' 190
Last Supper 140, 228 (Cup of The –) 234
Latona 176
Launcherly Hill 120
Laws of Creation 165
Laws of Medes and Persians 153
Laws of Molmutius 151
Layamon's Brut 139

Lazarus 235
Lear (or Llyr) King 209
Leda 92
Leland 141
Leo 62, 71-79, 85, 114, 173, 255, 256, 258, 263
Leodegrance 88
Lepus (The Hare) 64
Leucius (See also Lucius) 230, 244
Leviathon 111, 143
Leys 178, 251
Libra 25, 64, 74, 75, 77, 83, 91-97, 106, 255, 257, 259, 264
Lion 63, 74, 79, 116
Lion & Unicorn 23, 116, 118
Little Dog 63
Little King 228
Little Song of the World 194
Liver 58
Liver Moor 58
Lleu (Llew) The Long-Handed 74, 102, 130, 247
(Lleu Llaw Gyffes) 208
Llud & Llefelys 211, 212
Llyn Llion Lake 50, 111
Llyr (or Lear) King 204, 247
Loathly Damsel 220, 223
Logos 23, 83, 88, 92, 93 (See also Word)
Logres 88 (The Kingdom of –)
Lohengrin 92
Lollover 33, 50, 58, 70
London, Troy Novant 106
Longinus 58
Looe (Cornwall) 227, 246, 250
Lost Land of Ys 156, 157
Lot 102, 103, 106
Lottisham 102
Lucifer 102, 104
Lucius & Kerinus 237
Lud 102, 106
Lug 63, 74
Lugh 74, 102
Lugnasad 74, 78
Luristan Metalwork 153
Lydford 101, 106
Lynchets 50
Lyonesse 62, 69, 70, 79, 155, 157, 162, 170

Mabinogion 22, 46, 124, 130, 135, 139, 202
Mabon 139, 203
Macsen (Prince) 211
Madai 17
Maelgwyn 93, 242
Magi 22, 164
Magic, – Wand, 151
Magotty Pagotty 76
Maimed King 169, 240
Maltwood 31
Maltwood, K. 29-34
Maltwood Dove 91-2, 24

Maltwood Memorial Museum 31, 33
Man 163, 190, 203, 250
Manawydan 204, 205, 210, 247
Mandeville, Geoffrey 86
Mandeville, Sir John 86
Manger 163
Map (Walter) 240
Marseilles Druids & Joseph 235
Martha 235
Mary Magdalen 84, 235
Massacre of Innocents 103
Masons 61, 69
Math (Son of Mathonwy) 61, 151, 196, 206 207
Math Great Mathematician 196, 231
Math's Wand 151, 167
Matholuch (King of Ireland) 209
Matter of Britain 22
Maximin 235
May Day 67, 103, 191
May Eve 204, 212
Maypole Knap 78
Maze 162, 182, 184
Measuring Rod 151, 196
Medea 153, 174, 187, —'s Cauldron 153
Medes 111, —'s and Persians 111
Medusa the Gorgon 168, 172, 173
Meleager (Meleagant?) 168, 173
Melkin's Prophecy 242-243
Menai 69
Mendips 164, 247, 251
Menes 69, 114
Menu (The Measurer) 50, 69, 93, 157
Mercury 95, 161
Merddin 96, 197, —'s Avallenau 197
Merlin 22, 96, 103, 111, 124, 150, 196, 200, 237, 255, 265
Merton College 181
Mesolithic Britain 156
Messiah 54
Metal Mines 74, 158, 163, 237, 247-248, 250
Methuselah 165
'Mighty Virgin' 242
Milton 180
Minehead Ship 67
Minos 69, 93, 94, 160, 175
Minotaur 104, 175
Minyans 69
Miracles 76
Mistletoe 101
Mithraic Mysteries 51, 140
Mithraism 51
Mona 229
Molmutius (British Laws of) 151
'Monkish Inventions?' 241
Montacute's Legend 251
Montgomery 179
Moon 64, 68, 94, 149, 150

Moon Month 59, 60, 150
Mordred 102, 103
Morgan Le Faye 88, 102, 103
Morrigan, The 88
Morte D'Arthur 103, 116
Moses 52, 103, 105, 131, 189
Moses' and Jesus' Cradle 241
Mother Cary 23, 80, 96, 174
Mother Goddess 38, 92
Mound of Arberth 183, 203
Mount Ida 130, 163
Musical Scale 26
Myths 38, 39, Norse — 101
Myths Reflect Eternal Pattern
Mysteries 22, 25, 50, 61, 62, 68, 83, 86, 94, 113, 115, 121, 130, 132, 139, 150, 165, 168, 171, 185, 191, 196, 214, 249, Cabiric — 249, Druidic — 130-1, Glastonbury — 113, — Schools 165, — Kept Secret 185

Name of God 75, 78
Nasciens, Seraph 240, 241
Nature Pattern 35, 36, 37
Nave 241
Nemean Lion 79
Nennius (History of the Britons) 243
New Testament Apocrypha 229
Newton 25, 260
Nicodemus (Gospel of —) 229
Nightmare 68, 83
Nile 241
Nimrod 153, 155
Noah 39, 50, 61, 69, 78, 92, 93, 158, 163, 164, 166, 239
Nodens of Lydney 140
Normans 77
Norman French 22
Norse Myth 101
North Pole 223
November 102, 103

Oak of Dodona 174
Oannes 125, 139
Obed (Story of) 234
Oberon 161
Ocean 59, Atlantic — 157
Odin 150, Odin's Wagon 93
Odysseus 69, 170-172
Oedipus 103
Oestrymnides 213
Oeth & Anoeth, Charnel House of Bones 139
Ogygia 170
Olwen 214, 215
Olympus 39, 59, 115, 130, — A Giant 169
Orcus, Phorcys 172
'Origins of Christmas' 83
Orion 59, 61, 62
Orpheus 140, 174

Osiris 59, 62, 64, Car of – 93, 102, 111, 164
'Outlandish Knight' 226
Owein 218
Oxford 213
Ox-Hide 216
'Ox-Pen of the Bards (The Zodiac) 49, 217

Palestine 62, 143, 235, 236, 246
Palomedes 149
Pan 102, 124
Paps of Anu 85
Paradise 78, 123, 148, 231
Parbrook 101
Park Wood 94, 143, 144, 196
Paris 103
Par Rock 88, 101
Parrett River 44, 88, 147, 148, 149, 150, 151, 152
Parzifal 83
Paschal Lamb 43, 52, 105, 123
Passion 38, 39
Passover 52
Patron Saints 116
Pelasgian 162, 196
Penardin 246, 247
Penelope 172
Pennard Hills 111
Pentecost (Festival of –) 182
Perceval 44, 52, 63, 131, 133, 143, 144, 150, 153, 222, 237
Perceval's Key 143
Perceval's Sister 88
Peredur 219-225 (Son of Efrawg)
Perfected Man (Ganymede) 163, (Androgeus) 175
Persephone 87
Perseus 96, 161, 172, 173
Pesach 52
Peter's & John's Church 229
Petrus 240
Pheryllt 186, 199, 213
Philip the Fair, King of France, 119
Phoenician 59, 115, 148, 158, Proto – 159
Phoenician Maps 60
Phoenician Origin of the Britons 67, 74
Phoenicians 159, 160
Phoenicians Carry Christianity 235, 241, 251, 253
Phoenix 25, 39, 129, 130, 133
Phorcys 172
Physics 37, 113
Pilate 231, 234
Pillars of Hercules 161, 167, 253
Pineal 70, 251
Pirie Reis (Map) 60
Piscean Age 253, 254
Pisces 25, 95, 102, 114, 139-144, 223
Planets 164, 187

Planisphere 22
Plantagenet (Richard) 74, 83
Plantagenet. 107, 121, 244, 256
Plant of Eternal Life 154
Plato 156, 157, 160, 162, 165
Pleiades 51
Plough Stars 92, 93 (See Great Bear)
Plutarch 52, 102, 125, 157
Pluto 151
Polden Hills 33, 43
Pole Star 93, 143, 144, 151, 223
Pole Tree 94
Pollux 59
Polyolbion (Drayton's) 152
Pomparles Bridge 140
Ponter's Ball 118, 122
Pope (Gregory) 20
Portway 44
Poseidon 160
Precessional Ages 253
Precession of Equinoxes 172
Preiddu Annwn (Taliesin's Poem) 191
Pre-Roman Roads 177
Priddy (In Mendips) 247-251
Prince of Wales Feathers 116
Procopius on Bretons' Task 230
Prometheus 58, 115
Pryd 248
Pryderi 204, 205, 210, 247, 248
Prydwen 70, 190
Prytania 161
Pwyll Prince of Dyved 203, 204
Pwyll Mound 183
Pythagoras 25
Pythagorean Numerology 228
Pythagorean Cosmology 266
Pythoness 85
Pyramid 21, 141
Pyramid 141

Questing Beast 149, 150, 240
Questions of Bartholomew 231-233
Quest of Grail 20, 22, 23, 33, 63, 70, 74, 106, 133, 140, 150, 217, 240

Ra Egyptian Sun-God 59, 133
Rag Lane 87
Ras Shamra Tablets 159, 241
Rebirth 94
'Recognitions of Clement' 236
Red Sea 52
Red Lake 58
Redlands 50, 58, 239
Red Launde 50, 52
Religion 25
Regulus 74, 115
Resurrection 230
Rhiannon (Moon) 204

Richard I 74
Richard II 122, 257
Rich Fisher (Bron) 236, 239
Rigel 61
Ring of the Nibelungs 161
Robert De Borron's 'Joseph' 240
Roman Church 121, 228, 229, 237
Roman Emperor 211, 212, 234
Roman Phoenician Mines 251
Roma Secunda 121, 246
Rome 20, 121, 151, 228
Romans 76, 84, 92. — Zodiac 130
Roman Quarries 76
Round Table 20, 22, 44, 74, 103, 106, 111, 124, 132, 202, 240. — Mound, Windsor 119
Royal Secret 107

Royal Society of Arts 33
Royal Star Cross 74, 135
Runic 162
Rhydderch 199
Rhys Ap Tewdur 202

Sabitu 154
Sabrina (Severn Goddess) 154
Sacred Sites Found by Animals 252
Sagittarius 39, 51, 77, 101, 102, 108-117, 255, 257, 259
Salmon of Wisdom 23, 61, 69, 139, 189, 215, 236
Sanconiathon, Phoenician Historian 164
Sanctuary Knockers 78
Sang Real 225
Sanhedrin 230
Santorin 156 (Thera)
Saphat (Josaphat) 242
Sapphire Book 163
Saracens 240, 241
Sarra, Caiaphas' Daughter 233
Sarras, Grail City 153, 240
Sargon I of Akkad 67
Satan 74, 124, 158
Satanas 231-233
Satanas (City of) 232
Satans 74
Saturn 74, 75, 102, 124, 125, 255
Satyrs 102
Saxons 71, 151, — Kings 152, — Monks 155, 244
Scales 64 (See also Libra) 92
Science 37, 113
Sculptures 33
Scorpio 59, 77, 92, 101-107, 143, 219, 222, 223, 255, 257, 259, 266
Seasons 32, 44
Second Twin 63
Secret of the Lord 20, 21
Secret of the World 241

Seven Deadly Sins
Seven Heavens 113
Seven Lady Springs 80
Seven Words, Days 2, 97
Severed Head 220, 247
Sex 75
Severn River 68 (Sea) 70, 85, 68, 103, 113, 139, 147, 157, 158
Shakespeare 78
Sheru 163
Ship Nevydd Nav Neivion (Ark) 155
Ship 36, 37, 64 (Also see Cancer) 67, 69, 70, 94, 113, 147
Ship's Masts 59
Shoemaker, Wise 23
Siege Perilous 227 (Swallows Moses) 239
Silurian 20, 62, — Druids 235, 237
Silver Street 92
Sirens 171
Sirius 113, 148, 215
Skull in Well 124
Sleeping Beauty 23, 214
Snake 36
Snake Goddess 85
Snowdon (Eryri) 213
Sol 68, 130, 250
Solomon 163, 240, 250
Solomon's Ship 63, 68, 153, 240, 241, 250
Solomon's Temple 68
Solon 165
Somersault 116
Somerset 25, 67, 74, 85
Somerton 23, 71, 74, 77, 78
Somerton Lane 76
Sophia 122, 216
'Song of the Graves' 22
Song of the World 195
Sons of God (Genesis) 158
Sons of the King of Suffering 221
Space Time Pattern 35, 115, 132, 141, 227, 251, 253, 266
Spenser's Fairy Queen 119
'Spoils of Annwn' 51
St. Andrew 52, 116
St. Anne 85, 150, 246
St. Augustine 20
St. Beon (St. Benignus) 20
St. Bride's Well 20
St. Bridget 84
St. Christopher 104
St. Collen 19, 20
St. Columba 95
St. David 20, 116, 238, 252
St. Drennalus of Morlaix 236
St. Dunstan 255
St. Dunstan's Biographer 20, 36, 244
St. Erney 250
St. George & Dragon 23, 94, 115

St. John 75, 95
St. John's Day 67, 228
St. Keyne 85, 86, 94, 169
St. Michael 94, 115, 148
St. Nunn 95, 116
St. Padarn 231
St. Patrick 20, 58, 84, 116, 141
St. Peter 229
St. Philip in France 235, 244
St. Pol De Leon, Prince 112
St. Swithin 151
St. Veronica's Handkerchief 235
Star-Fall, Aries & Pisces 141
Stickle Bridge 84
Stoke Sub Hamden's Norman Tympanum 77
Stone 102
Stone Altars as Ships 138
Stone Circles, Astronomical 178
Stone (Holed) 210, Village of – 102
Stonehenge 103, 169, 176
Street Churchyard 43, 50
Stymphalian Birds 169
Styx 105, 230, 248
Sumeria 64, 74, 123, 148
Sumerians 35, 67, 69, 74, 147. – Paradise of Gilgamesh 152, 155, 159
Sumers' Seat 153
Sumer Town 180
Summerland 69, 118, 158. – Zodiac 159
Summer Stars 189
Sun 96, 102, 103, 111, 112, 132, 250
Sun & Moon 112, 179, 206
Sun-Gods 22, 94, 114, 115
Sun King 102, 135, 139, 214, 259
Sun Muth 44, 59, 83, 249
Sun Reborn 249
Sun Saviour 113, 191
Swallet (Priddy) 248
Sybil 85
Sybil of Cumae's Prophecy 180
Syweddyd (Druids) 151, 206, 215

Tadworth 32
Tailor 23, 139
Tailor of Gloucester 103
Taliesin 22, 46, 50, 58, 67, 71, 93, 96, 125, 150, 185 tale of, 210, 249
Talus 188
Tanit 248
Taranis (The Earth Mother) 62
Tartarus 231, 233
Taurean Age 52, 254
Taurobolium 51
Taurus 37, 49-53, 67, 143, 160, 168, 223
Tavy 97
Telescopes 177
'Temple of the Stars' 22, 36, 50, 63, 75, 86, 157, 164, 190

Templars 43, 59, 83, 86, 107, 121, 123, 150
Ten Commandments 95
Ten Zodiac Signs 94, 95
Teucros of Babylon 83
Theseus 94, 162, 174, 175
Thieves Good and Bad 39, 61, 233
Thirteenth Moon Month 59
Thirteen Treasures of Britain 22, 116, 242
Thorn Hedge (Ysbadadden) 247
Thor's Wagon 93
Thoth 59, 164 (Egyptian Hermes)
Three Bars of Light (diag.) 60, 68, 74, 75, 91, 92, 116, 163, 196, 253
Three Births 187
Three Doleful Uncoverings 211
Three Drops 68, 186
Three Frivolous Battles 101
Three Gold Shoemakers (The) 205, 208
Three Happy Astronomers 177, 196
Three Magi 165
Three Mary's 84
Three Plagues of Britain 212
Three Primary Bards 196
Three Spindles 68
Three Water Signs 101
Three Fire Signs at Stoke 77
Tiamat 153
Tiberius (The Healing of –) 234, 243, – Caesar
Time's Purpose 75, 143
Tin Islands 69, 237
Tin Track 44
Titans 74, 157, 158, – & Greek War, 158, 161, 162, 233
Titania 161
Titus 234
Toot, Tot 85 (twt)
Tower Hill (White Mound) 211
Tower of Babel 155
Tor 19, 21, 23, 38, 84, 125, 129, 130, 154, 175, 214, 227, –'s Cave 120, 121, – Hill 133, –'s Tower 96
Tovi, Canute's Standard Bearer 252
Towns and 'Tons' 182
Tree Alphabet 162, 193
Tree of Life 68, 144, 159, 210, 227
Triads 22, 103, 235
Trinity 38, 129, 193, 196, 202
Trinovantes (New Troy, London) 181
Triple Goddess 80, 84, 94, 111
Tripod 85
Tristram 79
Trojan 58, 151, – Law 153
Troy 52, 74, 106, 159, 160, 181
Tuath de Danaan 85
Tumulus 21, 58
Turning Castle 93, 149, 175
Turning Island 241
Turtle 96

Twelve Apostles, Gods of Olympus 52, 247
Twelve Hides of Glastonbury 20, 21, 141, 152, 228, 245, 246
Twelve Labours of Hercules 167
Twins 38, 59, 67, 131, 233
Two Cruets 132, 150
Two Thieves of Crucifixion 233
Twrch Trwyth, Chief Boar 215
Tycho Brahe 26
Tyre 69

Uffington (White Horse of) 68
Ulysses 171
Uncles 222, 223
Underworld 22, 46, 70, 74, 113, 139, 148, 150, 153
Unicorn 75, 78, 118, 122
Unicorn Horn 78
Union Jack 116
Upper Room 88
Uranus 132, 133, 254
Ursa Minor 143
Uther 150, 249
Utnapishtim 154

Vale of Avalon – See Avalon
Vengeance of the Saviour 234
Venus 223
Vessel 20
Vespasian 234, 251
Virago 83
Virgin 63, 83, 86, 122, 185
Virgin and Unicorn 122
Virgin Birth 83, 95
Virgin Mary 20, 62, 143, 228, 243
Virgo 37, 39, 50, 58, 74, 92, 164, 173, 243, 255, 257, 259, 263
Virgo 80-88
Vivien 124

Wagg 148
Wagon of Our Saviour 93 (also Thor's – , Odin's–)
Wales 249
Wallyers Bridge 143
Walter Map 240
Waltham 252, – Abbey 252
Walton 44
War of Titans and Greeks 158
Wassail Song 145
Waste Lane 45, 205, 218
Water Carrier 129, 234, 252
Water Carrier (St. Luke's Gospel) 233
Water of Life 201
Wattle Church 20, 243
Wearyall Hill 46, 131, 132, 139, 141, 222, 246, 251
Wells Clock 132
Wells Museum 248

Welsh Genealogy 143
Welsh Surnames 95
Whale 25, 37, 64, 68, 94, 96, 111, 139, 141, 147, 222
Wheatstraw Compass 177
Wheatsheaf 84, 86
Wheel of Fortune 116
Whit and Week 182
White Eve 88
White Hart 120
White Horse 68
Wick 43, 123, 133
William of Malmesbury 20, 22, 76
William of Malmesbury's Prophecy 244
Wimble Toot 84, 85
Winchester's Round Table 151
Winchester's Cathedral 151
'Winged Son of Avebury' 249
Winter Solstice 255
Witch 215, – of Wookey 248
Witches of Caer Loyw (Gloucester) 226
Witch of Wookey 248
Withial 101
Woodford Green 248
Word (The) 88, 92 160 (also see Logos)
Words (Seven, of creation) 97
Worley Hill 76, 78
Wul Mo Sarra 92

Yeovilton 78, 88
Ys, Lost Land of 156, 157
Ysbaddaden (Chief Giant) 214, 215, 247
Ysbidinongle 224
Ysu 83
Ywein (Owein) 227

Zeus 58, 124, 130, 160, 170, 174
Ziggurats 21
Zodiac 22, 23, 24, 25, 35, 50, 92, 163, 208, 253,
Zodiac Christianity 62, 75, 83, 228
Zodiac Clock 111, 131, 132, 141, 217, 219
Zodiac (Dendereh) 54
Zodiac Described 20, 23
Zodiac Effigies 64, 242, 247
Zodiac Geometry 51, 59, 112
Zodiac Giants 106, 214, 247
Zodiac in Atlantis 59, 161
Zodiac in Celtic Poetry 185-202
Zodiac in Egypt 133
Zodiac in Sumerian Myths 153-155
Zodiac in Greek Myth 167-177
Zodiac in Mabinogion 202-227
Zodiac is Natural 35
Zodiac, Kingston 76
Zodiac (Meaning of) 25, 57, 76, 114, 143, 202, 240, 266
Zodiac Mysteries 119, 121, 228, 239, 245
Zodiac Myth 68, 69, 94, 101, 247, 250, 266

Zodiac Philosophy 35, 38
Zodiac Stars 22, 69, 94, 144, 223, 241
Zohar 164
Zu 130 (Chaldean Eagle) 131

Jerusalem

And did those feet in ancient time
Walk upon England's mountains green
And was the Holy Lamb of God
On England's pleasant pastures seen

And did the Countenance Divine
Shine forth upon these clouded hills
And was Jerusalem builded here
Among these dark Satanic mills?

Bring me my bow of burning gold
Bring me my arrows of desire
Bring me my Spear! O clouds unfold!
Bring me my Chariot of Fire!

I will not cease from mental fight
Nor shall my sword sleep in my hand
Till we have built Jerusalem
In England's green and pleasant land.

William Blake.